X/1999™

VOL. 10
FUGUE
Shojo Edition

STORY & ART BY CLAMP

ENGLISH ADAPTATION BY FRED BURKE

Translation/Lillian Olsen
Touch-Up Art & Lettering/Stephen Dutro
Cover Design/Hidemi Sahara
Graphic Design/Carolina Ugalde
Supervising Editor/Julie Davis
Editor/P. Duffield

Managing Editor/Annette Roman
Editor in Chief/William Flanagan
Director of Licensing & Acquisitions/Rika Inouye
Sr. VP of Sales & Marketing/Rick Bauer
Sr. VP of Editorial/Hyoe Narita
Publisher/Seiji Horibuchi

X/1999 is rated "T+" for Older Teens. It may contain violence, language, alcohol or tobacco use, or suggestive situations.

Printed in Canada

Published by VIZ, LLC
P.O. Box 77010 • San Francisco, CA 94107

Shojo Edition
10 9 8 7 6 5 4 3 2 1
First printing, July 2004

www.viz.com

store.viz.com

X/1999 ™

Vol. 10
FUGUE
Shojo Edition

Story and Art by
CLAMP

X/1999

THE STORY THUS FAR

The End of the World has been prophesied
…and time is running out. Kamui Shiro is a
young man who was born with a special
power—the power to decide the fate of the
Earth itself.

Kamui had grown up in Tokyo, but had
fled with his mother after the suspicious death
of a family friend. Six years later, his mother
too, dies under suspicious circumstances,
engulfed in flames. Her last words to him are
that he should return to Tokyo…that his destiny
awaits.

Kamui obeys his mother's words, but
almost immediately upon his arrival, he's chal-
lenged to a psychic duel—a first warning that
others know of his power, and of his return.

Kamui is also reunited with his childhood
friends, Fuma and Kotori Monou. Although
Kamui attempts to push his friends away, hop-
ing to protect them, they too are soon drawn
into the web of destiny that surrounds him.

Meanwhile, the two sides to the great con-
flict to come are being drawn. On one side is
the dreamseer Hinoto, a blind princess who
lives beneath Japan's seat of government, the
Diet Building. On the other side is Kanoe,
Hinoto's dark sister with similar powers, but a
different vision of Earth's ultimate future.
Around these two women gather the Dragons of
Heaven and the Dragons of Earth, the forces
that will fight to decide the fate of the planet.
The only variable in the equation is Kamui,
whose fate it will be to choose which side he
will join.

And Kamui finally does make a choice. He
chooses to defend the Earth as it stands now.
But by making this choice, he pays a terrible
price. For fate has chosen his oldest friend to be
his "twin star"—the other "Kamui" who will
fight against him. And in this first battle, the
gentle Kotori is the first casualty.

Now Kamui must face the consequences of
his decision…and try to come to terms with not
only his ultimate fate, but that of the Earth.…

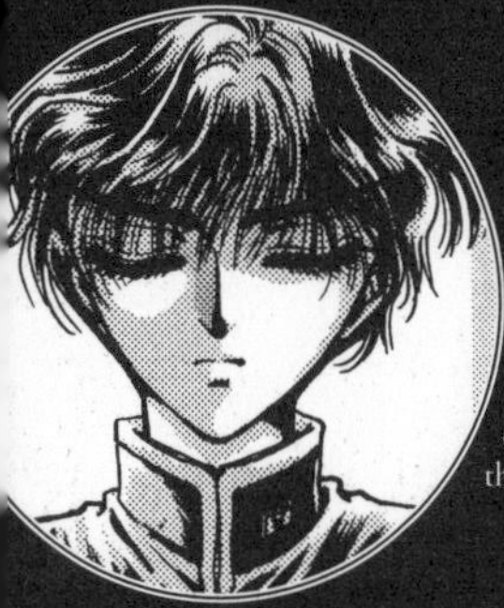

Kamui Shiro
A young man with psychic powers whose choice of destiny will decide the fate of the world.

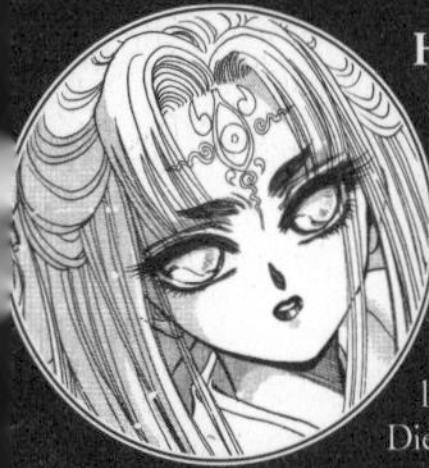

Hinoto
Blind, unable to speak or walk, Hinoto is a powerful prophetess, far older than she looks, who communicates with the power of her mind alone. She lives in a secret shrine located beneath Tokyo's Diet Building.

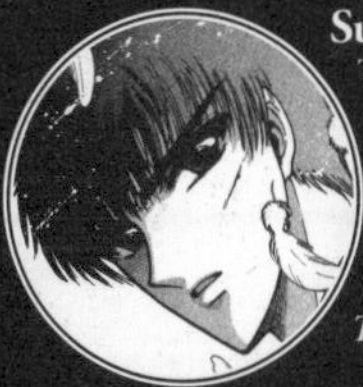

Subaru Sumeragi
The 13th family head of a long line of spiritualists and a powerful medium and exorcist. He is the lead character of another Clamp manga series, ***Tokyo Babylon***.

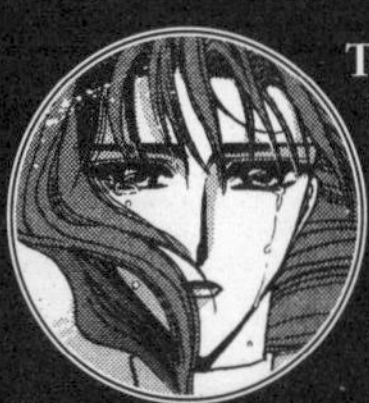

Toru
Kamui's mother was heir to the Magami clan, an ancient family of "Shadow Sacrifices," people who absorb the misfortunes of others.

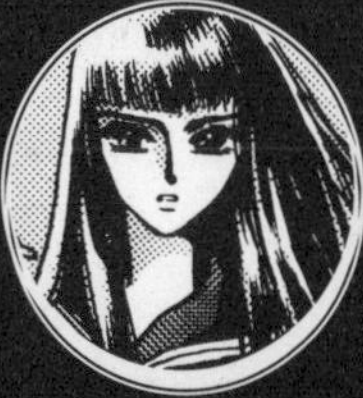

Arashi Kishu
Priestess of the Ise Shrine, Arashi can materialize a sword from the palm of her hand.

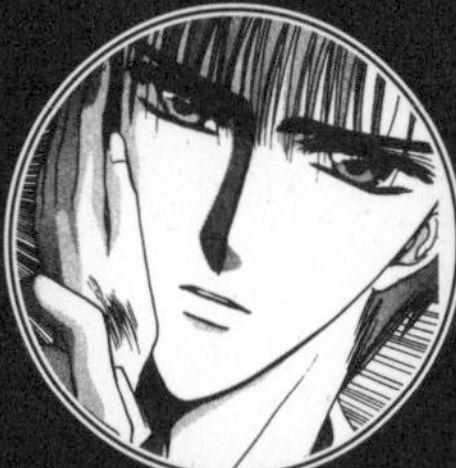

Fuma Monou
Kamui's childhood friend. When Kamui made his choice, Fuma was chosen by fate to become his "Twin Star" — the other "Kamui."

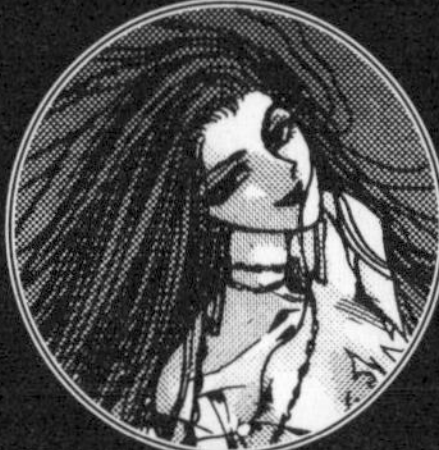

Kanoe
Hinoto's sister shares her ability to see the future… but Kanoe has predicted a different final result.

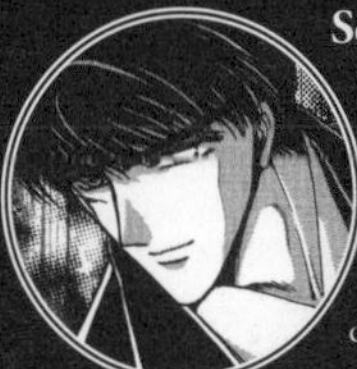

Seishiro Sakurazuka
Also called *Sakurazukamori*, the mysterious Seishiro is a crossover character from ***Tokyo Babylon***. He lost his sight in one eye during that series. He shares a deep rivalry with Subaru.

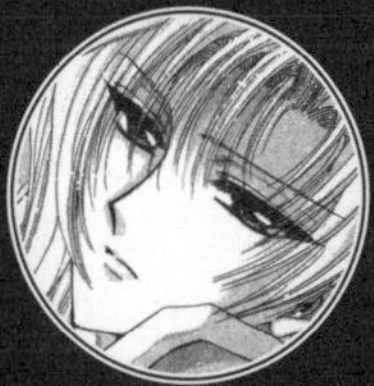

Kakyo Kuzuki
A dreamseer like Hinoto, Kakyo is a hospital-bound invalid kept alive by machines.

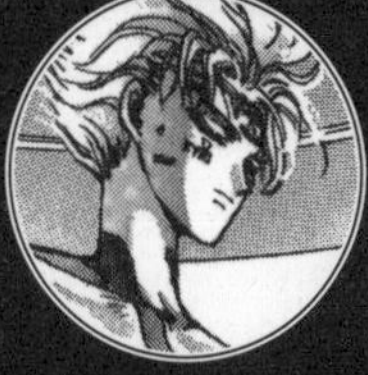

Nataku
A genetically engineered human, Nataku wields a ribbonlike piece of cloth.

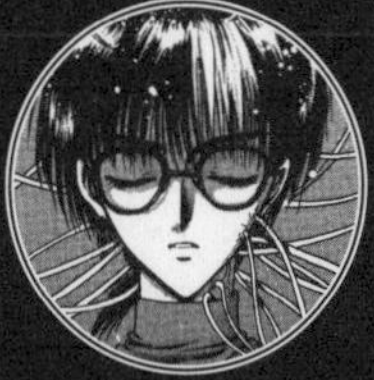

Satsuki Yatoji
A computer expert, Satsuki can interface directly with her personal machine, "The Beast."

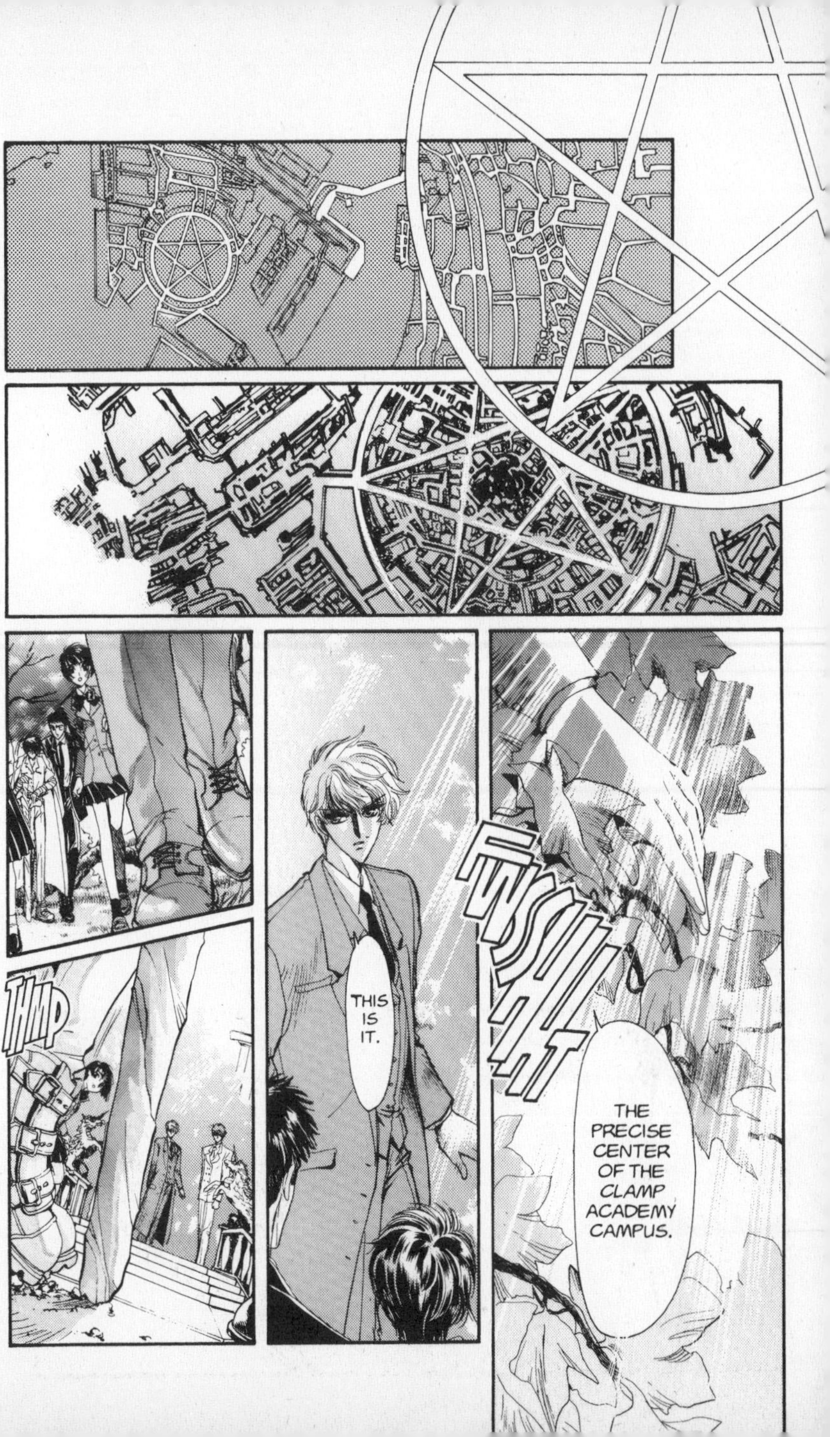
THMP
THIS IS IT.
FSSHHT
THE PRECISE CENTER OF THE CLAMP ACADEMY CAMPUS.

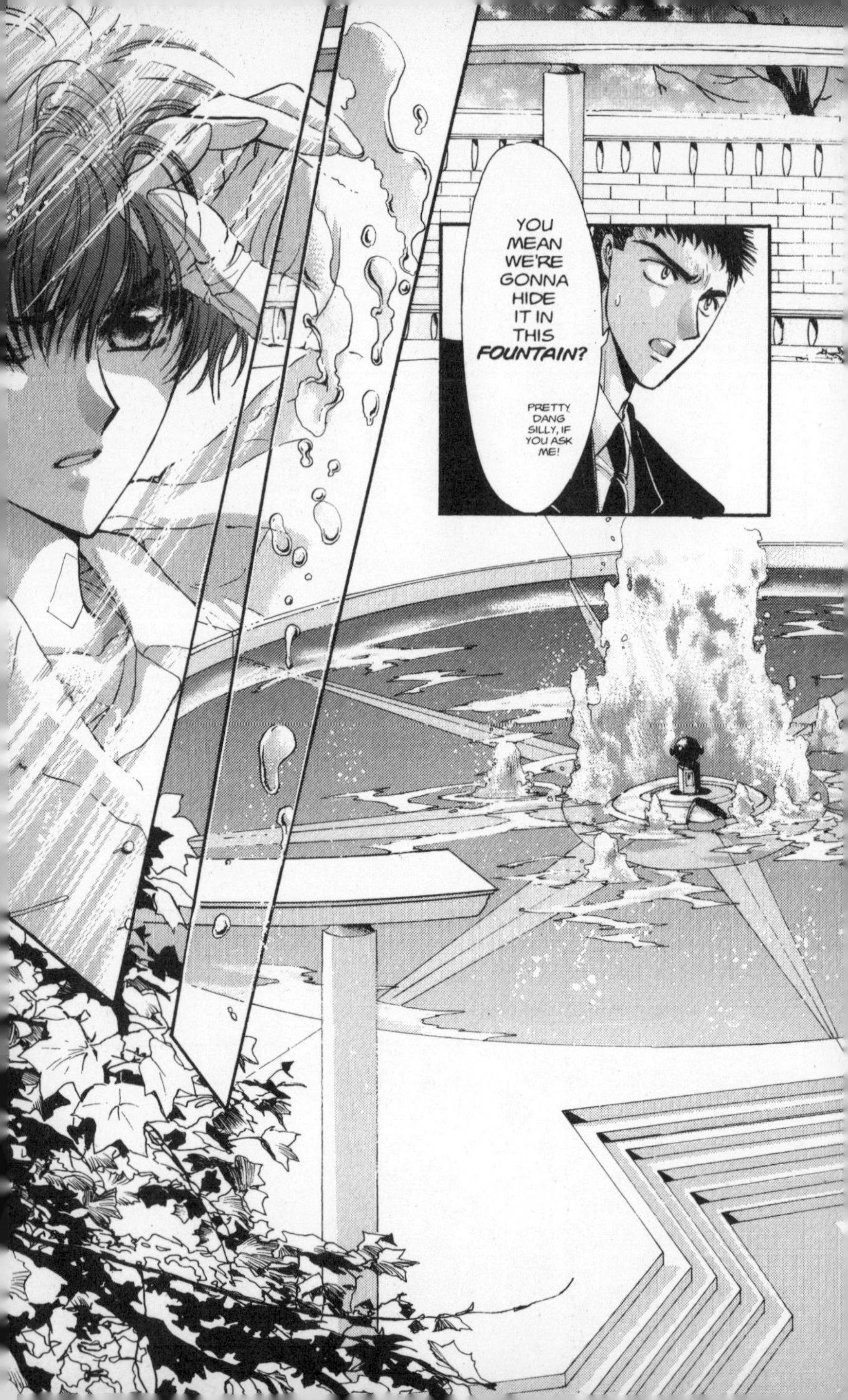
YOU MEAN WE'RE GONNA HIDE IT IN THIS *FOUNTAIN?*
PRETTY DANG SILLY, IF YOU ASK ME!

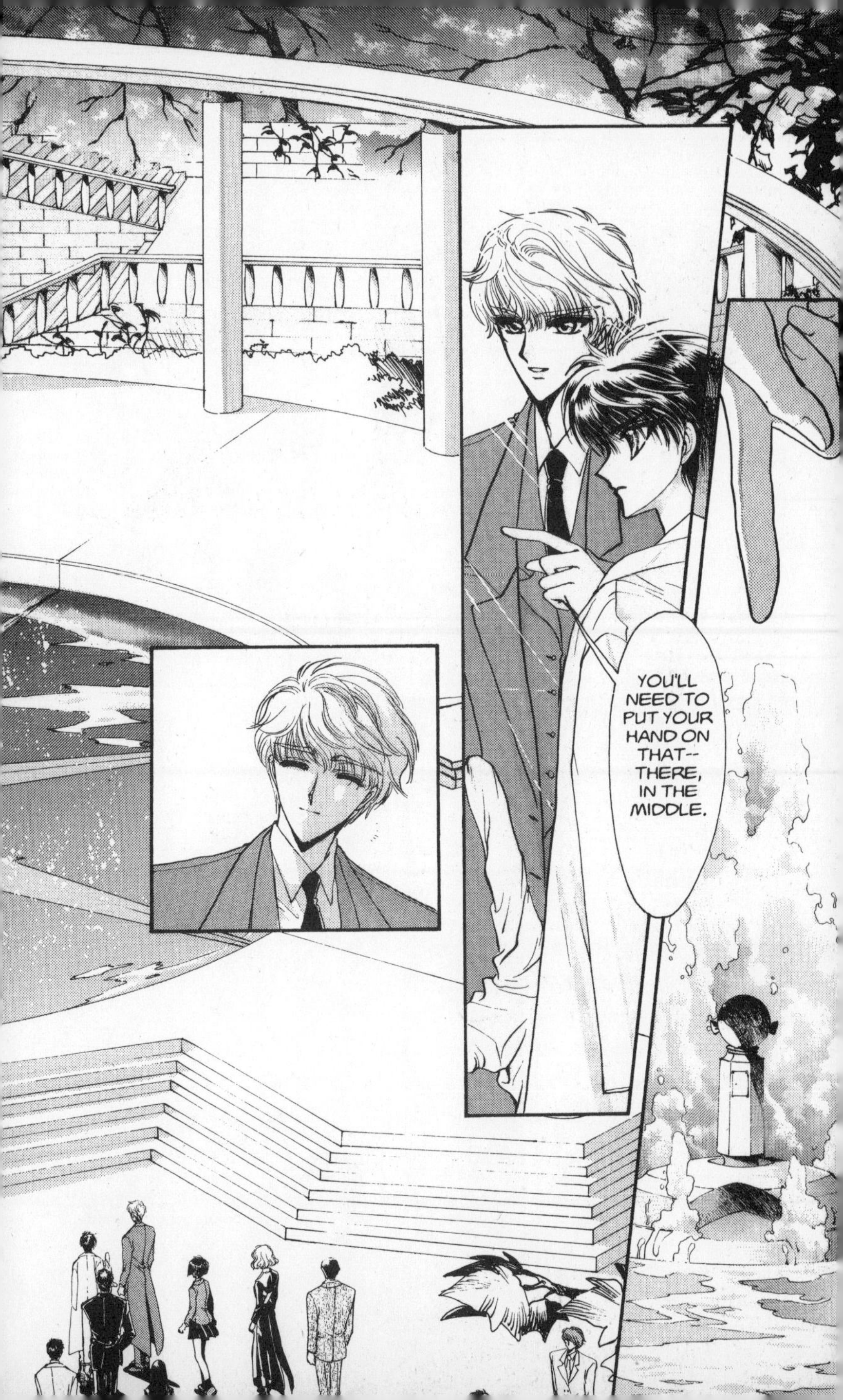
YOU'LL NEED TO PUT YOUR HAND ON THAT-- THERE, IN THE MIDDLE.

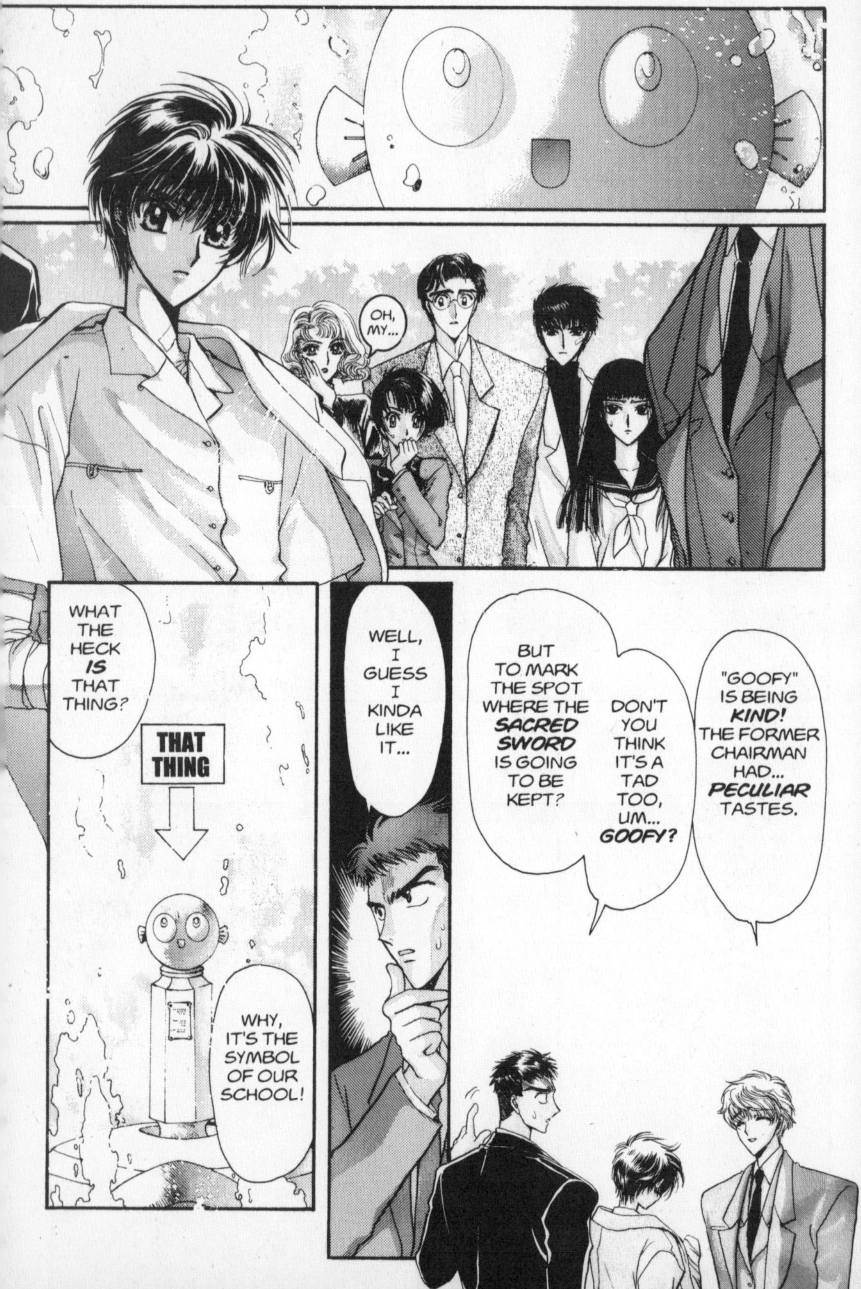
OH, MY...
WHAT THE HECK IS THAT THING?
THAT THING
WHY, IT'S THE SYMBOL OF OUR SCHOOL!
WELL, I GUESS I KINDA LIKE IT...
BUT TO MARK THE SPOT WHERE THE SACRED SWORD IS GOING TO BE KEPT? DON'T YOU THINK IT'S A TAD TOO, UM... GOOFY?
"GOOFY" IS BEING KIND! THE FORMER CHAIRMAN HAD... PECULIAR TASTES.

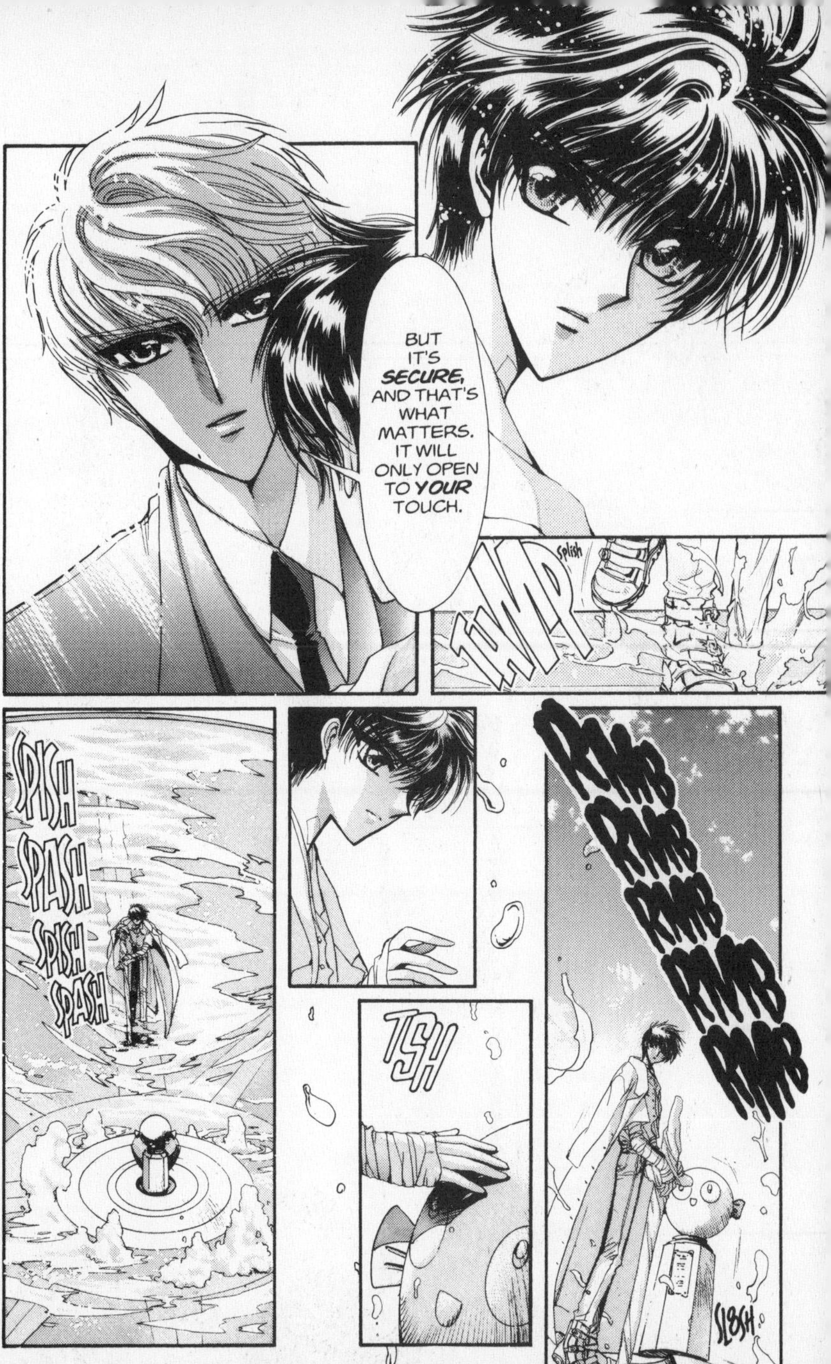
BUT IT'S **SECURE,** AND THAT'S WHAT MATTERS. IT WILL ONLY OPEN TO **YOUR** TOUCH.
splish
SPISH SPASH SPISH SPASH
TSH
SLOSH

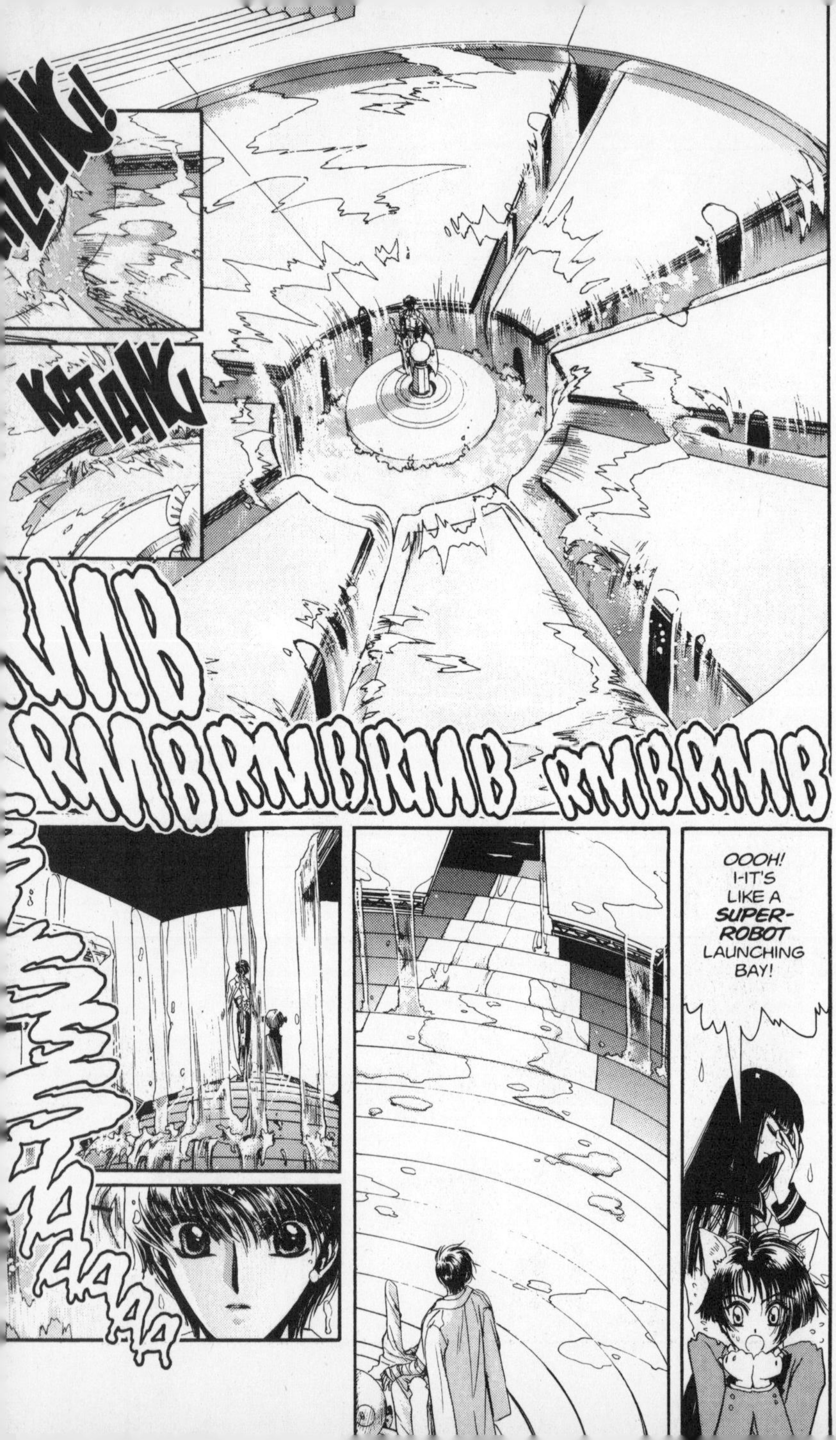
KATANG
RMBRMBRMBRMB RMBRMB
OOOH! I-IT'S LIKE A SUPER-ROBOT LAUNCHING BAY!

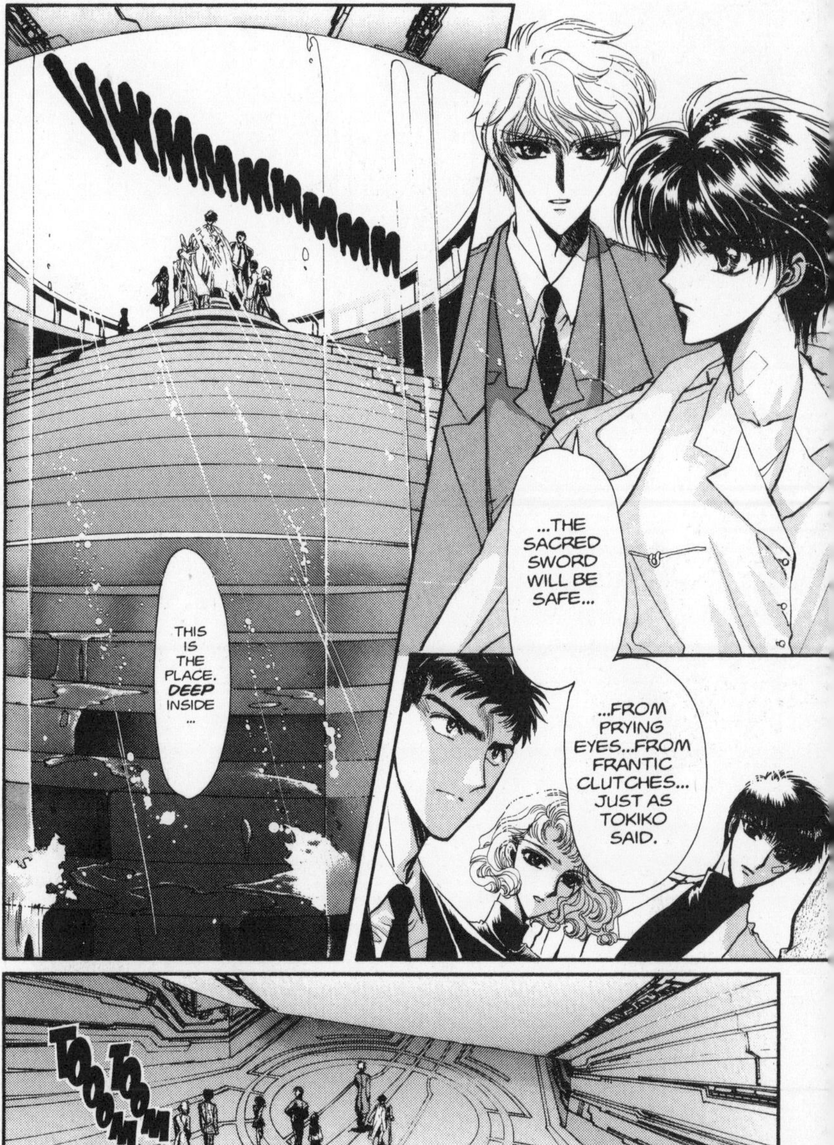
VWMMMMMMMMMM
THIS IS THE PLACE. DEEP INSIDE ...
...THE SACRED SWORD WILL BE SAFE...
...FROM PRYING EYES...FROM FRANTIC CLUTCHES... JUST AS TOKIKO SAID.
TOOOOM TOOM

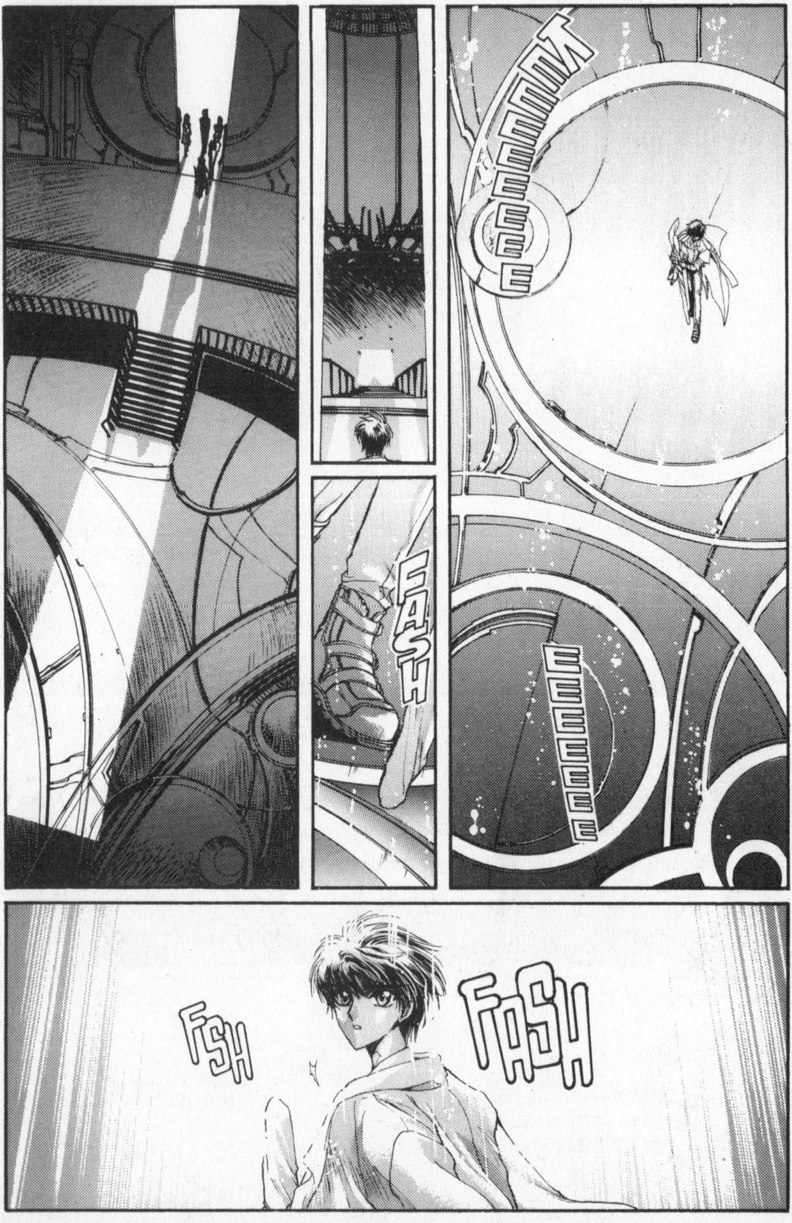
FASH
KEEEEEEE
EEEEEEEEE
FSH
FASH

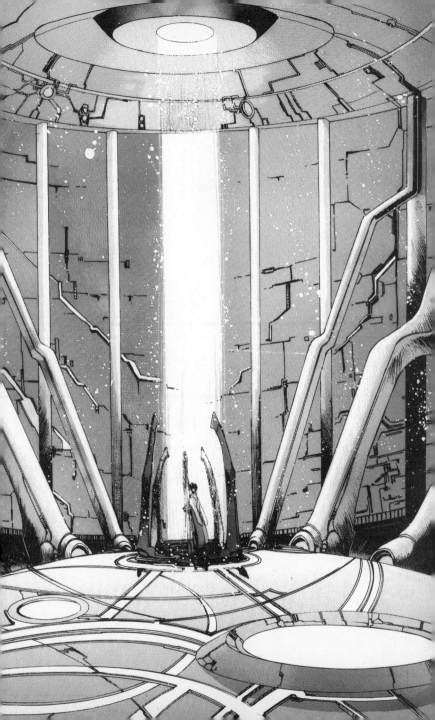

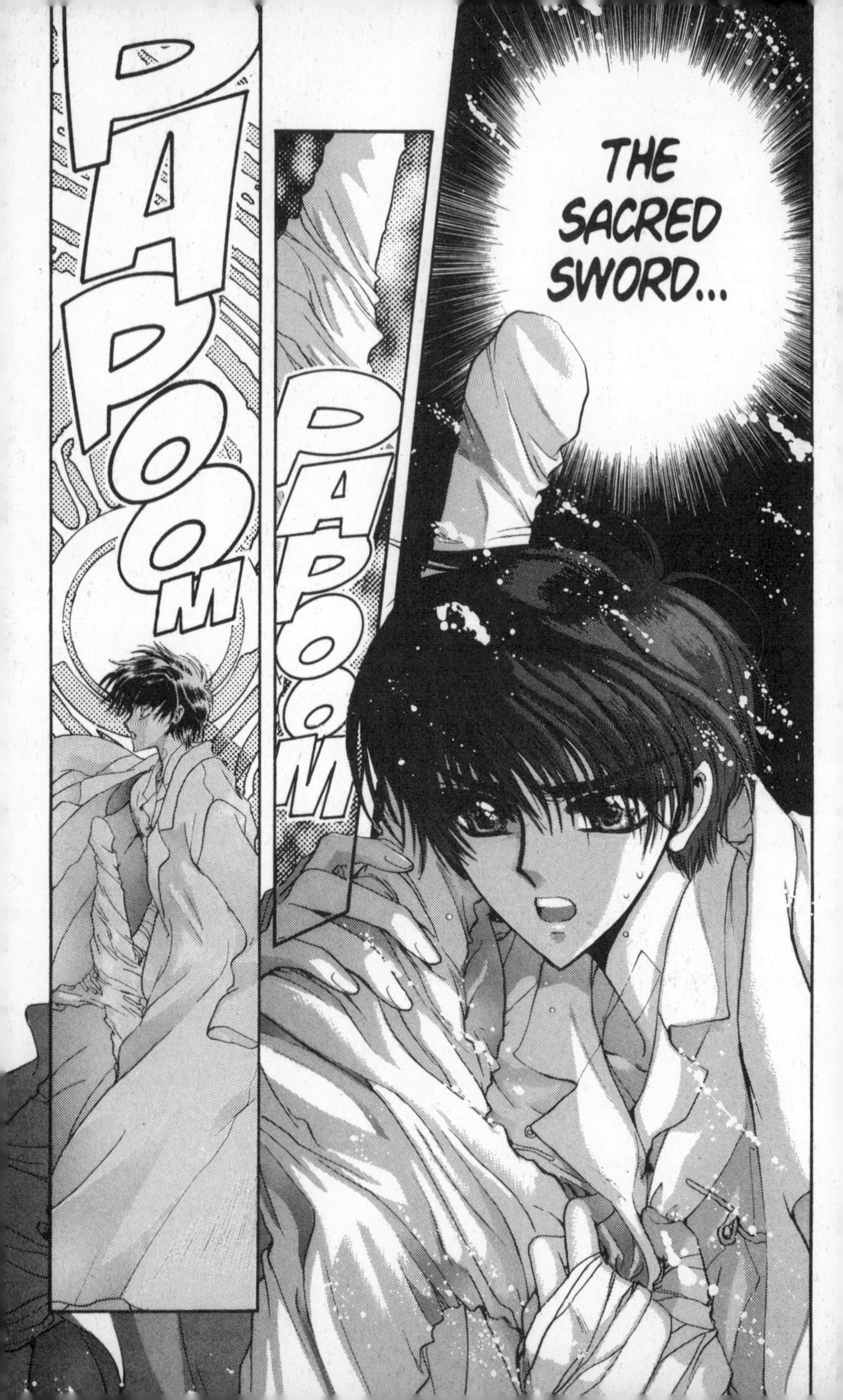
PADOOM
PADOOM
THE SACRED SWORD...

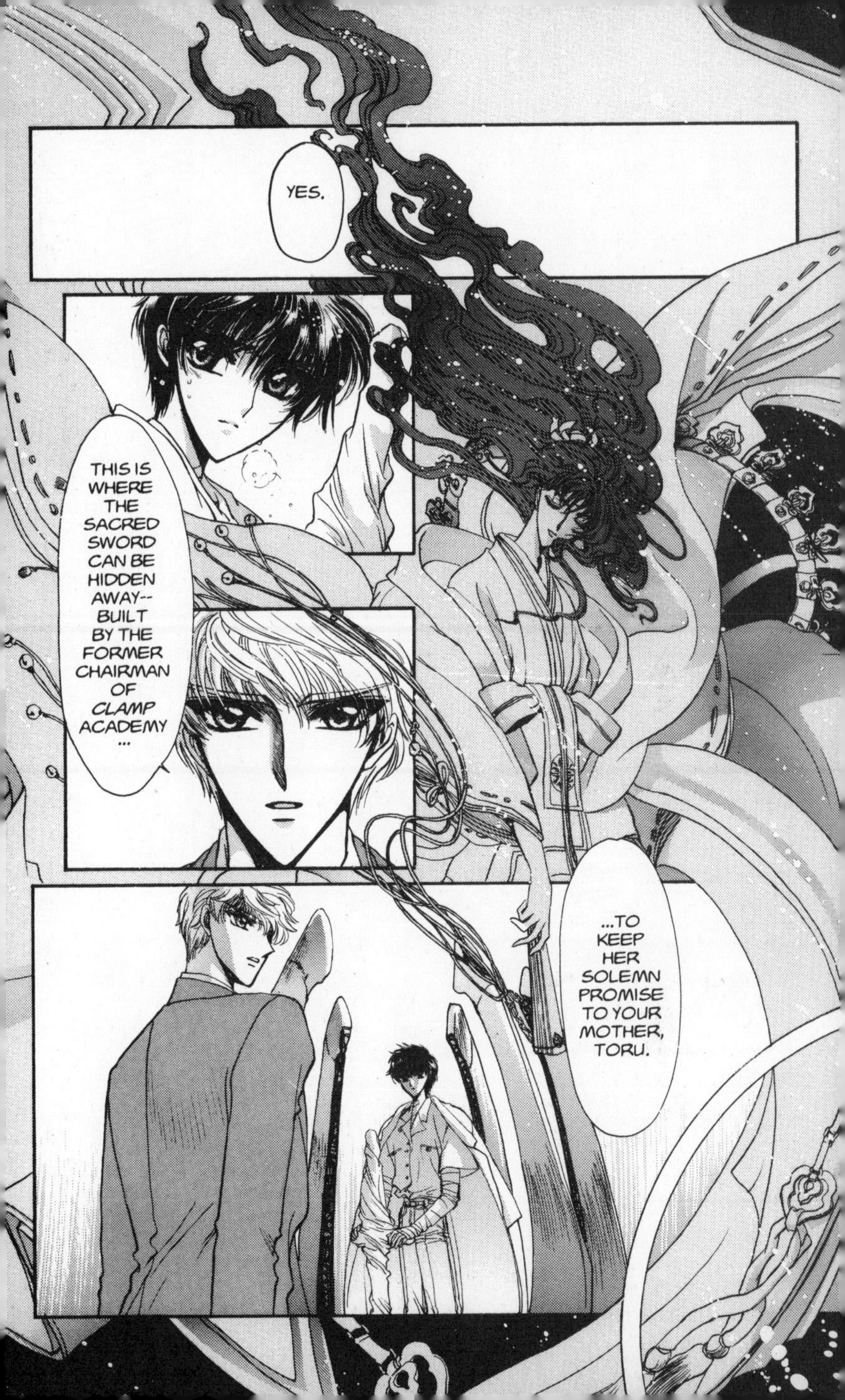
YES.
THIS IS WHERE THE SACRED SWORD CAN BE HIDDEN AWAY-- BUILT BY THE FORMER CHAIRMAN OF CLAMP ACADEMY ...
...TO KEEP HER SOLEMN PROMISE TO YOUR MOTHER, TORU.

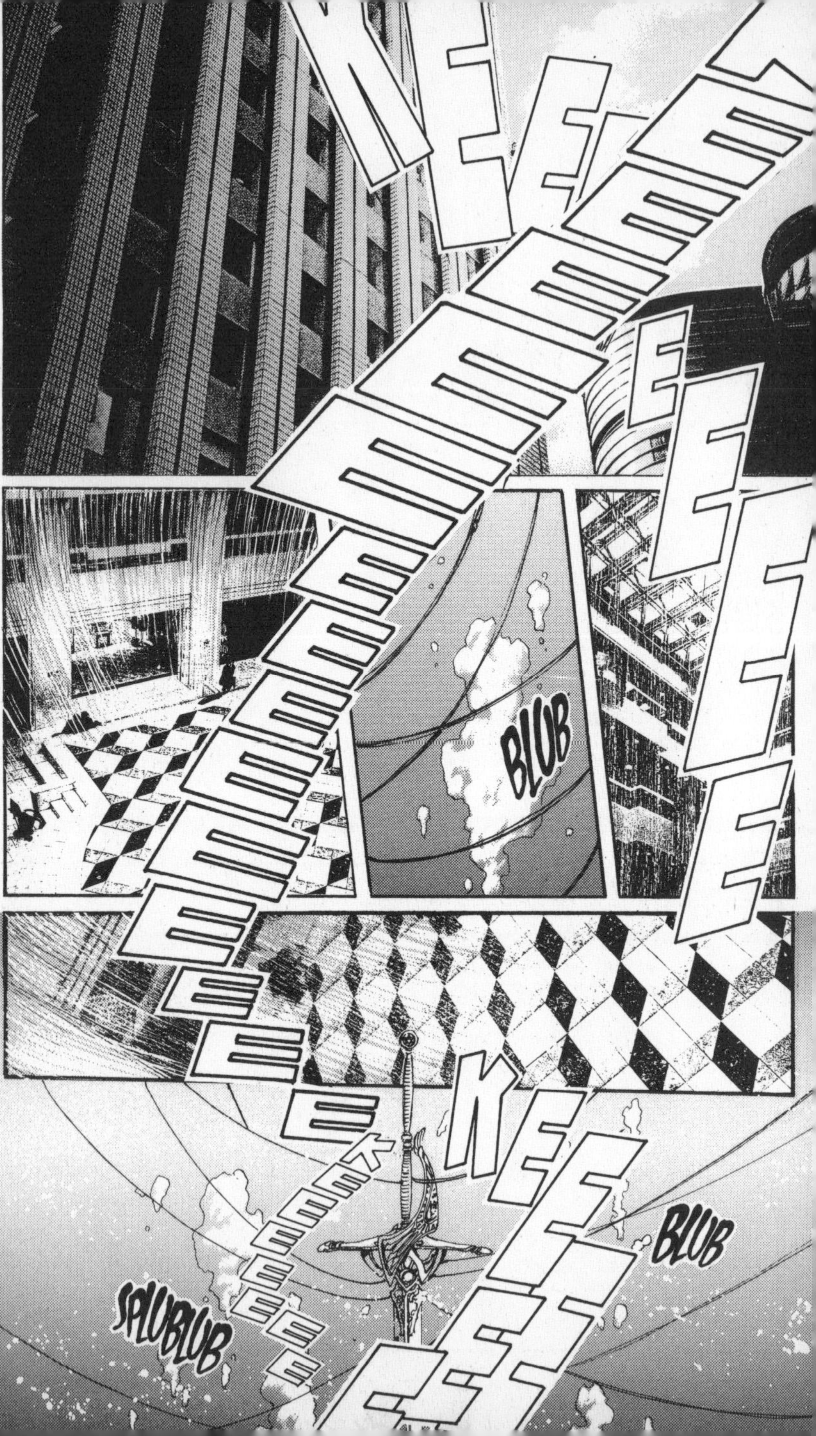
KEEEEEEEEEEEEEEEEEEEEEEEEEEEEE
BLUB
KEEEEEEEEE
KEEEEEEE
BLUB
SPLUBLUB

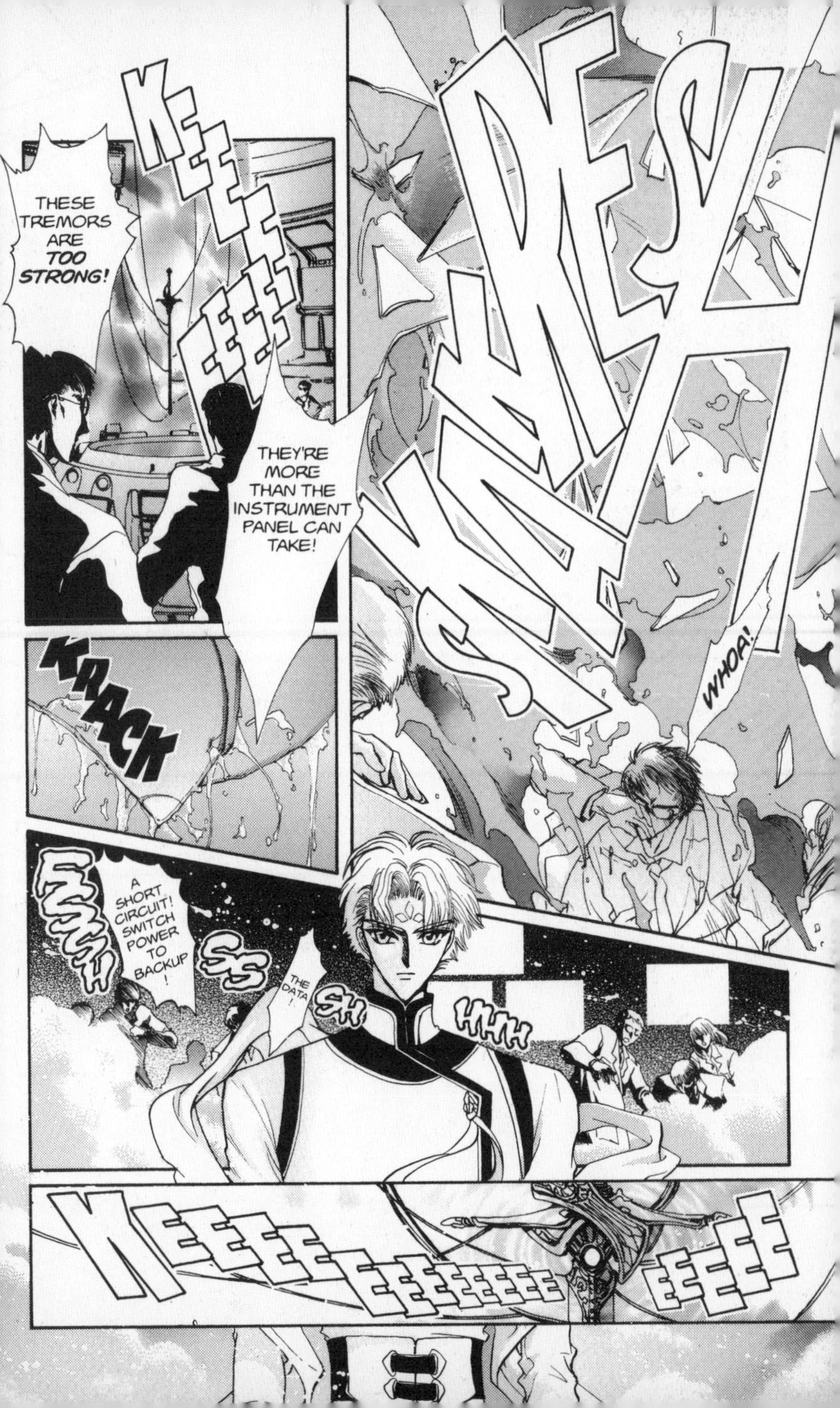

THESE TREMORS ARE TOO STRONG!
THEY'RE MORE THAN THE INSTRUMENT PANEL CAN TAKE!
KRACK
WHOA!
A SHORT CIRCUIT! SWITCH POWER TO BACKUP!
THE DATA!

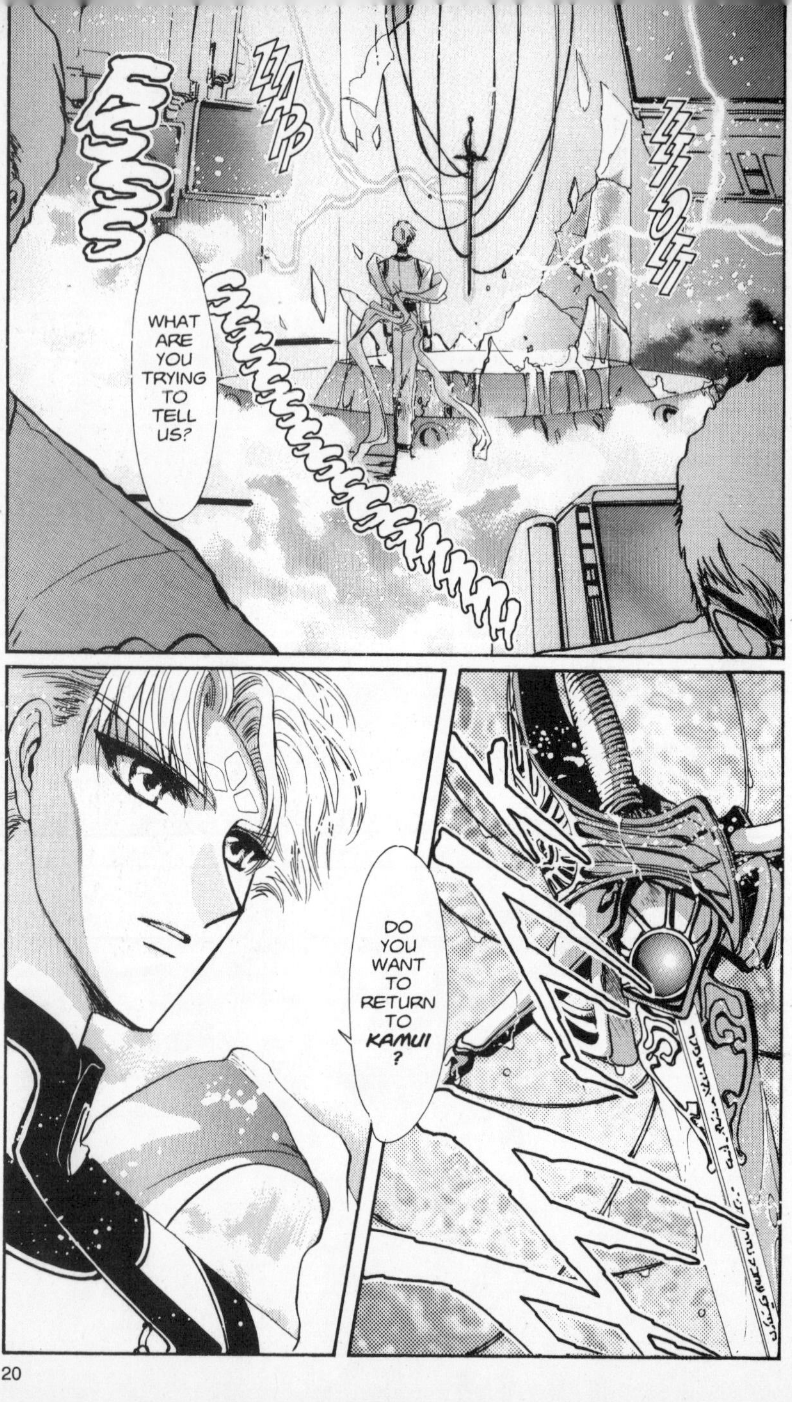
FSSS
ZZAPP
WHAT ARE YOU TRYING TO TELL US?
DO YOU WANT TO RETURN TO *KAMUI* ?

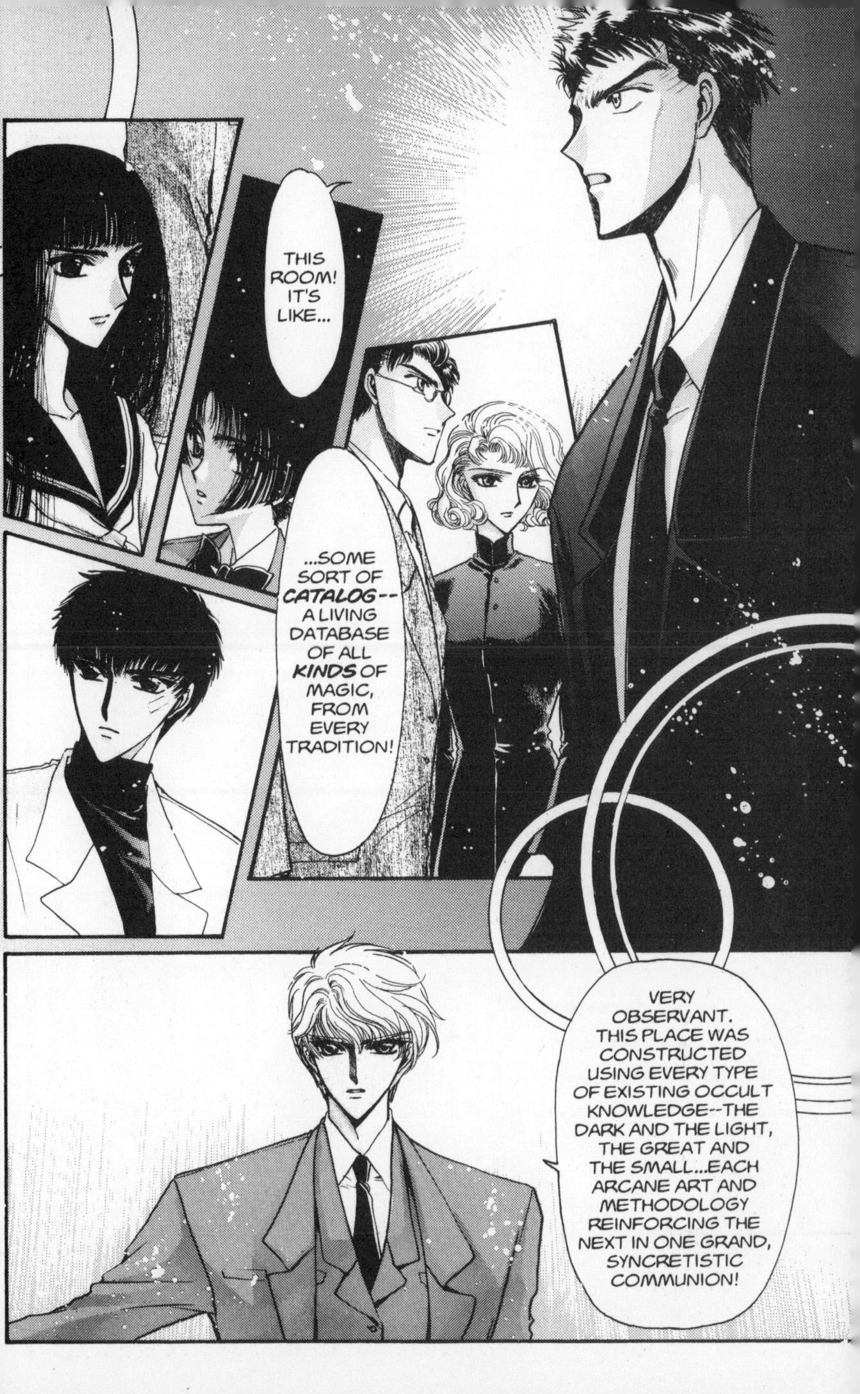
THIS ROOM! IT'S LIKE...
...SOME SORT OF CATALOG-- A LIVING DATABASE OF ALL KINDS OF MAGIC, FROM EVERY TRADITION!
VERY OBSERVANT. THIS PLACE WAS CONSTRUCTED USING EVERY TYPE OF EXISTING OCCULT KNOWLEDGE--THE DARK AND THE LIGHT, THE GREAT AND THE SMALL...EACH ARCANE ART AND METHODOLOGY REINFORCING THE NEXT IN ONE GRAND, SYNCRETISTIC COMMUNION!

THE *CLAMP ACADEMY* MONORAIL RUNNING IN THE SHAPE OF A FIVE-POINTED STAR...

...JUST *ONE* OF THE SPELLS WHICH PROTECTS THIS ROOM.

HEH

THE MONORAIL ONLY RUNS IN ONE DIRECTION, YOU KNOW.

AND EVER SO SLOWLY-- ONLY A LITTLE FASTER THAN RUNNING SPEED.

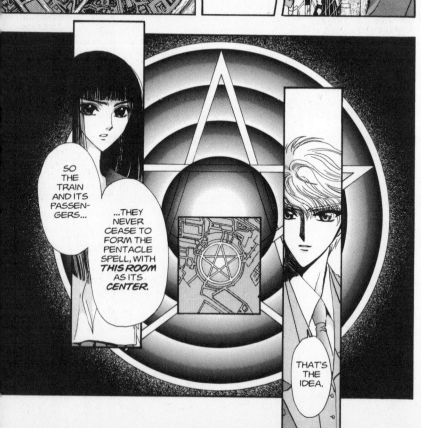

SO THE TRAIN AND ITS PASSEN-GERS...

...THEY NEVER CEASE TO FORM THE PENTACLE SPELL, WITH *THIS ROOM* AS ITS *CENTER.*

THAT'S THE IDEA.

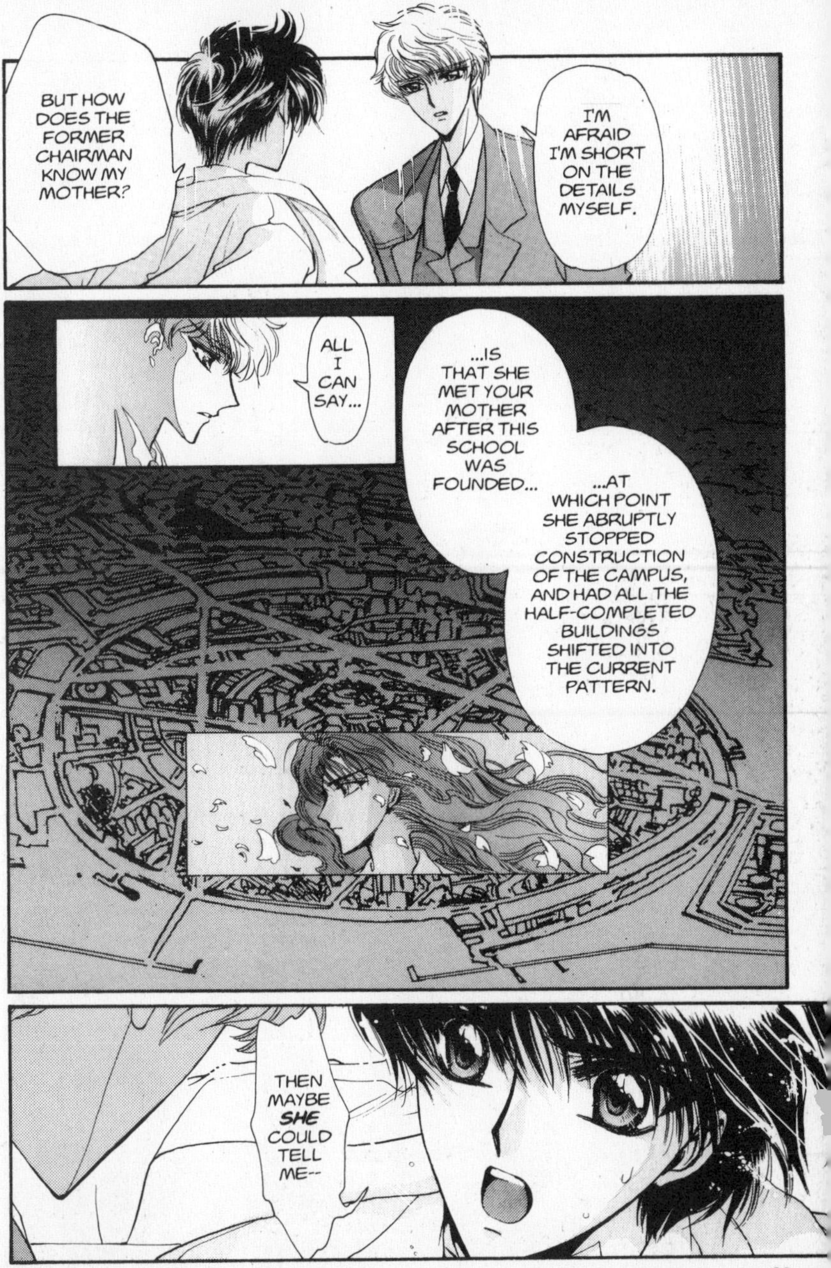
BUT HOW DOES THE FORMER CHAIRMAN KNOW MY MOTHER?
I'M AFRAID I'M SHORT ON THE DETAILS MYSELF.
ALL I CAN SAY...
...IS THAT SHE MET YOUR MOTHER AFTER THIS SCHOOL WAS FOUNDED...
...AT WHICH POINT SHE ABRUPTLY STOPPED CONSTRUCTION OF THE CAMPUS, AND HAD ALL THE HALF-COMPLETED BUILDINGS SHIFTED INTO THE CURRENT PATTERN.
THEN MAYBE ***SHE*** COULD TELL ME--

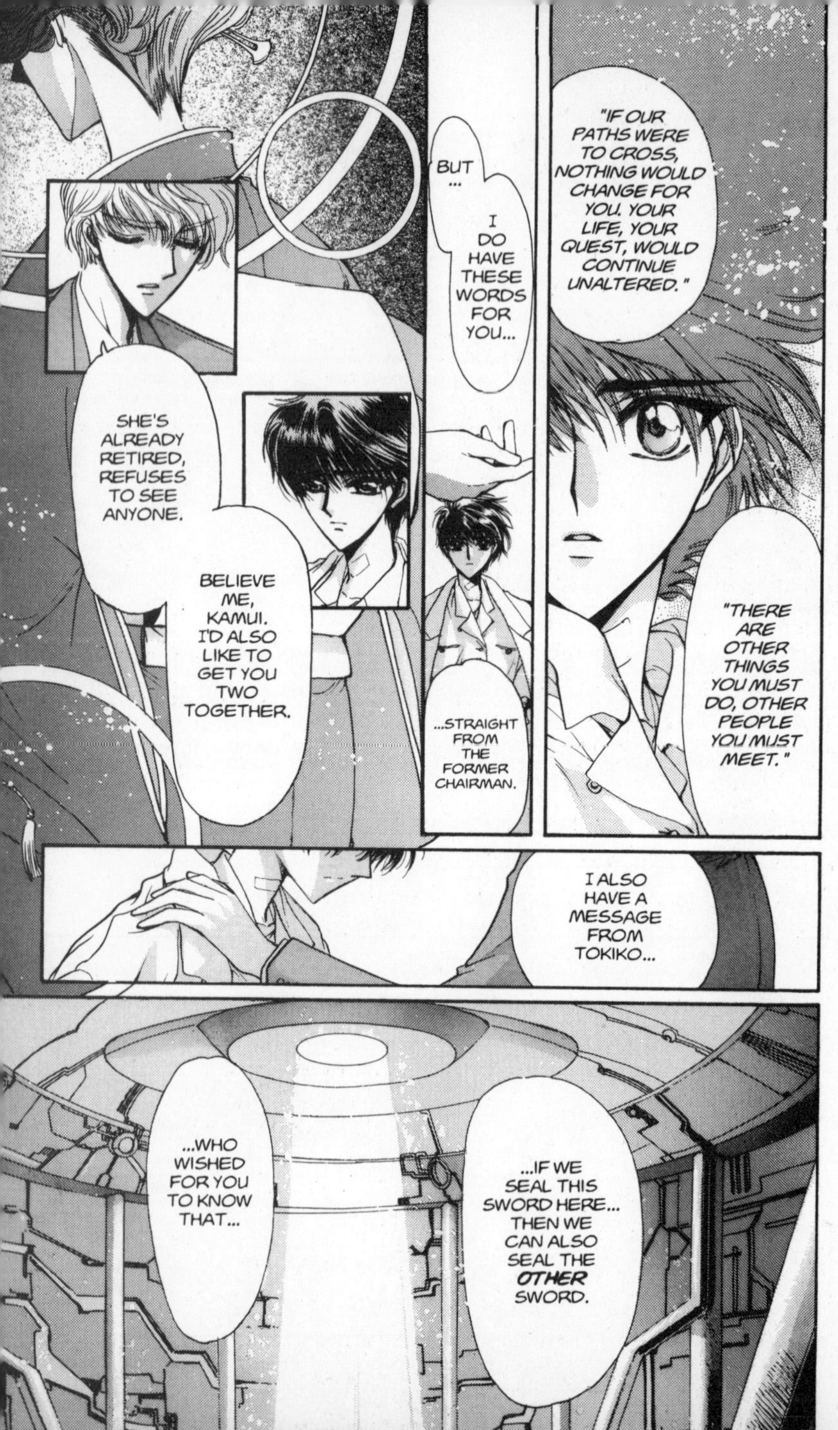
SHE'S ALREADY RETIRED, REFUSES TO SEE ANYONE.
BELIEVE ME, KAMUI. I'D ALSO LIKE TO GET YOU TWO TOGETHER.
BUT ...
I DO HAVE THESE WORDS FOR YOU...
...STRAIGHT FROM THE FORMER CHAIRMAN.
"IF OUR PATHS WERE TO CROSS, NOTHING WOULD CHANGE FOR YOU. YOUR LIFE, YOUR QUEST, WOULD CONTINUE UNALTERED."
"THERE ARE OTHER THINGS YOU MUST DO, OTHER PEOPLE YOU MUST MEET."
I ALSO HAVE A MESSAGE FROM TOKIKO...
...WHO WISHED FOR YOU TO KNOW THAT...
...IF WE SEAL THIS SWORD HERE... THEN WE CAN ALSO SEAL THE *OTHER* SWORD.

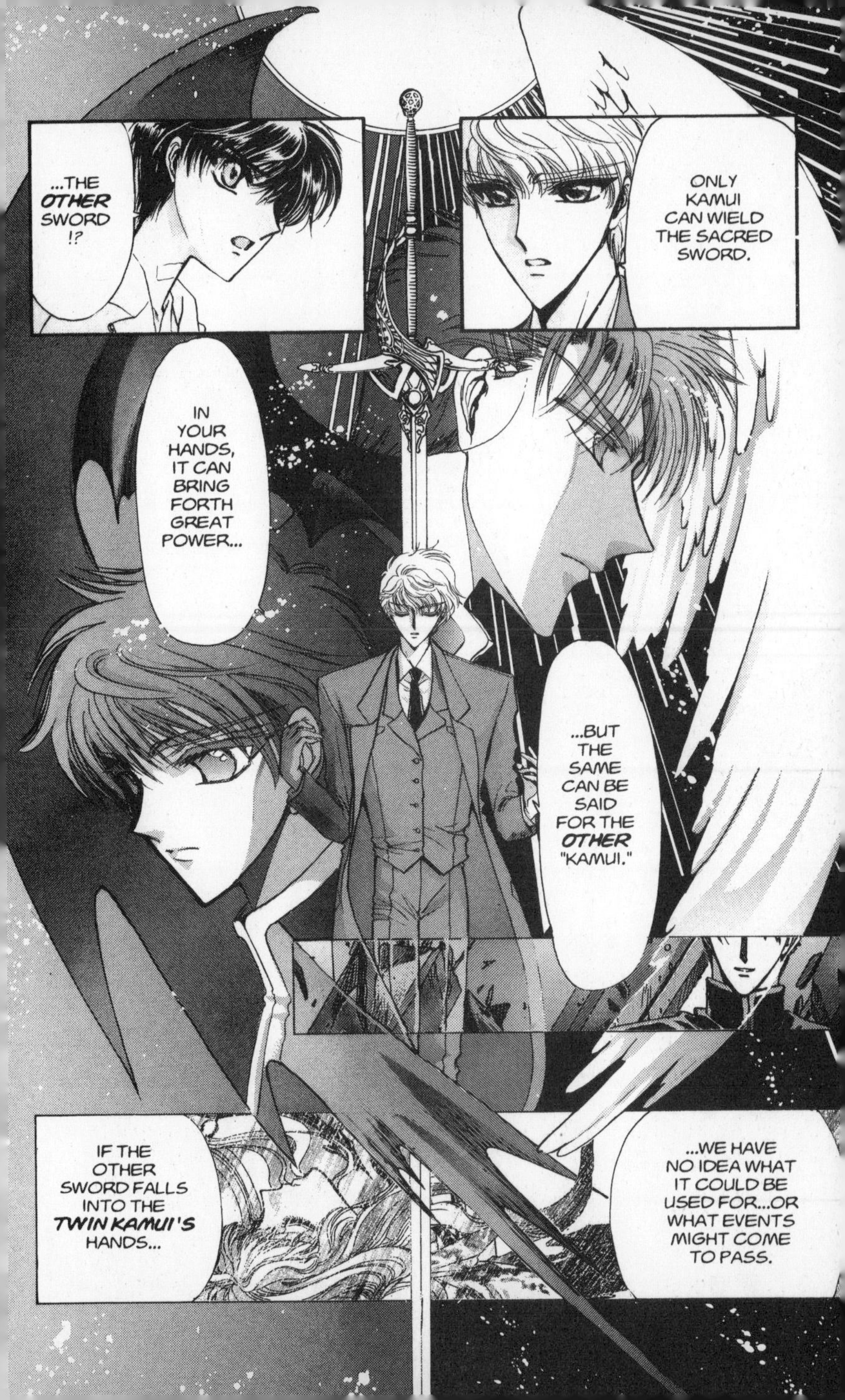
...THE OTHER SWORD !?
ONLY KAMUI CAN WIELD THE SACRED SWORD.
IN YOUR HANDS, IT CAN BRING FORTH GREAT POWER...
...BUT THE SAME CAN BE SAID FOR THE OTHER "KAMUI."
IF THE OTHER SWORD FALLS INTO THE TWIN KAMUI'S HANDS...
...WE HAVE NO IDEA WHAT IT COULD BE USED FOR...OR WHAT EVENTS MIGHT COME TO PASS.

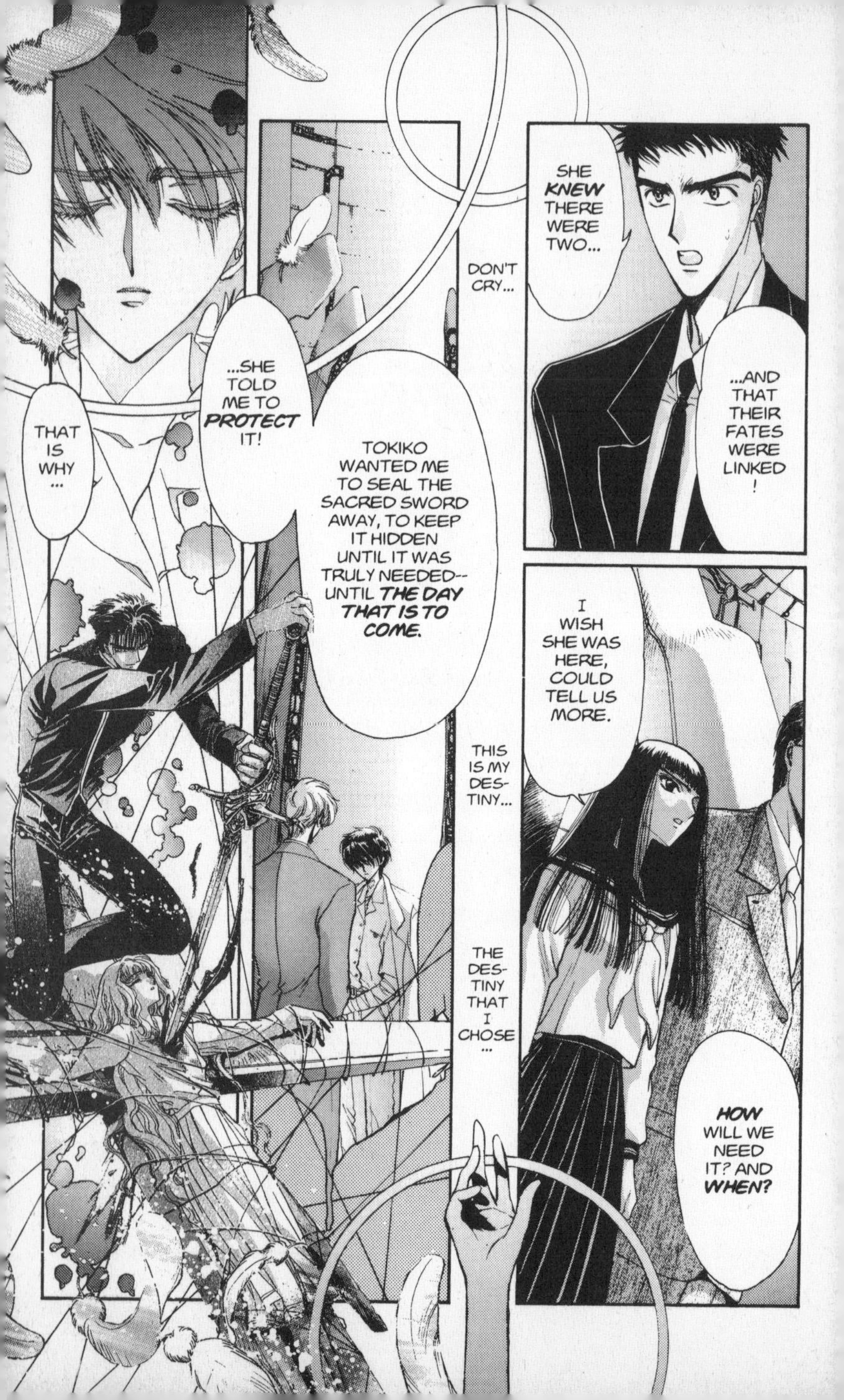
THAT IS WHY...
...SHE TOLD ME TO PROTECT IT!
TOKIKO WANTED ME TO SEAL THE SACRED SWORD AWAY, TO KEEP IT HIDDEN UNTIL IT WAS TRULY NEEDED-- UNTIL THE DAY THAT IS TO COME.
DON'T CRY...
SHE KNEW THERE WERE TWO...
...AND THAT THEIR FATES WERE LINKED!
I WISH SHE WAS HERE, COULD TELL US MORE.
THIS IS MY DES-TINY...
THE DES-TINY THAT I CHOSE...
HOW WILL WE NEED IT? AND WHEN?

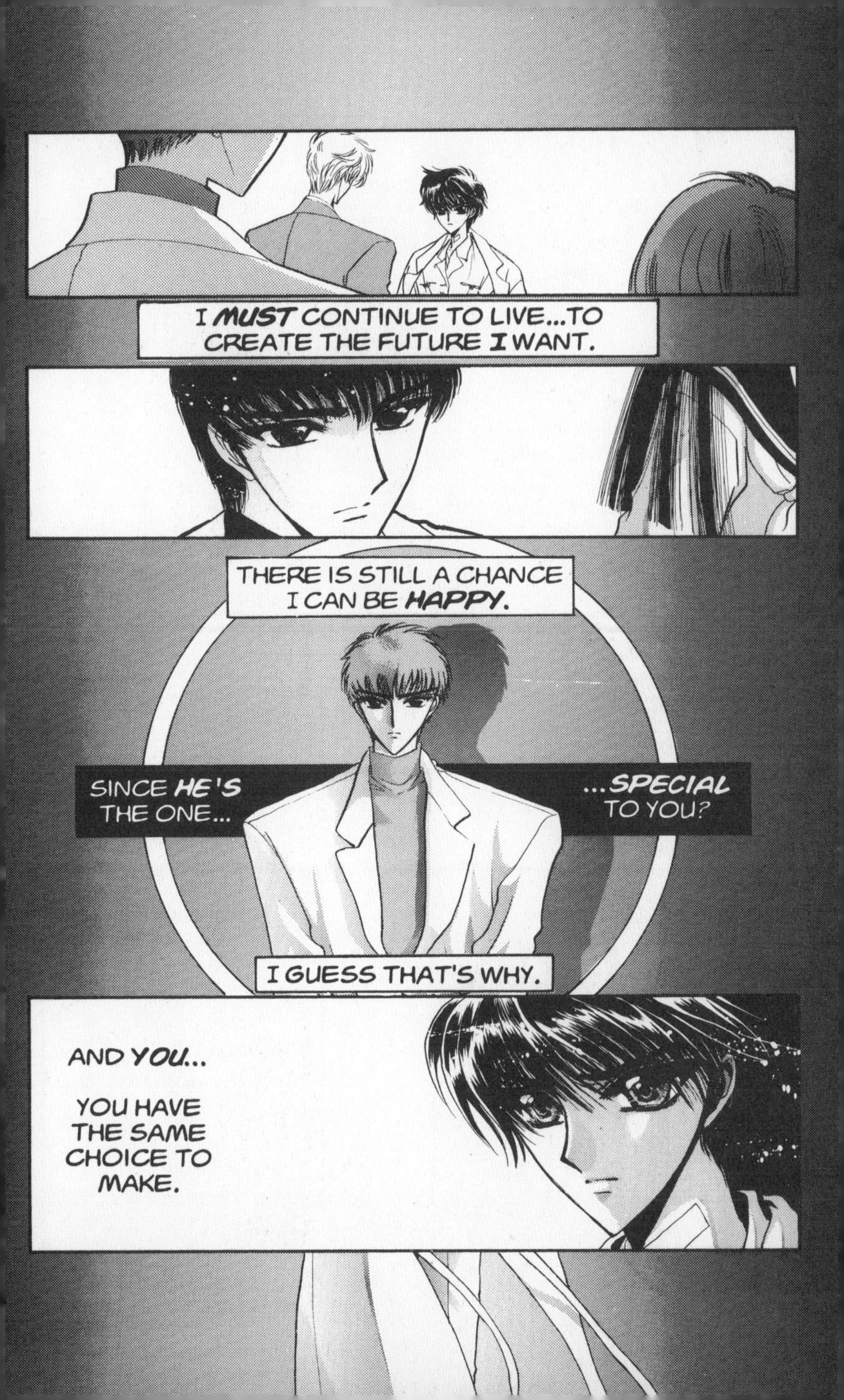
I MUST CONTINUE TO LIVE...TO CREATE THE FUTURE I WANT.
THERE IS STILL A CHANCE I CAN BE HAPPY.
SINCE HE'S THE ONE...
...SPECIAL TO YOU?
I GUESS THAT'S WHY.
AND YOU...
YOU HAVE THE SAME CHOICE TO MAKE.

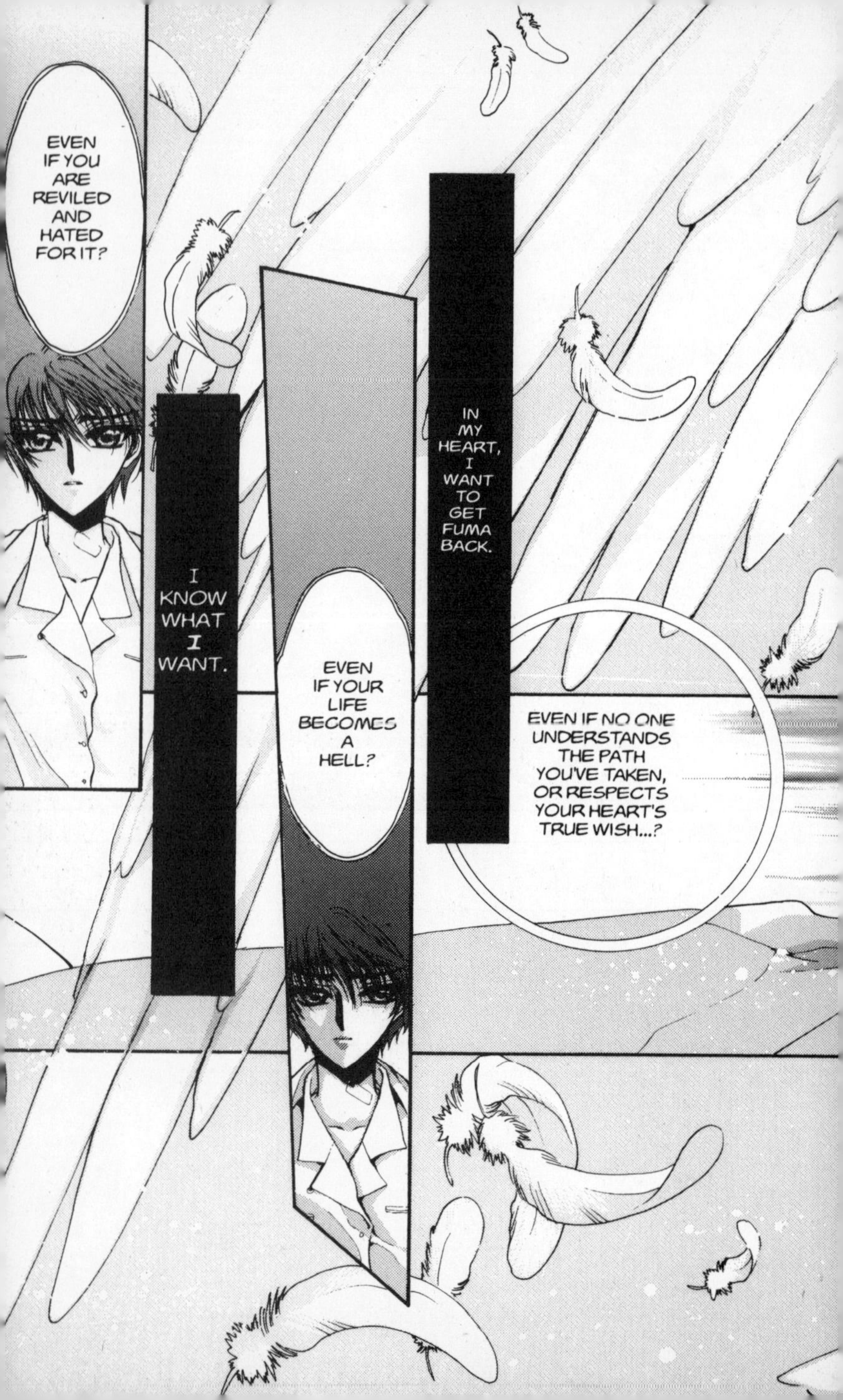
EVEN IF YOU ARE REVILED AND HATED FOR IT?
I KNOW WHAT I WANT.
EVEN IF YOUR LIFE BECOMES A HELL?
IN MY HEART, I WANT TO GET FUMA BACK.
EVEN IF NO ONE UNDERSTANDS THE PATH YOU'VE TAKEN, OR RESPECTS YOUR HEART'S TRUE WISH...?

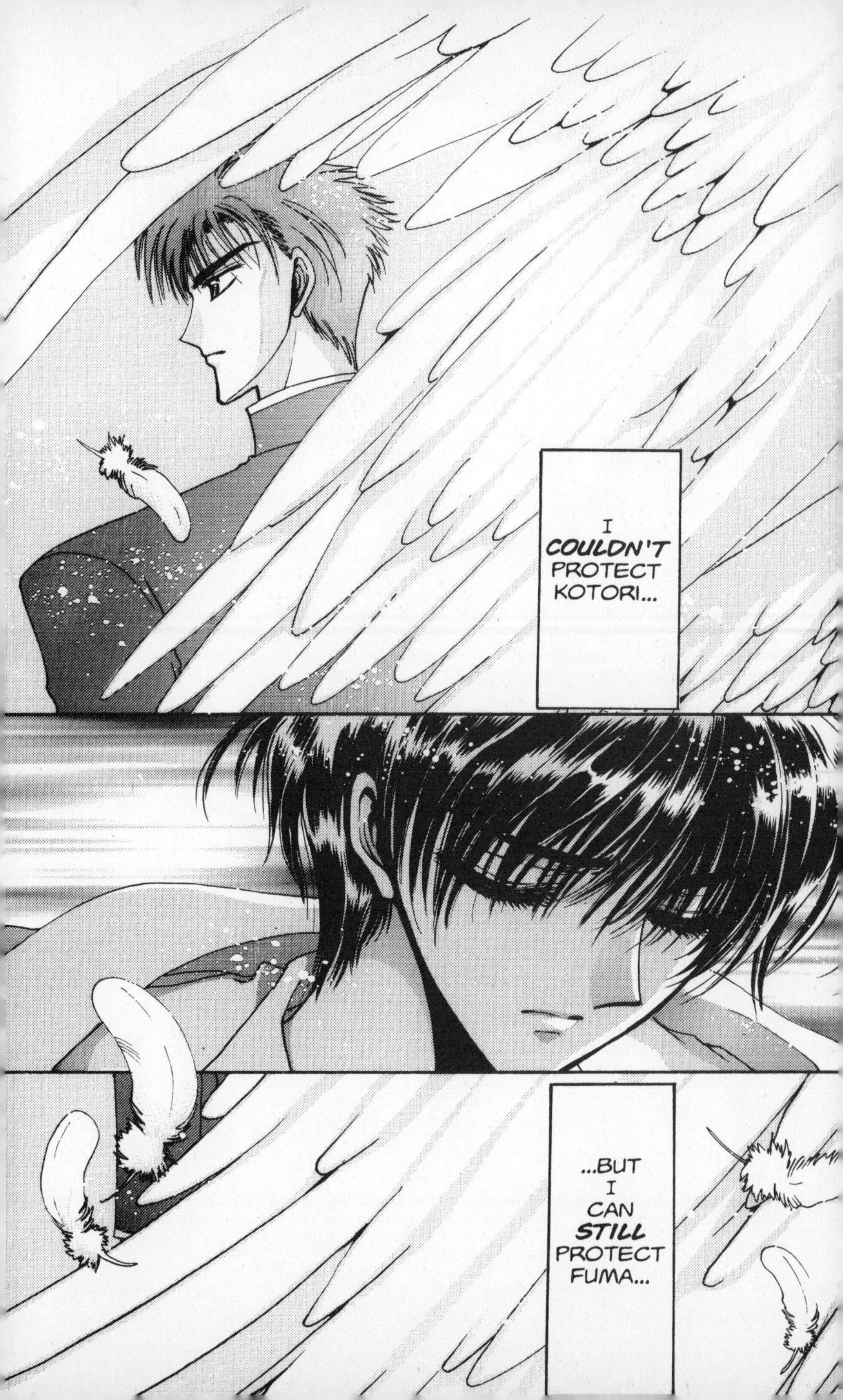
I COULDN'T PROTECT KOTORI...
...BUT I CAN STILL PROTECT FUMA...

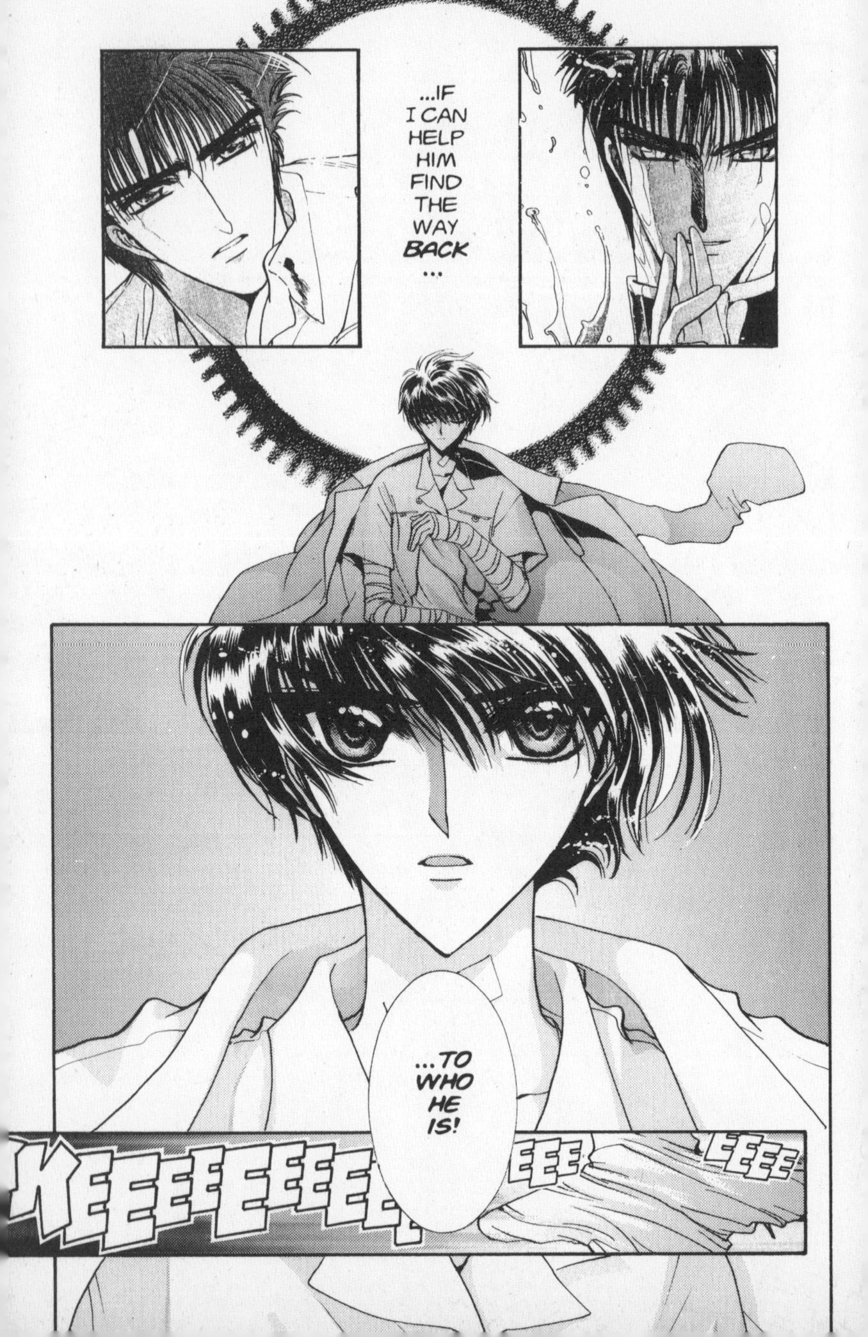
...IF I CAN HELP HIM FIND THE WAY BACK...
...TO WHO HE IS!
KEEEEEEEEEEEEEEEE

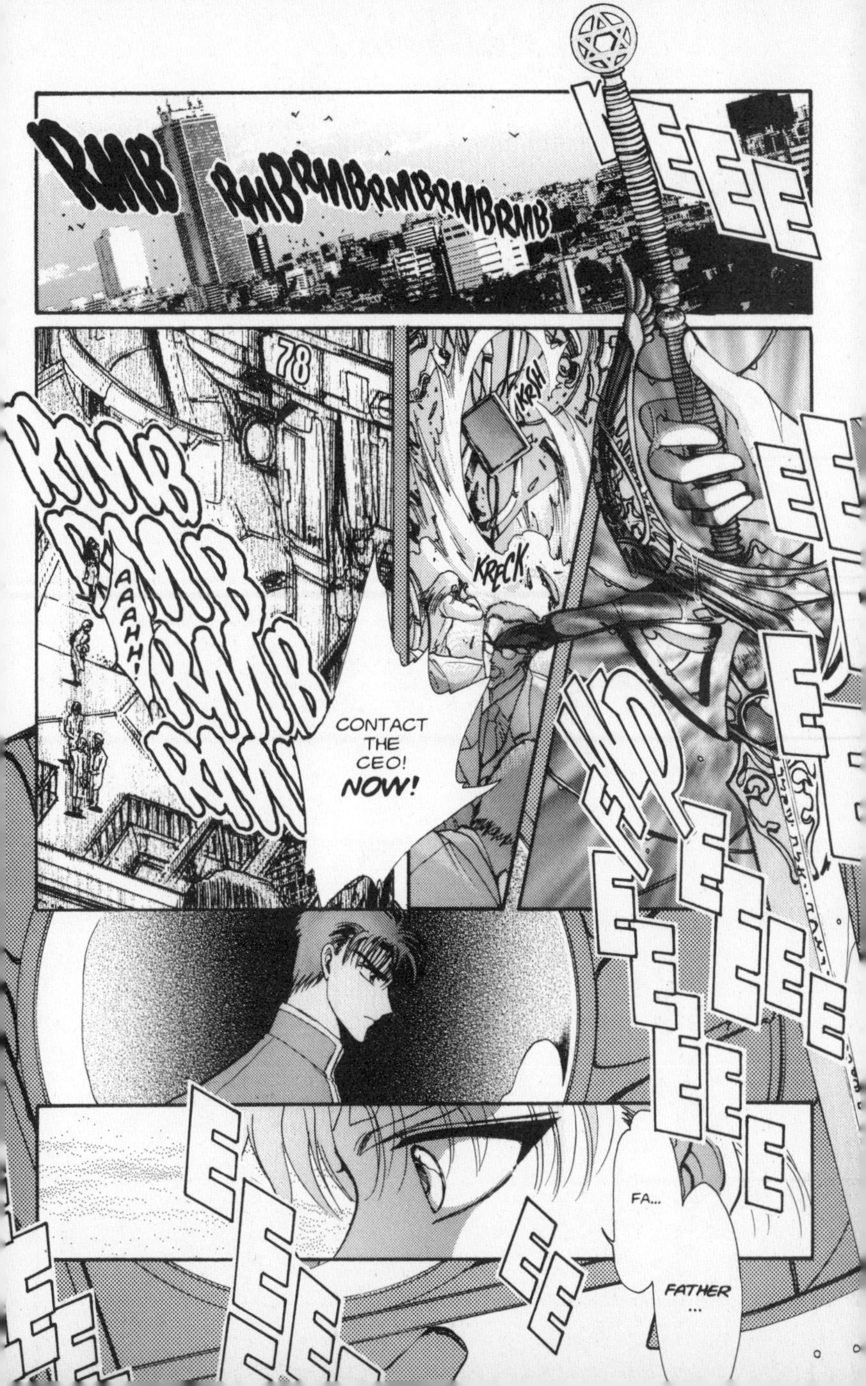

RMB RMBRMBRMBRMBRMB
YEEEE
RMB RMB RMB RMB
AAAHH!
CONTACT THE CEO! NOW!
KRSH
KRECK
EEE
EEE
EEEE
FA...
FATHER ...

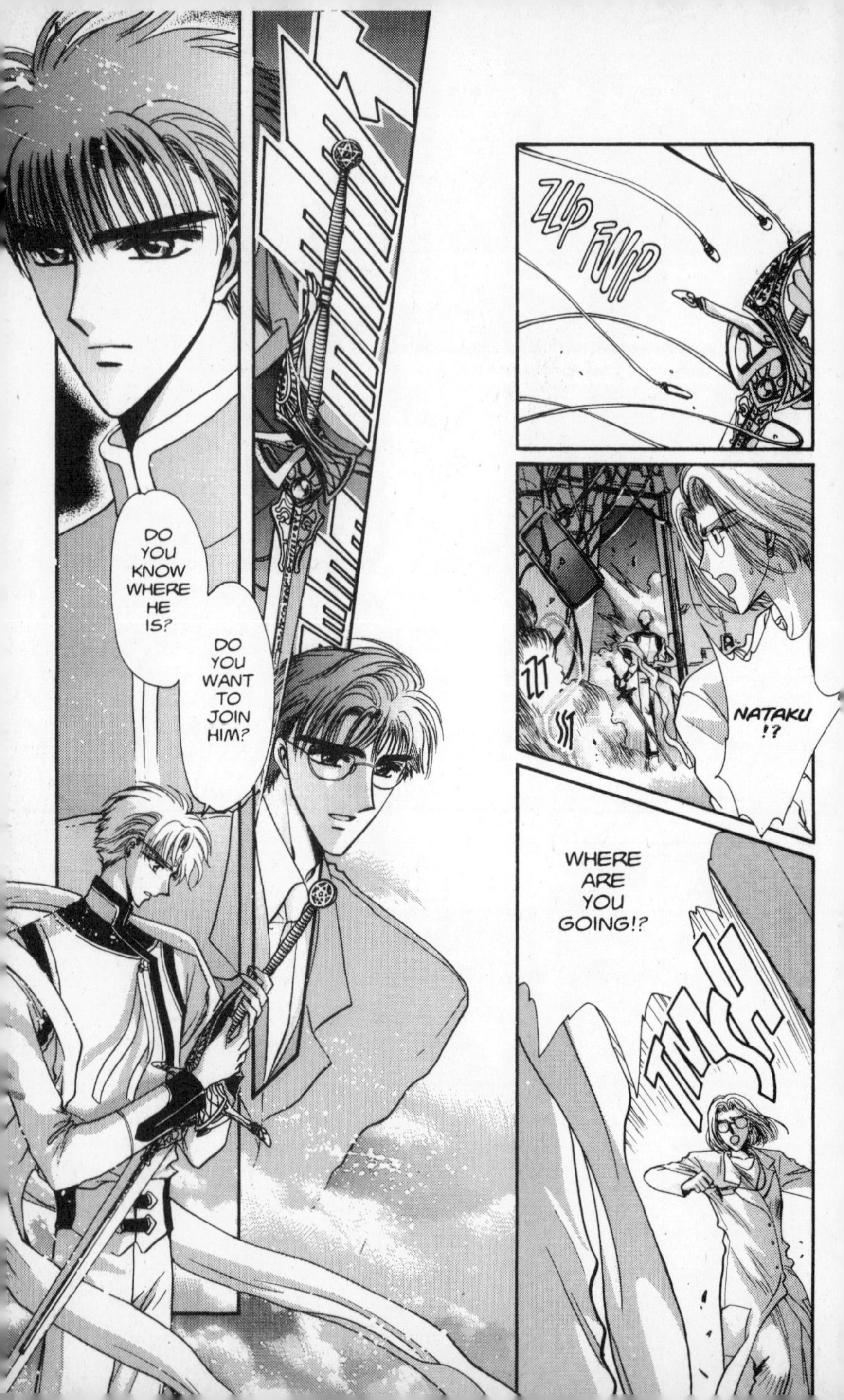
DO YOU KNOW WHERE HE IS?
DO YOU WANT TO JOIN HIM?
ZZT
SST
NATAKU!?
WHERE ARE YOU GOING!?

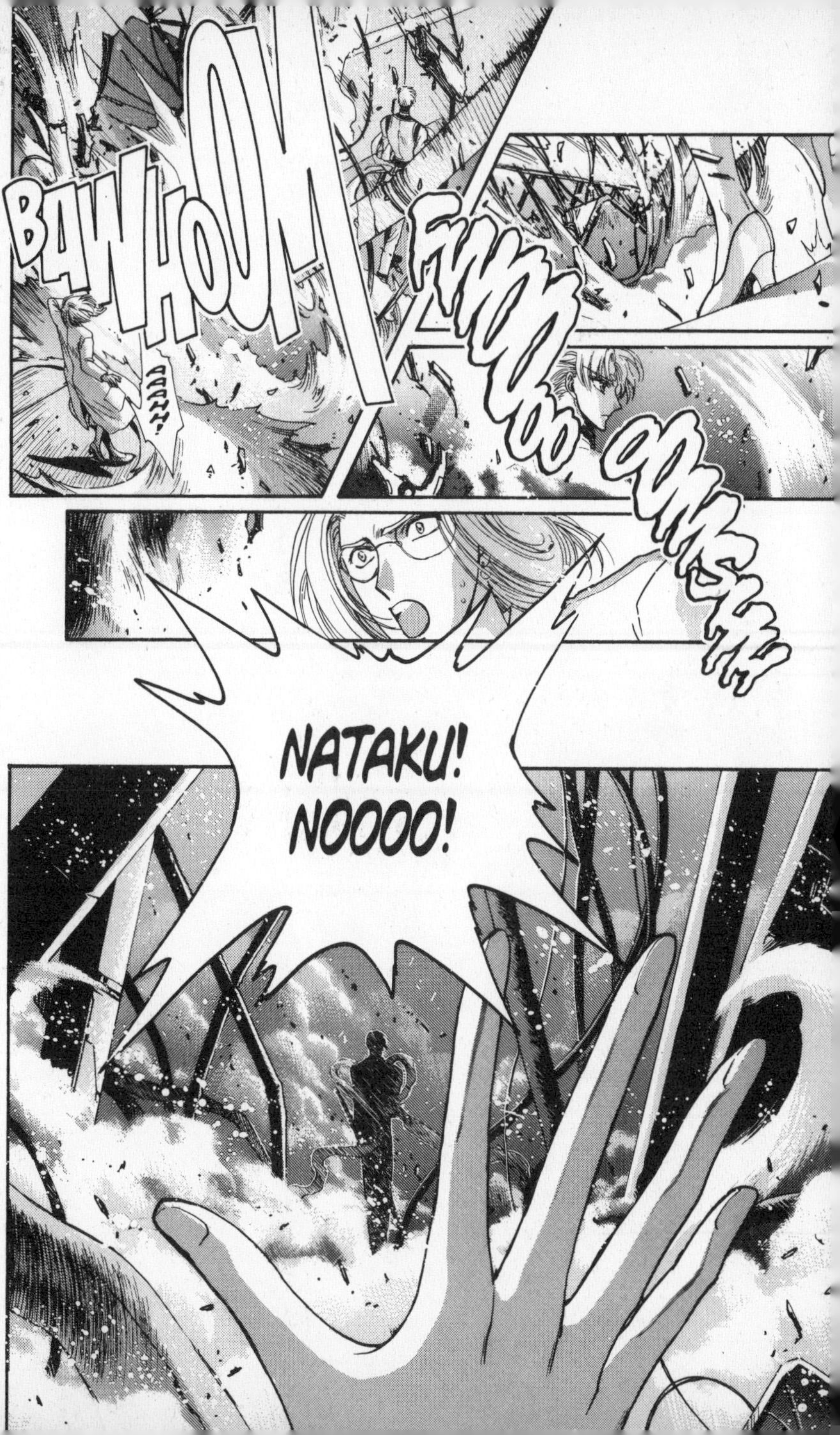
BAWHOOM
AAAHH!
FWOOOOOOMSHH
NATAKU! NOOOO!

SHWIP
SHWIP
SHWIP
SHWIP

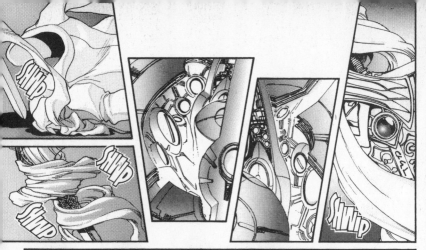

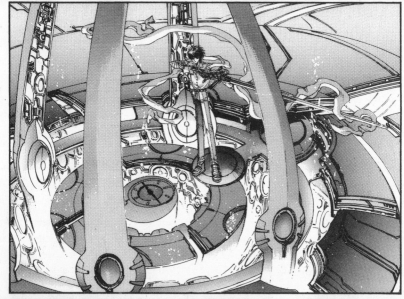

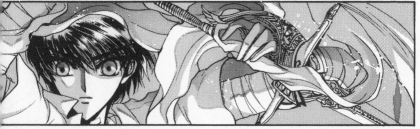

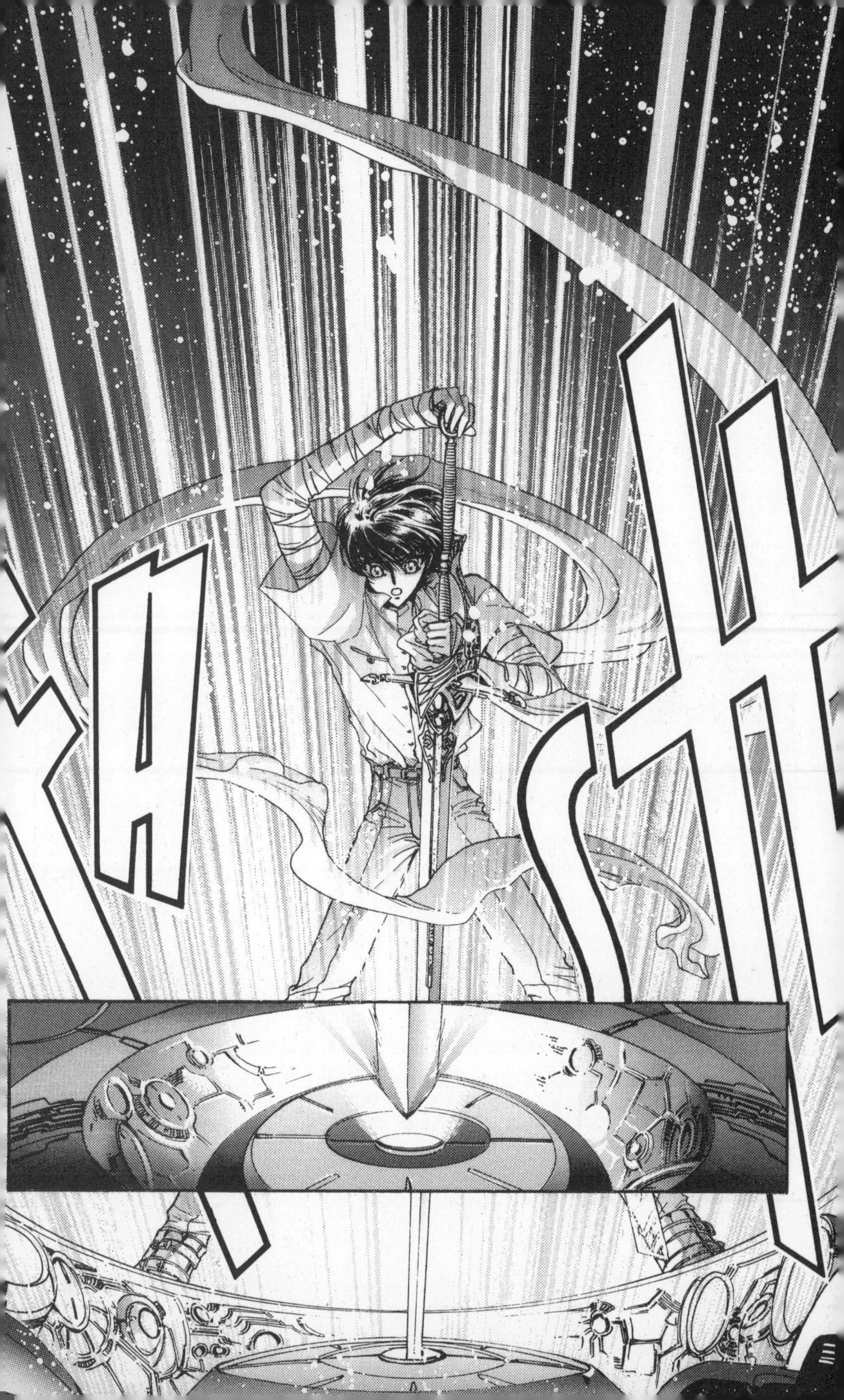
KASH

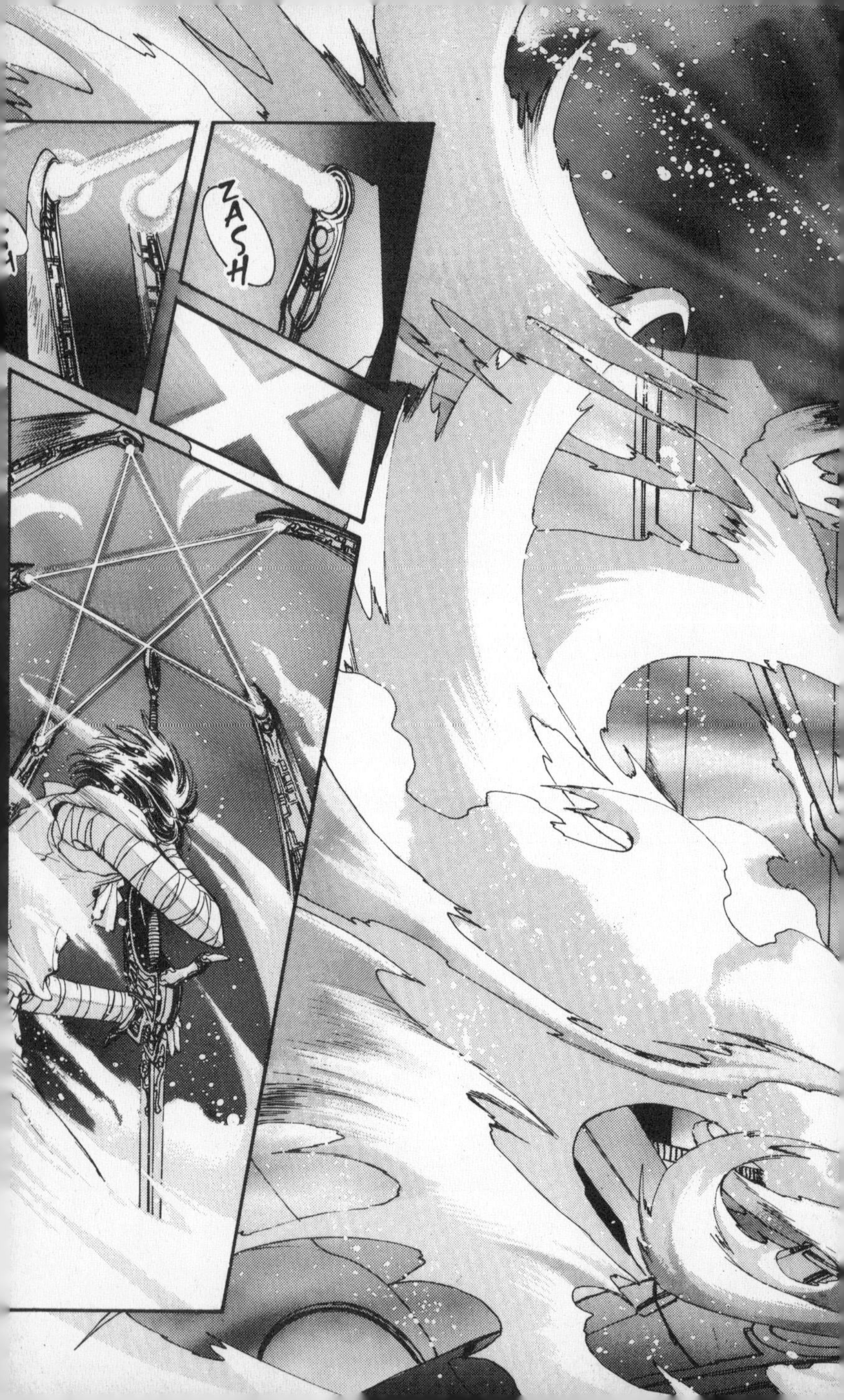
ZASH

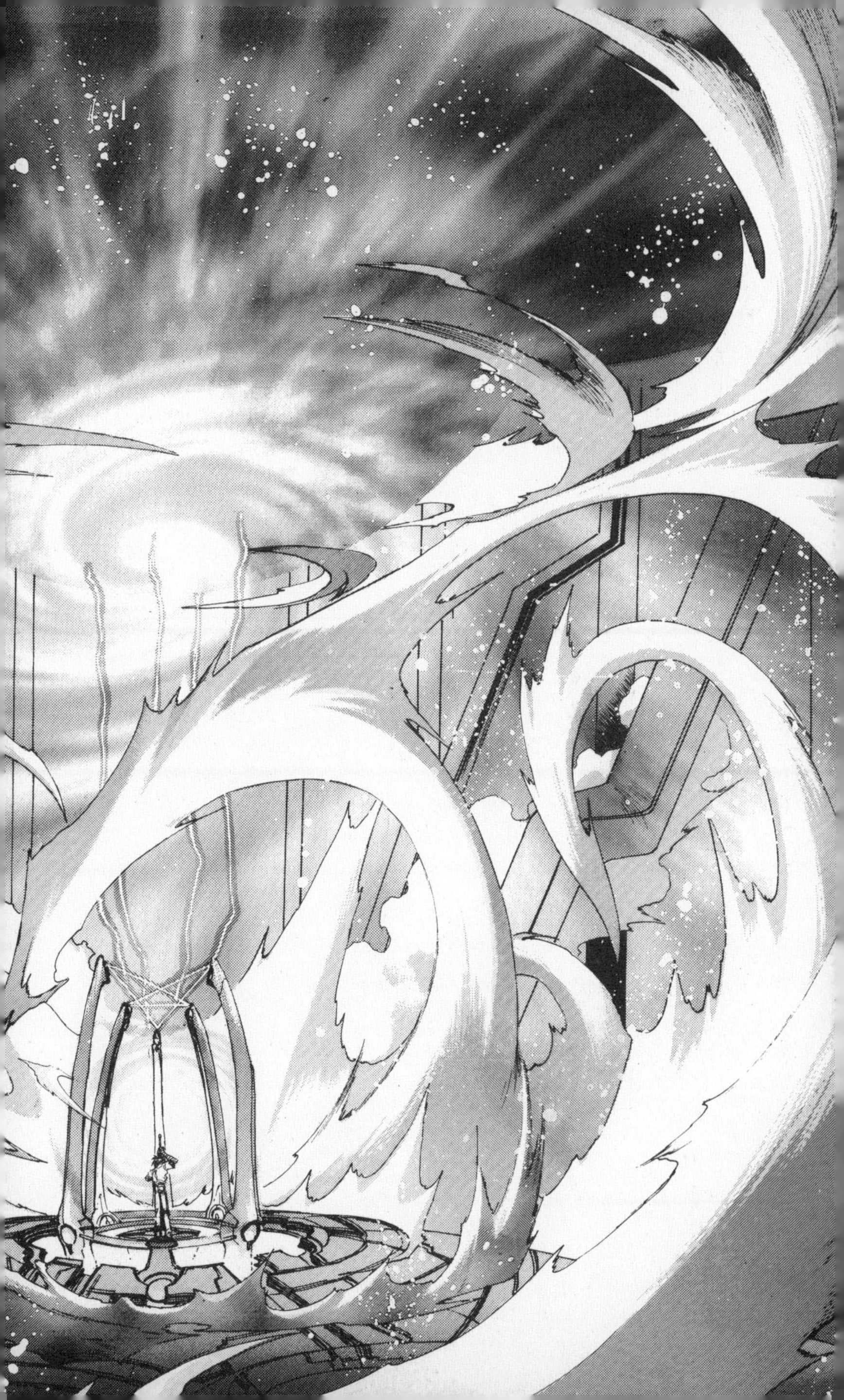

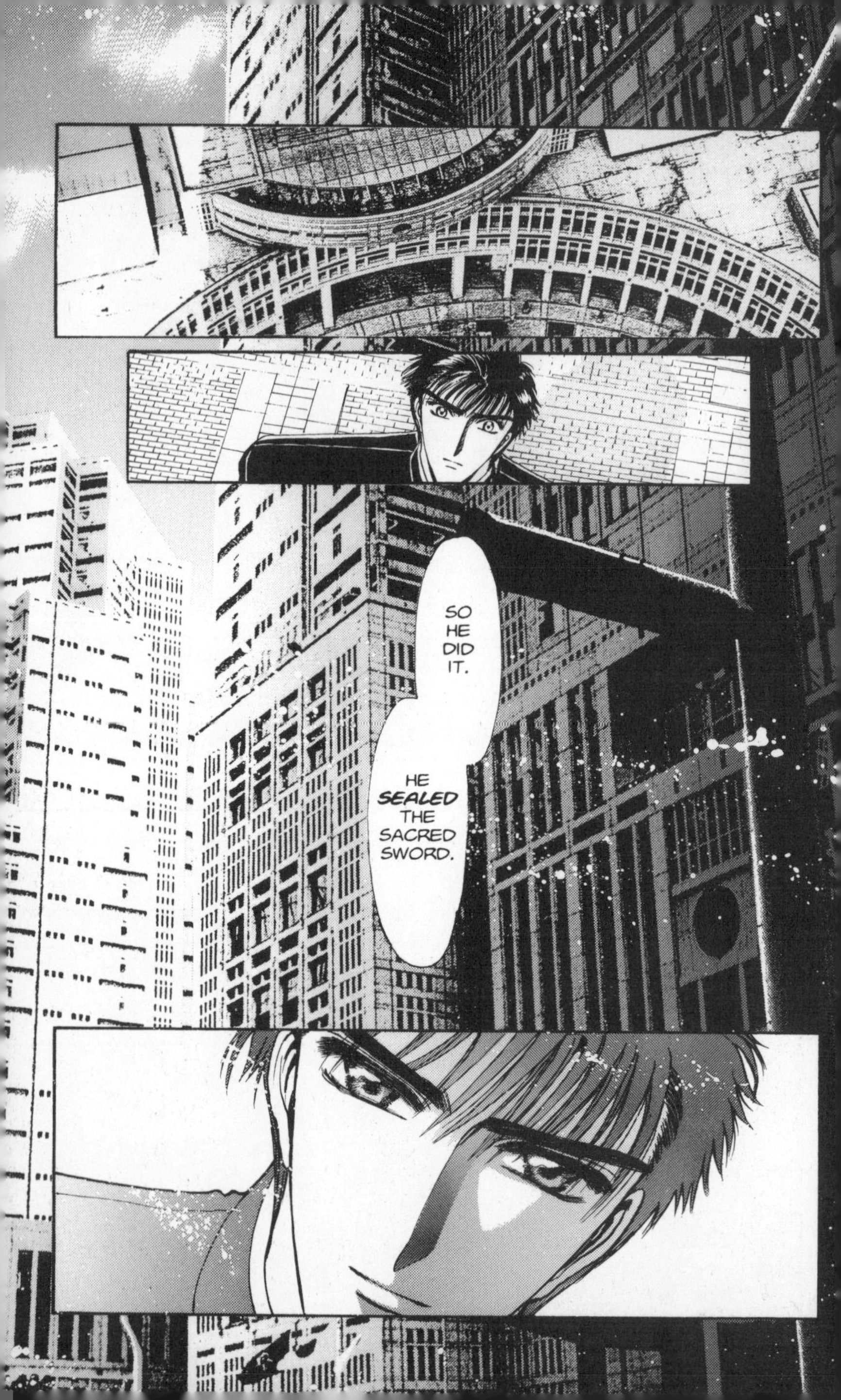
SO HE DID IT.
HE **SEALED** THE SACRED SWORD.

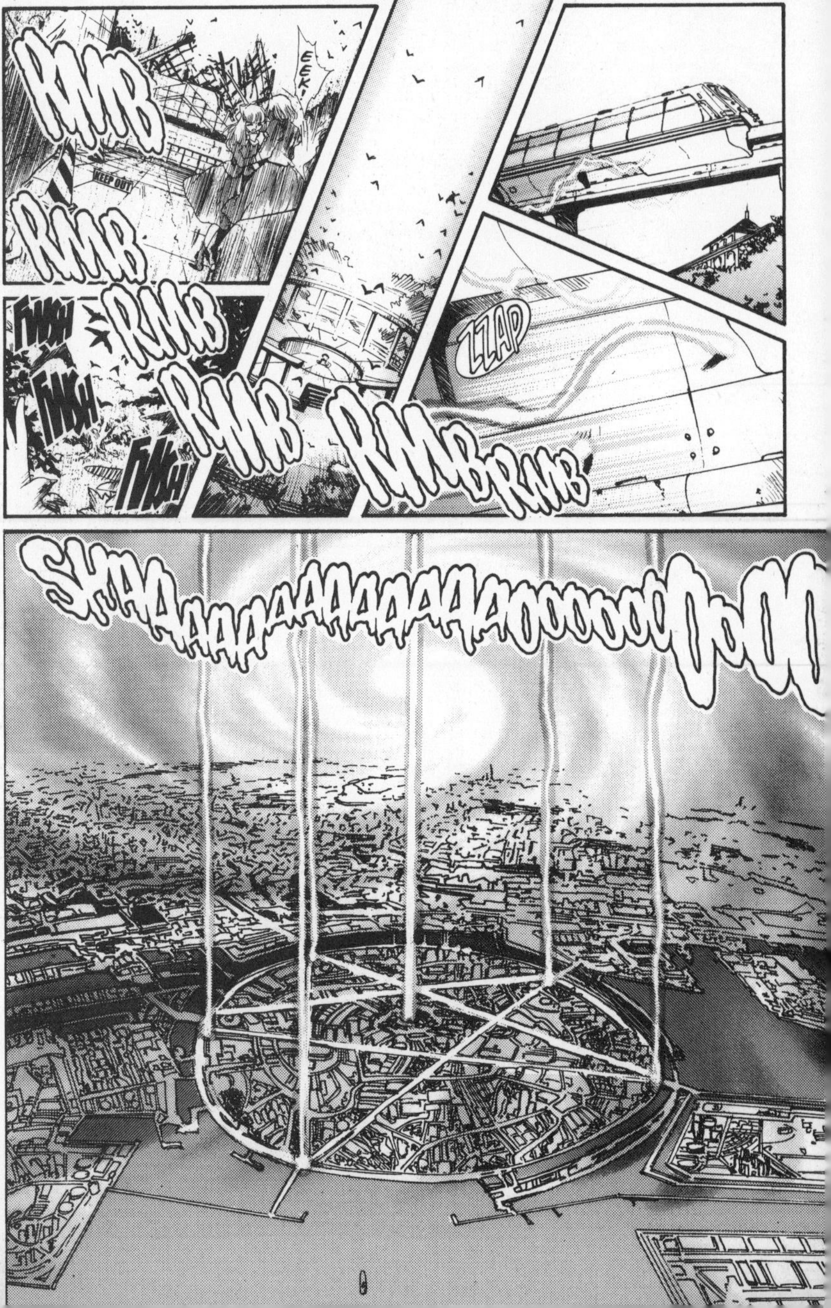
RMB
RMB
EEK!
KEEP OUT
FWSH
RMB
FWSH
RMB
FWSH
RMB
ZZAP
RMB RMB
SHAAAAAAAAAAAAOOOOOOOOO

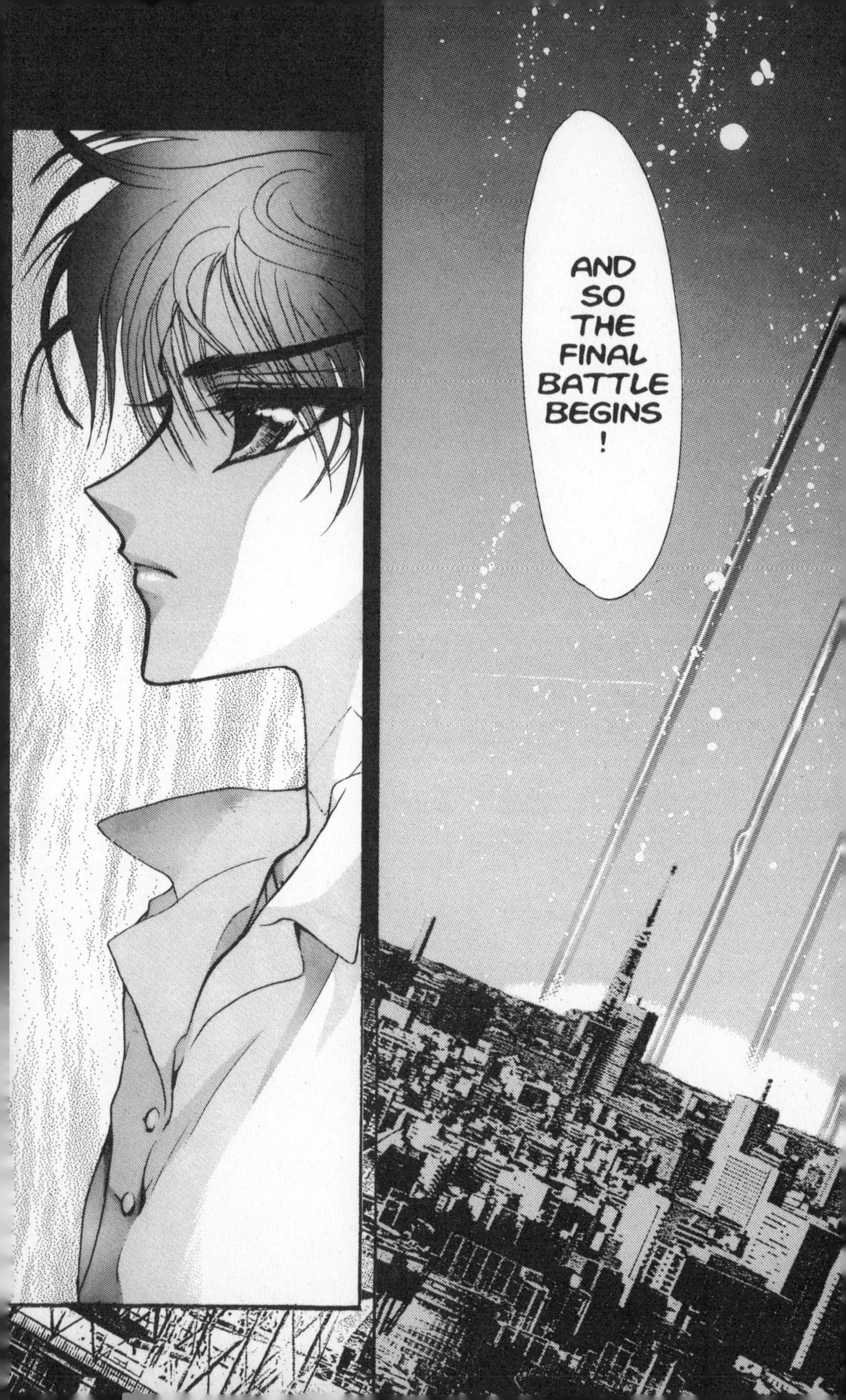
AND SO THE FINAL BATTLE BEGINS!

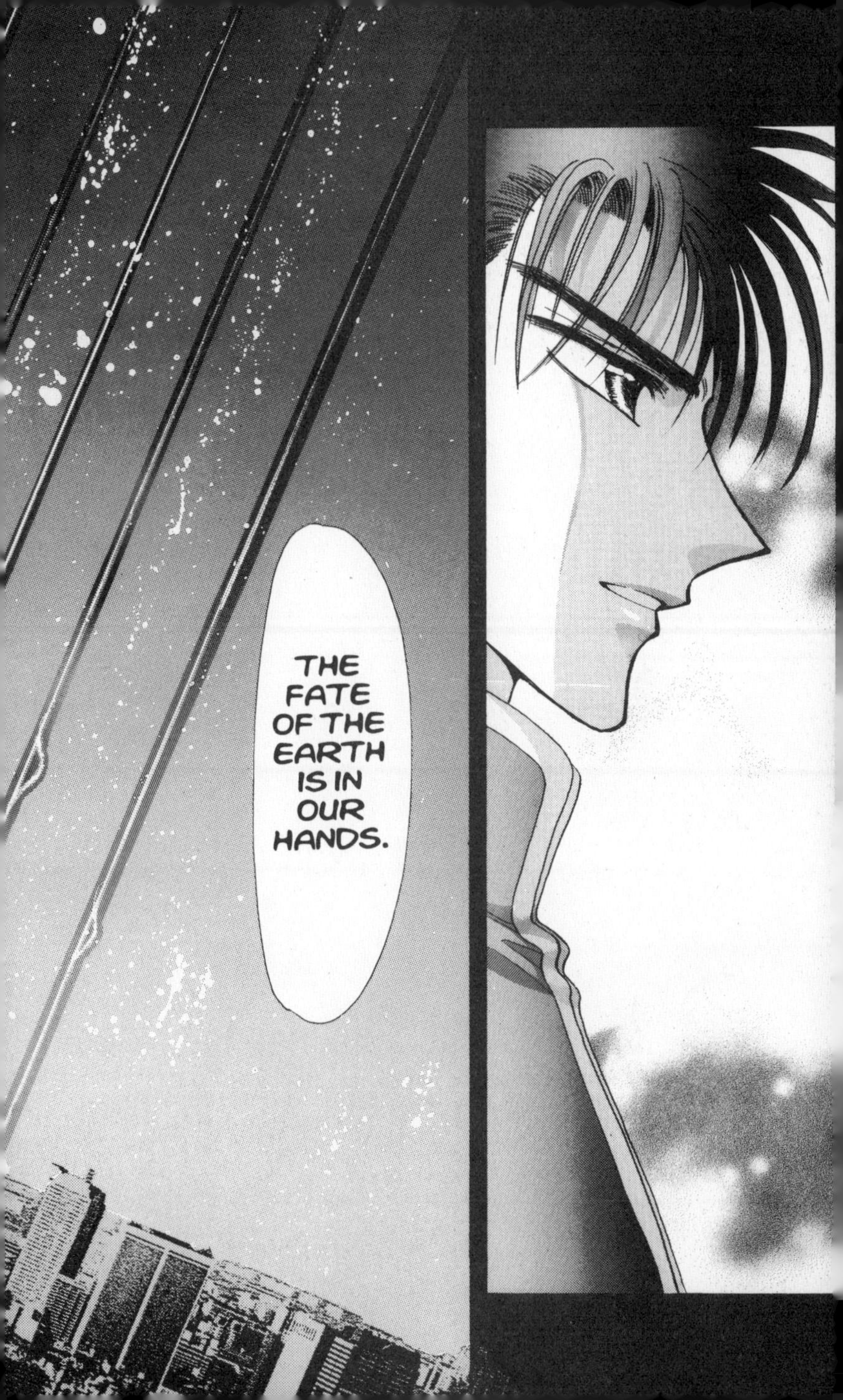
THE FATE OF THE EARTH IS IN OUR HANDS.

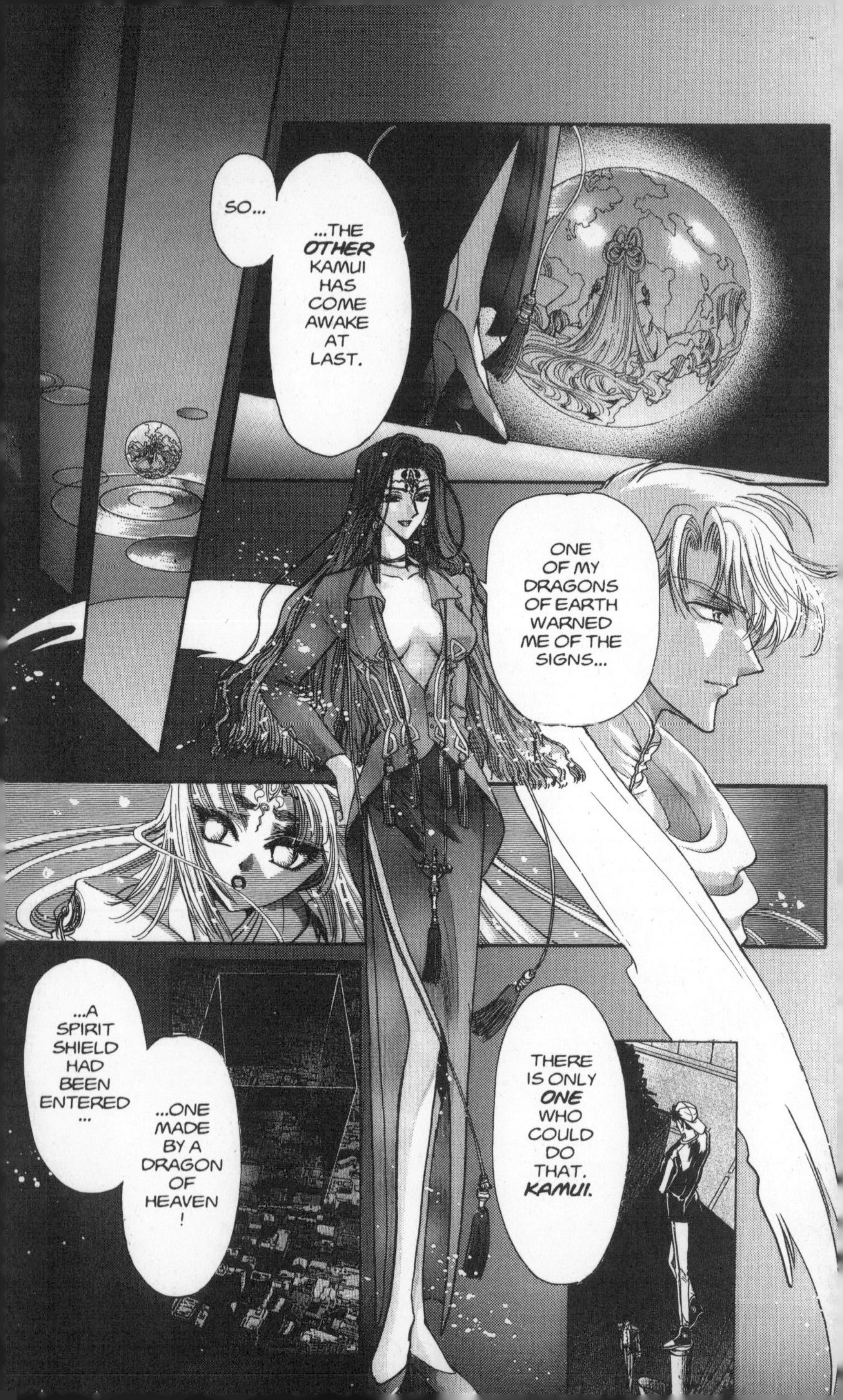
SO...
...THE OTHER KAMUI HAS COME AWAKE AT LAST.
ONE OF MY DRAGONS OF EARTH WARNED ME OF THE SIGNS...
...A SPIRIT SHIELD HAD BEEN ENTERED ...
...ONE MADE BY A DRAGON OF HEAVEN!
THERE IS ONLY ONE WHO COULD DO THAT. KAMUI.

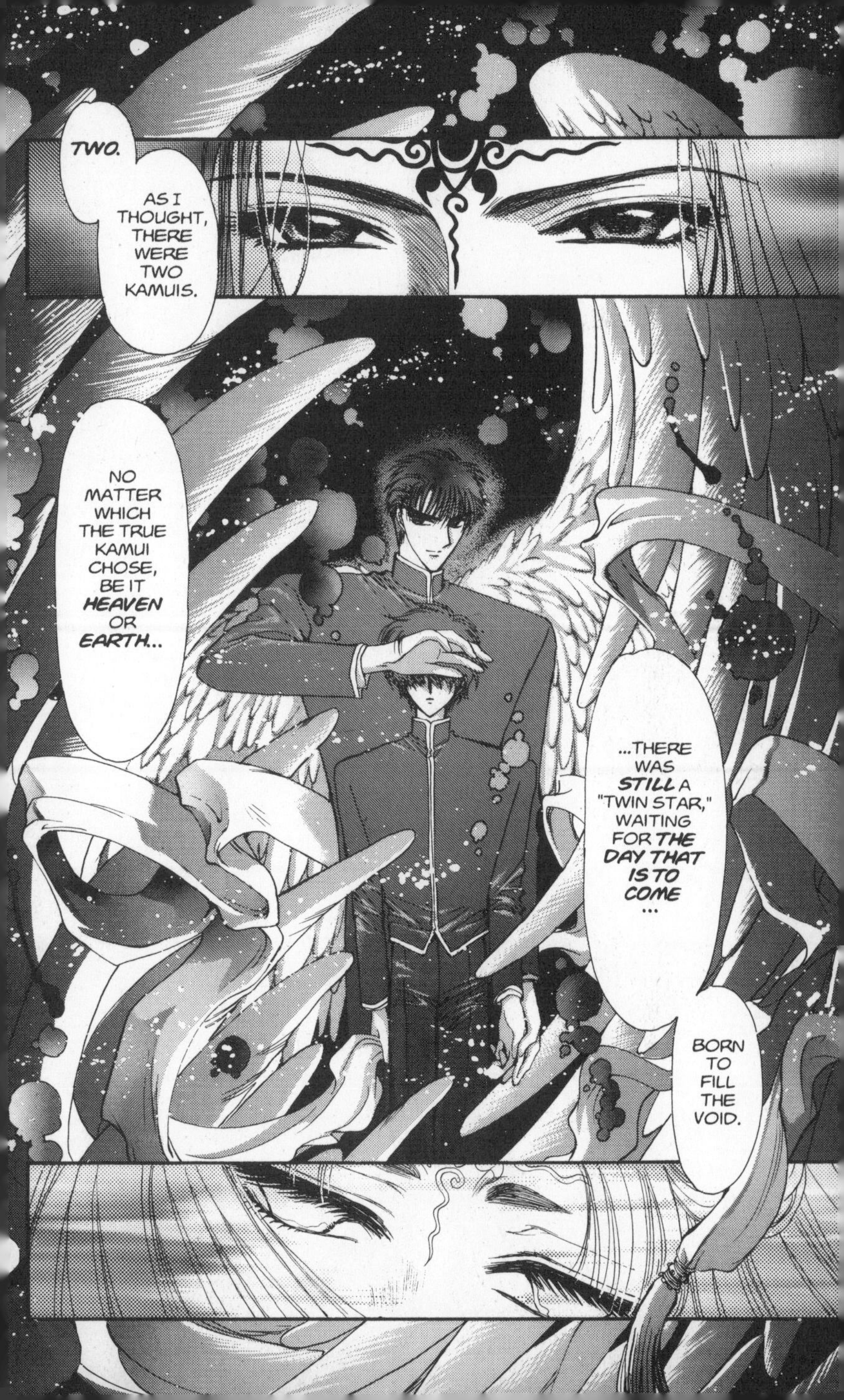
TWO.
AS I THOUGHT, THERE WERE TWO KAMUIS.
NO MATTER WHICH THE TRUE KAMUI CHOSE, BE IT HEAVEN OR EARTH...
...THERE WAS STILL A "TWIN STAR," WAITING FOR THE DAY THAT IS TO COME...
BORN TO FILL THE VOID.

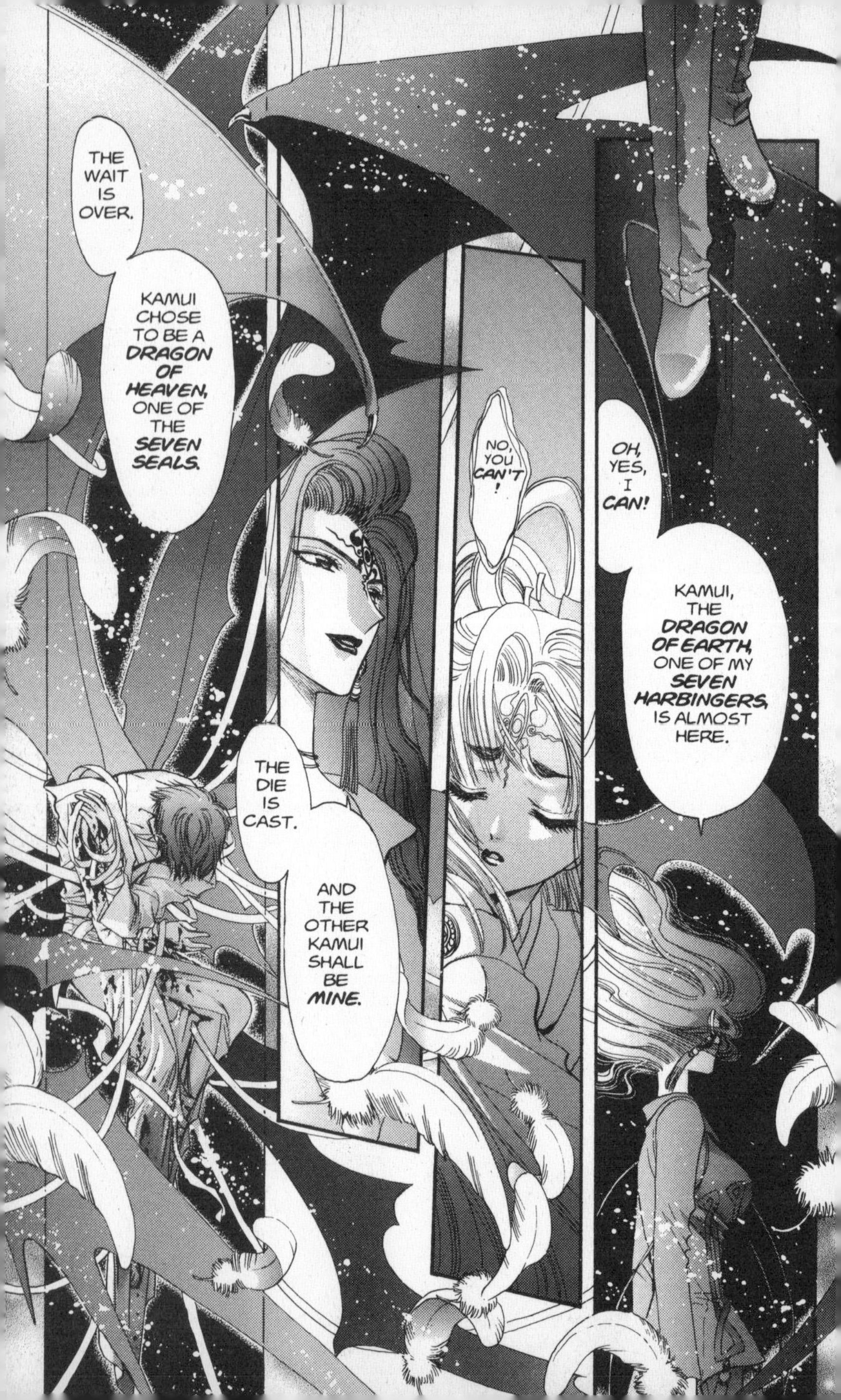
THE WAIT IS OVER.
KAMUI CHOSE TO BE A DRAGON OF HEAVEN, ONE OF THE SEVEN SEALS.
THE DIE IS CAST.
AND THE OTHER KAMUI SHALL BE MINE.
NO, YOU CAN'T!
OH, YES, I CAN!
KAMUI, THE DRAGON OF EARTH, ONE OF MY SEVEN HARBINGERS, IS ALMOST HERE.

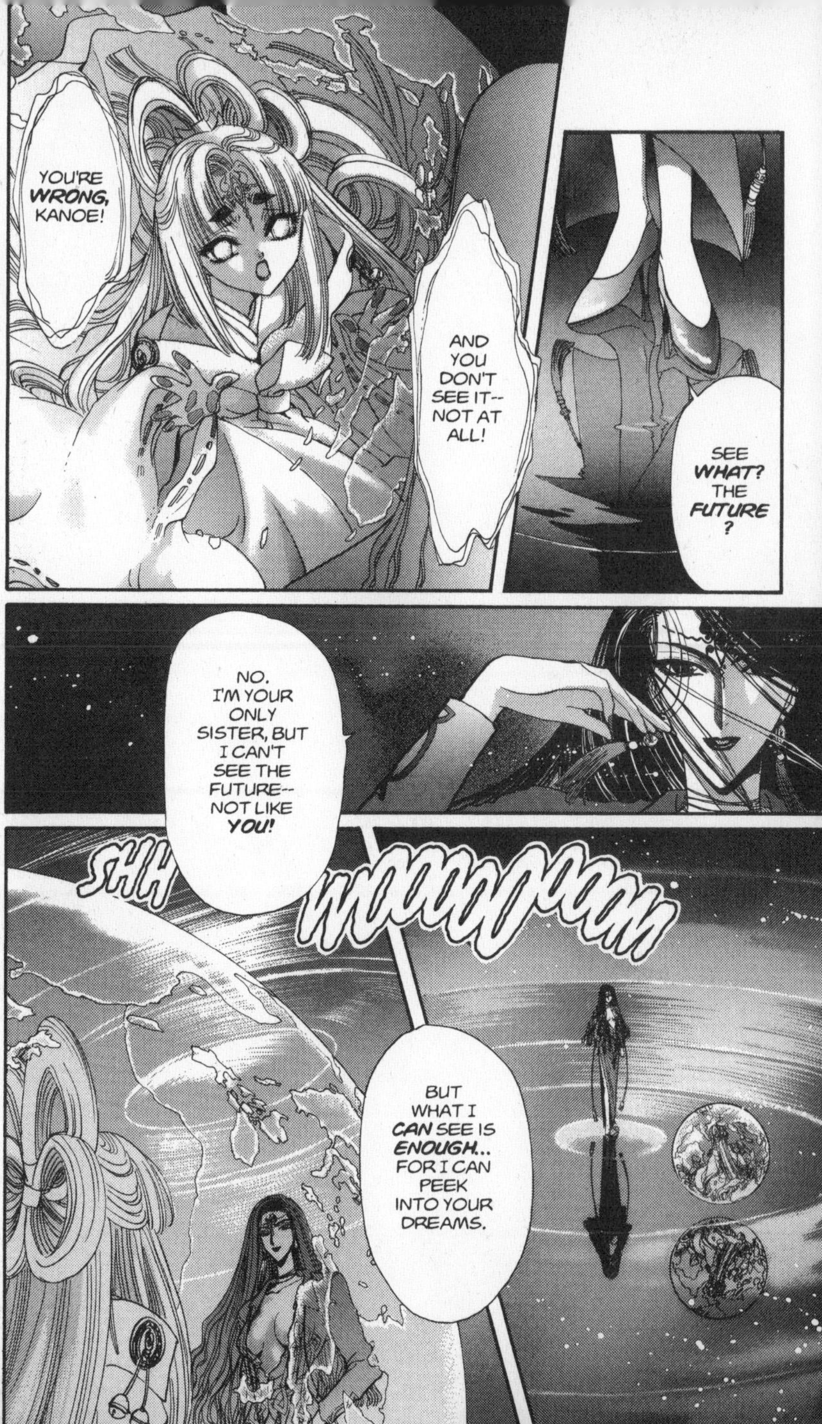

YOU'RE WRONG, KANOE!
AND YOU DON'T SEE IT-- NOT AT ALL!
SEE WHAT? THE FUTURE ?
NO. I'M YOUR ONLY SISTER, BUT I CAN'T SEE THE FUTURE-- NOT LIKE YOU!
SHH WOOOOOOOOM
BUT WHAT I CAN SEE IS ENOUGH... FOR I CAN PEEK INTO YOUR DREAMS.

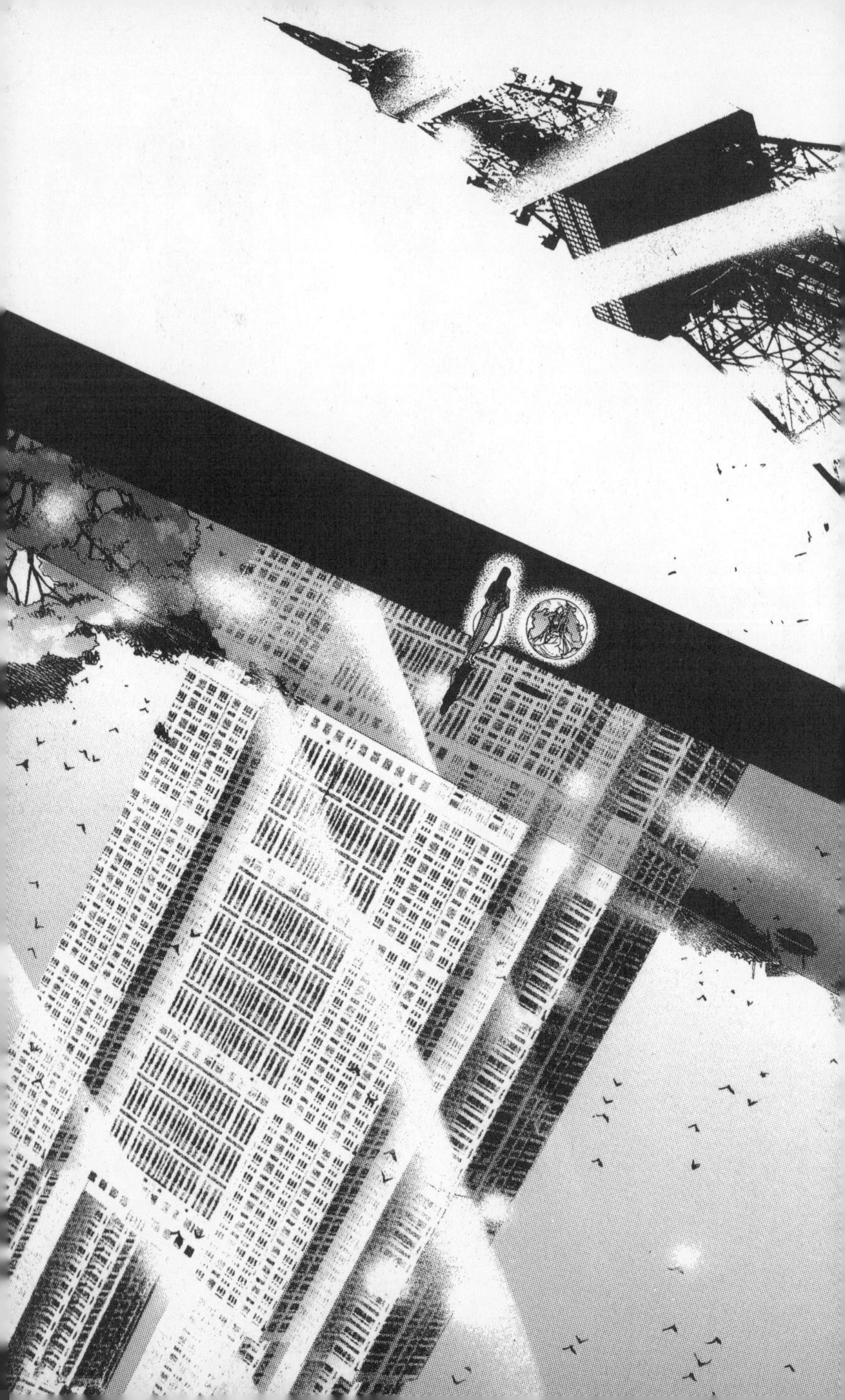

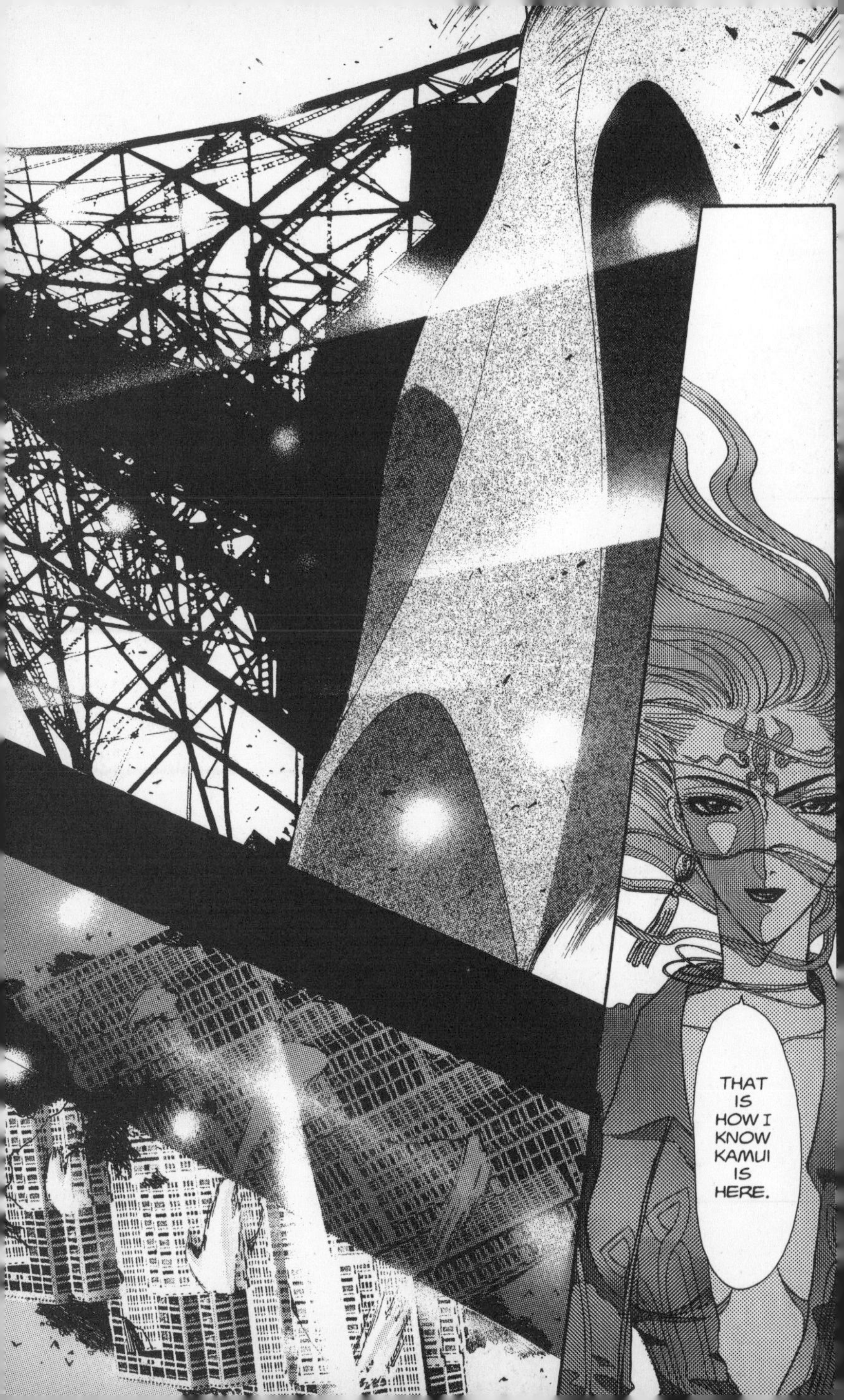
THAT IS HOW I KNOW KAMUI IS HERE.

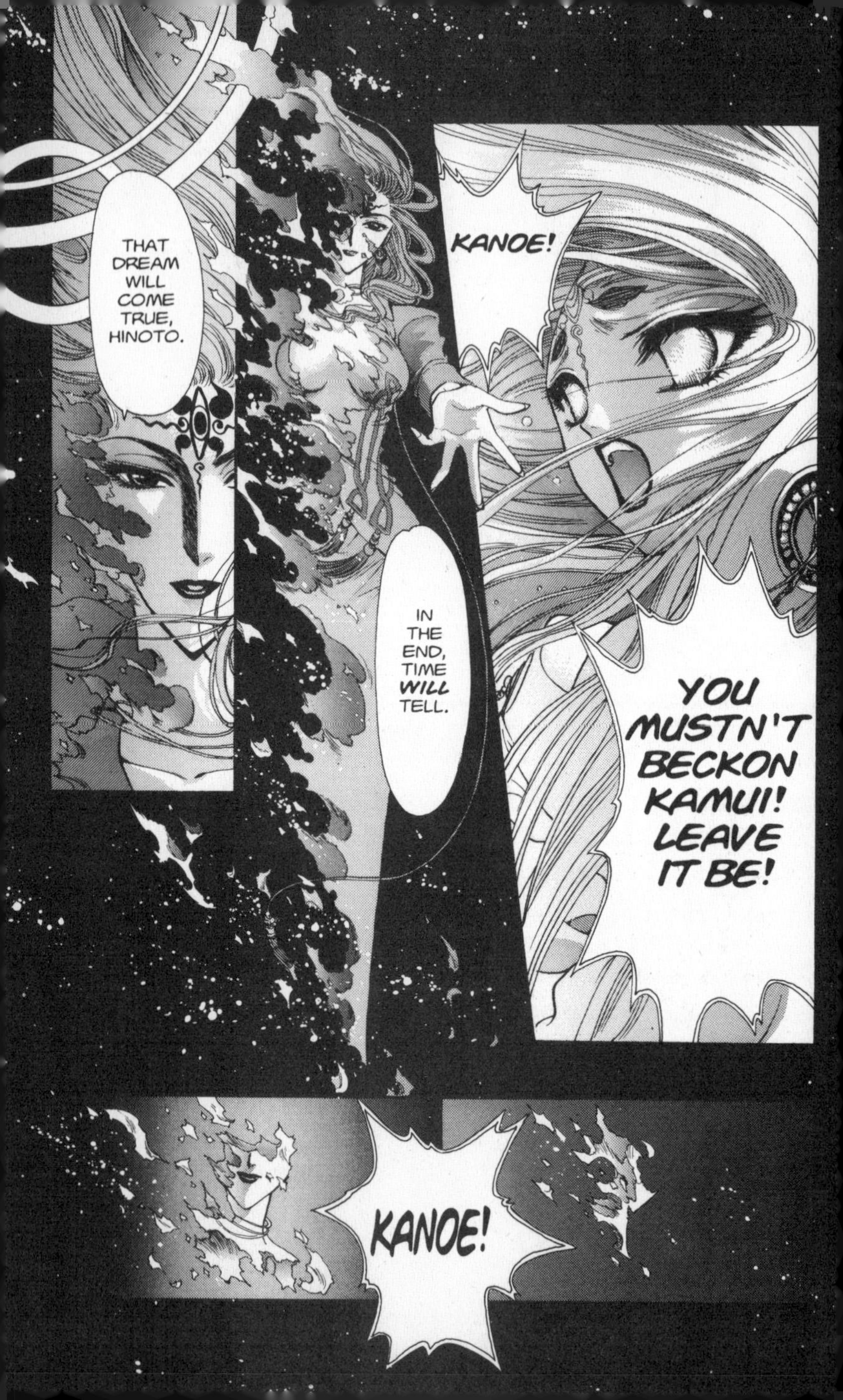
KANOE!
YOU MUSTN'T BECKON KAMUI! LEAVE IT BE!
THAT DREAM WILL COME TRUE, HINOTO.
IN THE END, TIME *WILL* TELL.
KANOE!

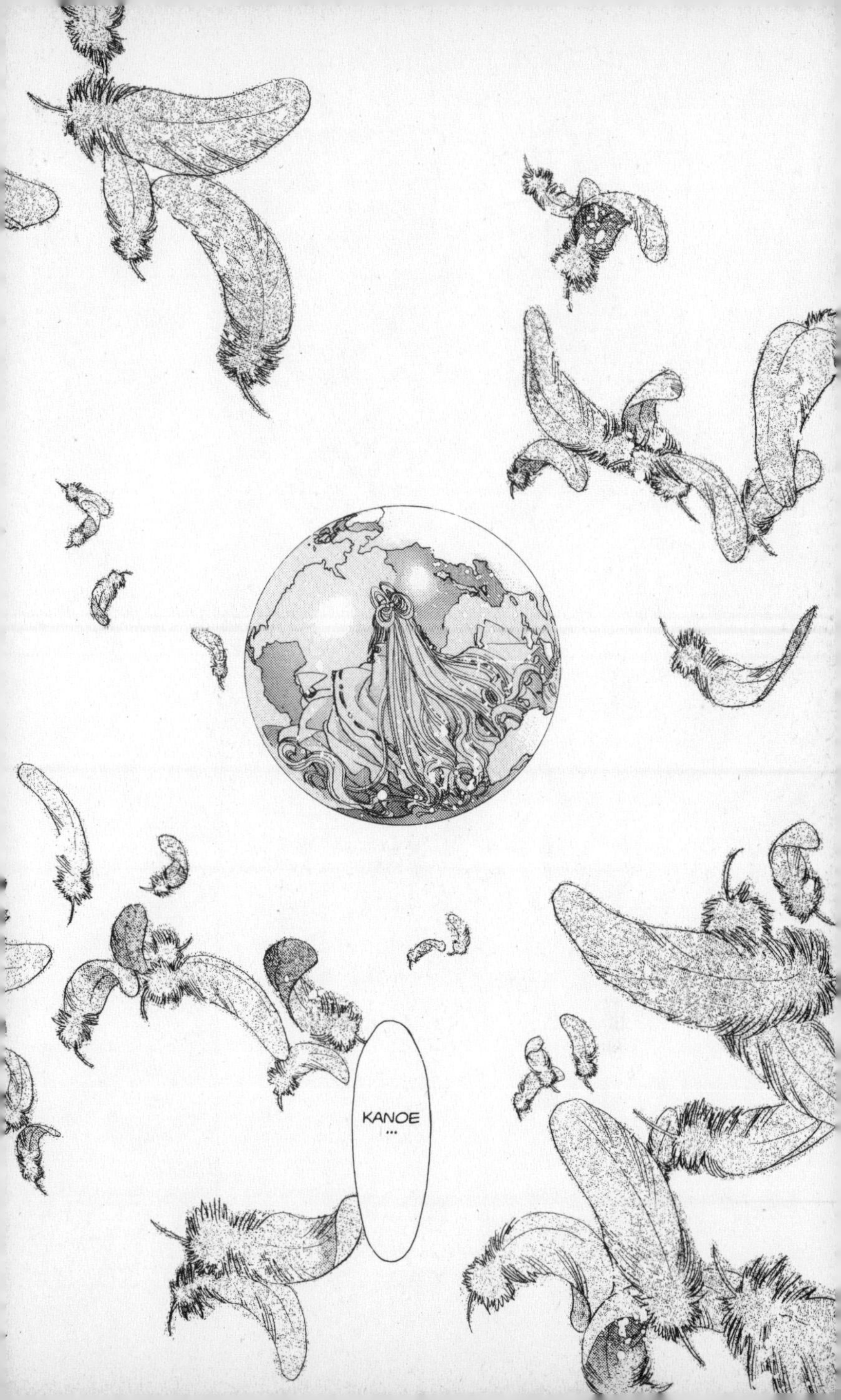
KANOE
...

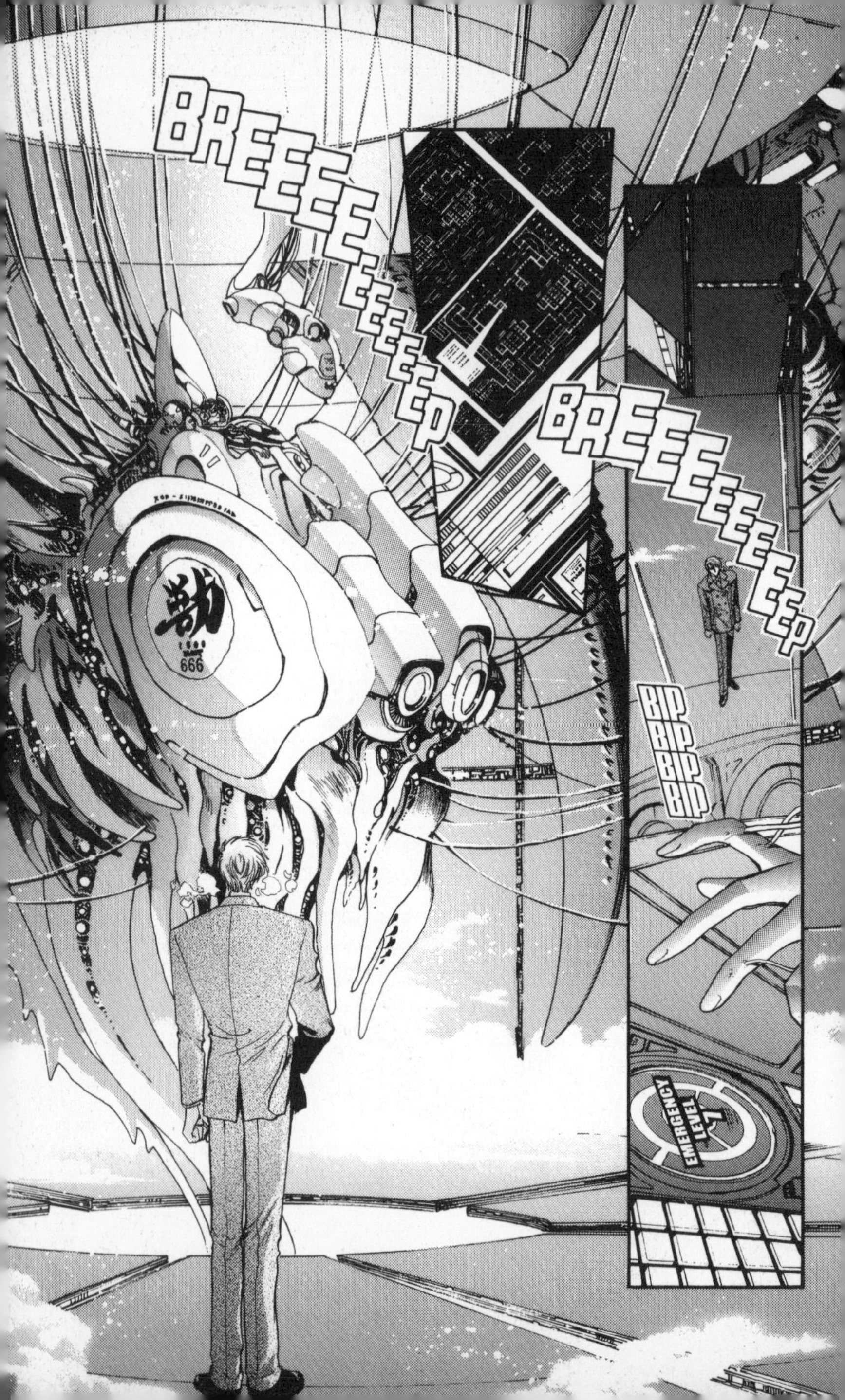
BREEEEEEEEEP
BREEEEEEEEP
BIP BIP BIP BIP
EMERGENCY LEVEL 7

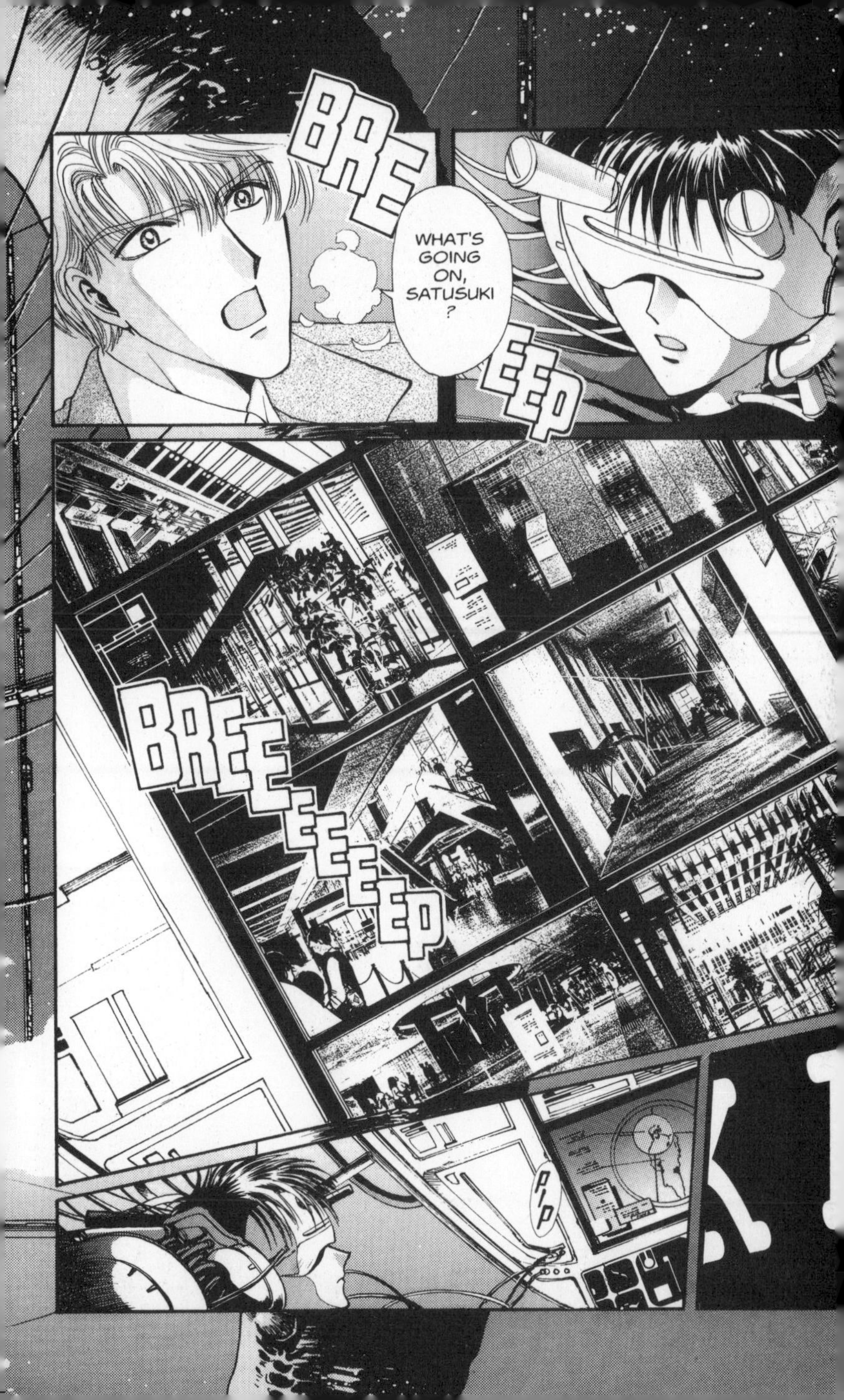
BREEEP
WHAT'S GOING ON, SATUSUKI ?
BREEEEEEEP
PIP

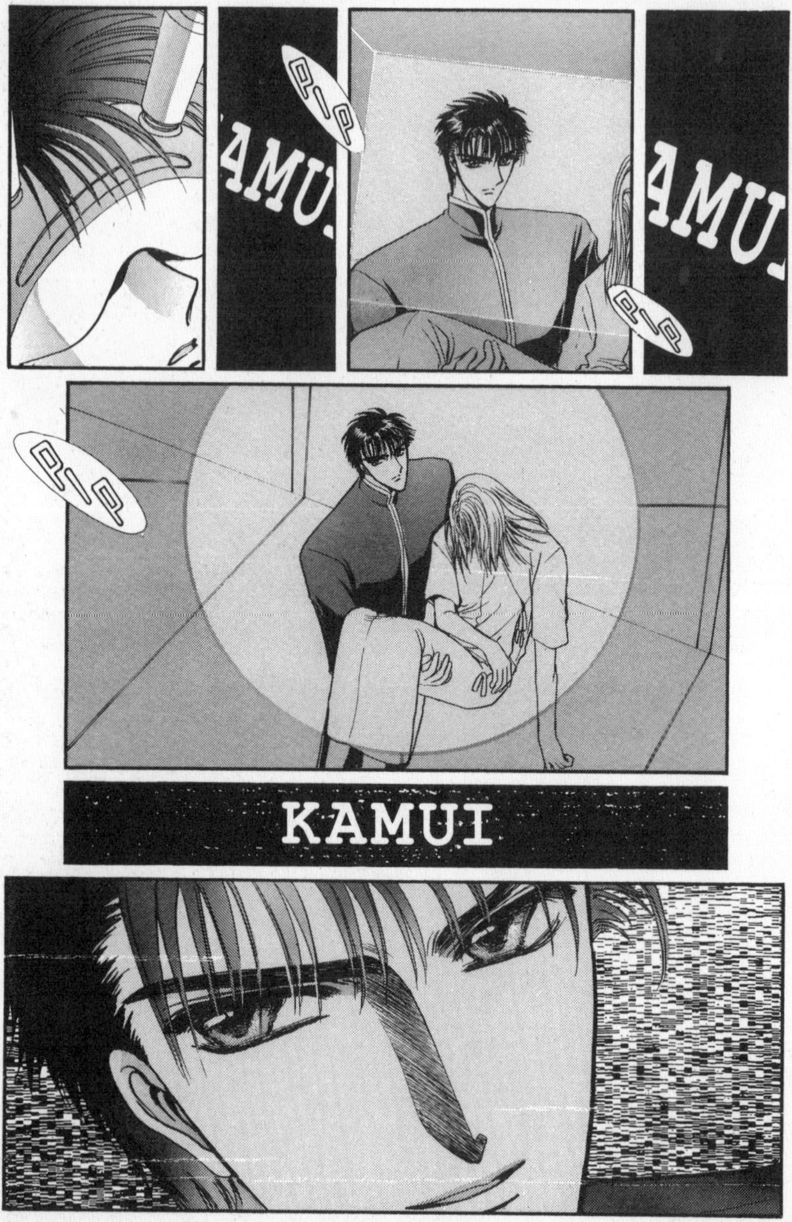
KAMUI

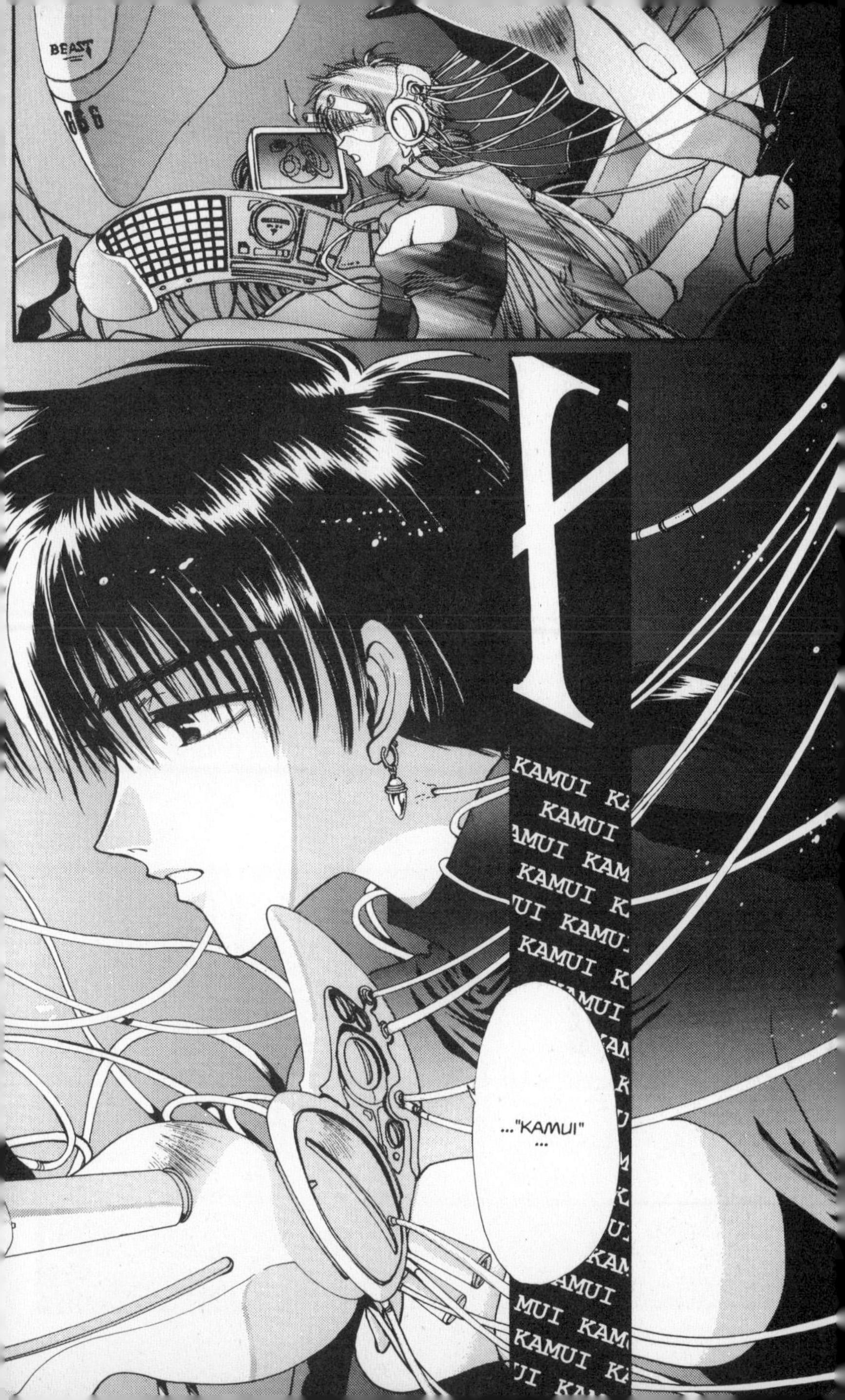
BEAST
666
F
KAMUI KA
KAMUI
AMUI KAM
KAMUI K
UI KAMUI
KAMUI K
..."KAMUI"
...

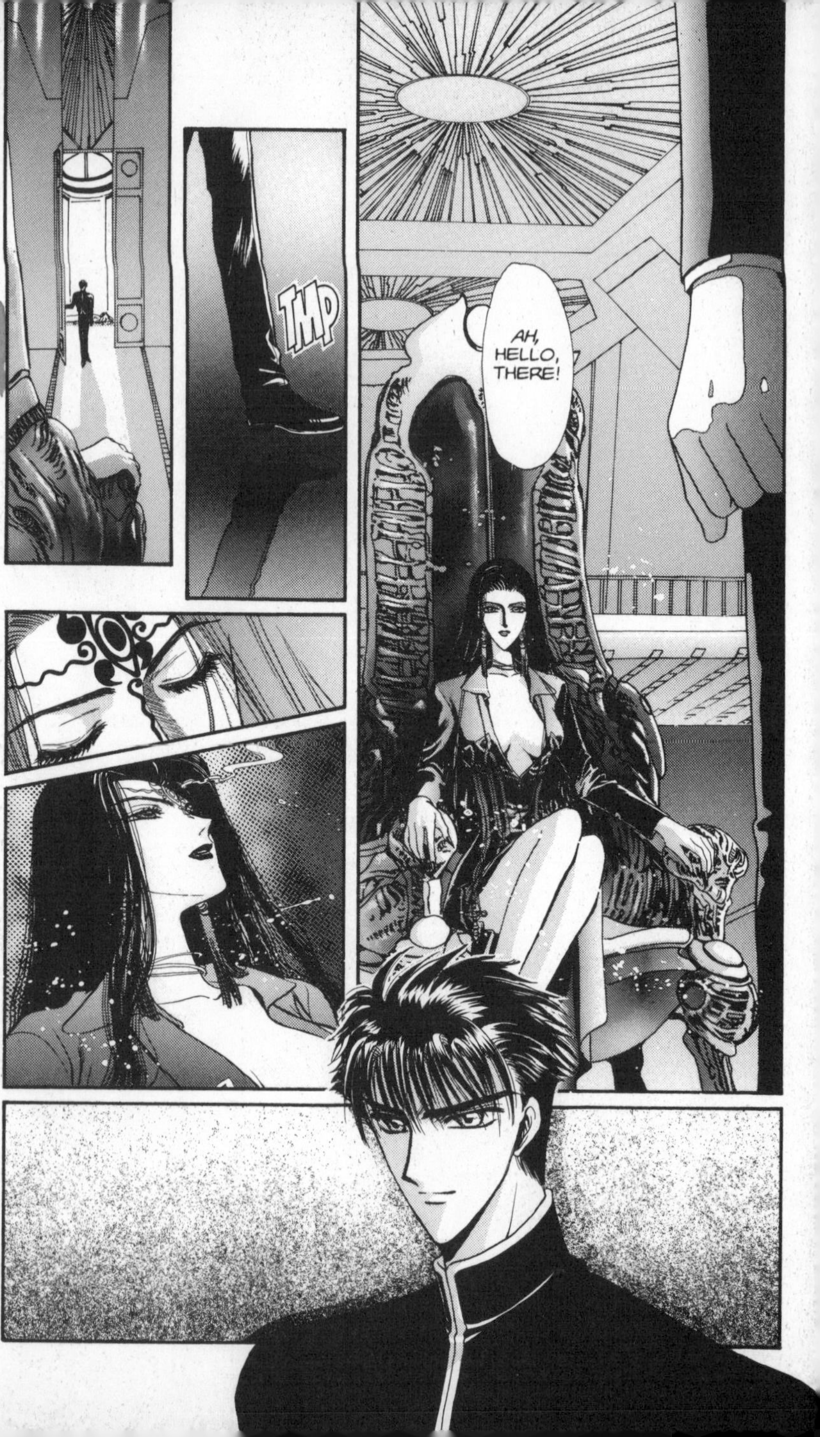
TMP
AH, HELLO, THERE!

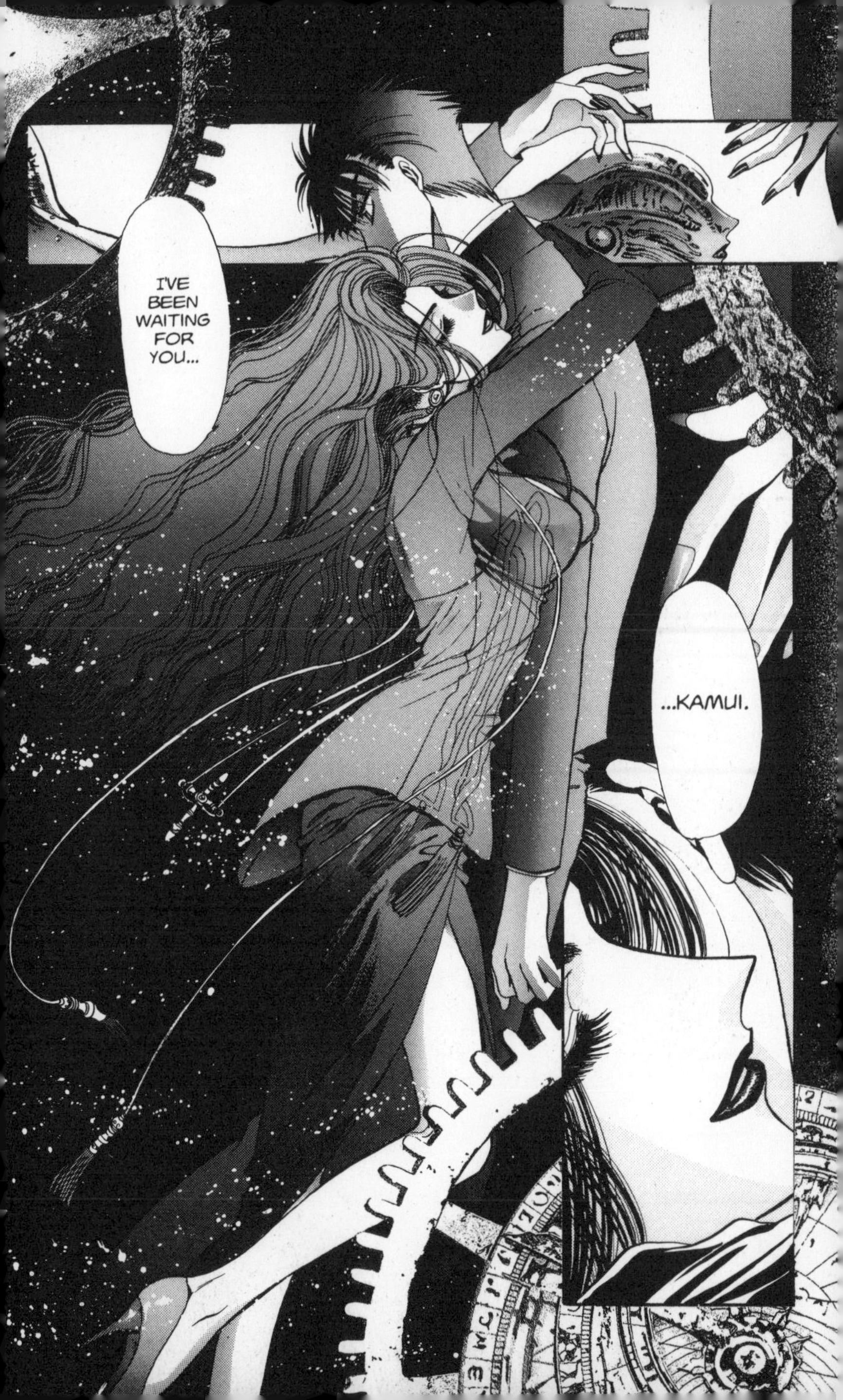
I'VE BEEN WAITING FOR YOU...
...KAMUI.

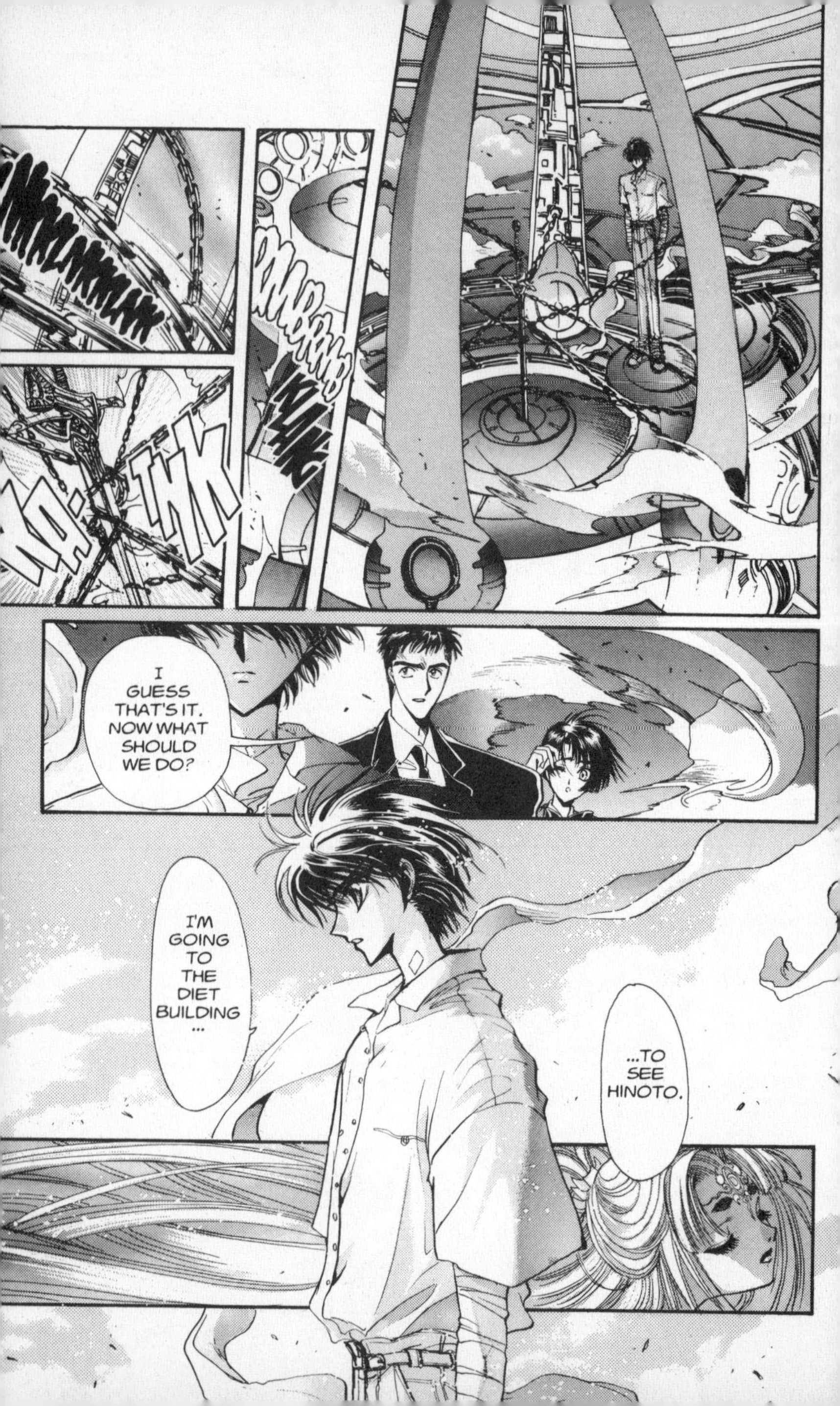
I GUESS THAT'S IT. NOW WHAT SHOULD WE DO?
I'M GOING TO THE DIET BUILDING ...
...TO SEE HINOTO.

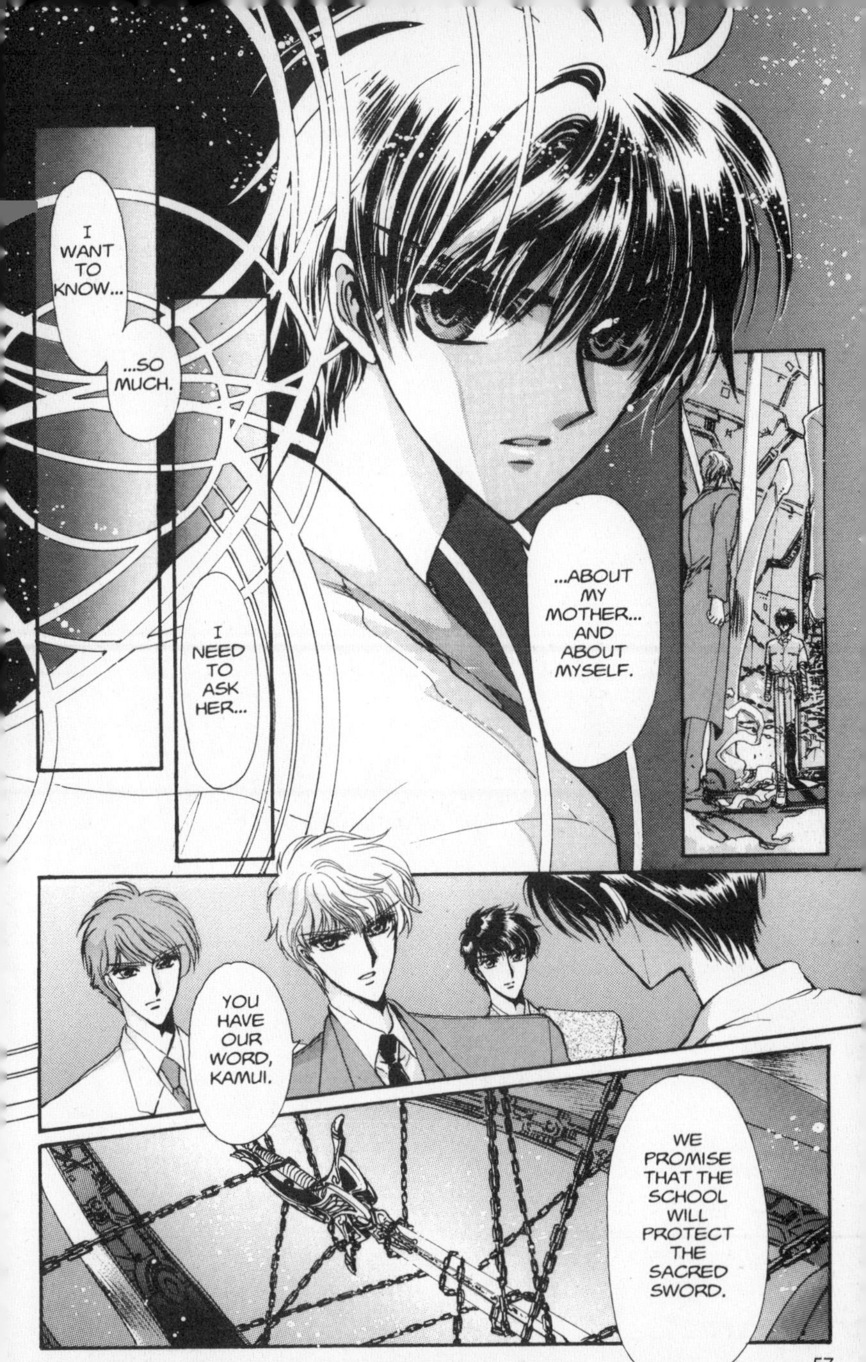
I WANT TO KNOW...
...SO MUCH.
I NEED TO ASK HER...
...ABOUT MY MOTHER... AND ABOUT MYSELF.
YOU HAVE OUR WORD, KAMUI.
WE PROMISE THAT THE SCHOOL WILL PROTECT THE SACRED SWORD.

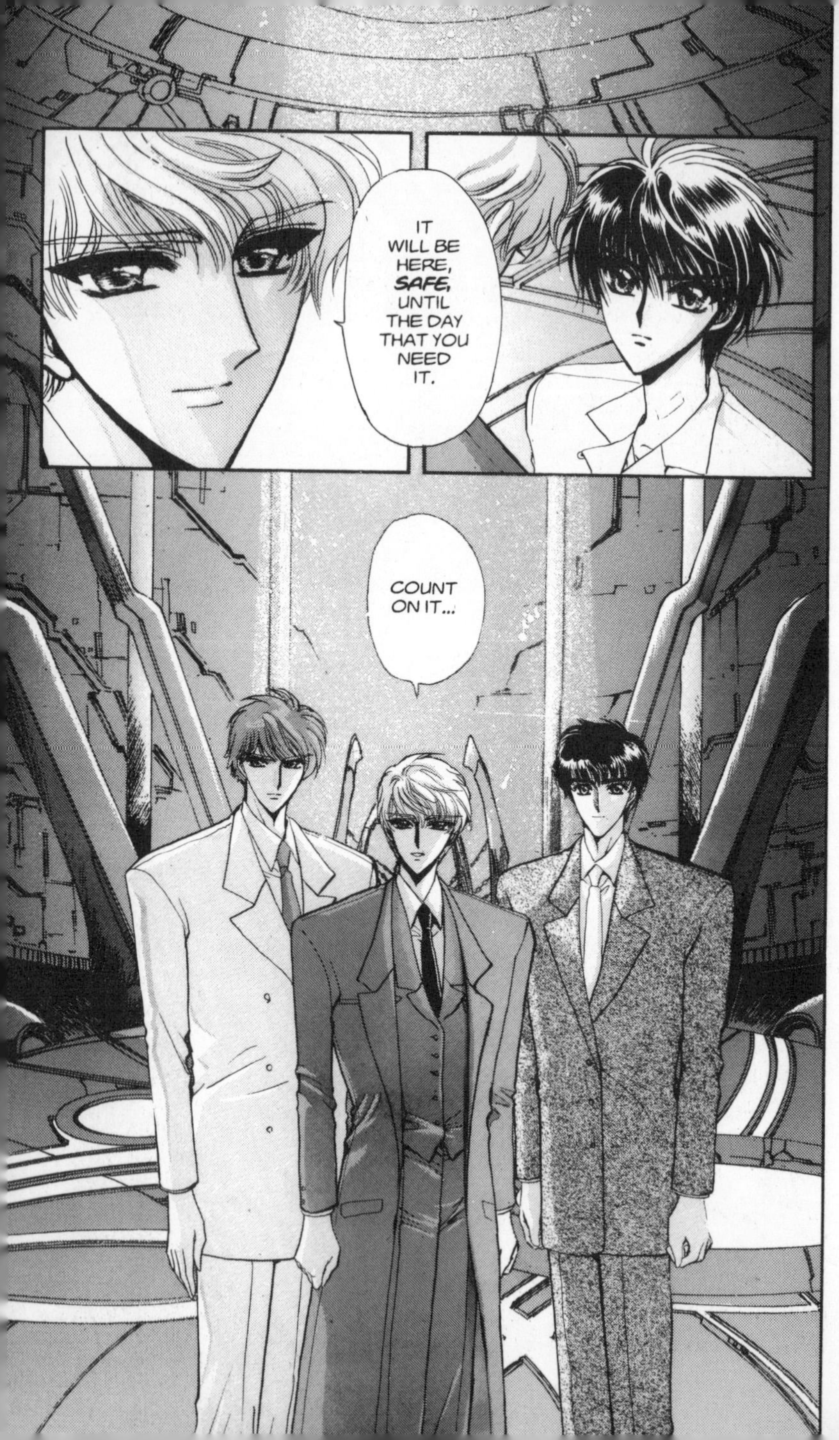
IT WILL BE HERE, ***SAFE,*** UNTIL THE DAY THAT YOU NEED IT.
COUNT ON IT...

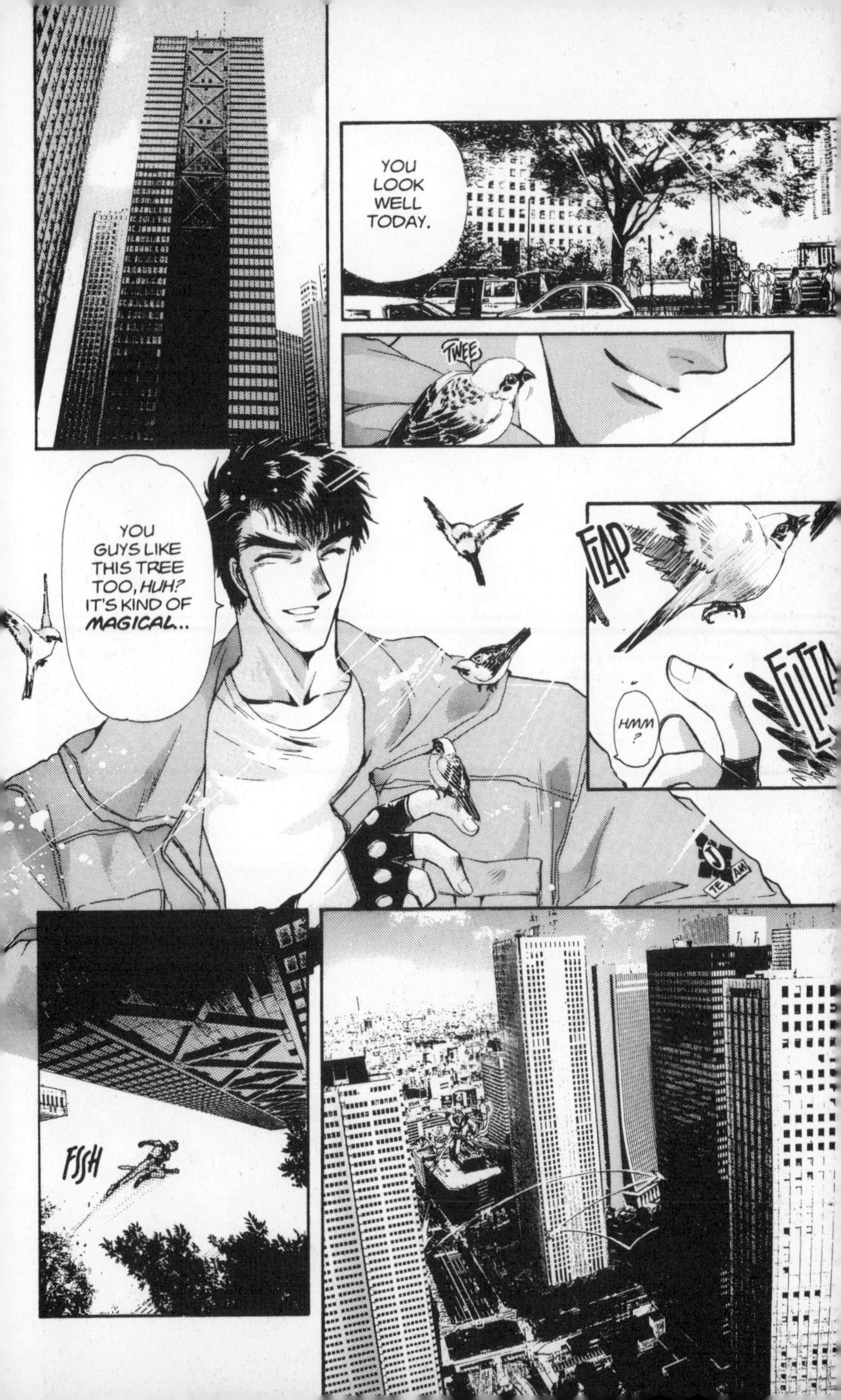
YOU LOOK WELL TODAY.
TWEE
YOU GUYS LIKE THIS TREE TOO, HUH? IT'S KIND OF MAGICAL...
FLAP
HMM?
FLITTA
FSSH

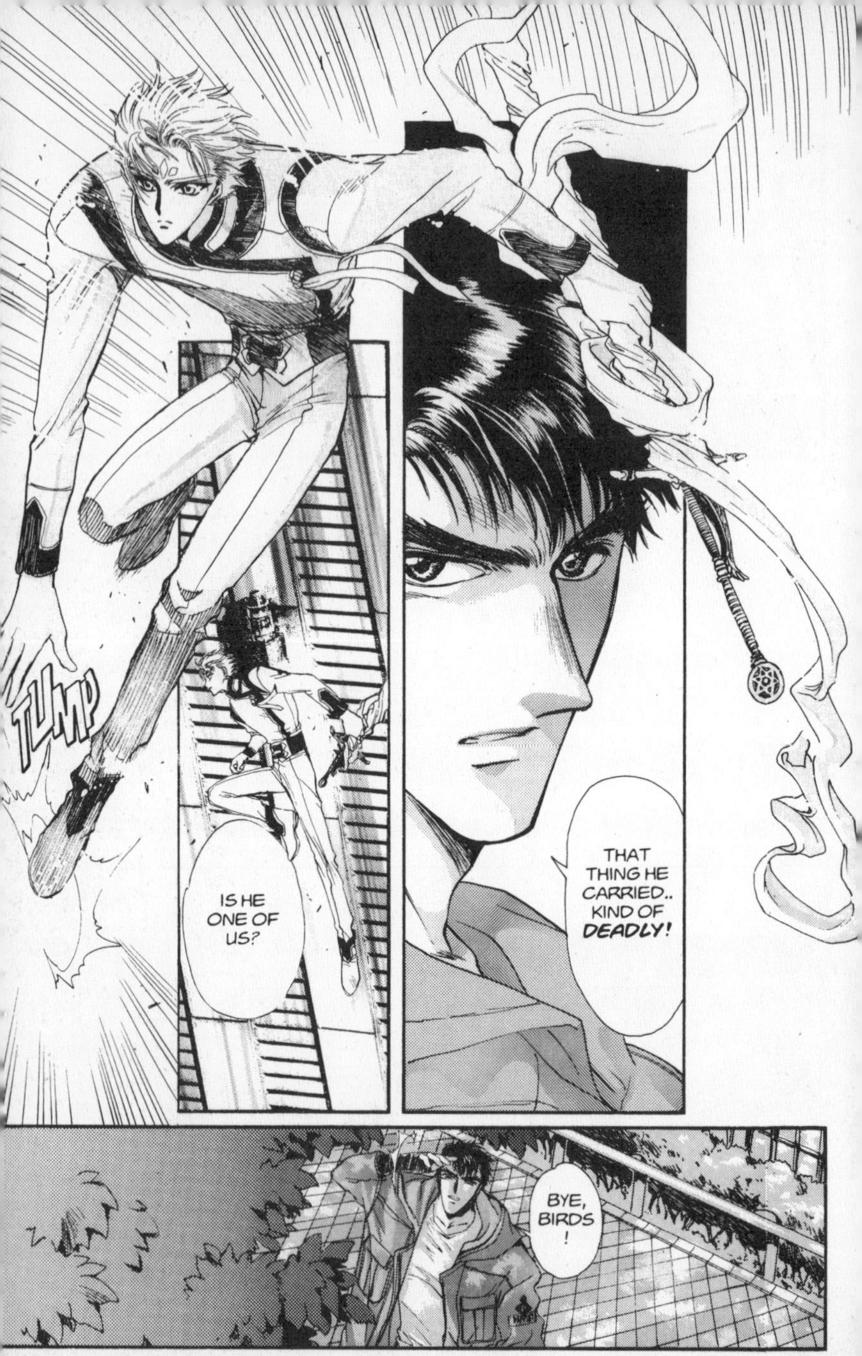
TUMP
IS HE ONE OF US?
THAT THING HE CARRIED.. KIND OF DEADLY!
BYE, BIRDS!

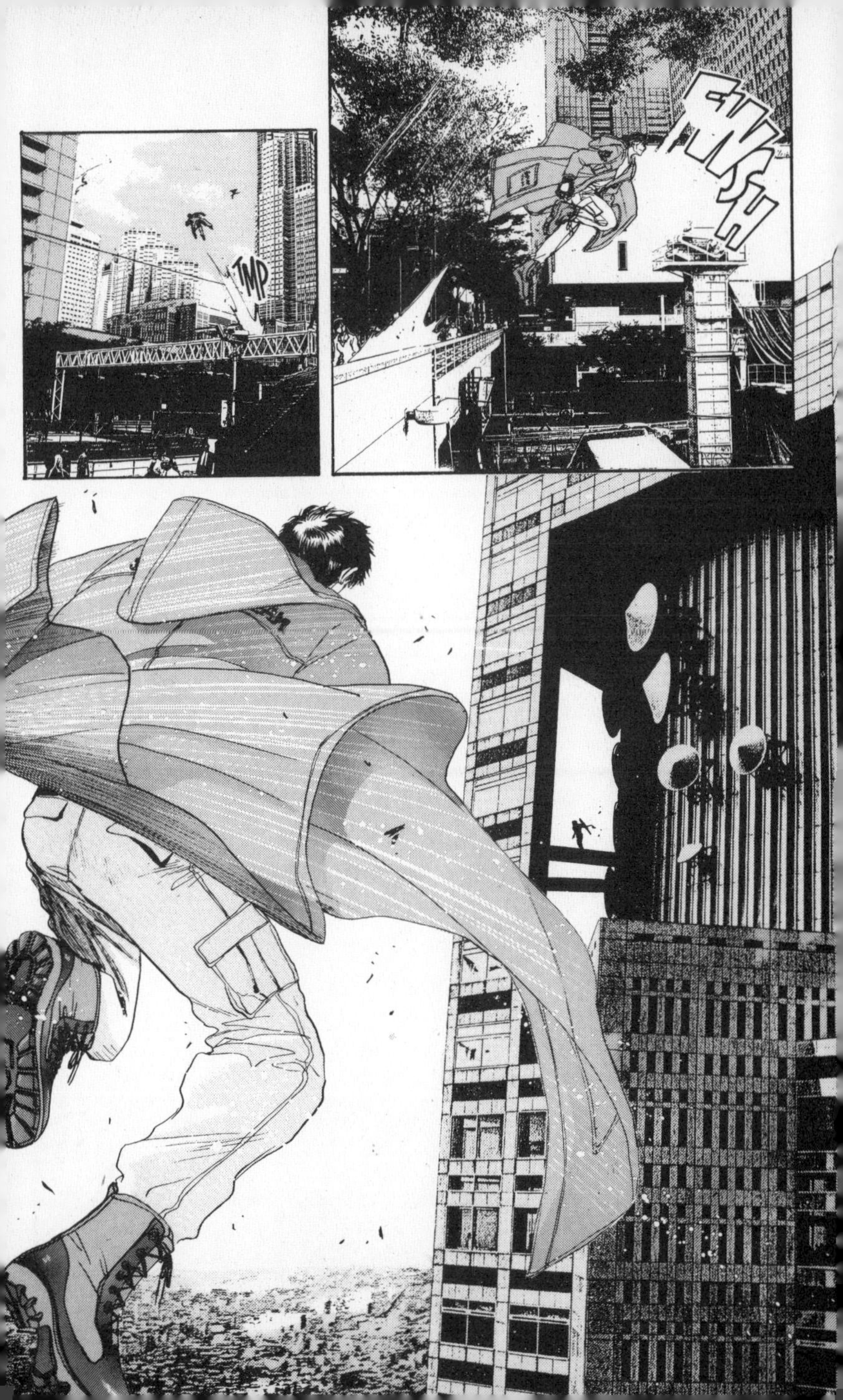
TMP
FWUSH

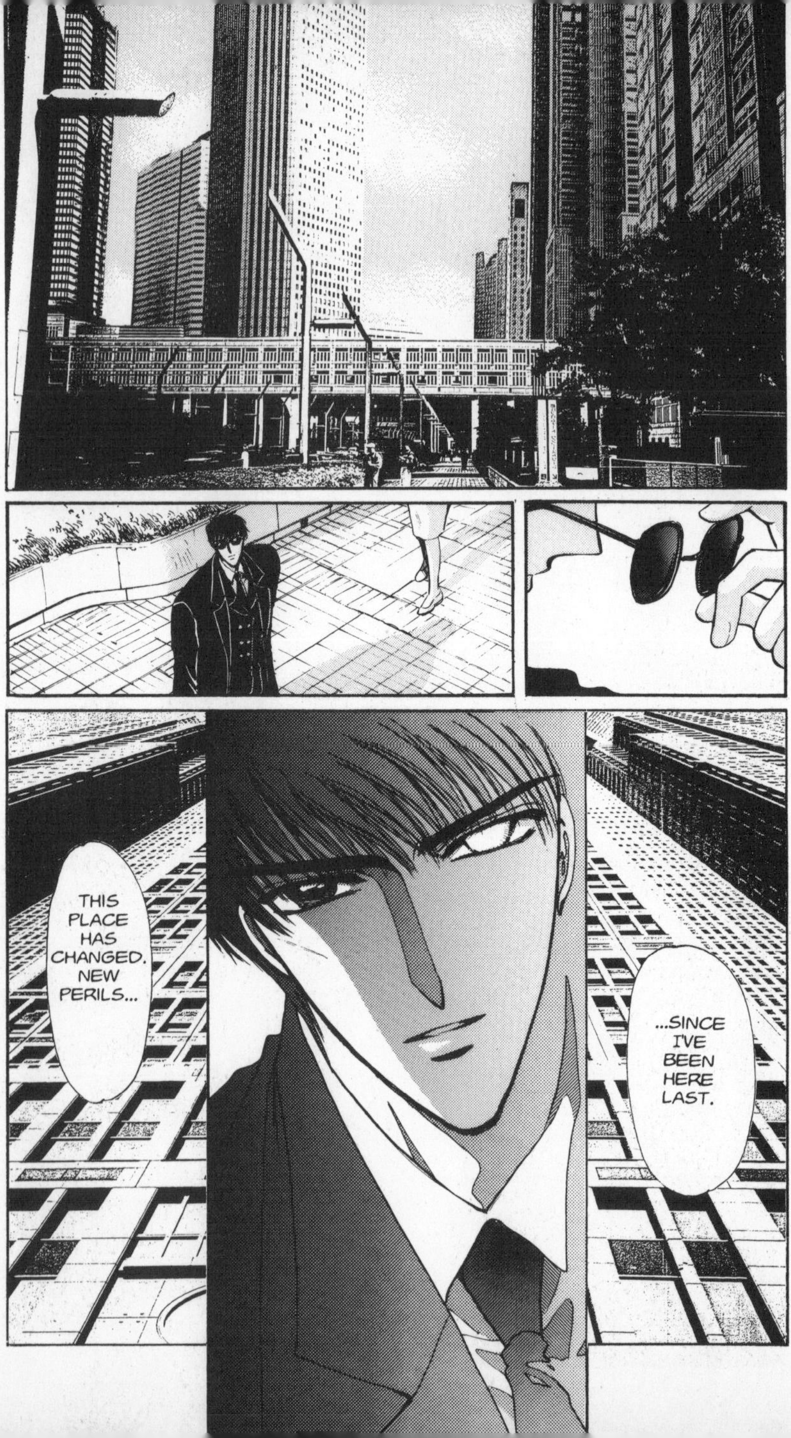
THIS PLACE HAS CHANGED. NEW PERILS...
...SINCE I'VE BEEN HERE LAST.

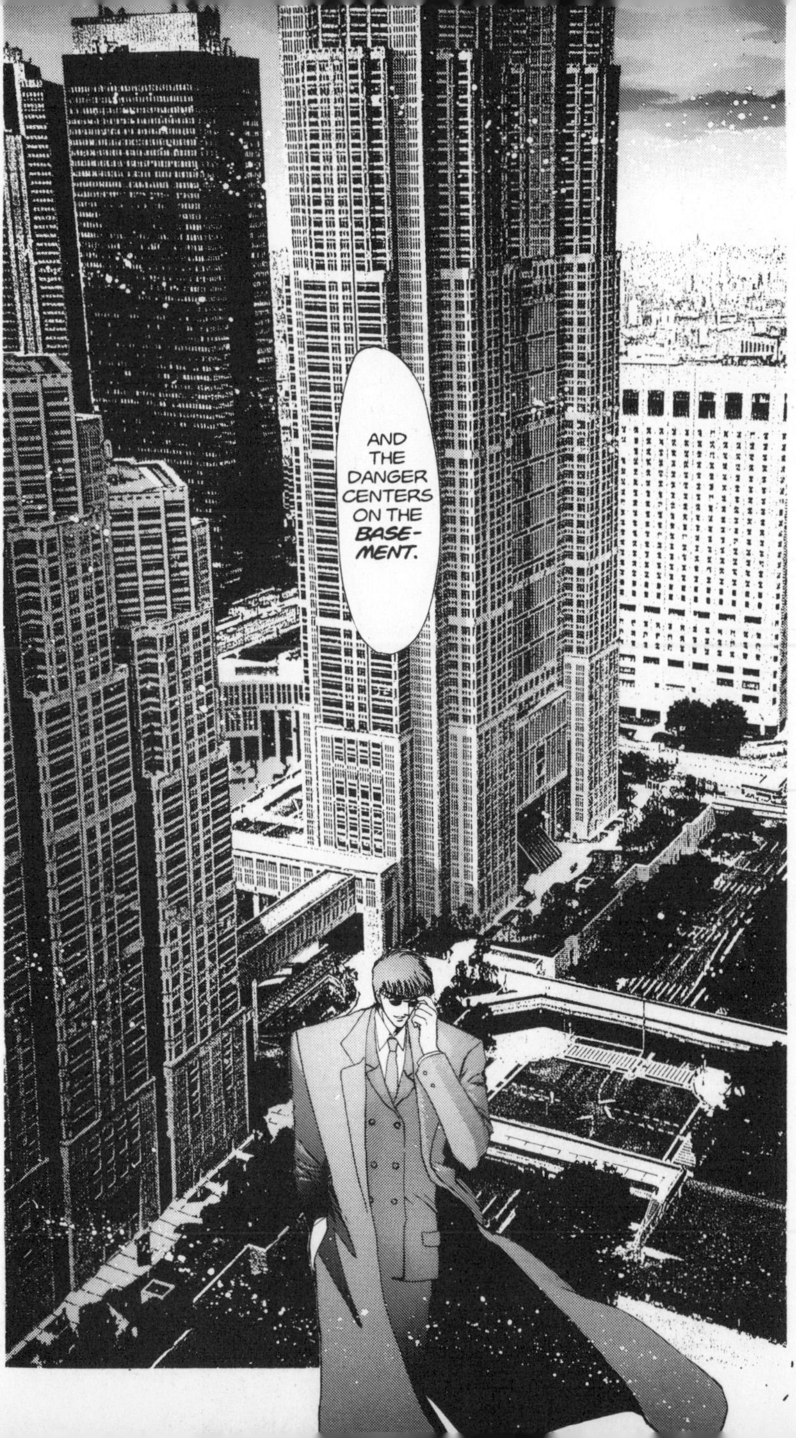
AND THE DANGER CENTERS ON THE BASE-MENT.

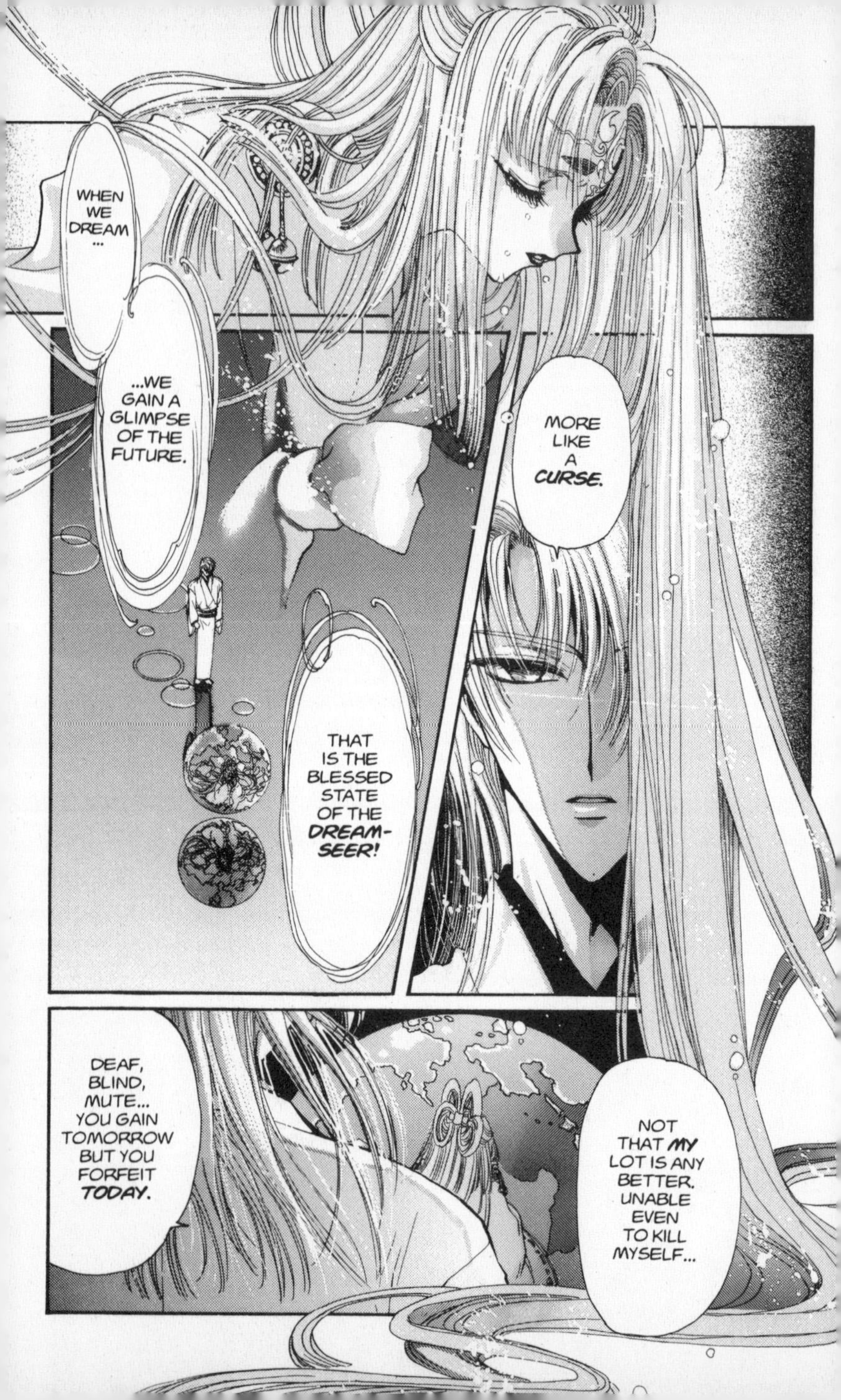
WHEN WE DREAM...
...WE GAIN A GLIMPSE OF THE FUTURE.
THAT IS THE BLESSED STATE OF THE *DREAM-SEER!*
MORE LIKE A *CURSE.*
DEAF, BLIND, MUTE... YOU GAIN TOMORROW BUT YOU FORFEIT *TODAY.*
NOT THAT *MY* LOT IS ANY BETTER. UNABLE EVEN TO KILL MYSELF...

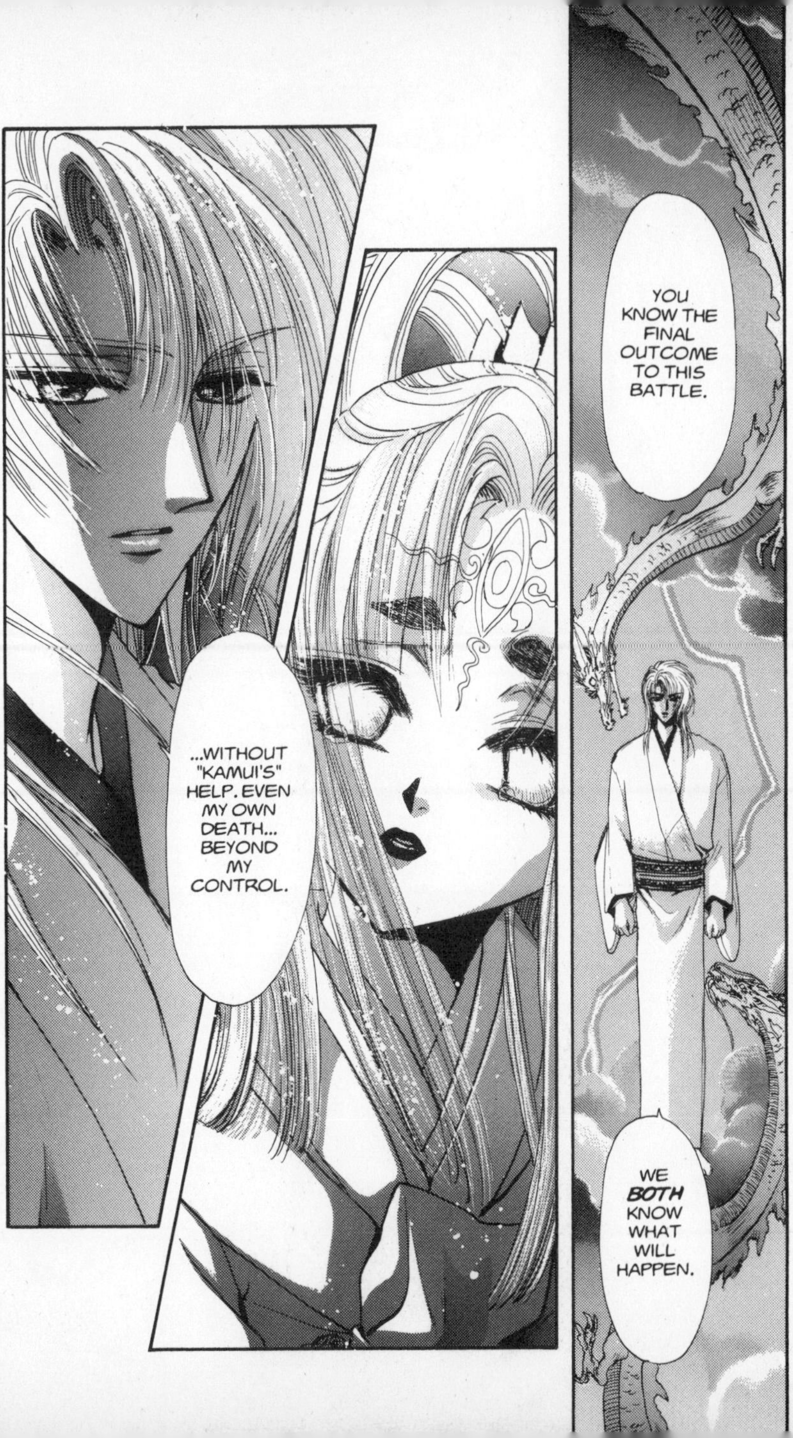
...WITHOUT "KAMUI'S" HELP. EVEN MY OWN DEATH... BEYOND MY CONTROL.
YOU KNOW THE FINAL OUTCOME TO THIS BATTLE.
WE ***BOTH*** KNOW WHAT WILL HAPPEN.

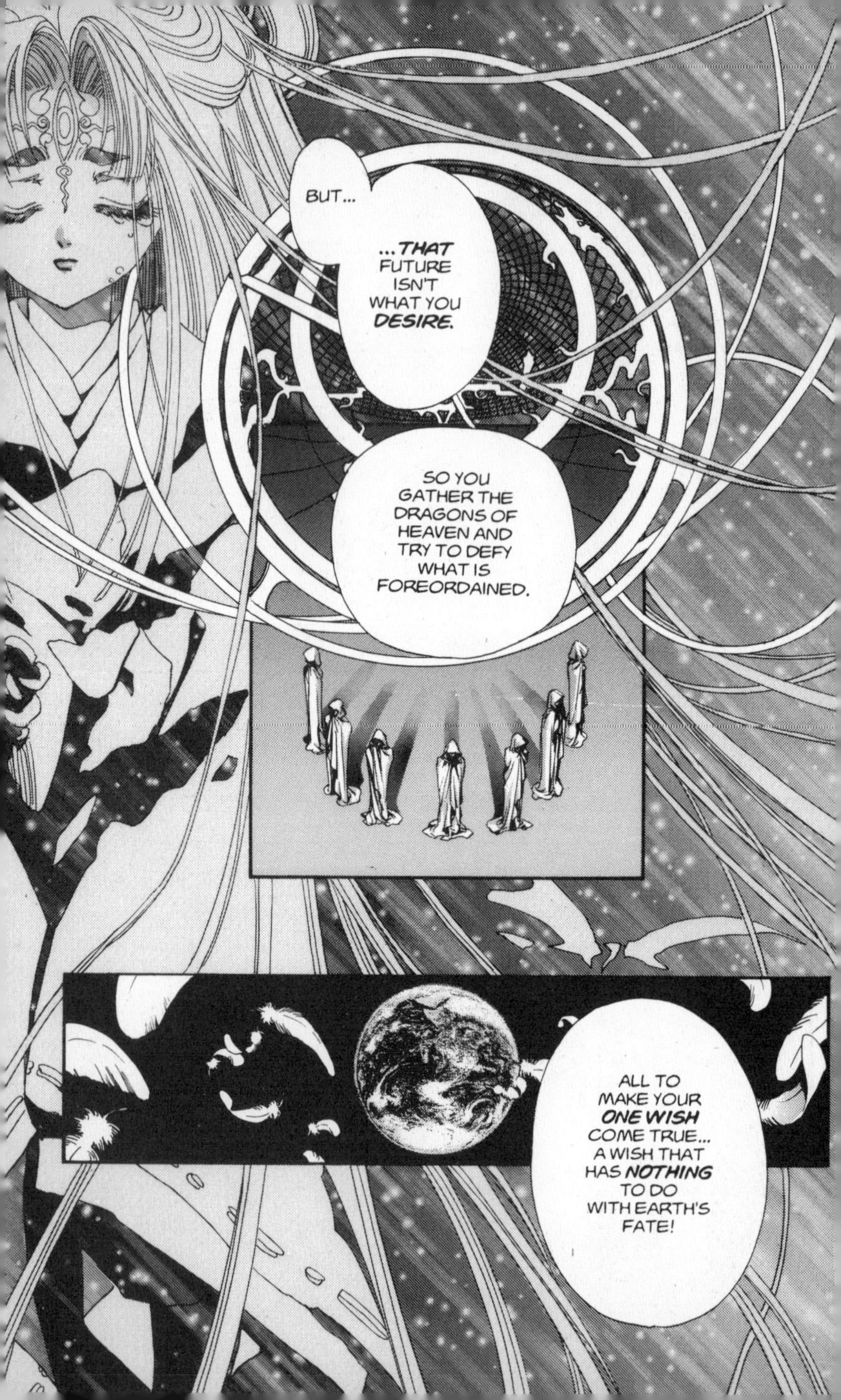

BUT...
...*THAT* FUTURE ISN'T WHAT YOU *DESIRE.*
SO YOU GATHER THE DRAGONS OF HEAVEN AND TRY TO DEFY WHAT IS FOREORDAINED.
ALL TO MAKE YOUR *ONE WISH* COME TRUE... A WISH THAT HAS *NOTHING* TO DO WITH EARTH'S FATE!

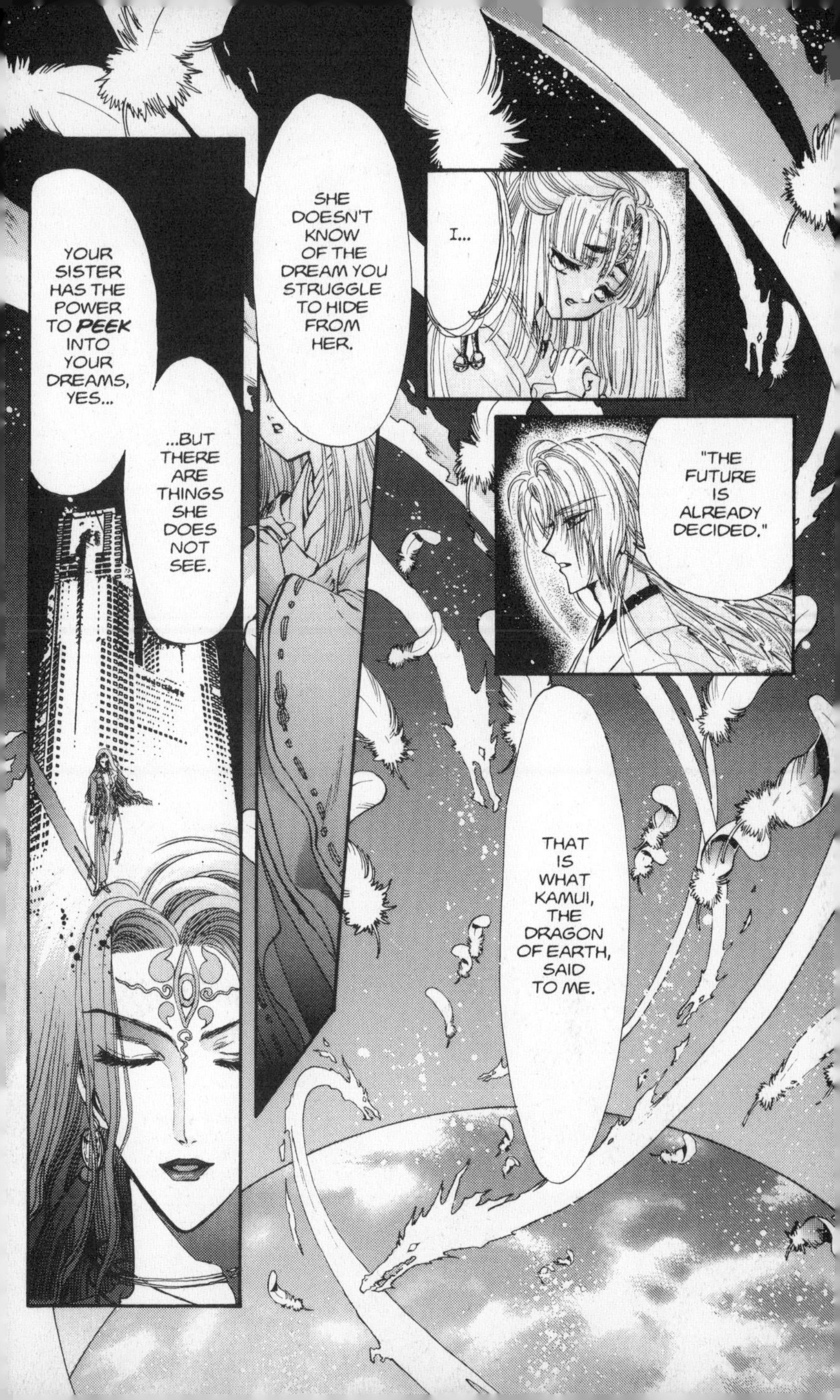
YOUR SISTER HAS THE POWER TO **PEEK** INTO YOUR DREAMS, YES...
...BUT THERE ARE THINGS SHE DOES NOT SEE.
SHE DOESN'T KNOW OF THE DREAM YOU STRUGGLE TO HIDE FROM HER.
I...
"THE FUTURE IS ALREADY DECIDED."
THAT IS WHAT KAMUI, THE DRAGON OF EARTH, SAID TO ME.

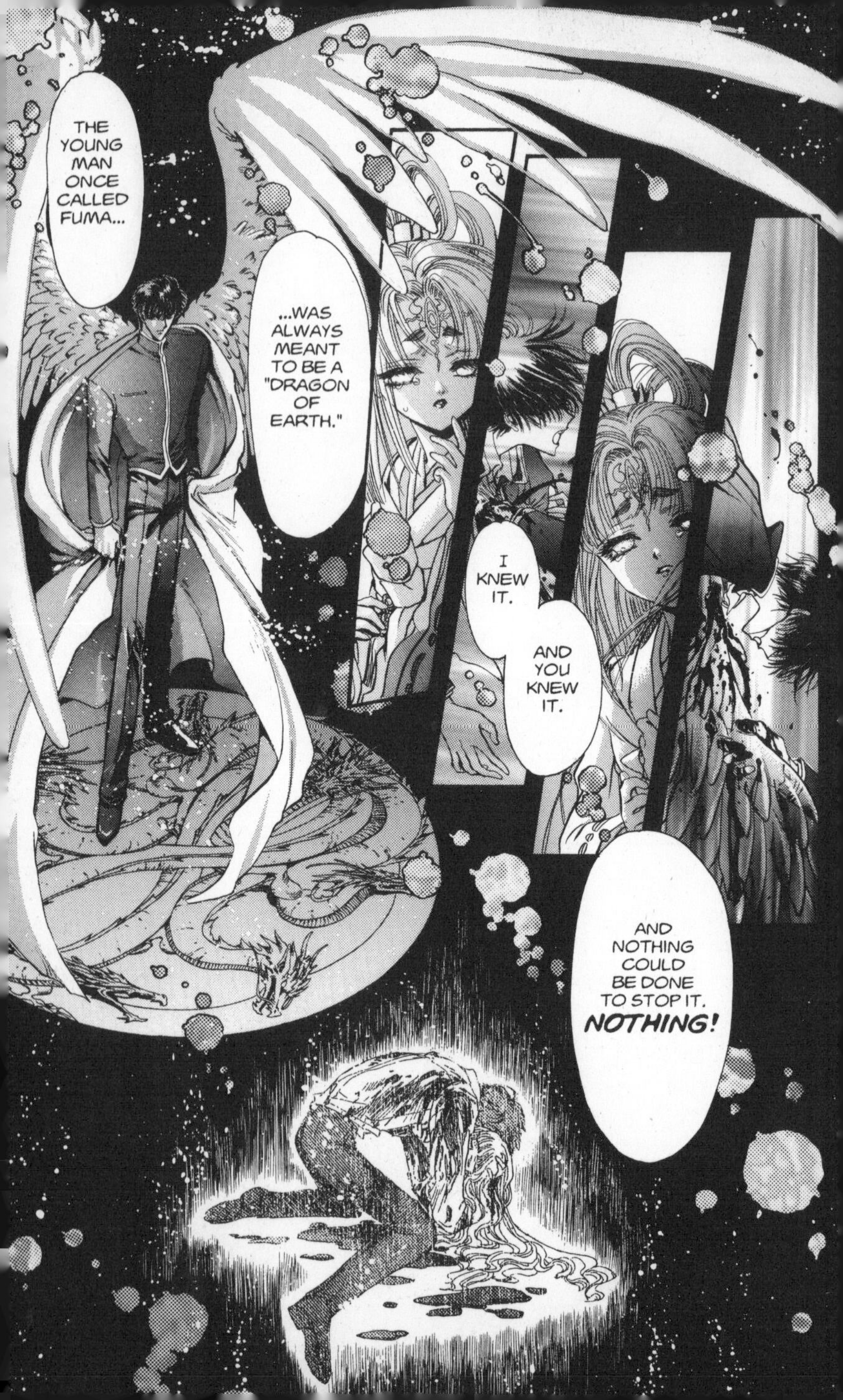
THE YOUNG MAN ONCE CALLED FUMA...
...WAS ALWAYS MEANT TO BE A "DRAGON OF EARTH."
I KNEW IT.
AND YOU KNEW IT.
AND NOTHING COULD BE DONE TO STOP IT. NOTHING!

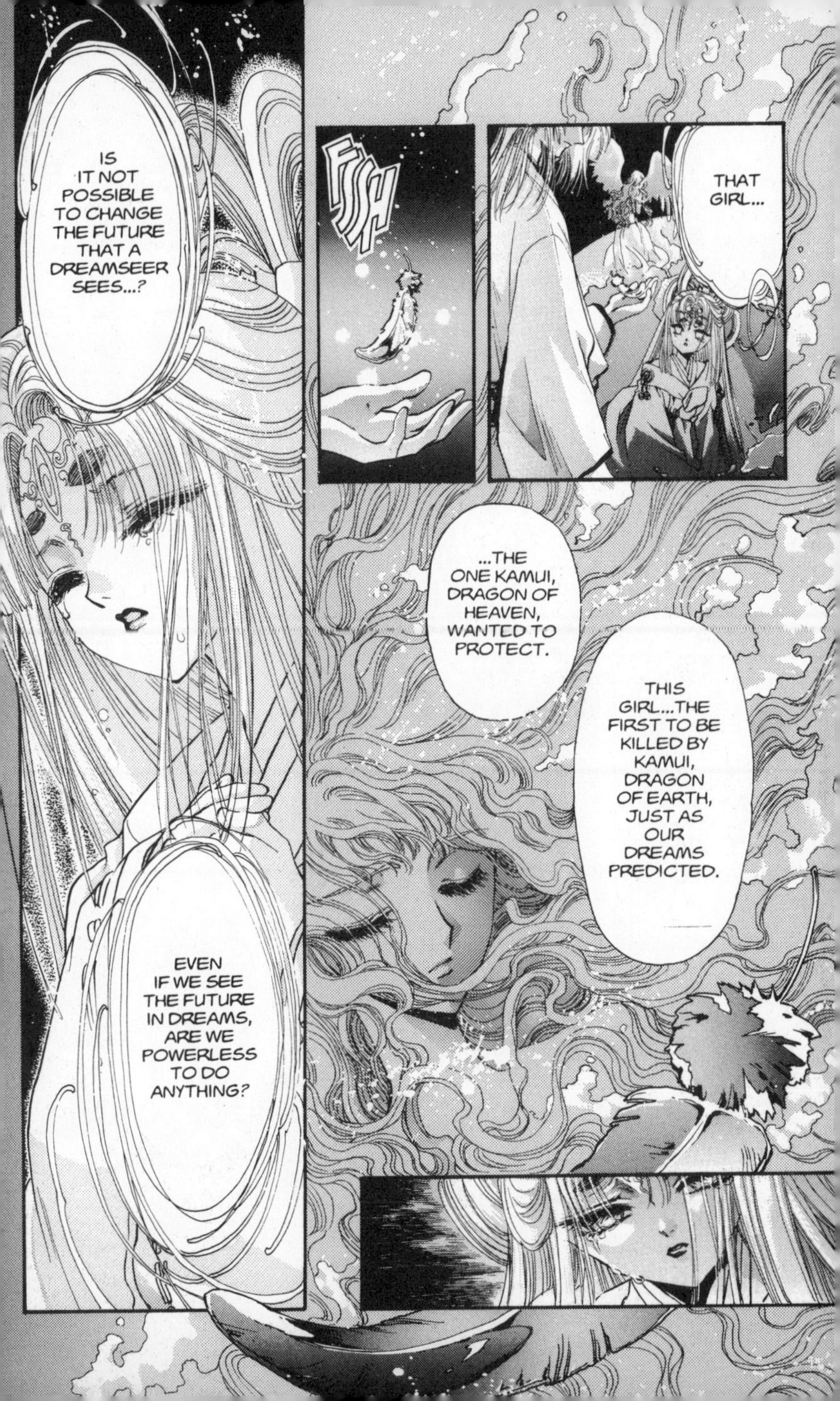
IS IT NOT POSSIBLE TO CHANGE THE FUTURE THAT A DREAMSEER SEES...?
EVEN IF WE SEE THE FUTURE IN DREAMS, ARE WE POWERLESS TO DO ANYTHING?
FISH
THAT GIRL...
...THE ONE KAMUI, DRAGON OF HEAVEN, WANTED TO PROTECT.
THIS GIRL...THE FIRST TO BE KILLED BY KAMUI, DRAGON OF EARTH, JUST AS OUR DREAMS PREDICTED.

SHE WAS BORN WITH THE CAPACITY OF A DREAMSEER...

..BUT DIED WITHOUT ROUSING HER FULL POWERS.

SHE WAS UNSKILLED, NOT YET A DREAM-SEER.

YET THIS IS THE DREAM THAT SHE SAW...IN HER MOMENT OF *DEATH*.

...THE *FUTURE* ...HAS YET TO BE DECIDED...

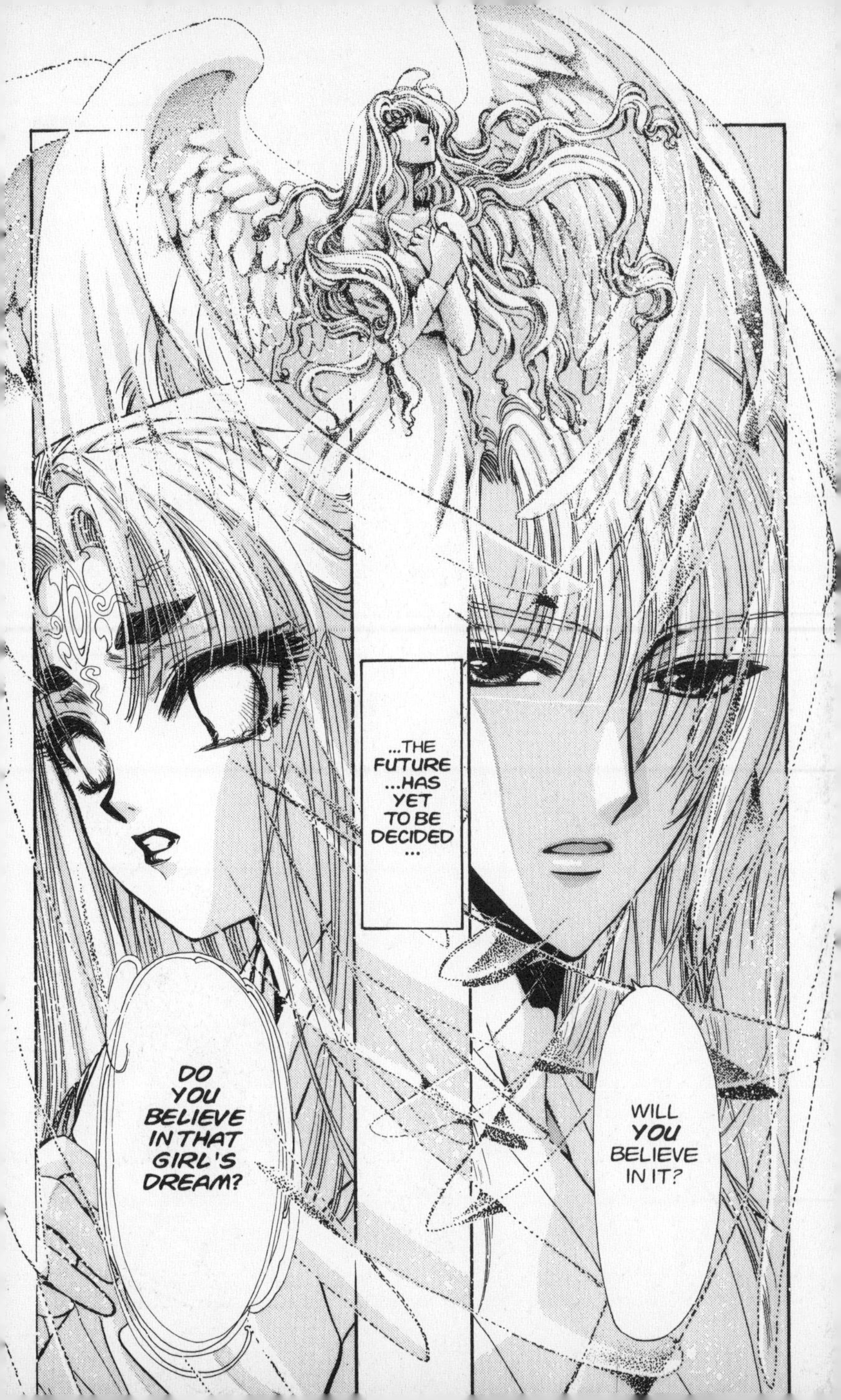
DO YOU BELIEVE IN THAT GIRL'S DREAM?
...THE FUTURE ...HAS YET TO BE DECIDED ...
WILL YOU BELIEVE IN IT?

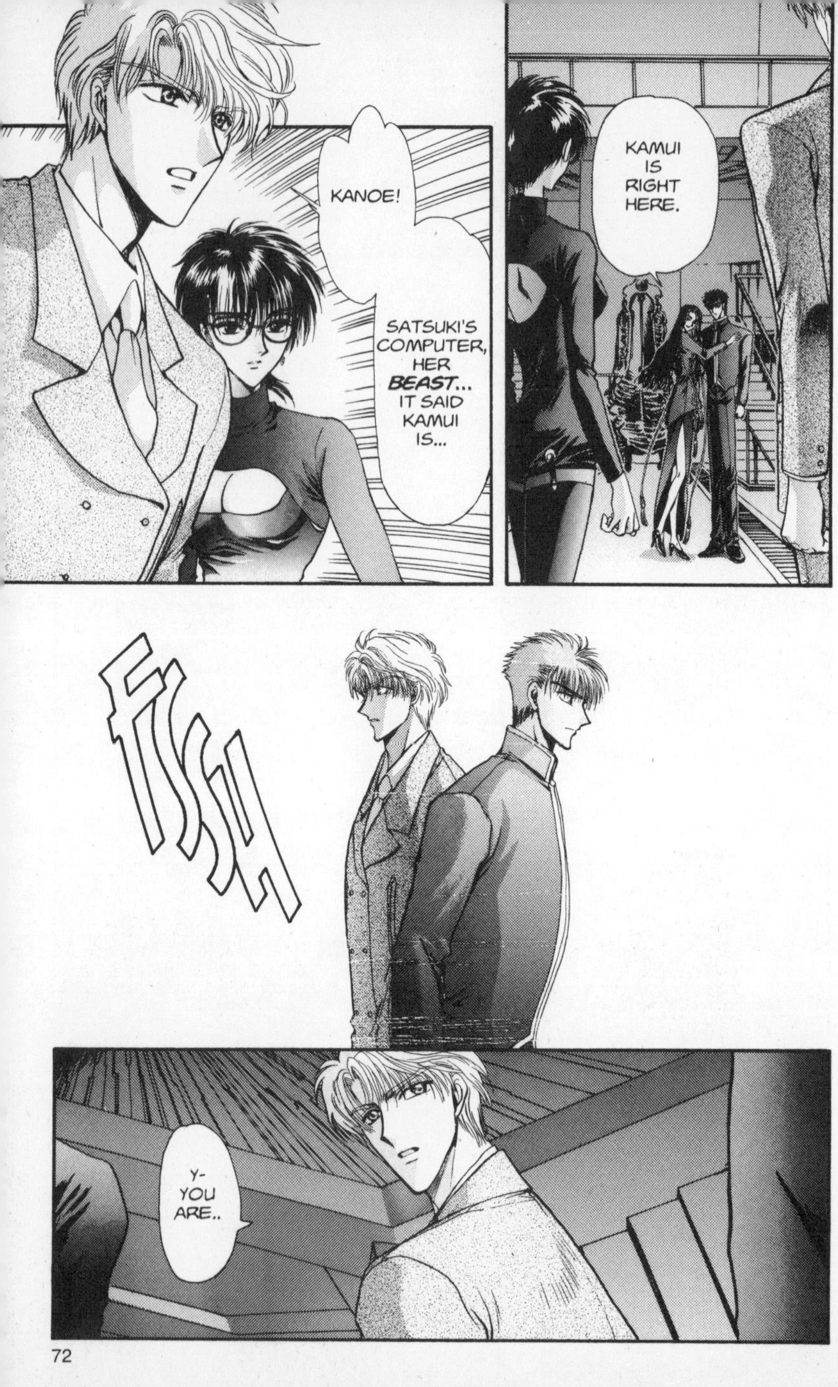
KANOE!
SATSUKI'S COMPUTER, HER *BEAST*... IT SAID KAMUI IS...
KAMUI IS RIGHT HERE.
FSSH
Y-YOU ARE..

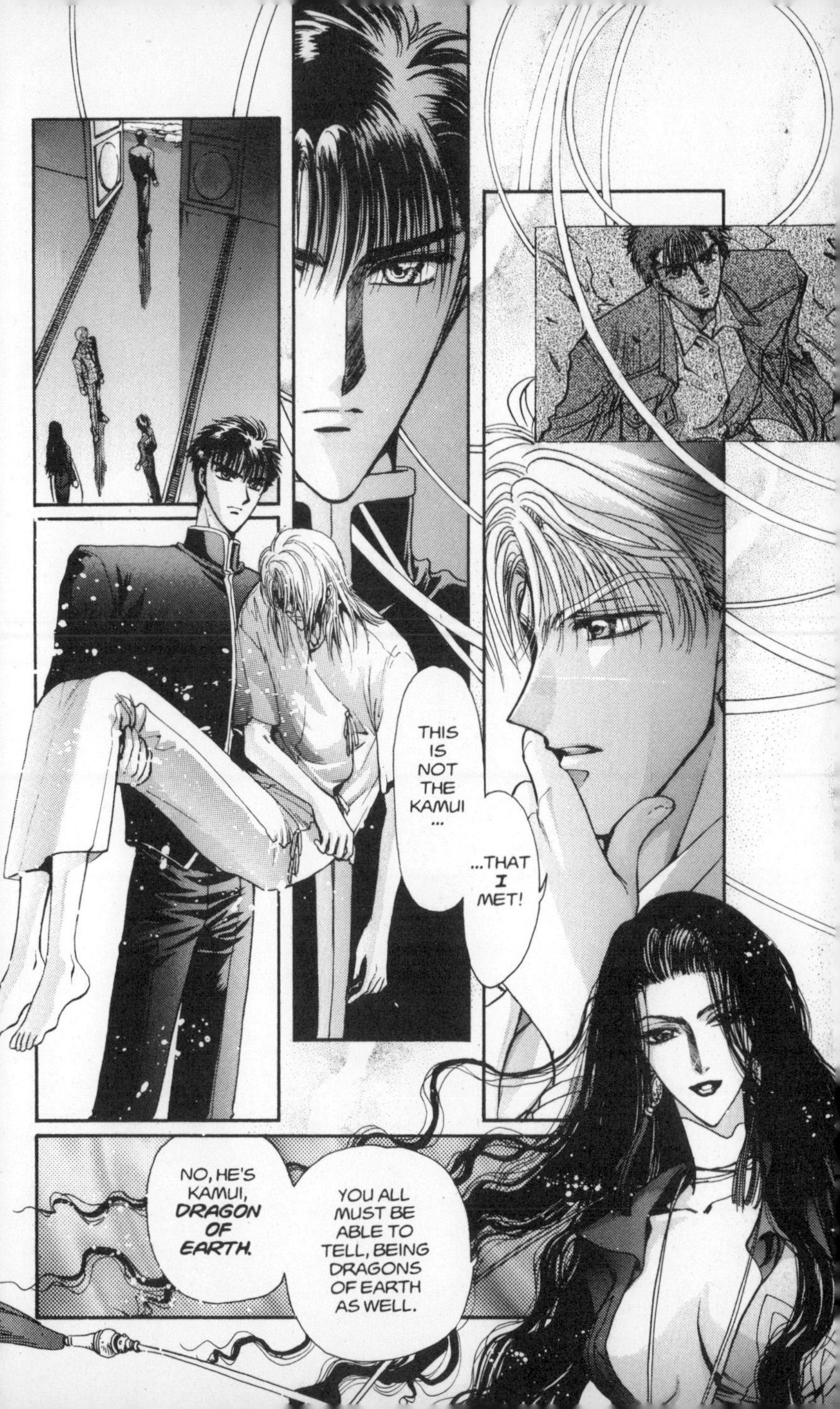
THIS IS NOT THE KAMUI ...
...THAT I MET!
NO, HE'S KAMUI, DRAGON OF EARTH.
YOU ALL MUST BE ABLE TO TELL, BEING DRAGONS OF EARTH AS WELL.

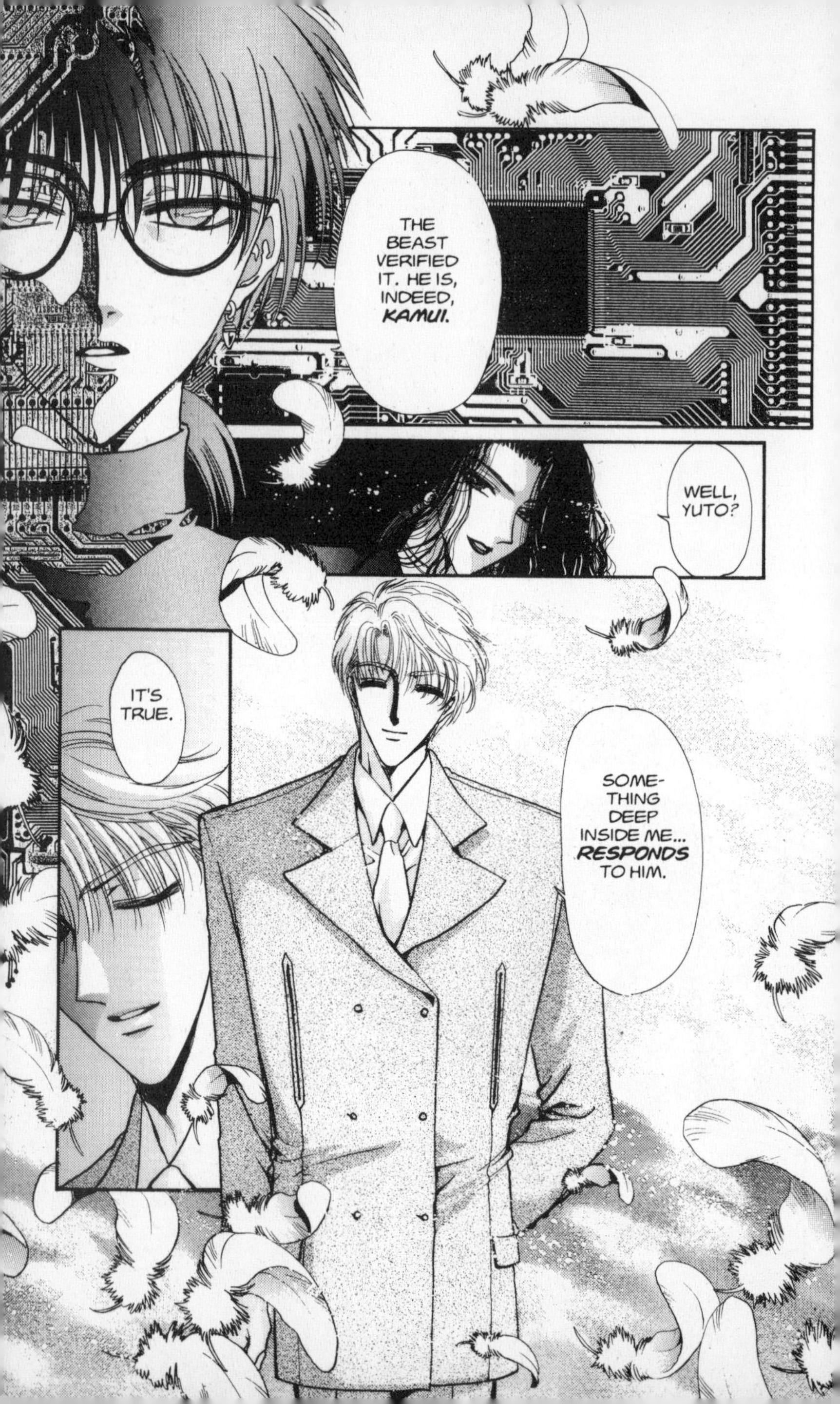
THE BEAST VERIFIED IT. HE IS, INDEED, KAMUI.
WELL, YUTO?
IT'S TRUE.
SOME-THING DEEP INSIDE ME... RESPONDS TO HIM.

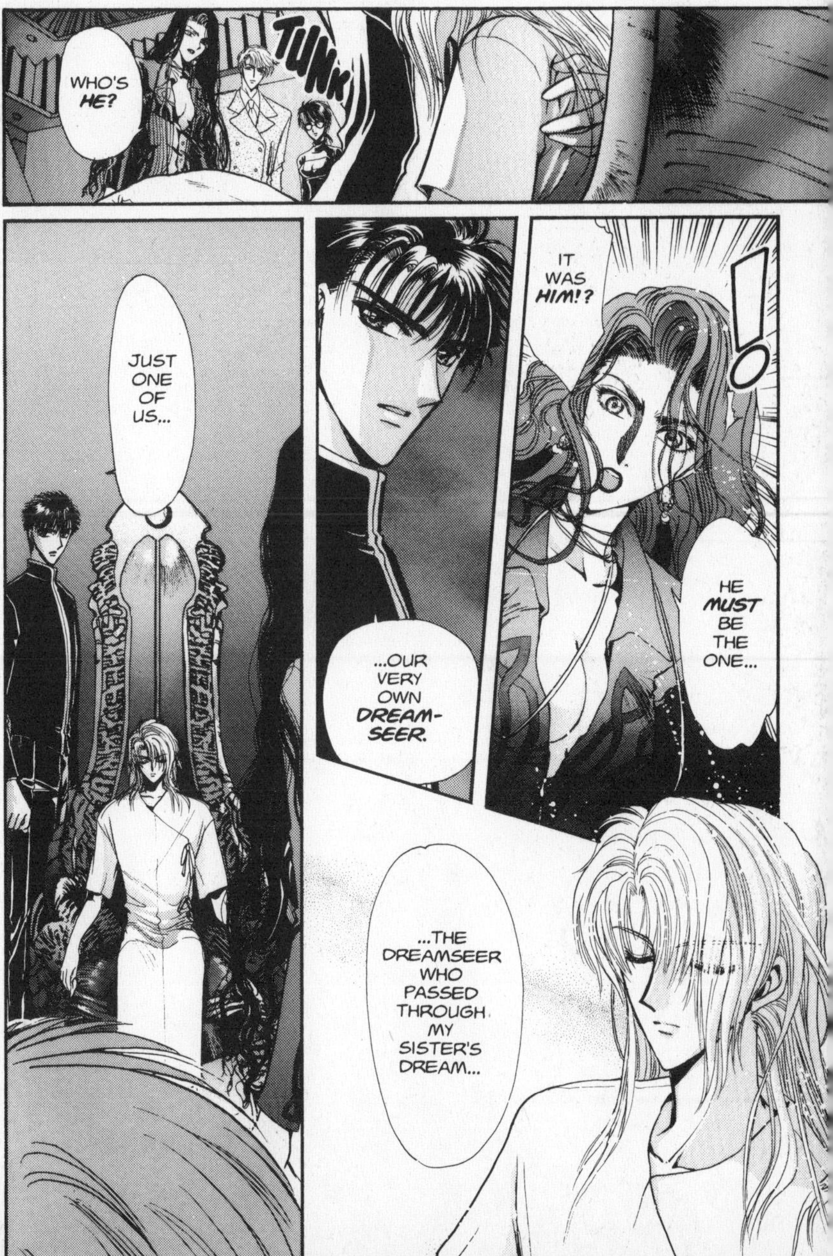

WHO'S HE?
TUNK
JUST ONE OF US...
...OUR VERY OWN DREAMSEER.
IT WAS HIM!?
!
HE MUST BE THE ONE...
...THE DREAMSEER WHO PASSED THROUGH MY SISTER'S DREAM...

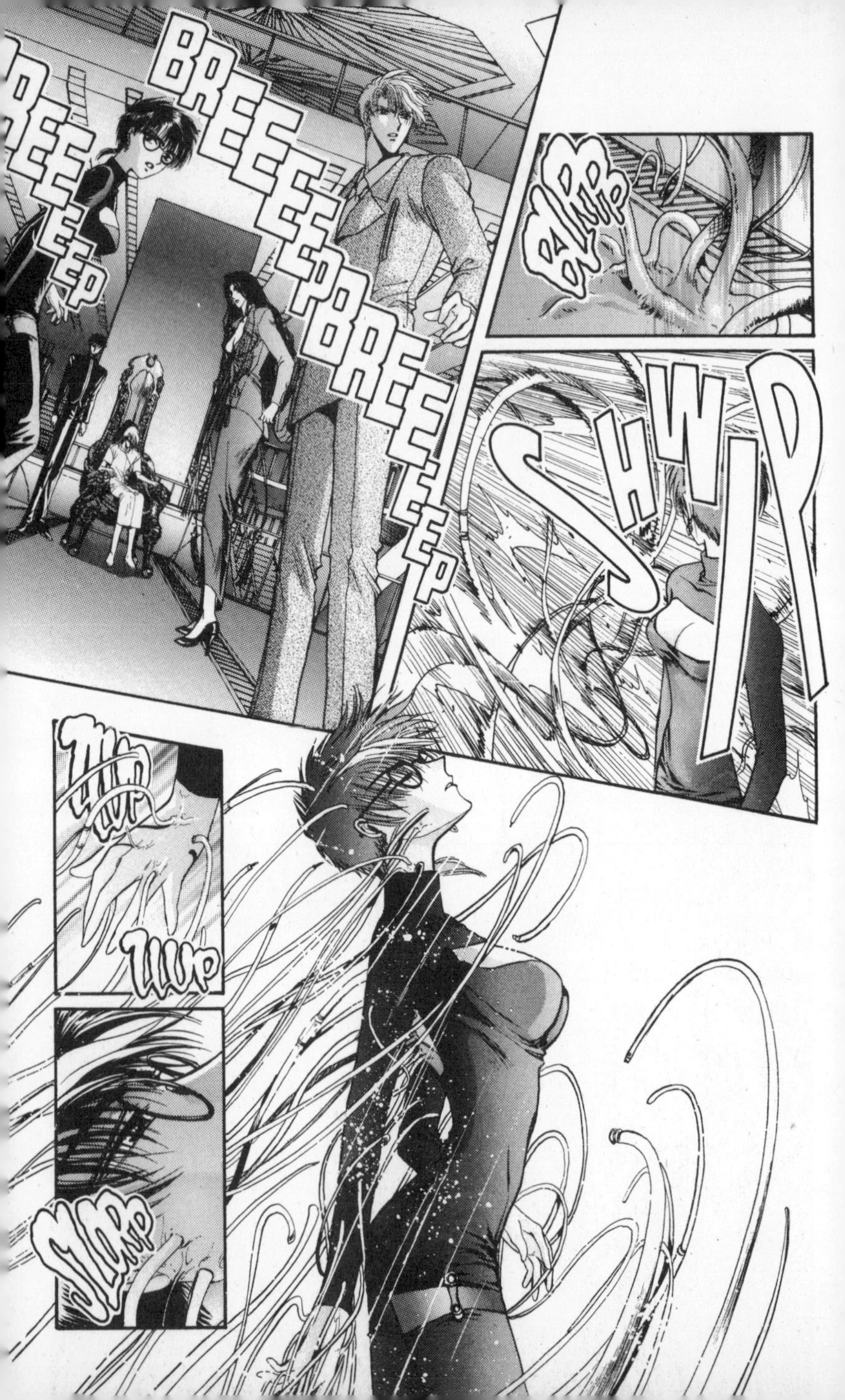
BREEEEEP
BREEEEP
SHWIP

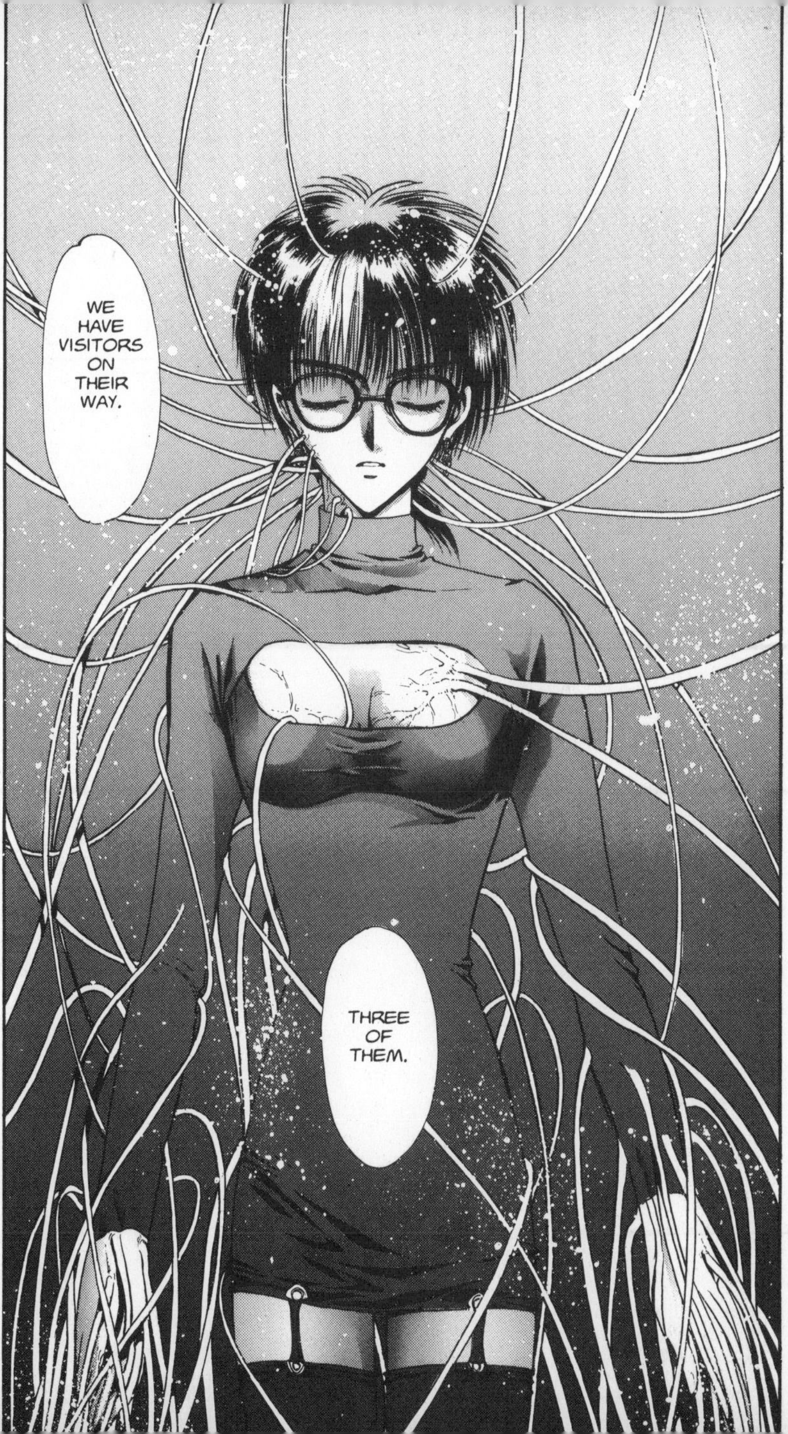
WE HAVE VISITORS ON THEIR WAY.
THREE OF THEM.

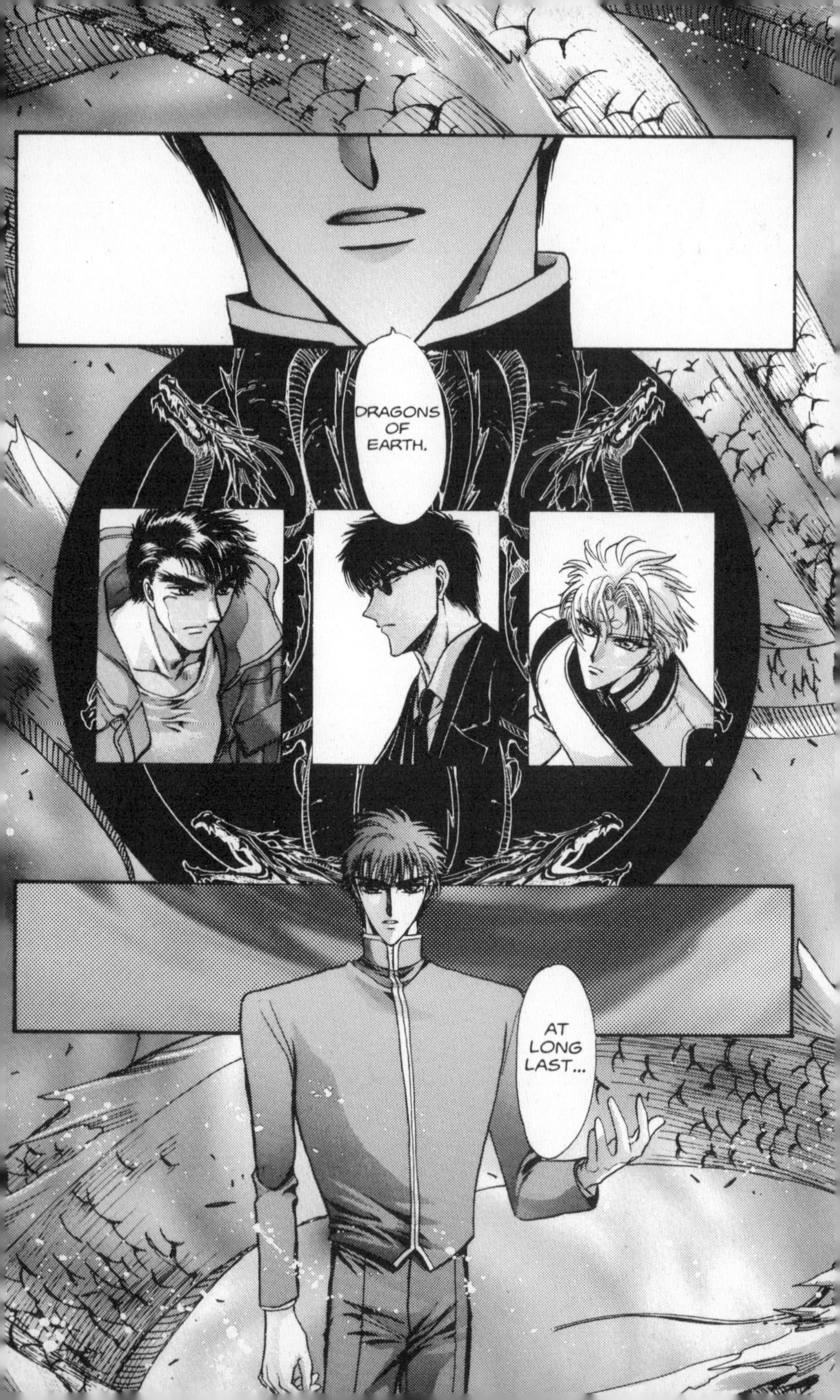
DRAGONS OF EARTH.
AT LONG LAST...

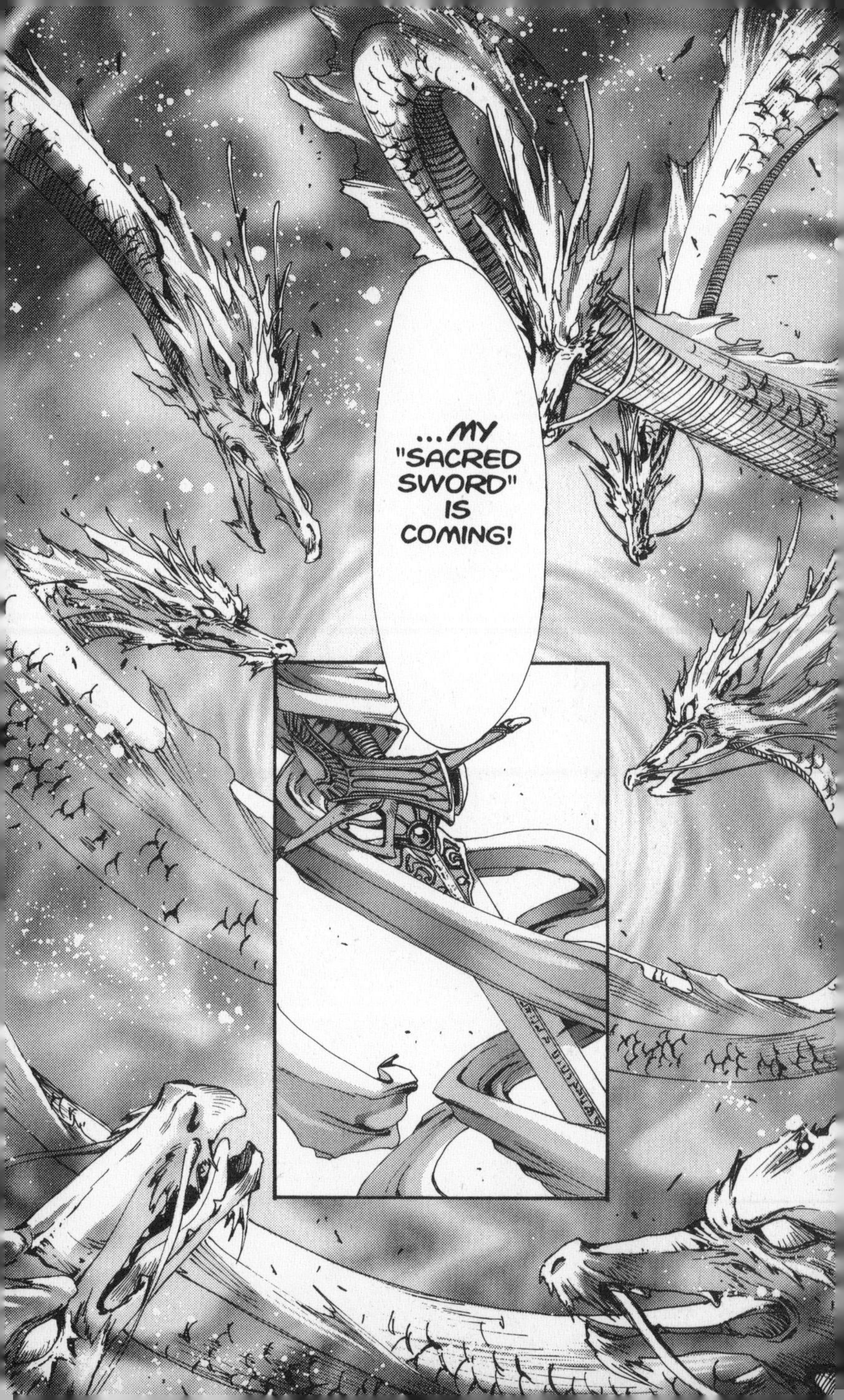
...MY "SACRED SWORD" IS COMING!

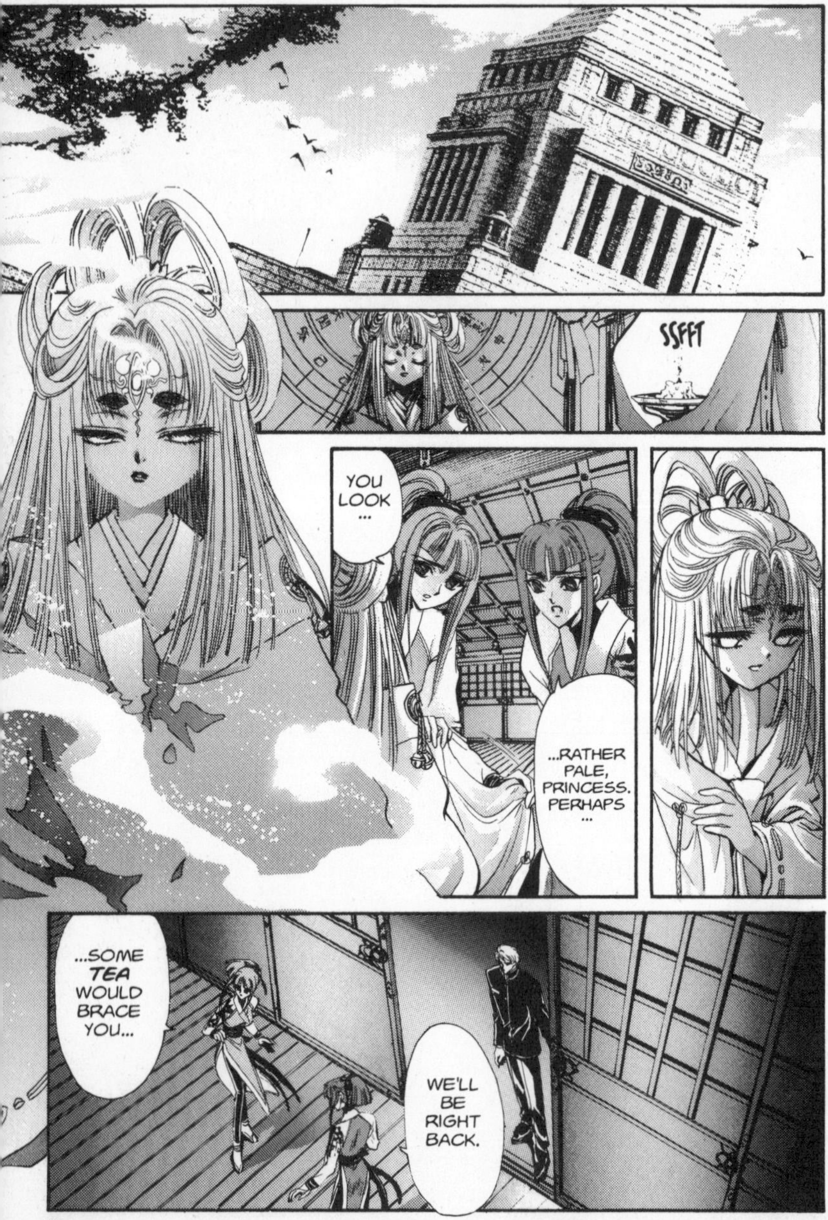
SSFFT
YOU LOOK ...
...RATHER PALE, PRINCESS. PERHAPS ...
...SOME TEA WOULD BRACE YOU...
WE'LL BE RIGHT BACK.

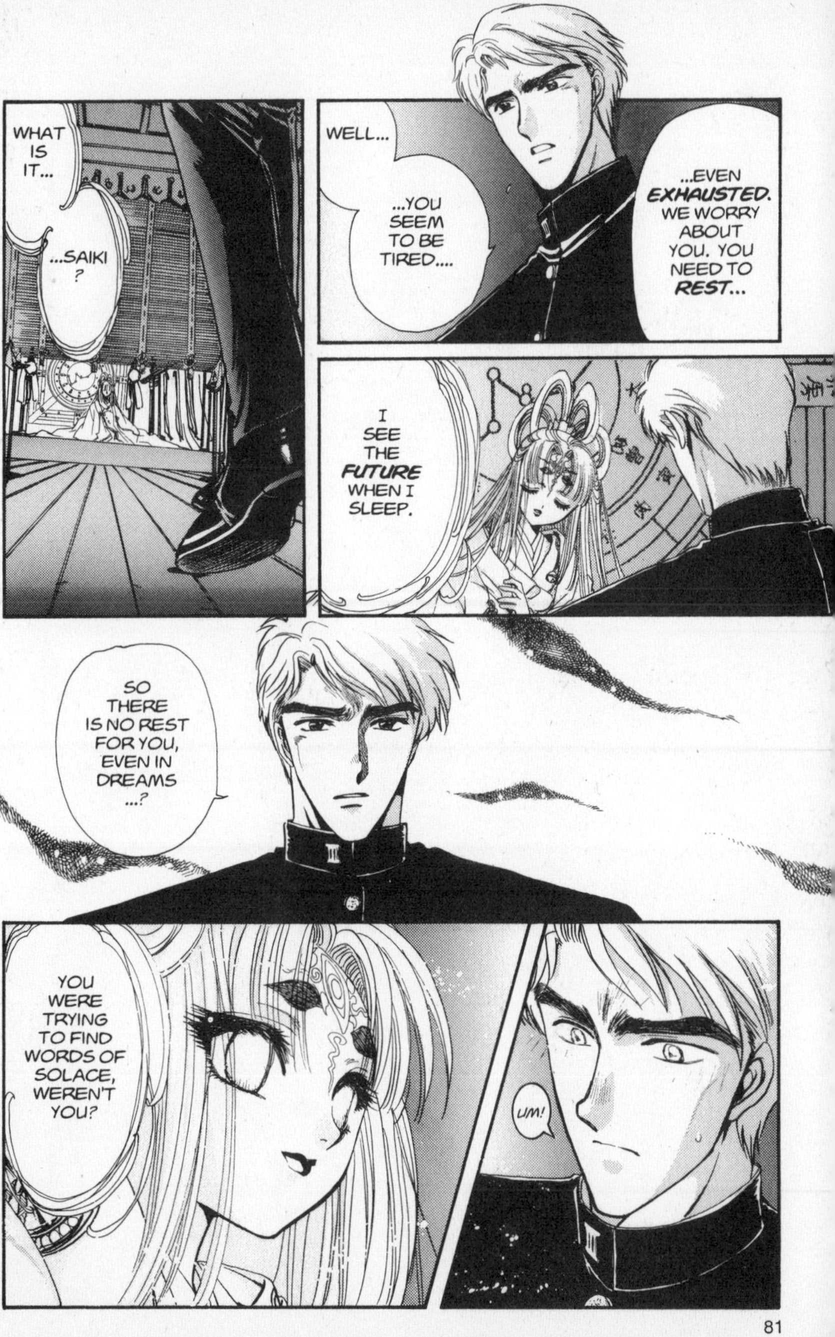
WHAT IS IT...
...SAIKI?
WELL...
...YOU SEEM TO BE TIRED....
...EVEN **EXHAUSTED.** WE WORRY ABOUT YOU. YOU NEED TO **REST...**
I SEE THE **FUTURE** WHEN I SLEEP.
SO THERE IS NO REST FOR YOU, EVEN IN DREAMS ...?
YOU WERE TRYING TO FIND WORDS OF SOLACE, WEREN'T YOU?
UM!

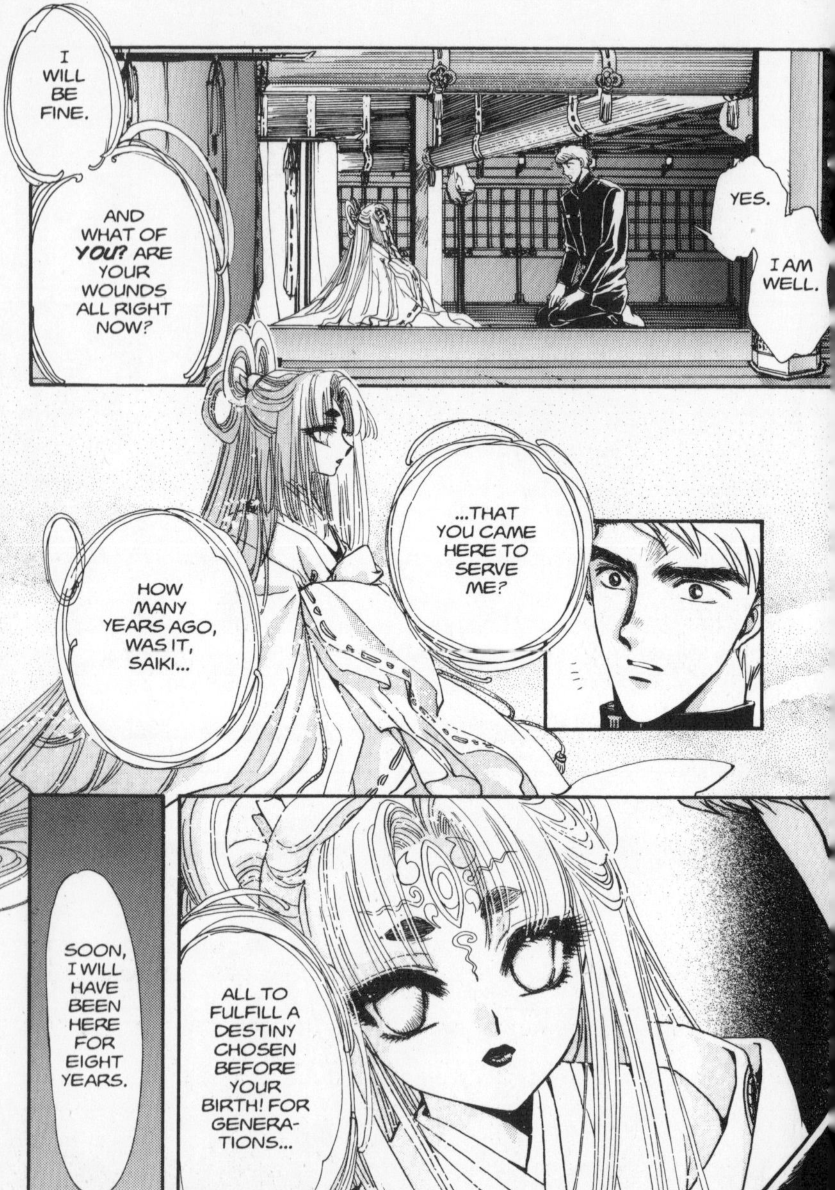
I WILL BE FINE.
AND WHAT OF ***YOU?*** ARE YOUR WOUNDS ALL RIGHT NOW?
YES.
I AM WELL.
HOW MANY YEARS AGO, WAS IT, SAIKI...
...THAT YOU CAME HERE TO SERVE ME?
SOON, I WILL HAVE BEEN HERE FOR EIGHT YEARS.
ALL TO FULFILL A DESTINY CHOSEN BEFORE YOUR BIRTH! FOR GENERA-TIONS...

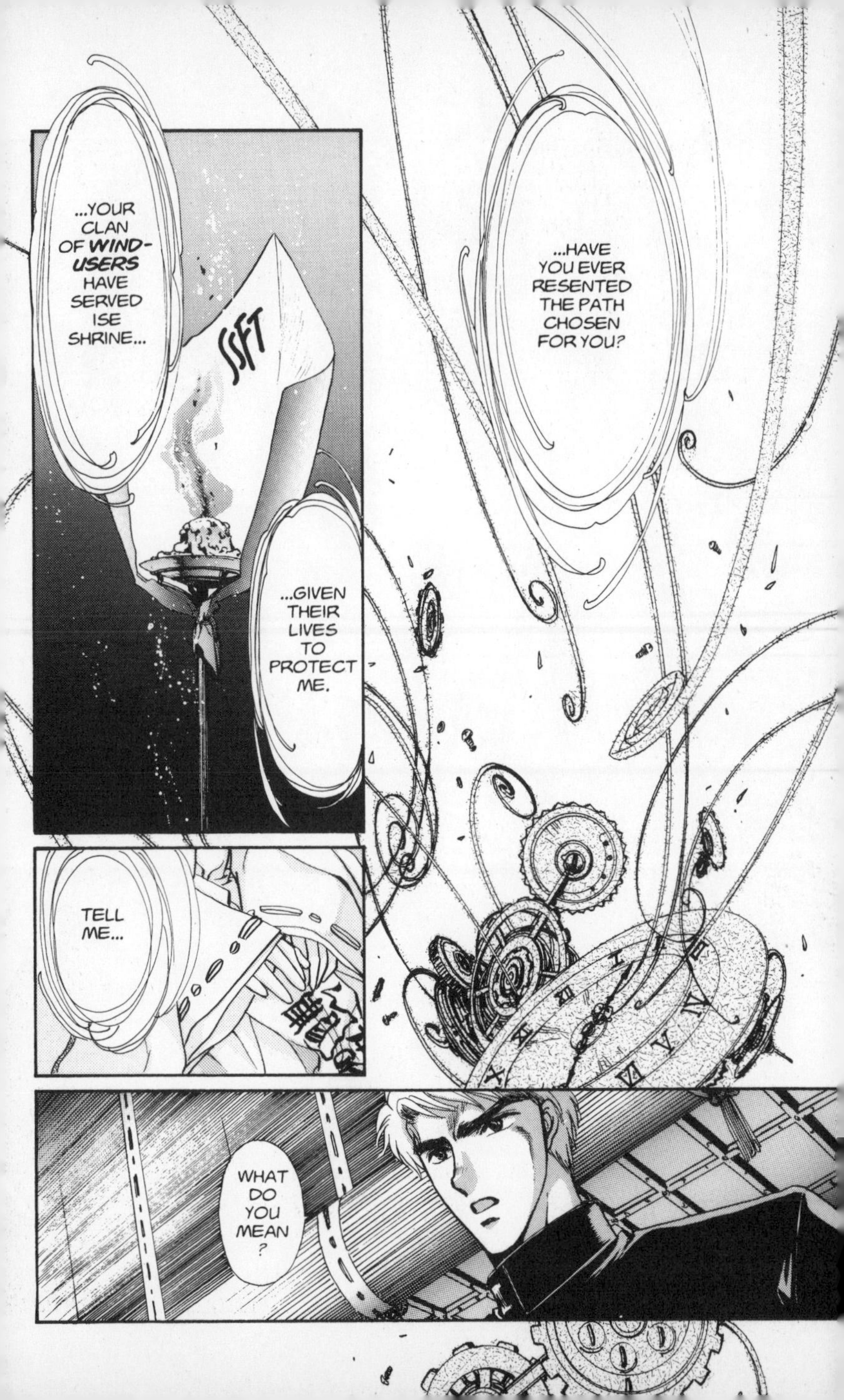
...YOUR CLAN OF **WIND-USERS** HAVE SERVED ISE SHRINE...
SSFT
...GIVEN THEIR LIVES TO PROTECT ME.
TELL ME...
...HAVE YOU EVER RESENTED THE PATH CHOSEN FOR YOU?
WHAT DO YOU MEAN?

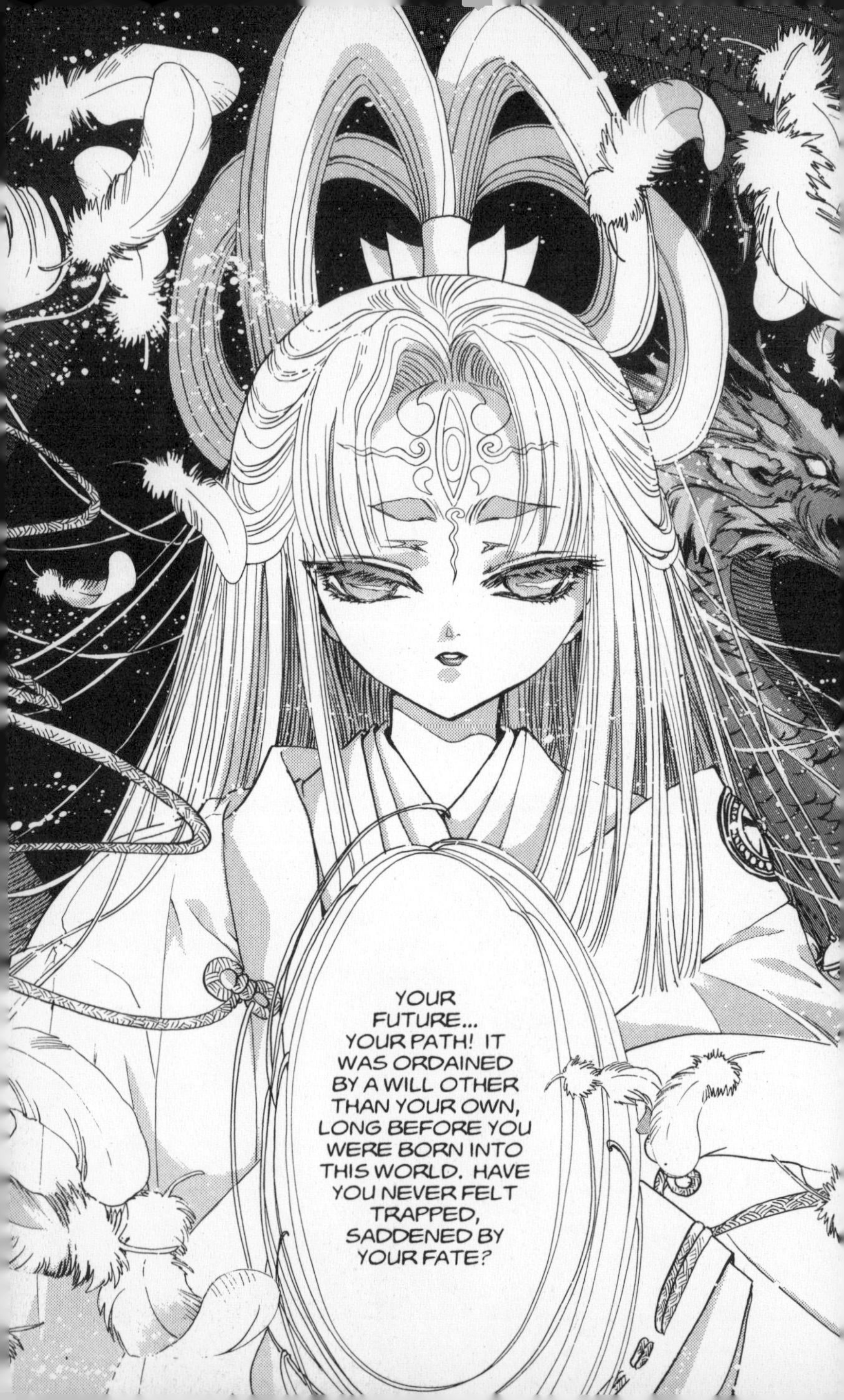
YOUR FUTURE... YOUR PATH! IT WAS ORDAINED BY A WILL OTHER THAN YOUR OWN, LONG BEFORE YOU WERE BORN INTO THIS WORLD. HAVE YOU NEVER FELT TRAPPED, SADDENED BY YOUR FATE?

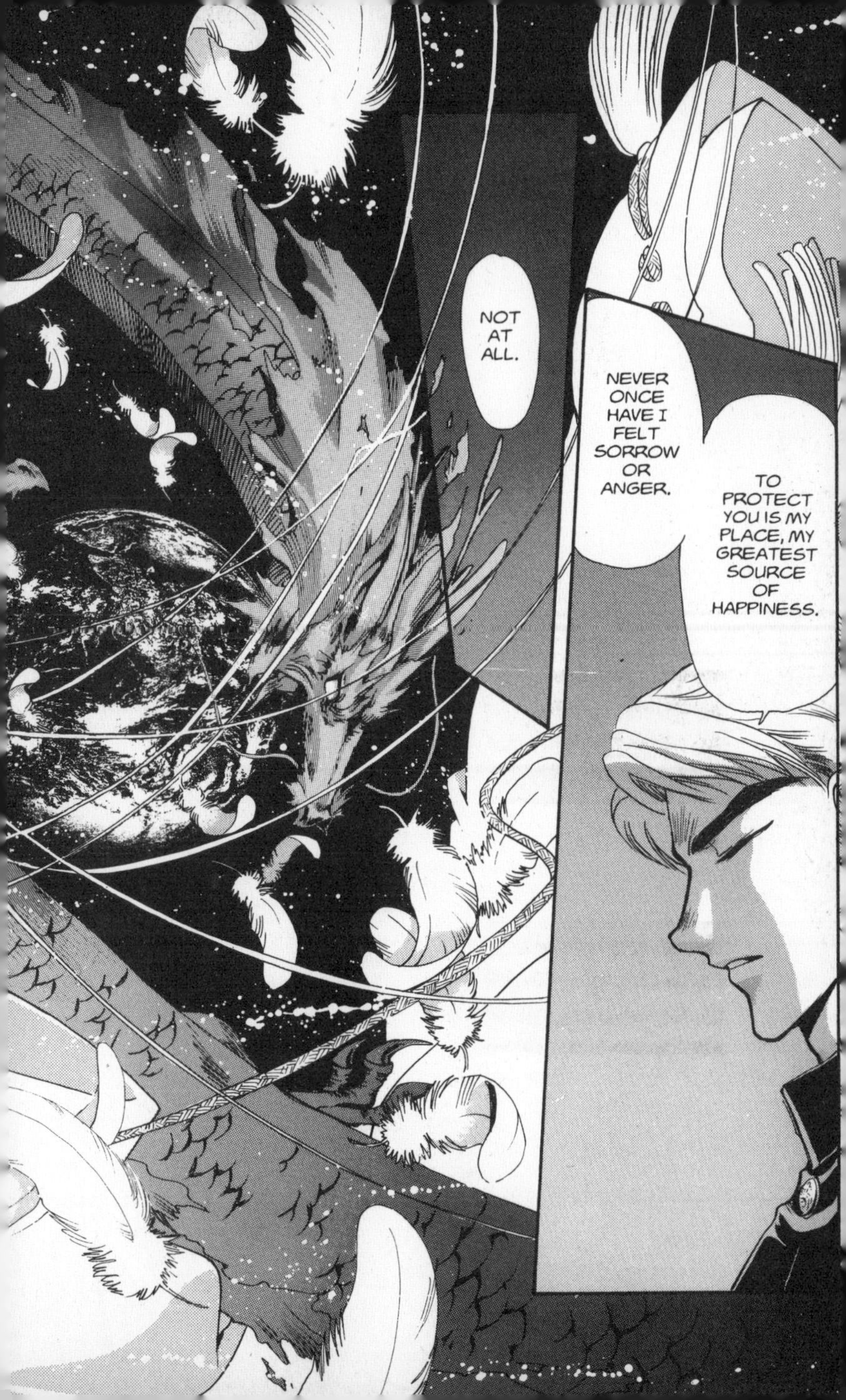
NOT AT ALL.
NEVER ONCE HAVE I FELT SORROW OR ANGER.
TO PROTECT YOU IS MY PLACE, MY GREATEST SOURCE OF HAPPINESS.

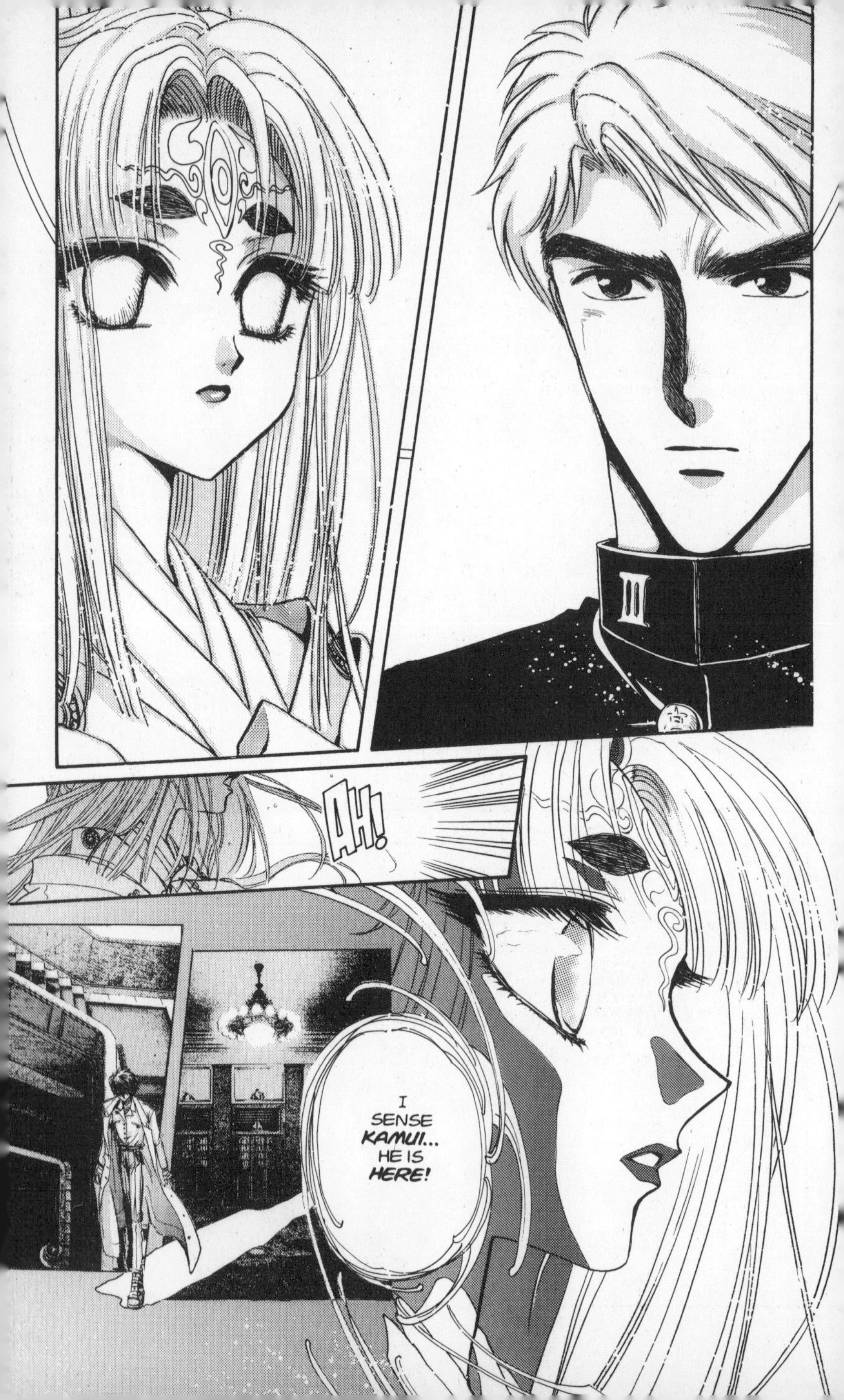
AH!
I SENSE KAMUI... HE IS HERE!

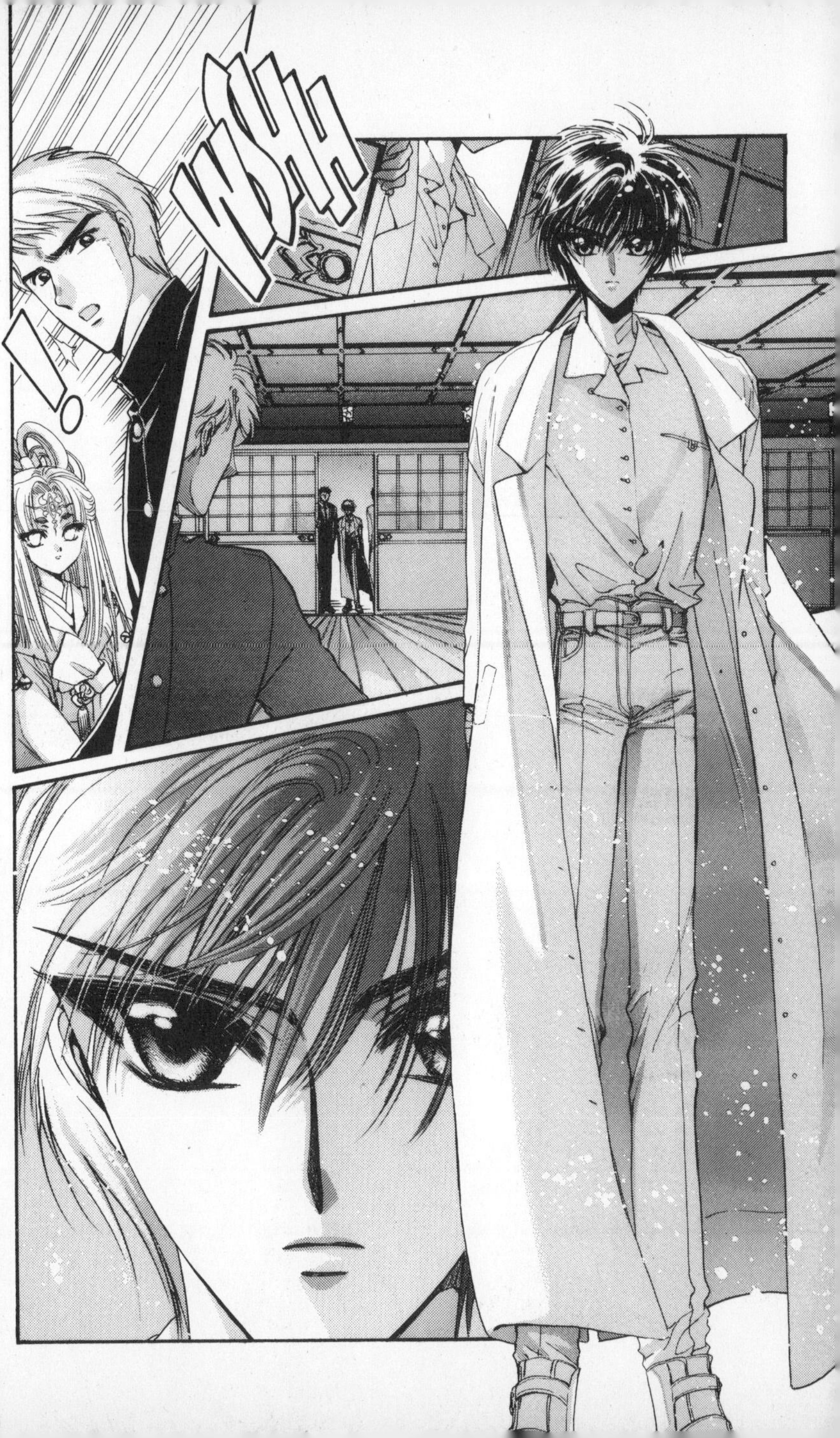
WSHH
!?

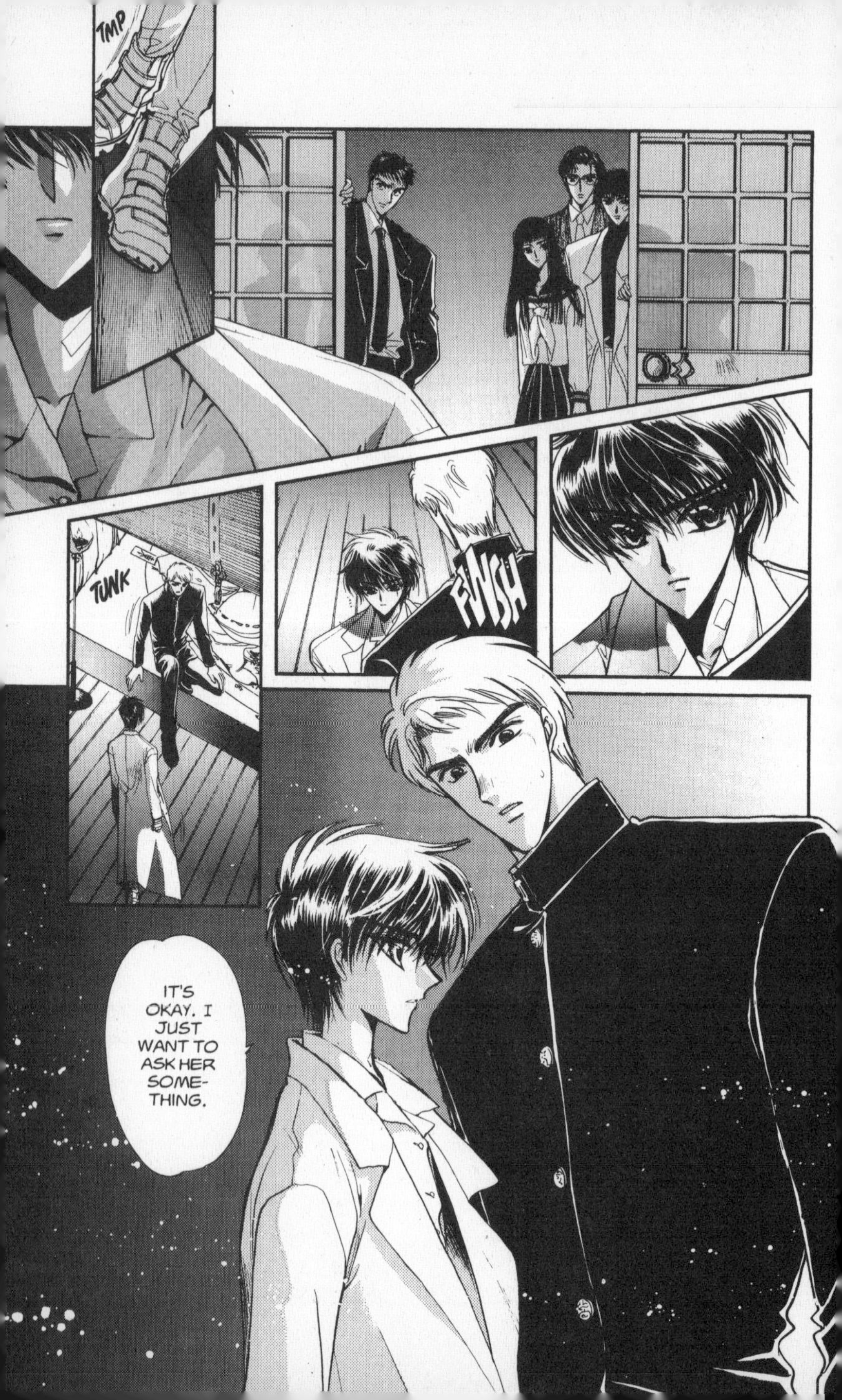
TMP
TUNK
FWISH
IT'S OKAY. I JUST WANT TO ASK HER SOME-THING.

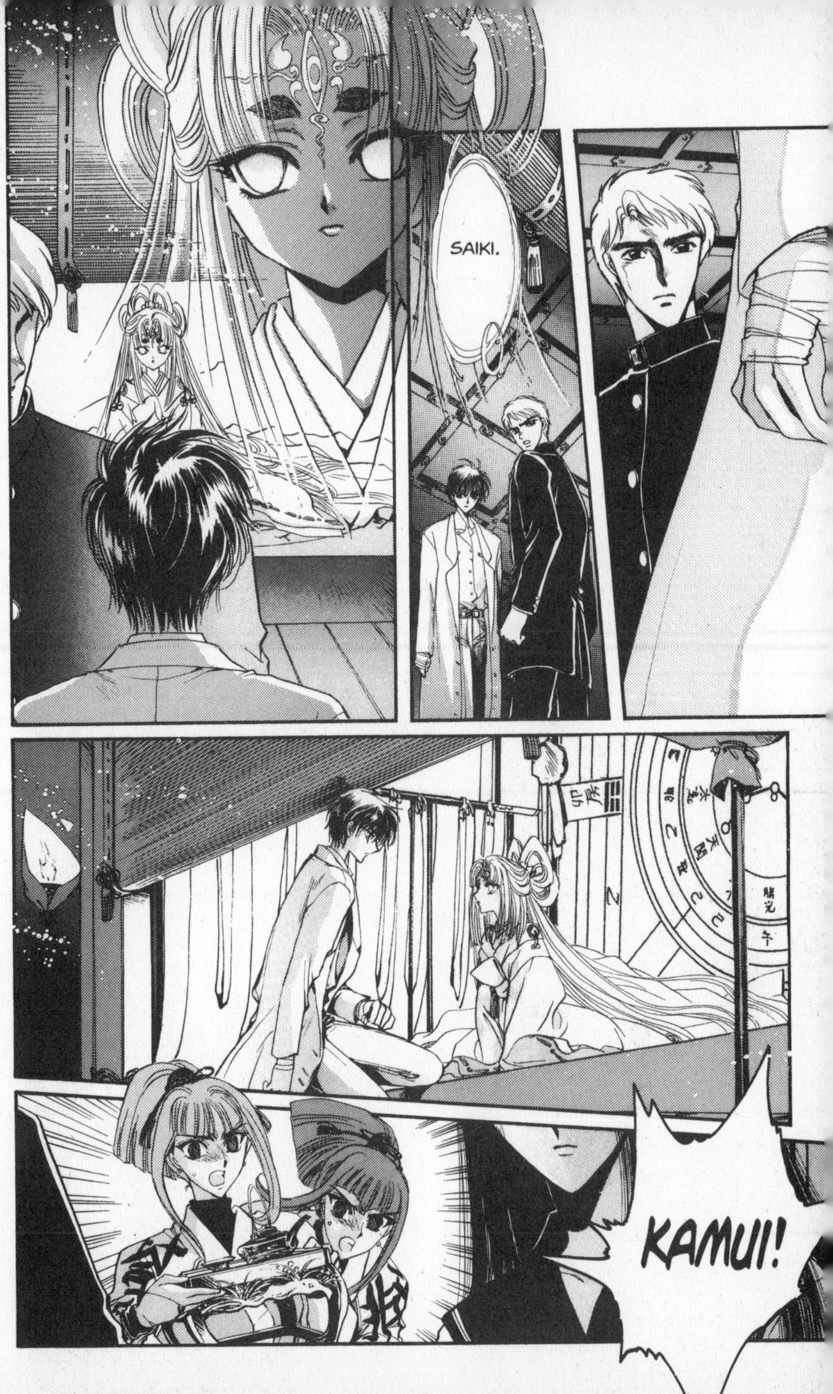
SAIKI.
KAMUI!

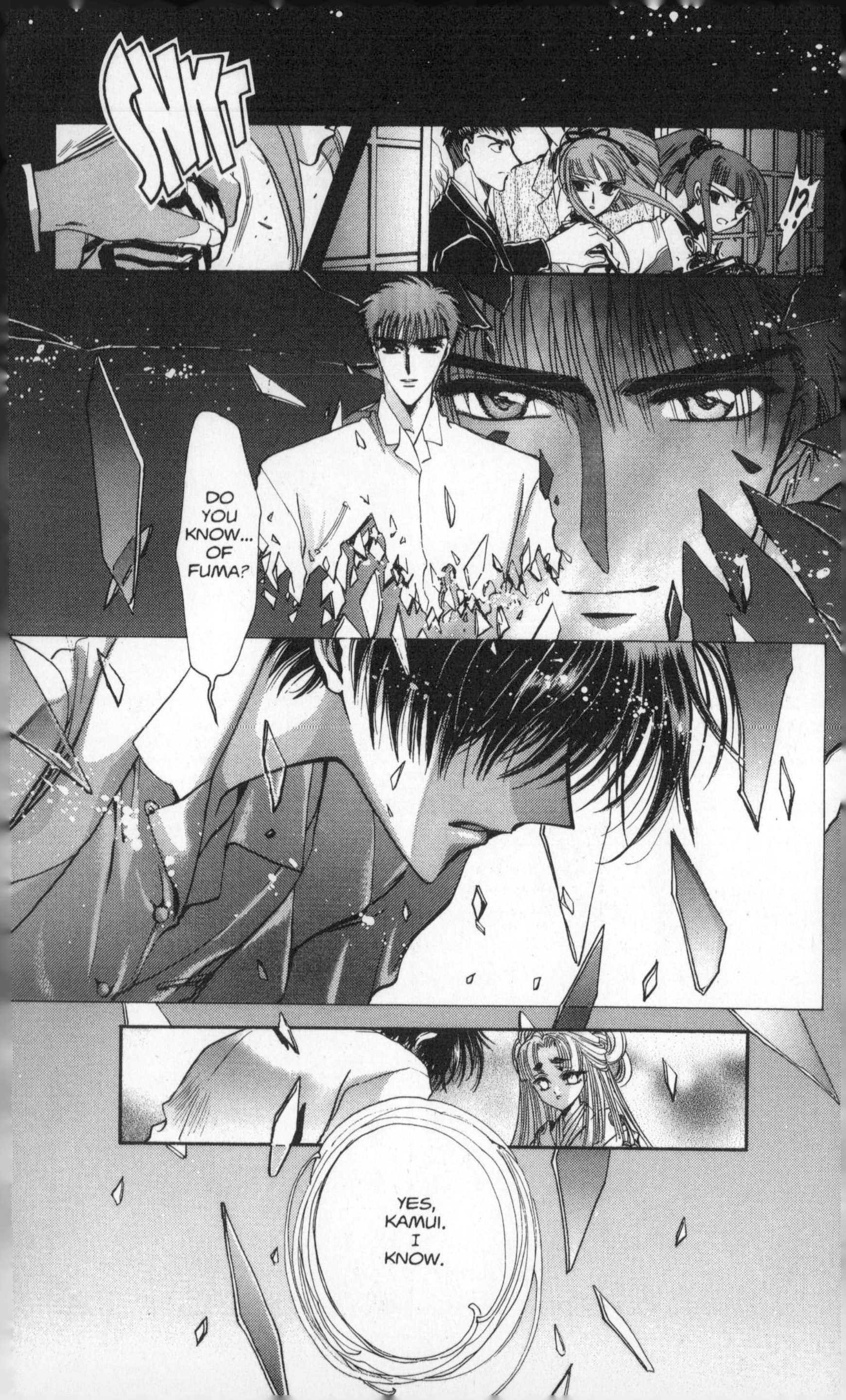

SHKT
!?
DO YOU KNOW... OF FUMA?
YES, KAMUI. I KNOW.

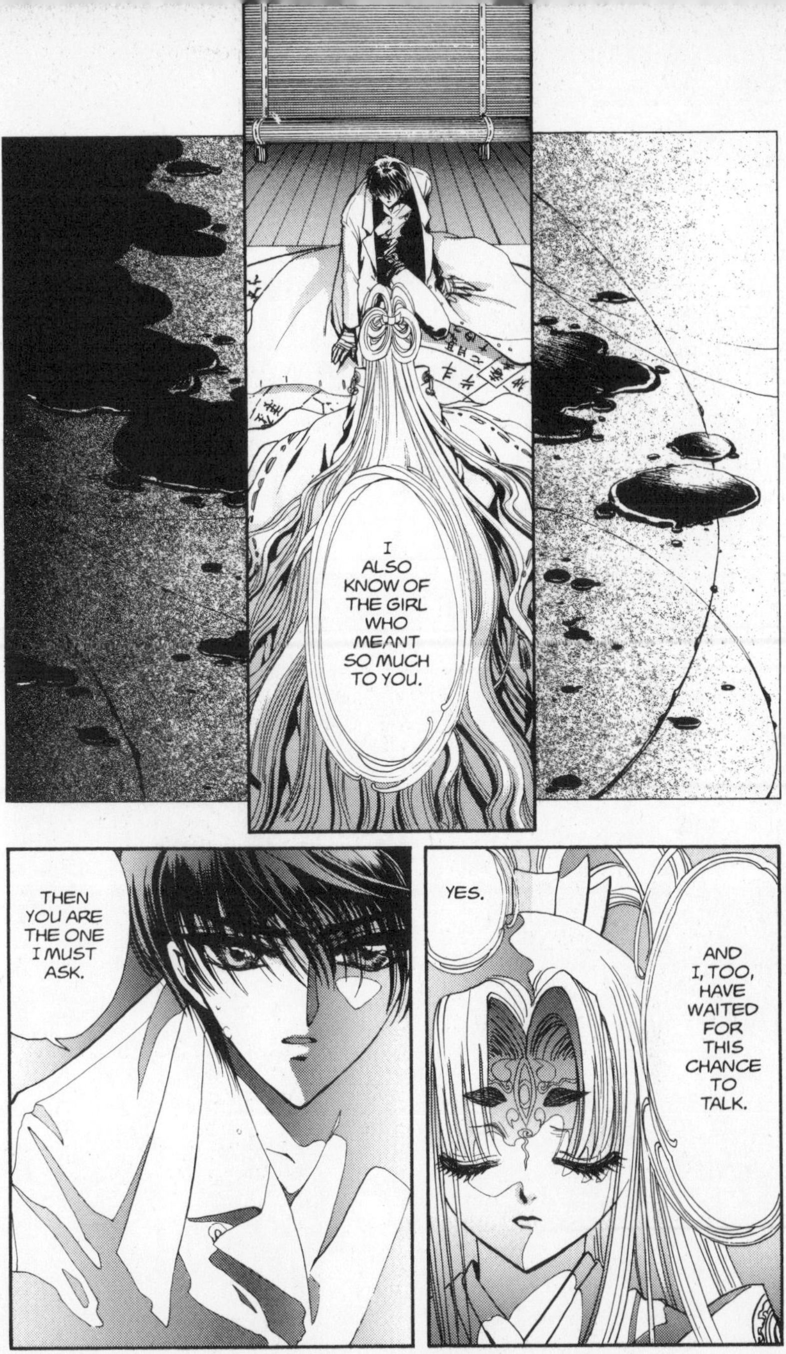
I ALSO KNOW OF THE GIRL WHO MEANT SO MUCH TO YOU.
THEN YOU ARE THE ONE I MUST ASK.
YES.
AND I, TOO, HAVE WAITED FOR THIS CHANCE TO TALK.

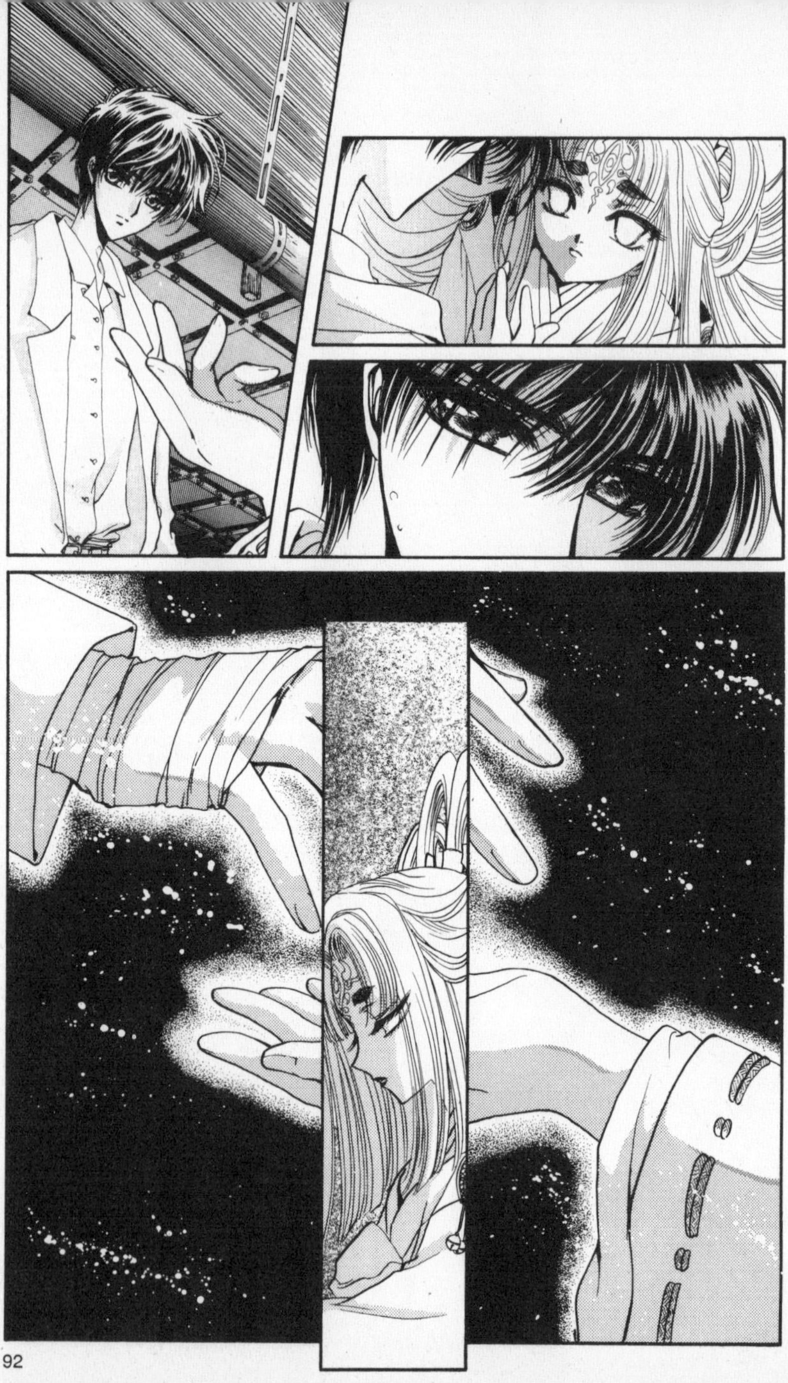

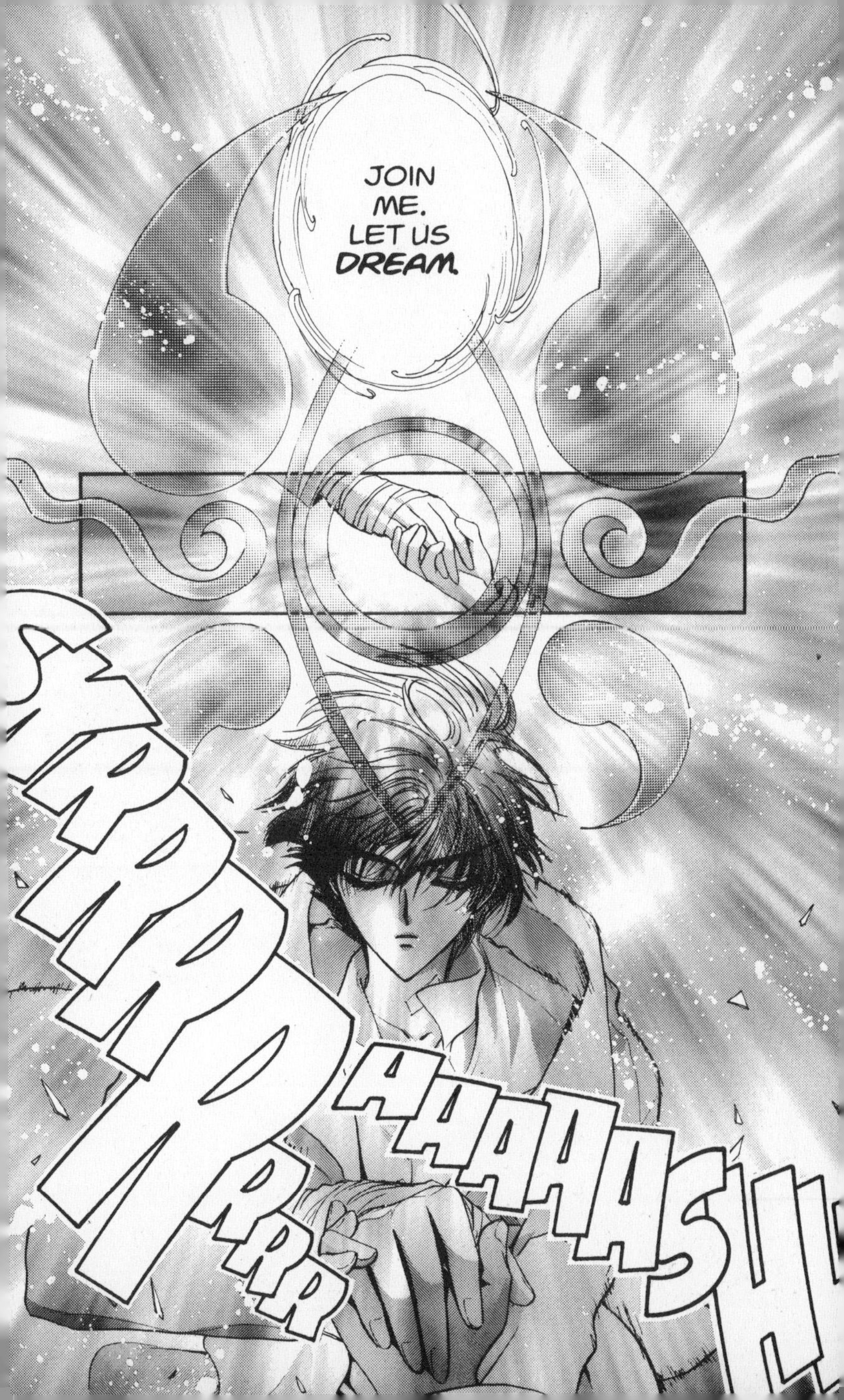
JOIN ME. LET US DREAM.
SKRRRRRR
AAAAASH!

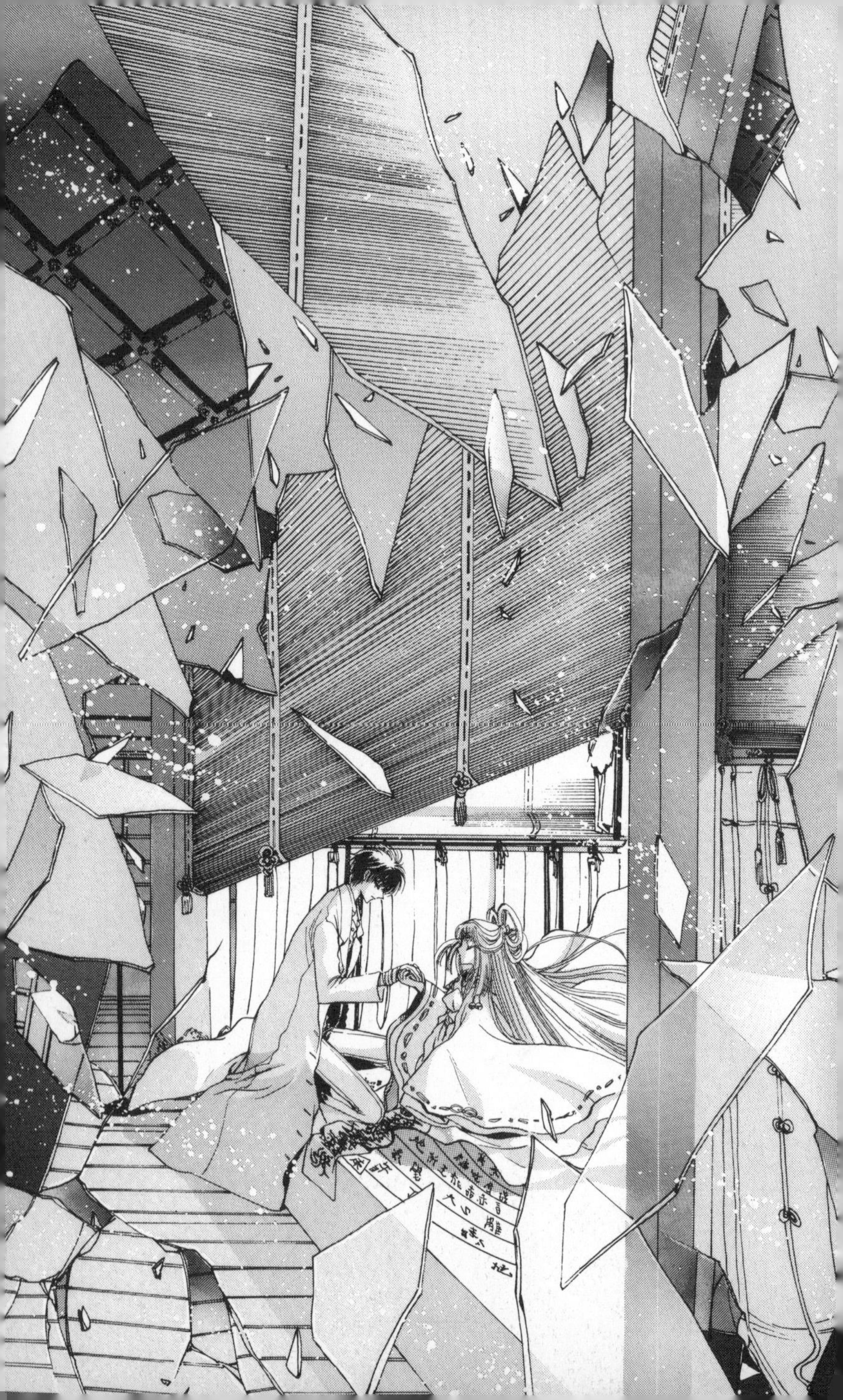

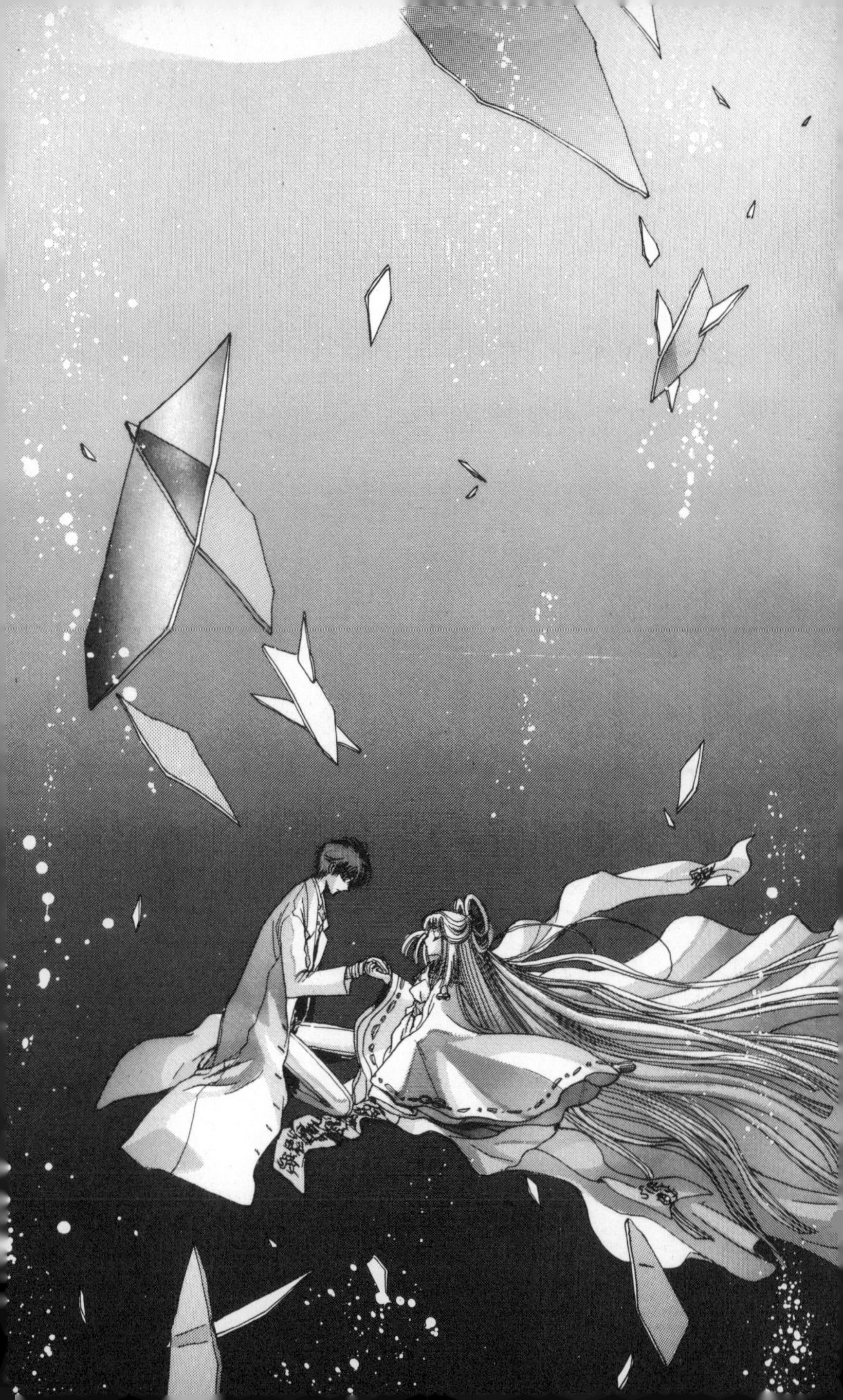

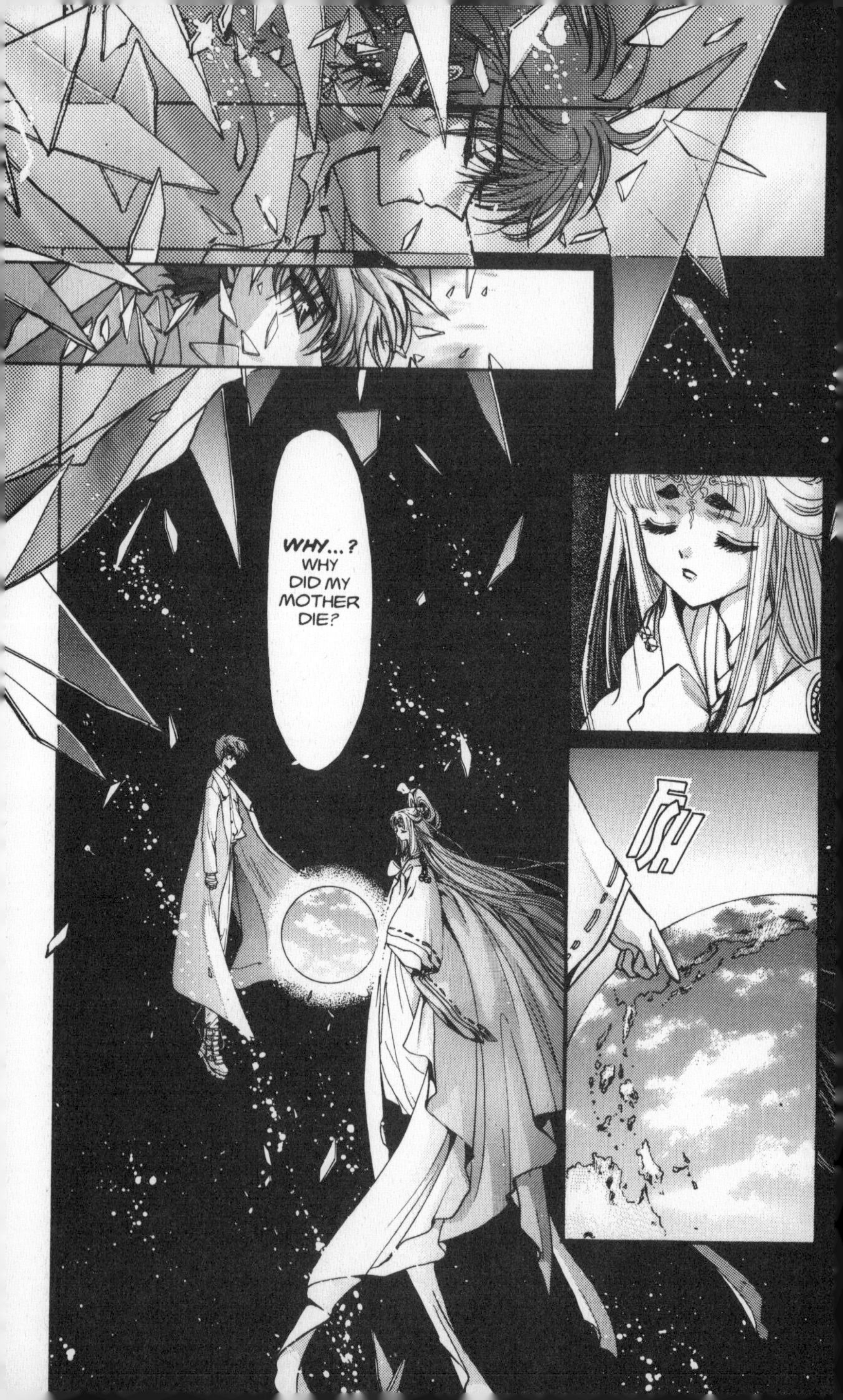

WHY...? WHY DID MY MOTHER DIE?
FSH

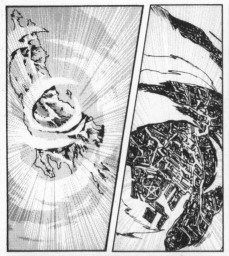

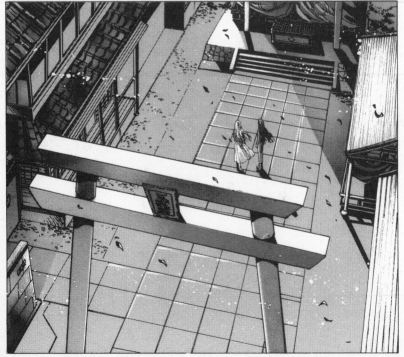

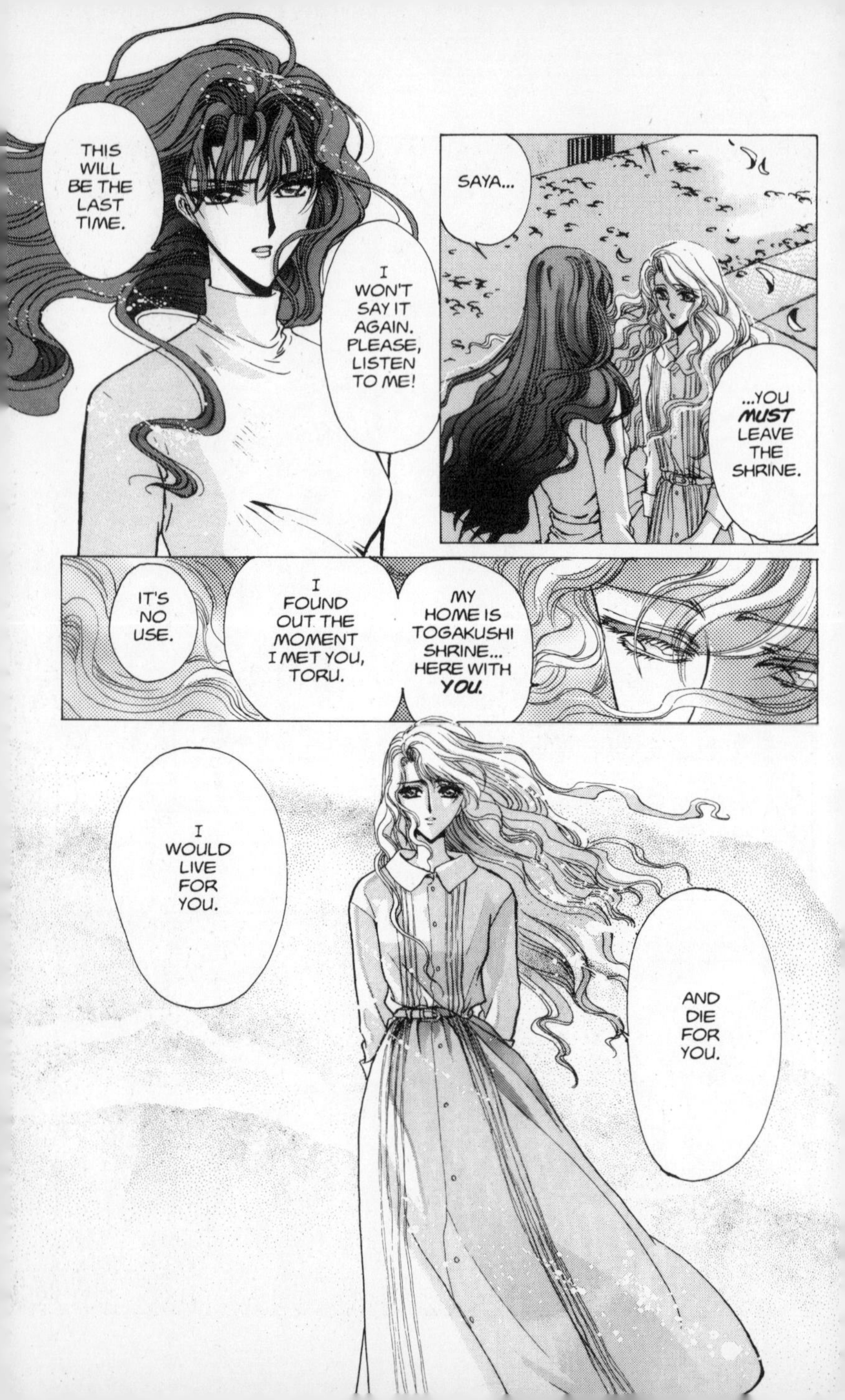
THIS WILL BE THE LAST TIME.
I WON'T SAY IT AGAIN. PLEASE, LISTEN TO ME!
SAYA...
...YOU **MUST** LEAVE THE SHRINE.
IT'S NO USE.
I FOUND OUT THE MOMENT I MET YOU, TORU.
MY HOME IS TOGAKUSHI SHRINE... HERE WITH ***YOU.***
I WOULD LIVE FOR YOU.
AND DIE FOR YOU.

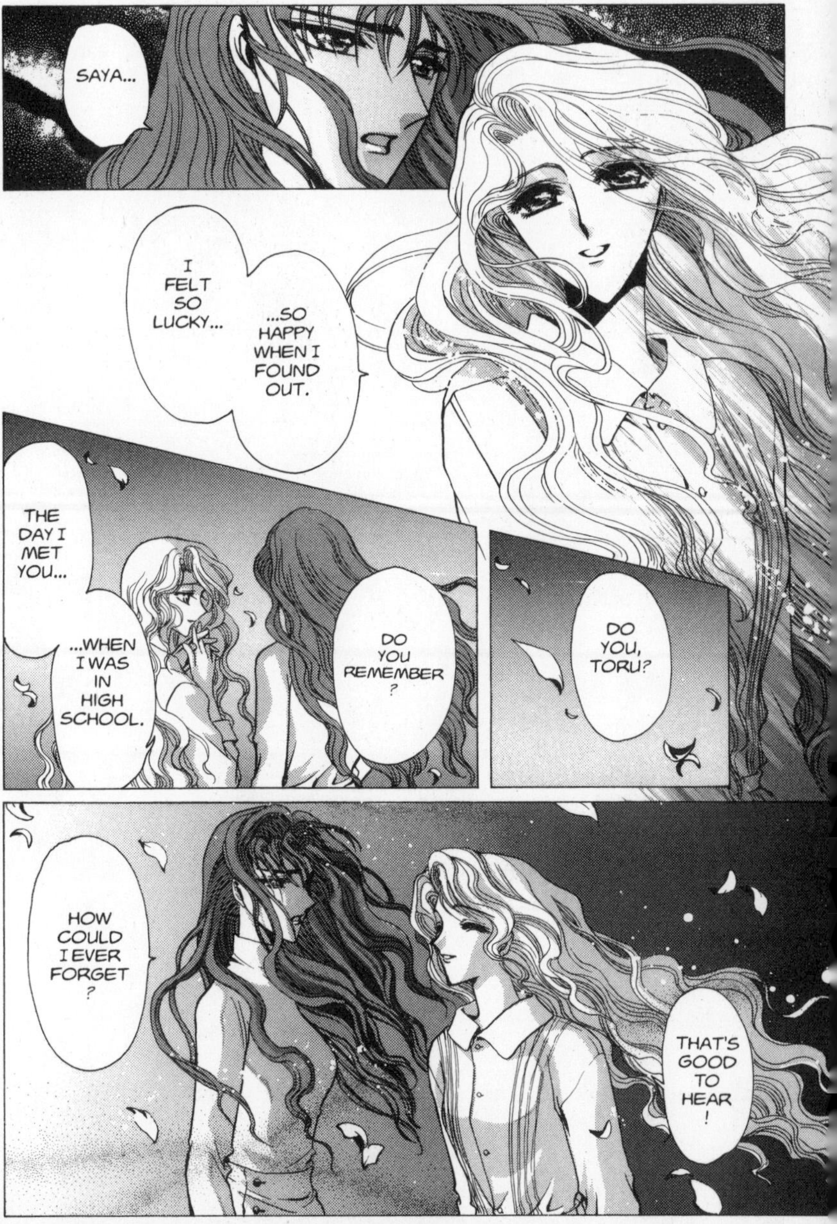
SAYA...
I FELT SO LUCKY...
...SO HAPPY WHEN I FOUND OUT.
THE DAY I MET YOU...
...WHEN I WAS IN HIGH SCHOOL.
DO YOU REMEMBER?
DO YOU, TORU?
HOW COULD I EVER FORGET?
THAT'S GOOD TO HEAR!

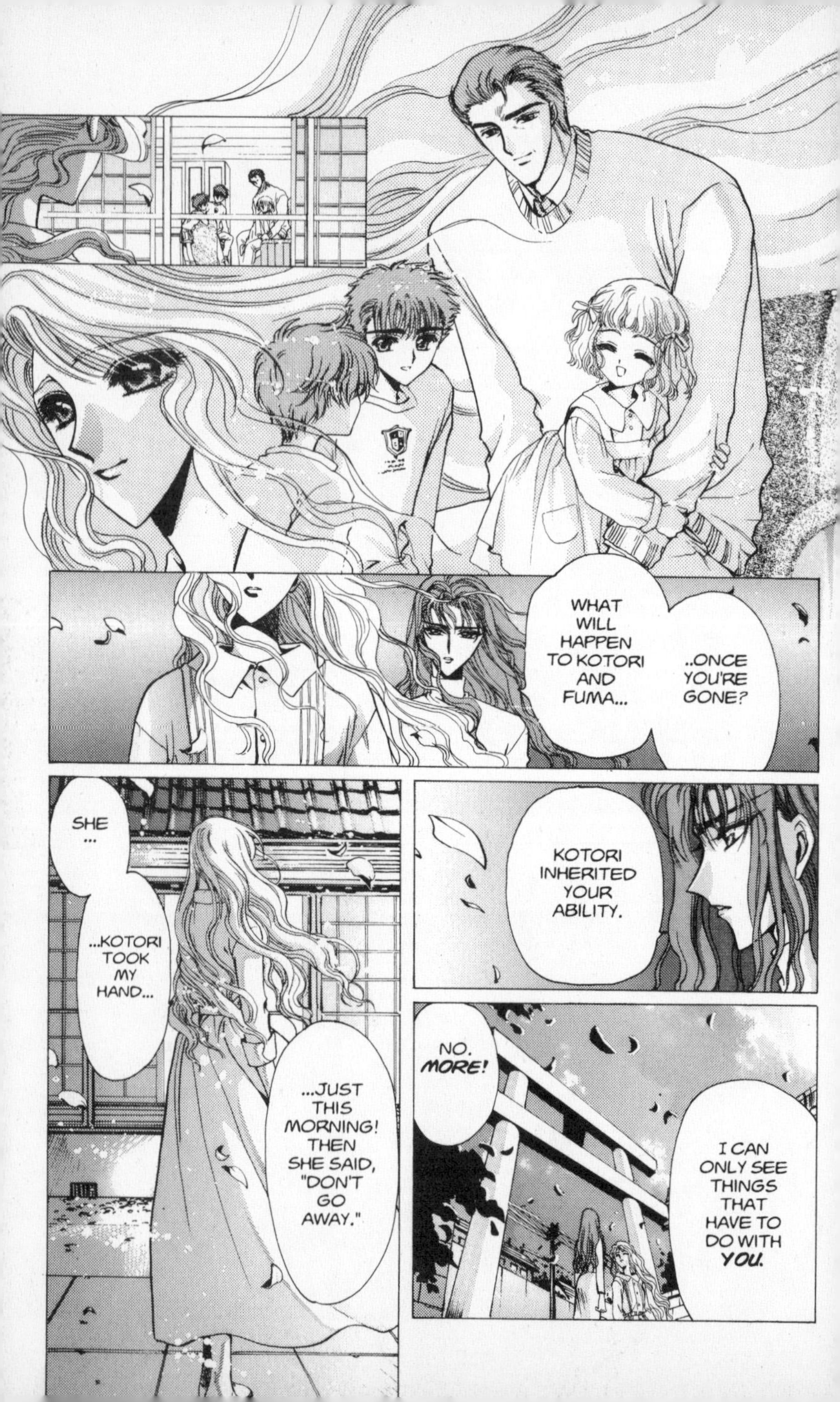
WHAT WILL HAPPEN TO KOTORI AND FUMA...
..ONCE YOU'RE GONE?
SHE ...
...KOTORI TOOK MY HAND...
...JUST THIS MORNING! THEN SHE SAID, "DON'T GO AWAY."
KOTORI INHERITED YOUR ABILITY.
NO. *MORE!*
I CAN ONLY SEE THINGS THAT HAVE TO DO WITH ***YOU.***

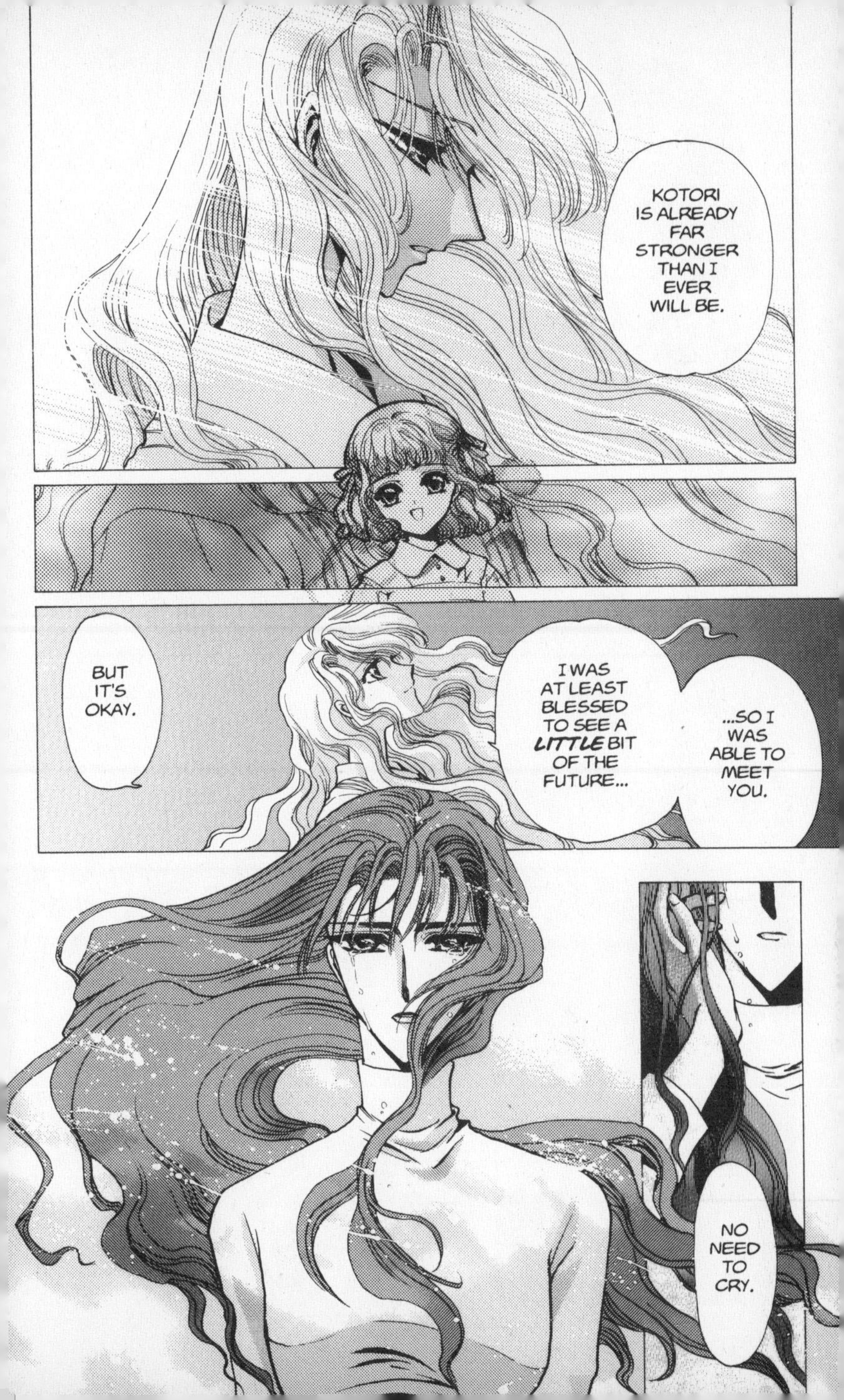

KOTORI IS ALREADY FAR STRONGER THAN I EVER WILL BE.
BUT IT'S OKAY.
I WAS AT LEAST BLESSED TO SEE A *LITTLE* BIT OF THE FUTURE...
...SO I WAS ABLE TO MEET YOU.
NO NEED TO CRY.

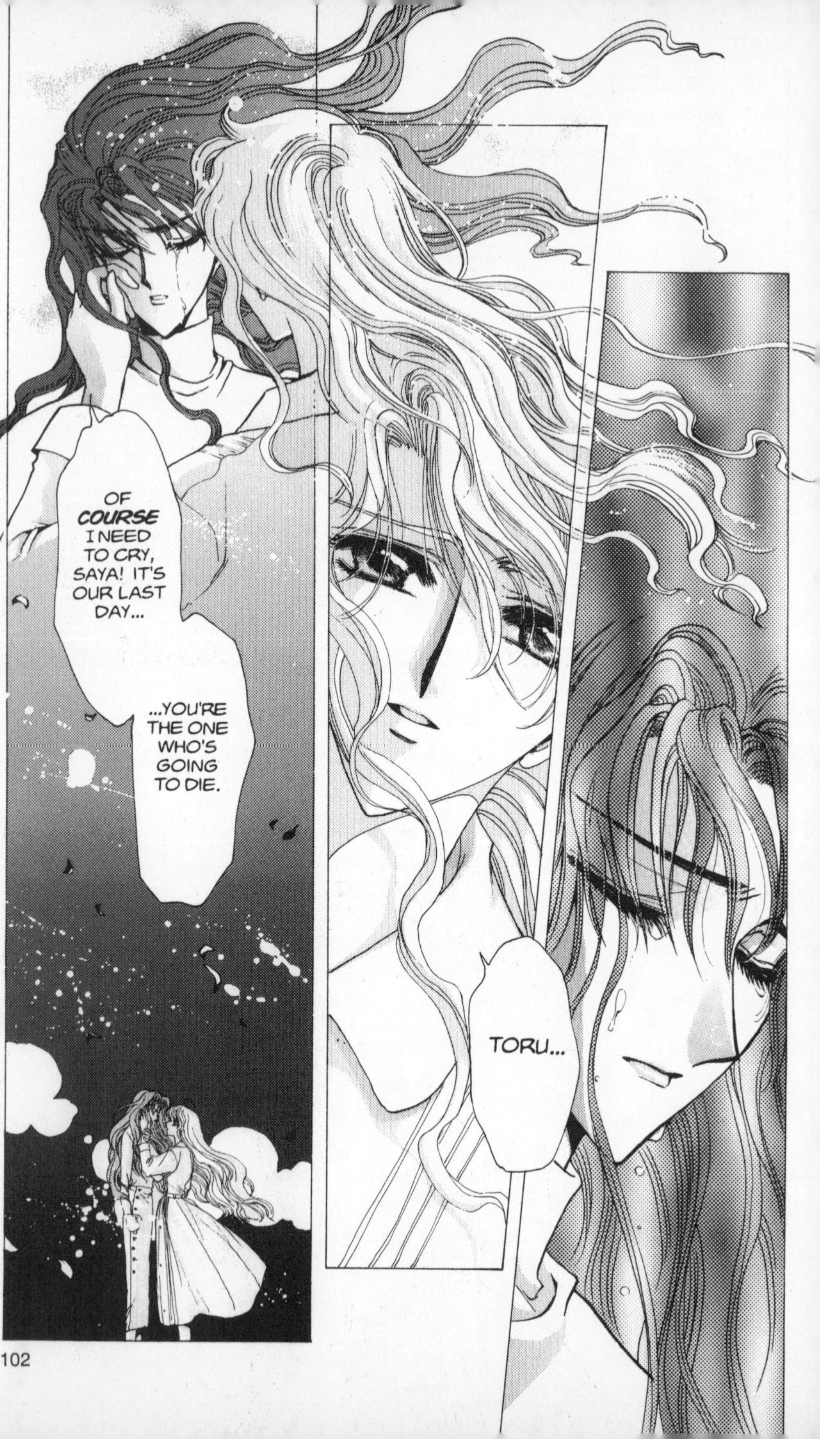

OF COURSE I NEED TO CRY, SAYA! IT'S OUR LAST DAY...
...YOU'RE THE ONE WHO'S GOING TO DIE.
TORU...

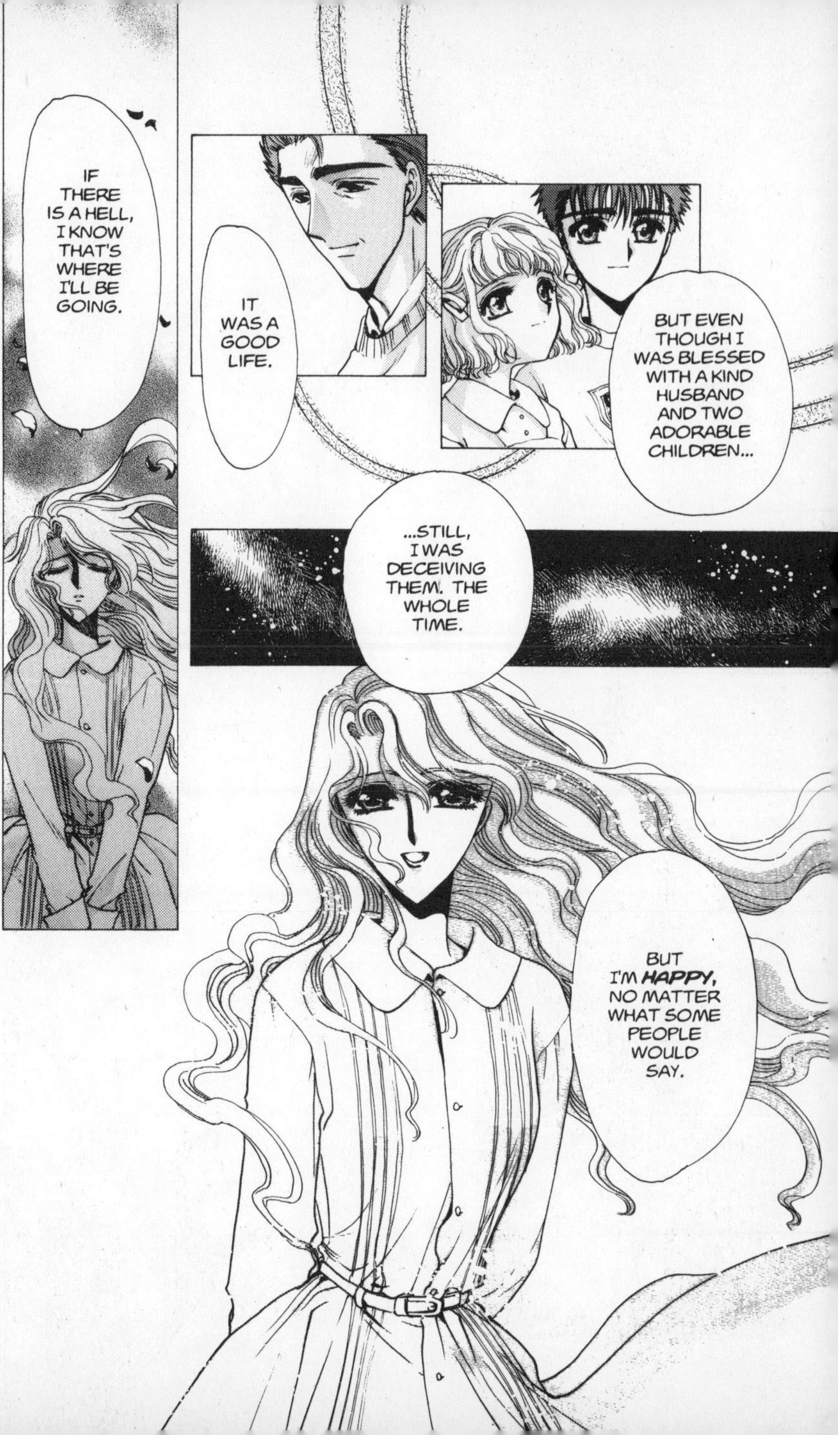

IF THERE IS A HELL, I KNOW THAT'S WHERE I'LL BE GOING.
IT WAS A GOOD LIFE.
BUT EVEN THOUGH I WAS BLESSED WITH A KIND HUSBAND AND TWO ADORABLE CHILDREN...
...STILL, I WAS DECEIVING THEM. THE WHOLE TIME.
BUT I'M **HAPPY**, NO MATTER WHAT SOME PEOPLE WOULD SAY.

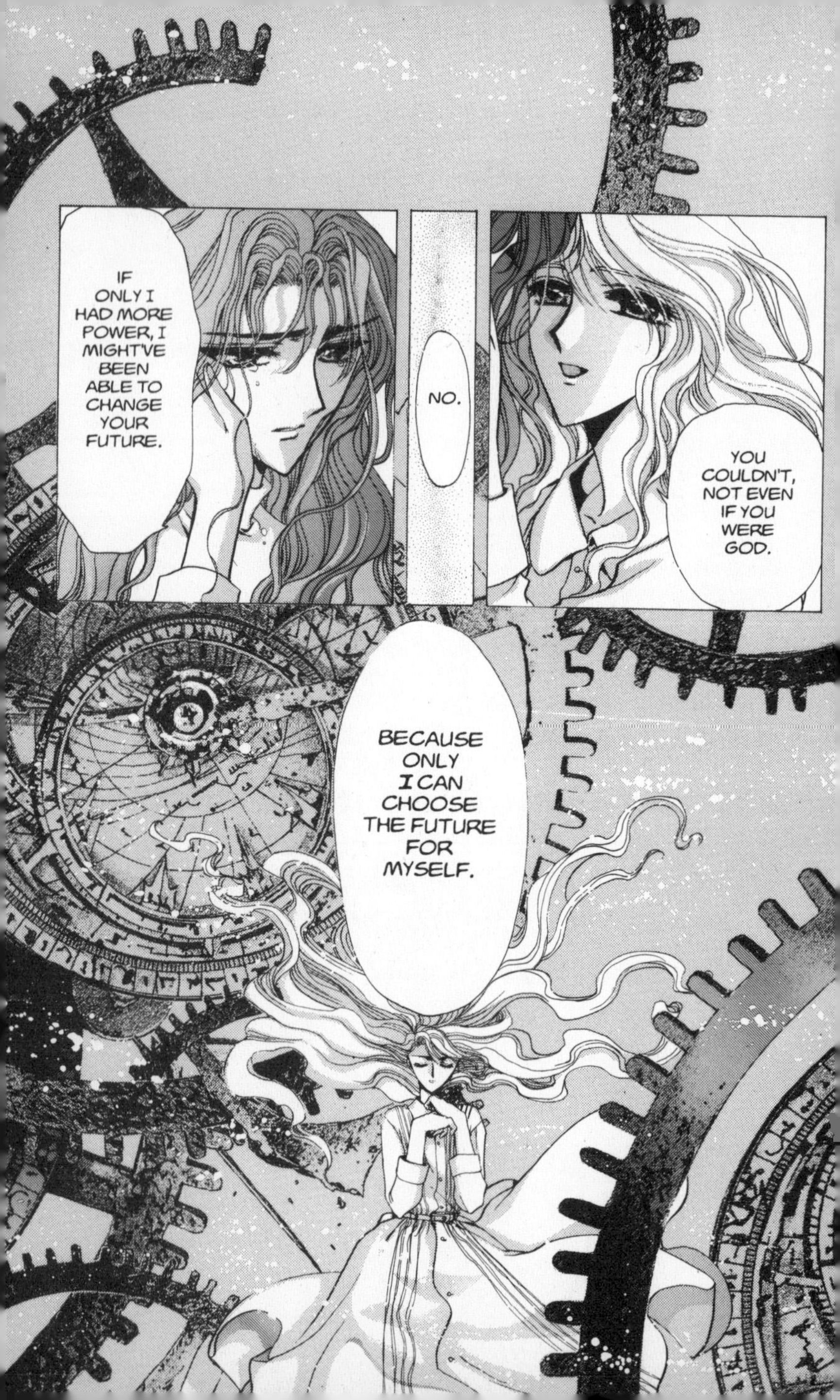
IF ONLY I HAD MORE POWER, I MIGHT'VE BEEN ABLE TO CHANGE YOUR FUTURE.
NO.
YOU COULDN'T, NOT EVEN IF YOU WERE GOD.
BECAUSE ONLY I CAN CHOOSE THE FUTURE FOR MYSELF.

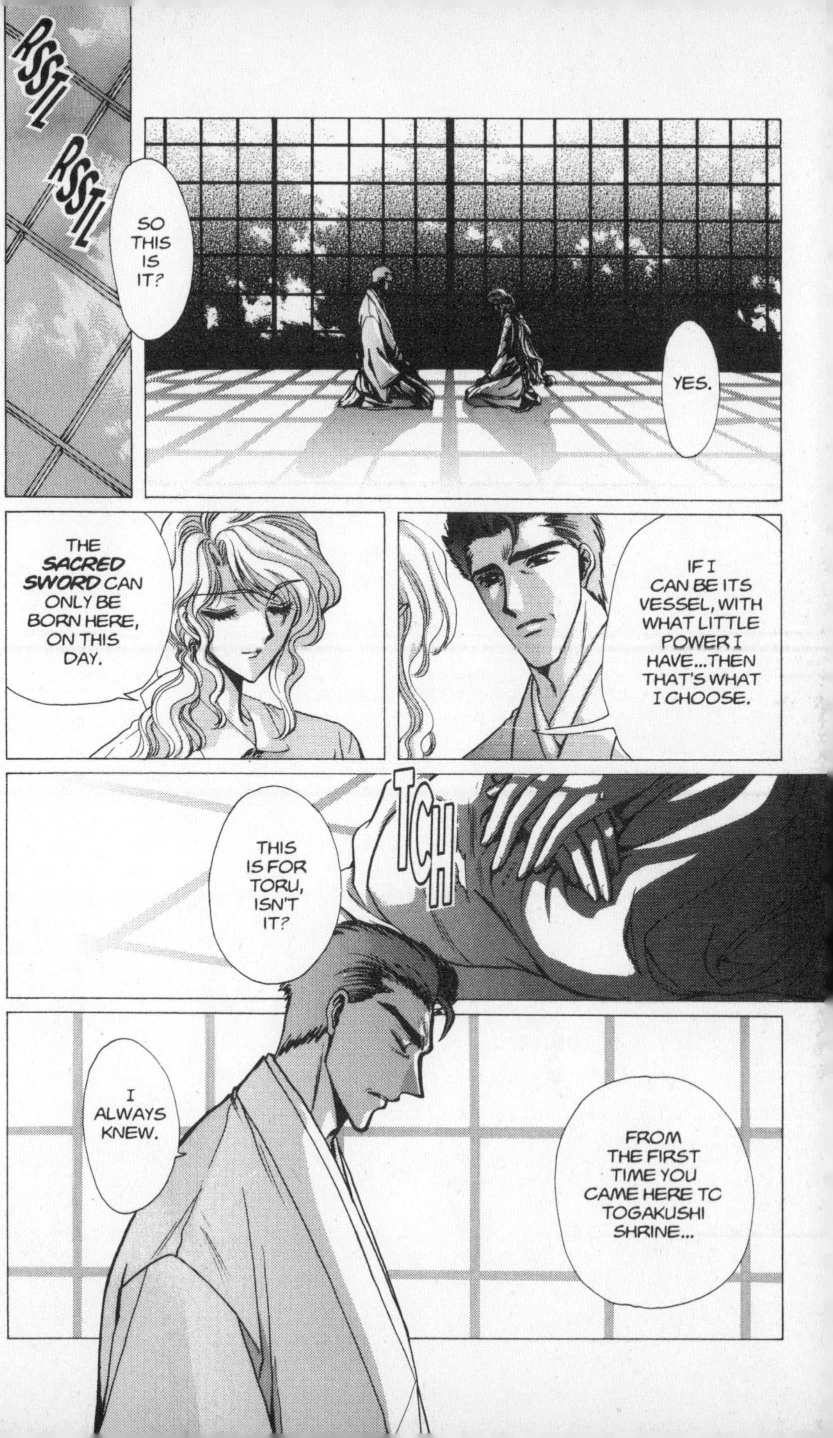
RSSTL RSSTL
SO THIS IS IT?
YES.
THE SACRED SWORD CAN ONLY BE BORN HERE, ON THIS DAY.
IF I CAN BE ITS VESSEL, WITH WHAT LITTLE POWER I HAVE...THEN THAT'S WHAT I CHOOSE.
THIS IS FOR TORU, ISN'T IT?
TCH
I ALWAYS KNEW.
FROM THE FIRST TIME YOU CAME HERE TO TOGAKUSHI SHRINE...

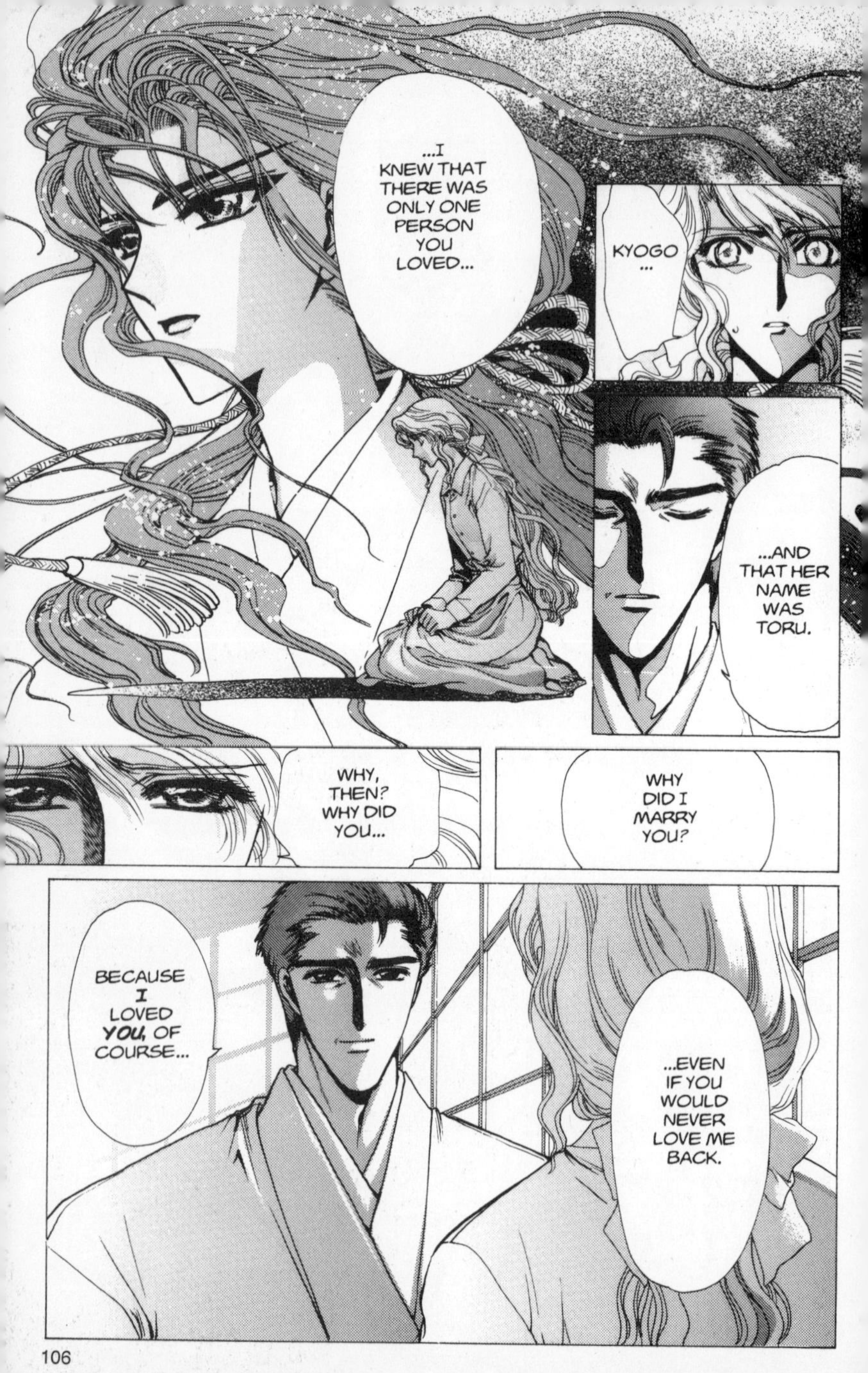
...I KNEW THAT THERE WAS ONLY ONE PERSON YOU LOVED...
KYOGO ...
...AND THAT HER NAME WAS TORU.
WHY, THEN? WHY DID YOU...
WHY DID I MARRY YOU?
BECAUSE I LOVED YOU, OF COURSE...
...EVEN IF YOU WOULD NEVER LOVE ME BACK.

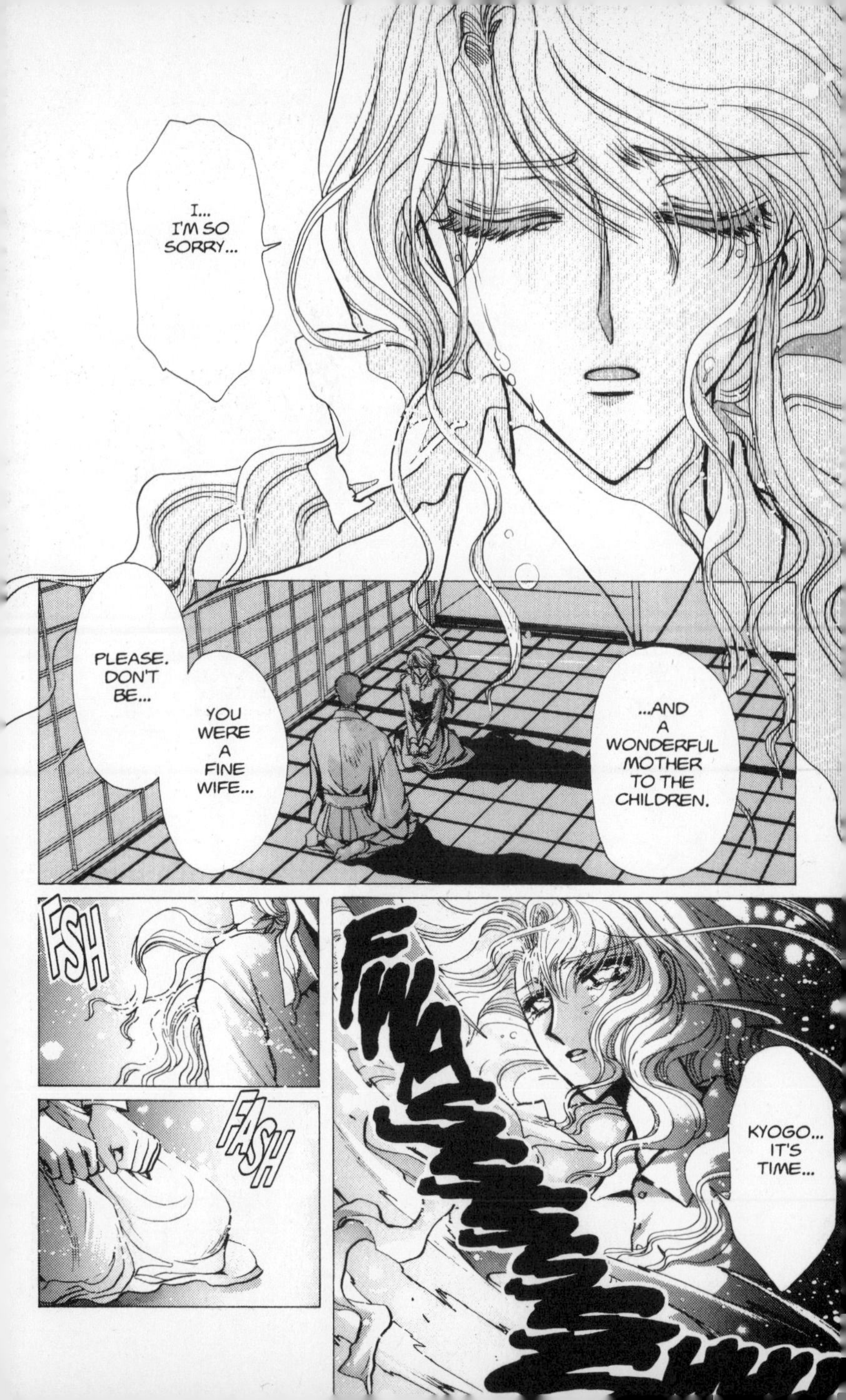
I... I'M SO SORRY...
PLEASE. DON'T BE...
YOU WERE A FINE WIFE...
...AND A WONDERFUL MOTHER TO THE CHILDREN.
FSH
FASH
FWASSSSHHH
KYOGO... IT'S TIME...

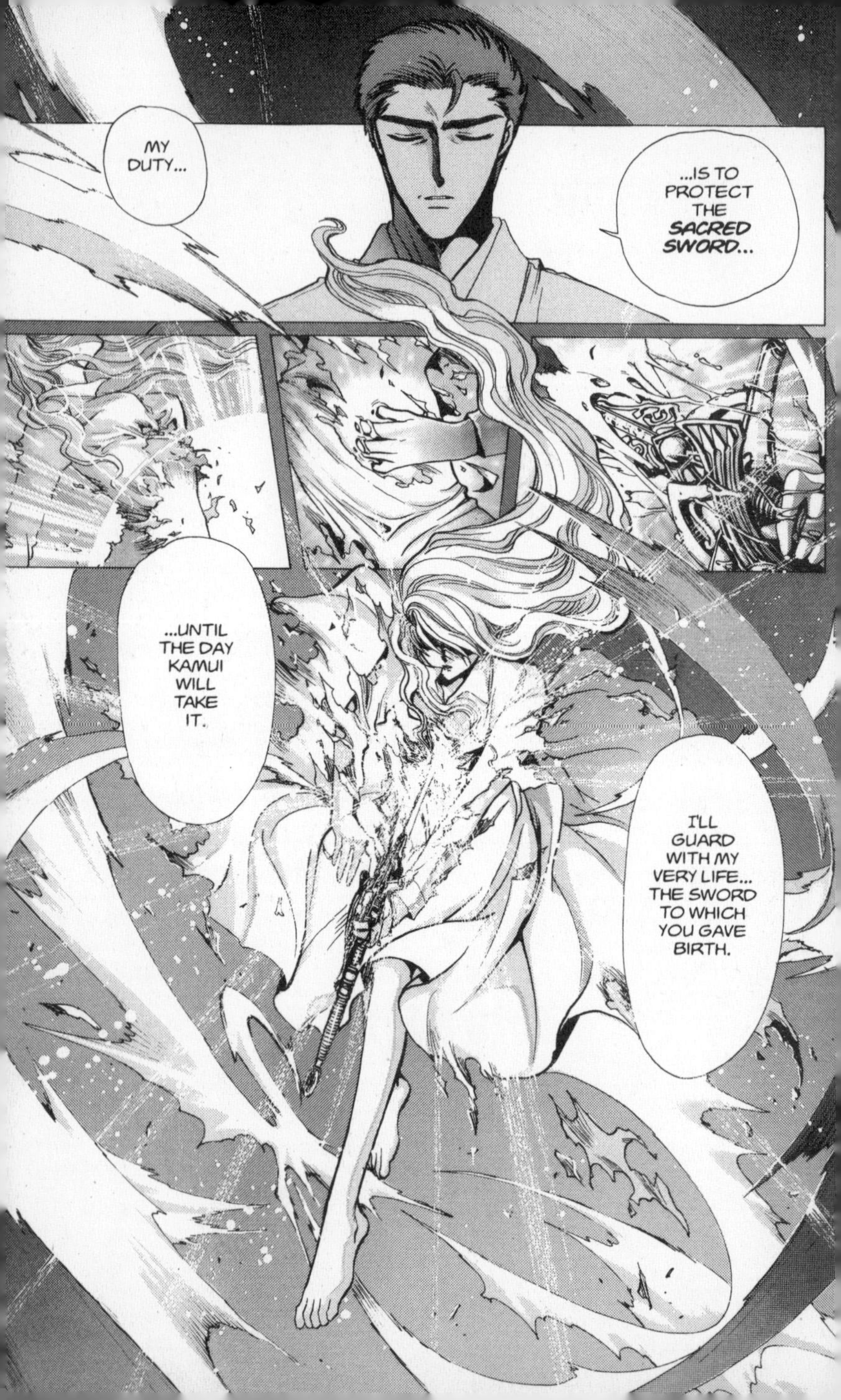
MY DUTY...
...IS TO PROTECT THE SACRED SWORD...
...UNTIL THE DAY KAMUI WILL TAKE IT.
I'LL GUARD WITH MY VERY LIFE... THE SWORD TO WHICH YOU GAVE BIRTH.

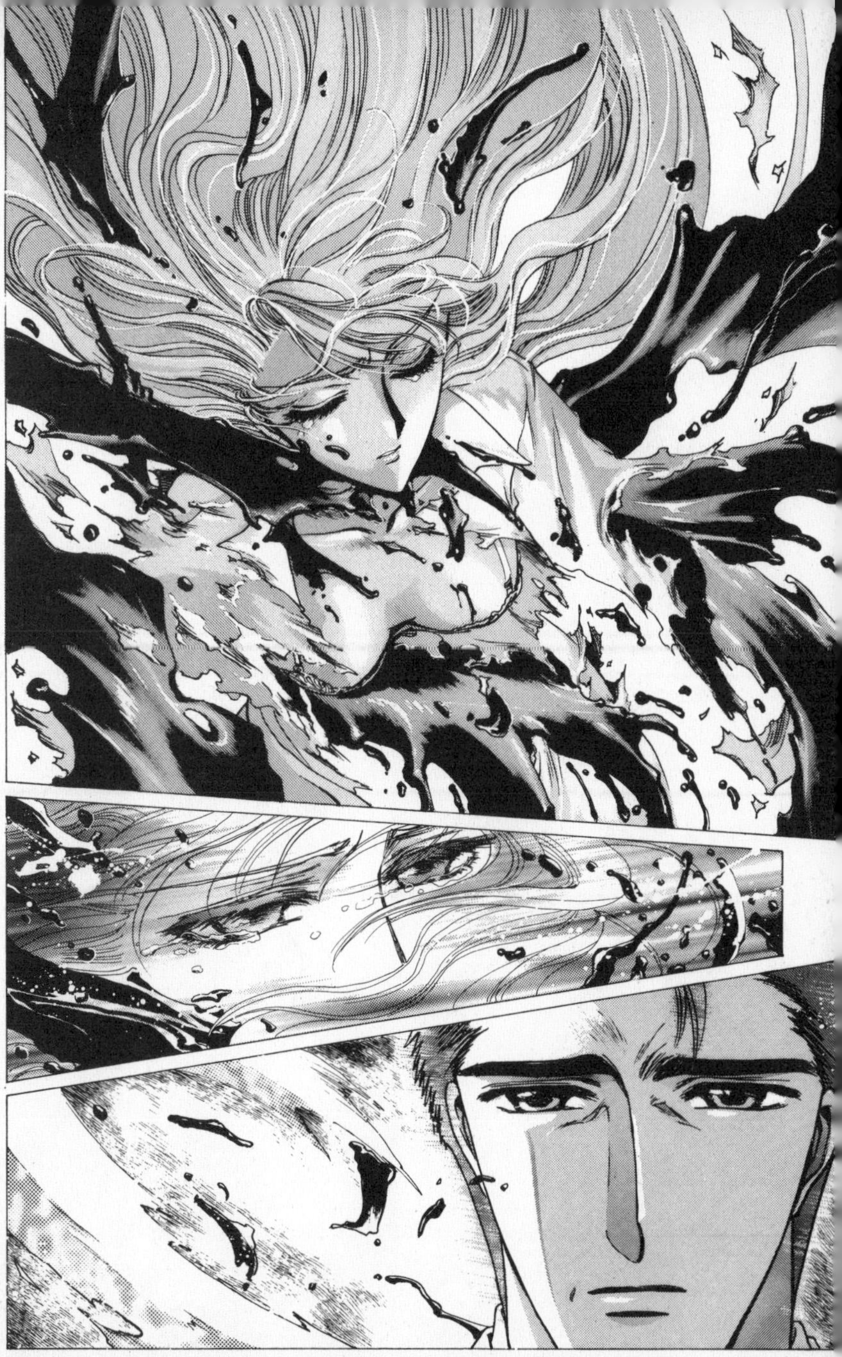

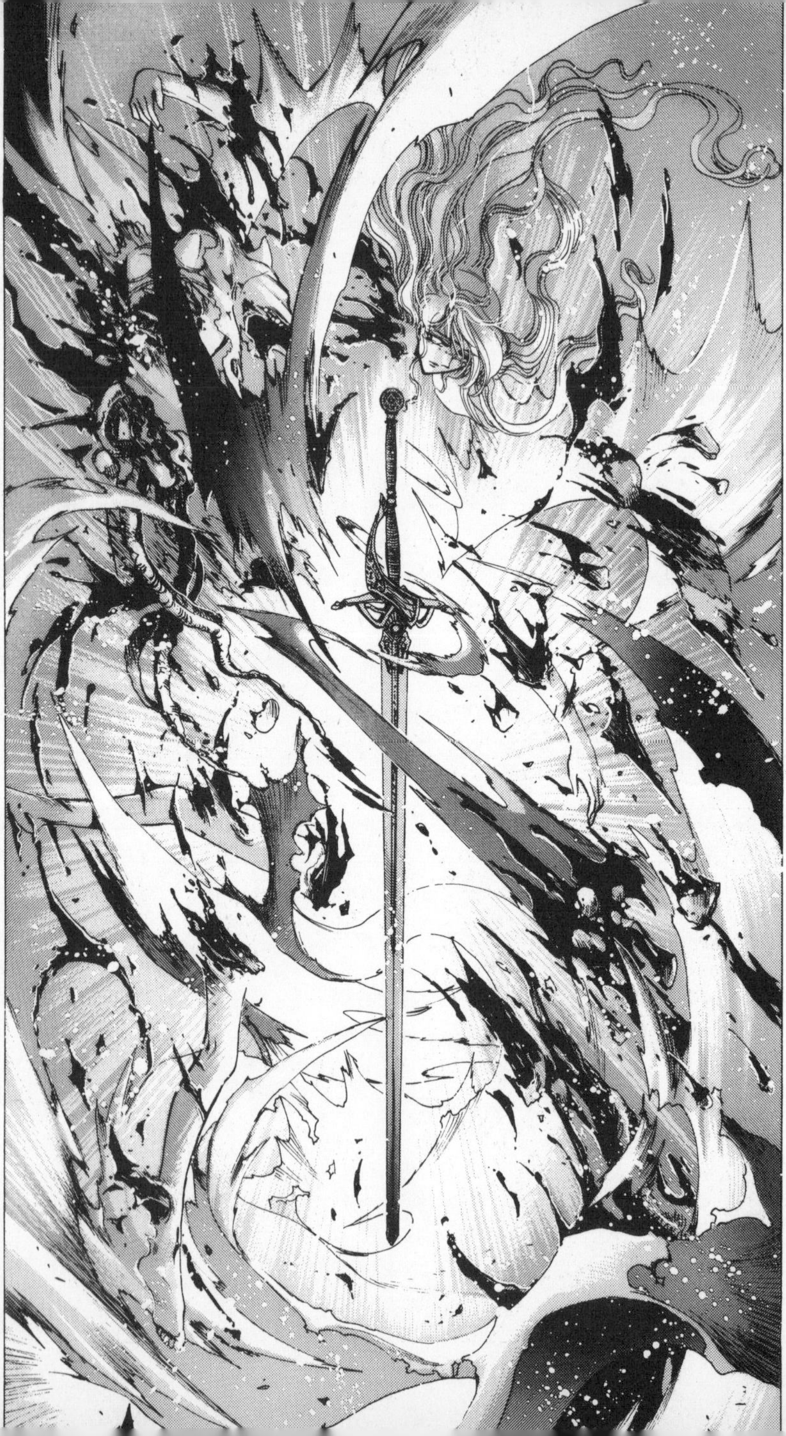

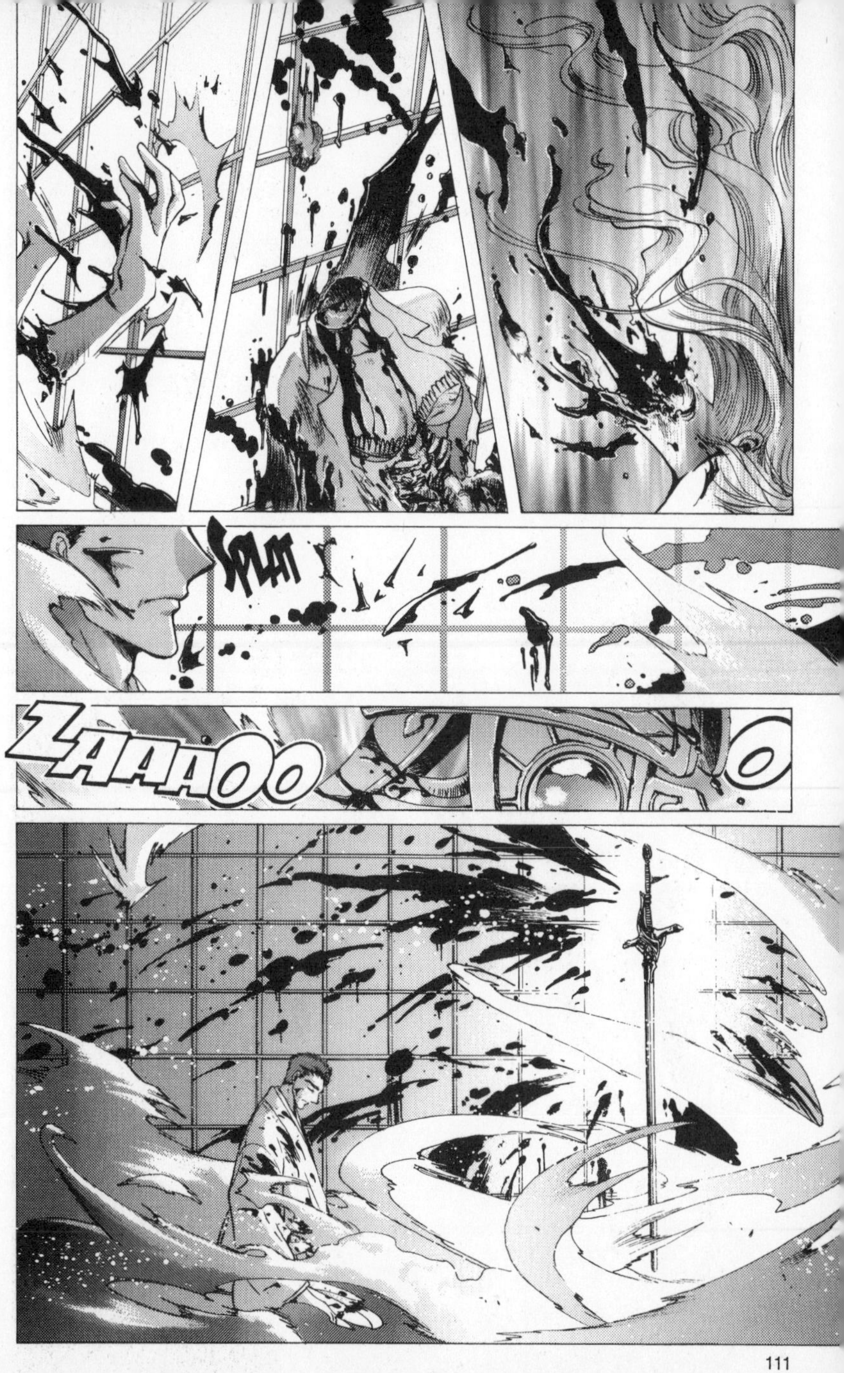
SPLAT
ZAAAOOO

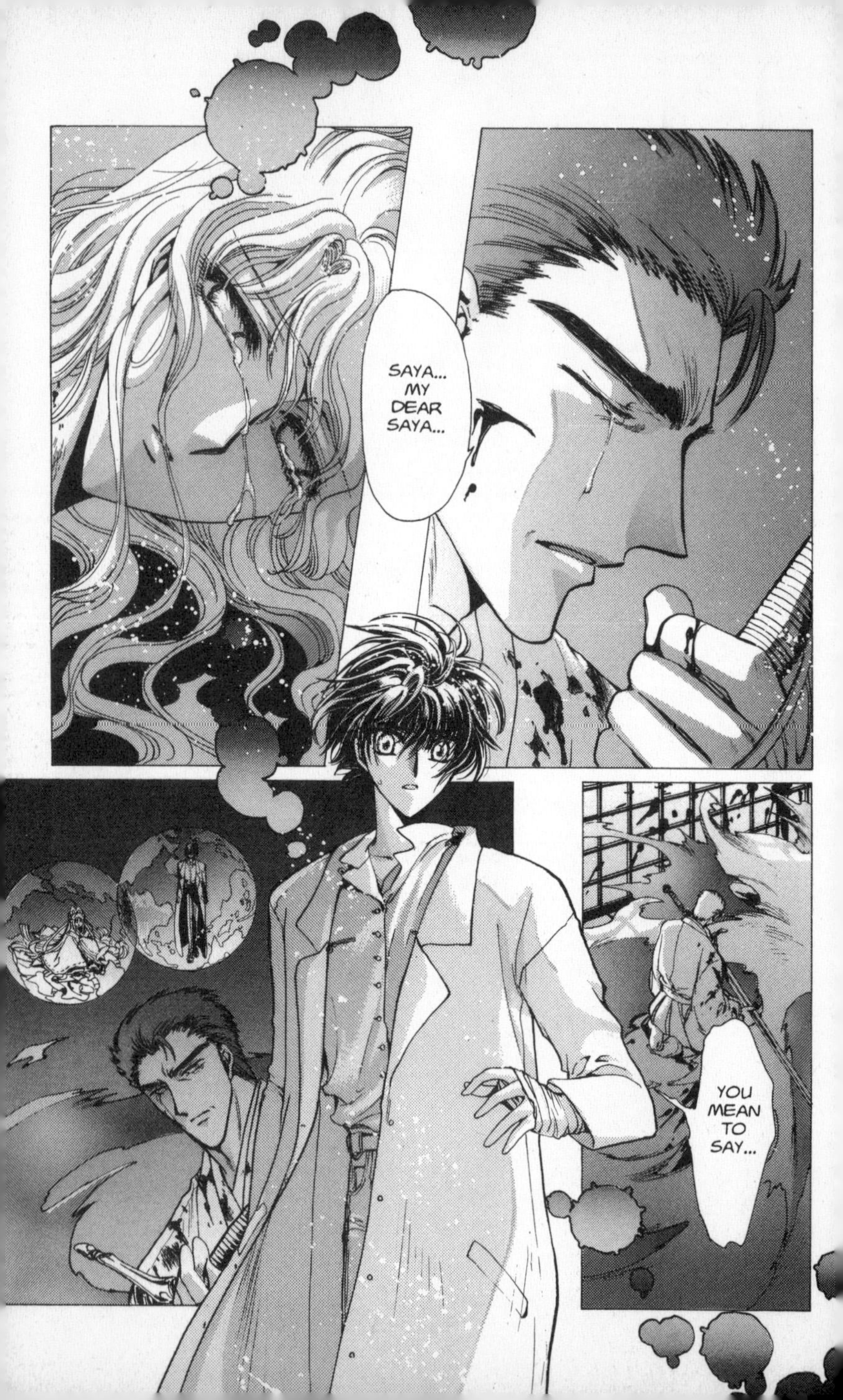
SAYA... MY DEAR SAYA...
YOU MEAN TO SAY...

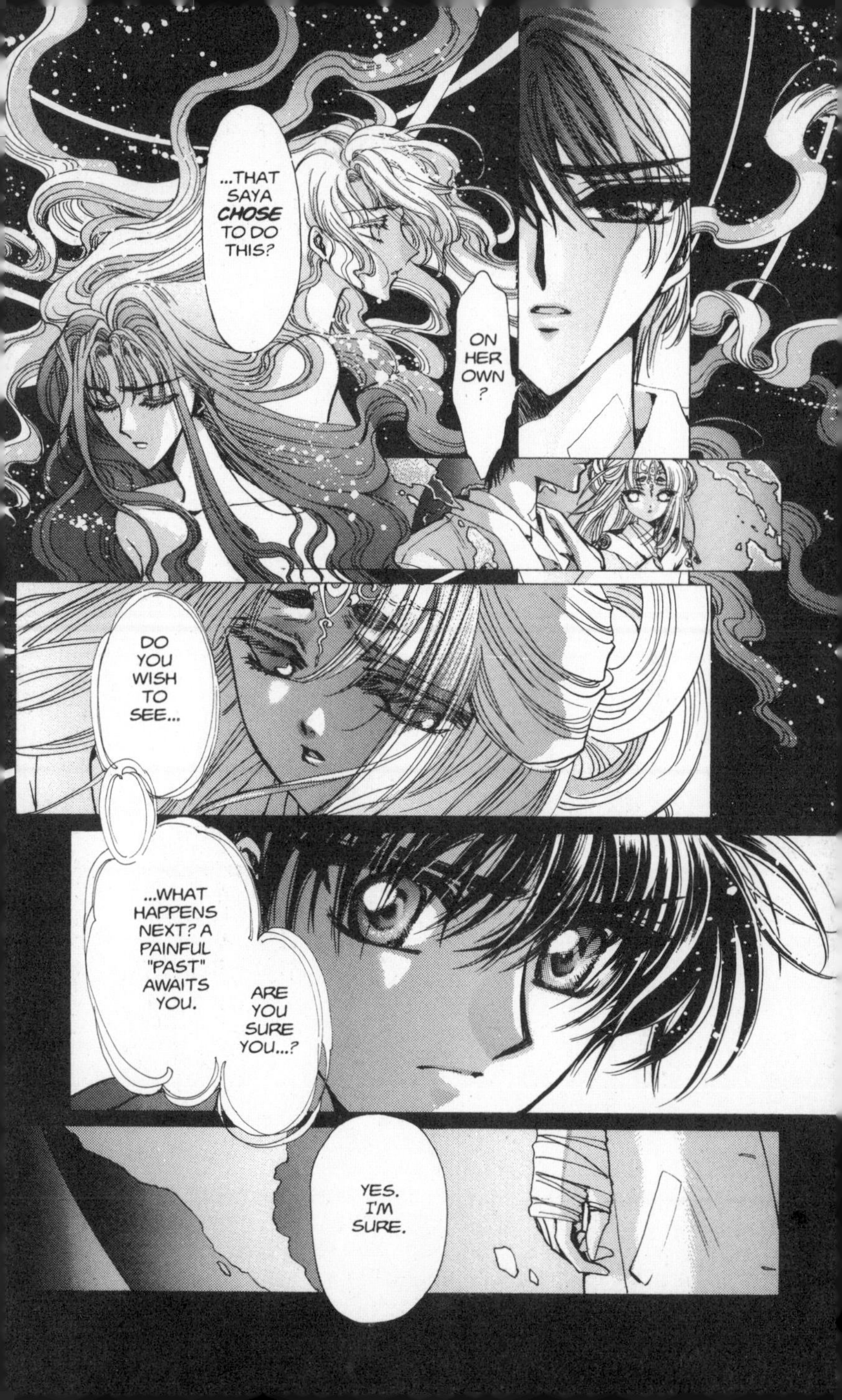
...THAT SAYA *CHOSE* TO DO THIS?
ON HER OWN?
DO YOU WISH TO SEE...
...WHAT HAPPENS NEXT? A PAINFUL "PAST" AWAITS YOU.
ARE YOU SURE YOU...?
YES. I'M SURE.

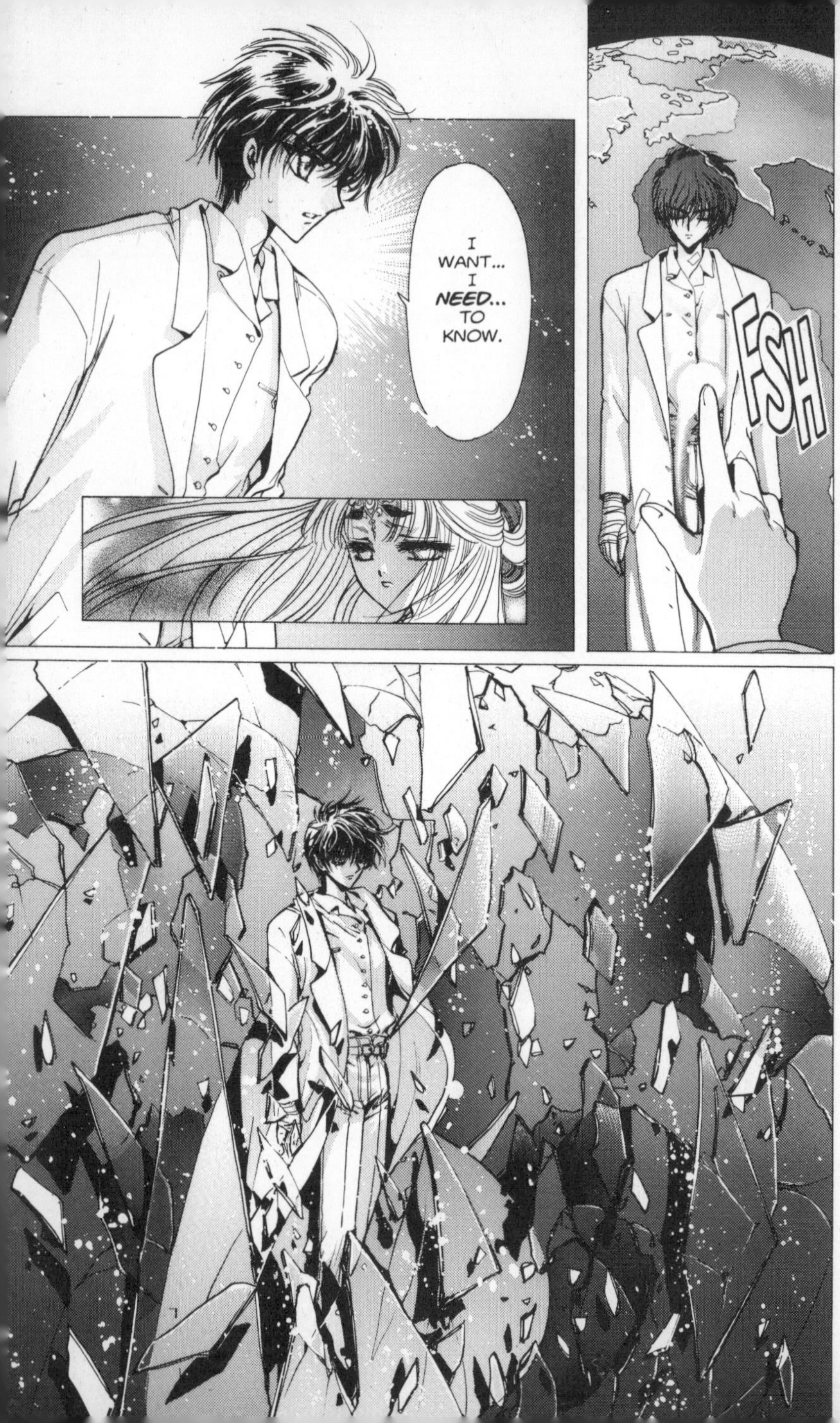
I WANT... I NEED... TO KNOW.
FSH

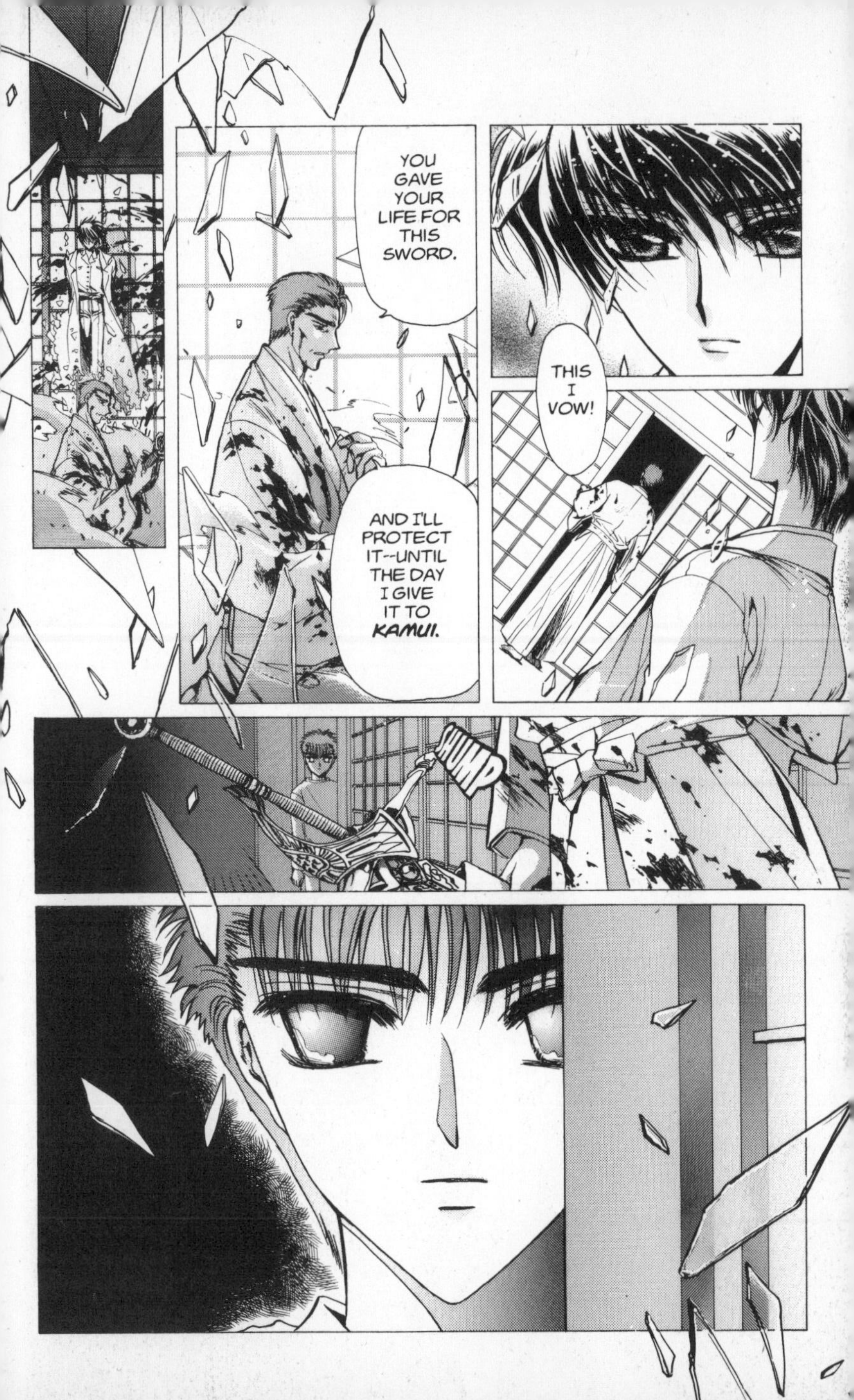
YOU GAVE YOUR LIFE FOR THIS SWORD.
AND I'LL PROTECT IT--UNTIL THE DAY I GIVE IT TO *KAMUI.*
THIS I VOW!
SHUMP

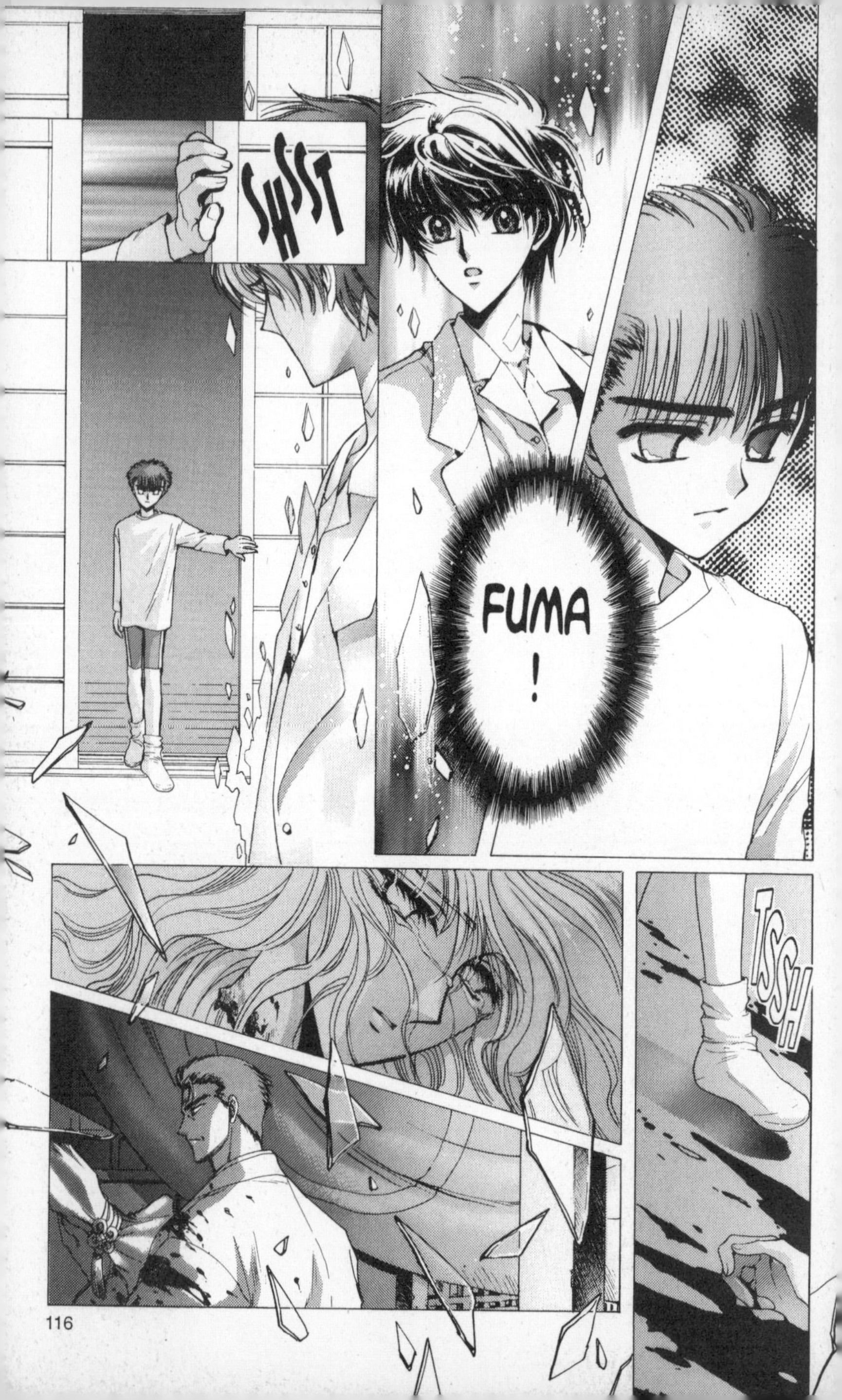
SHSST
FUMA
!
TSSH

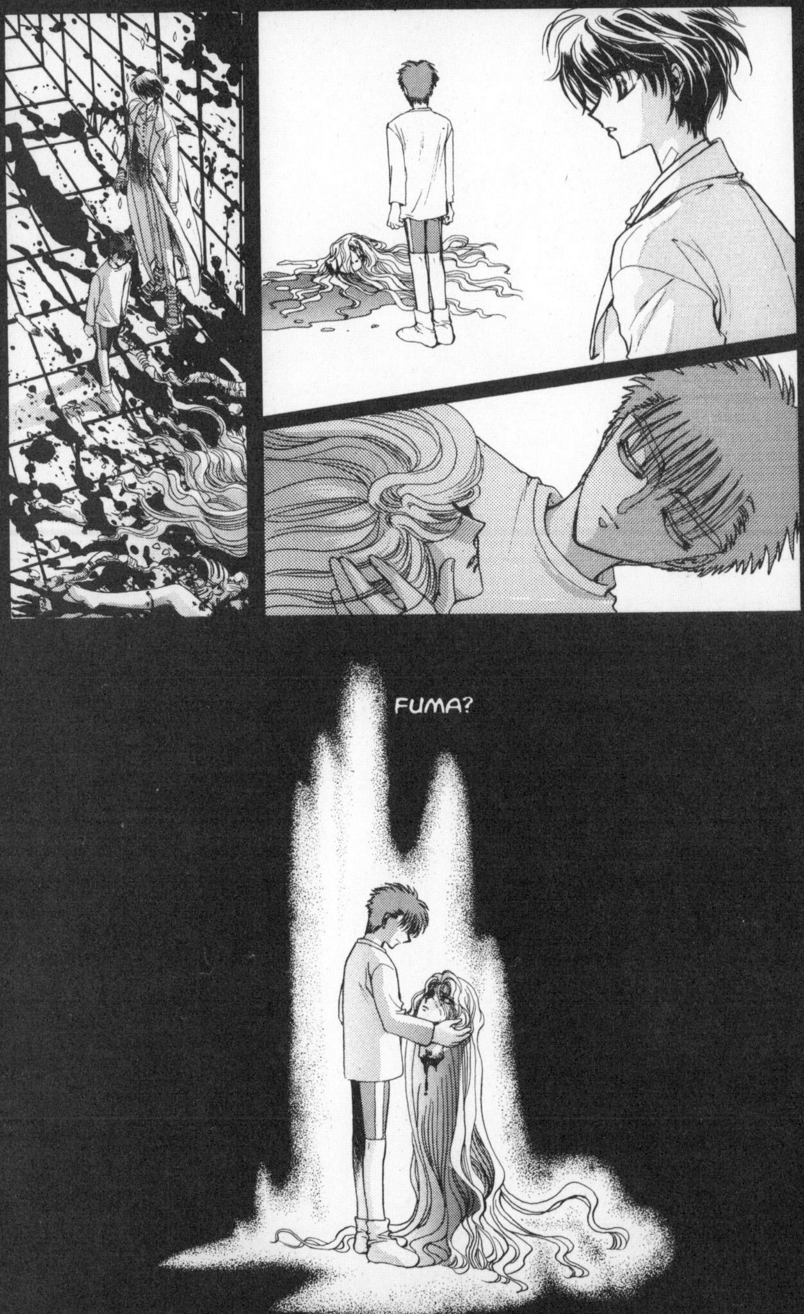
FUMA?

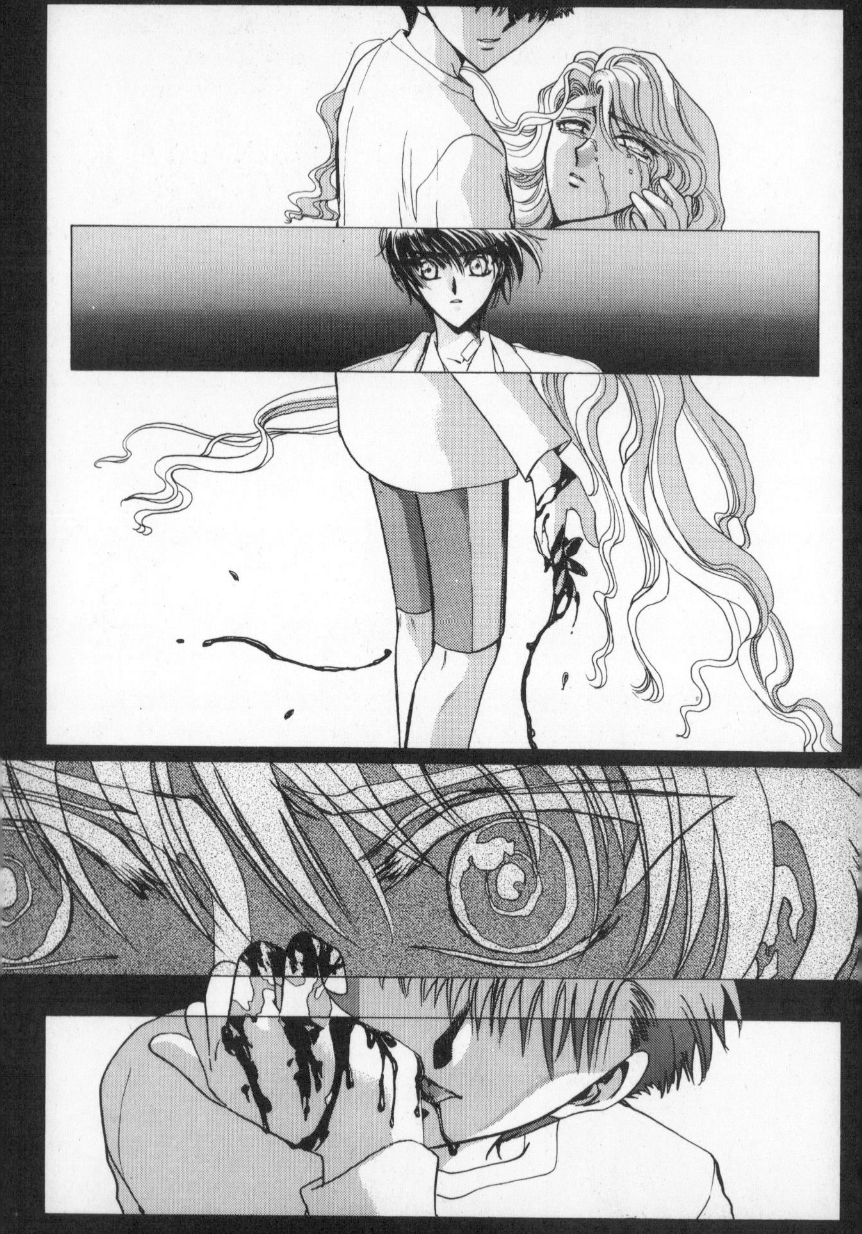

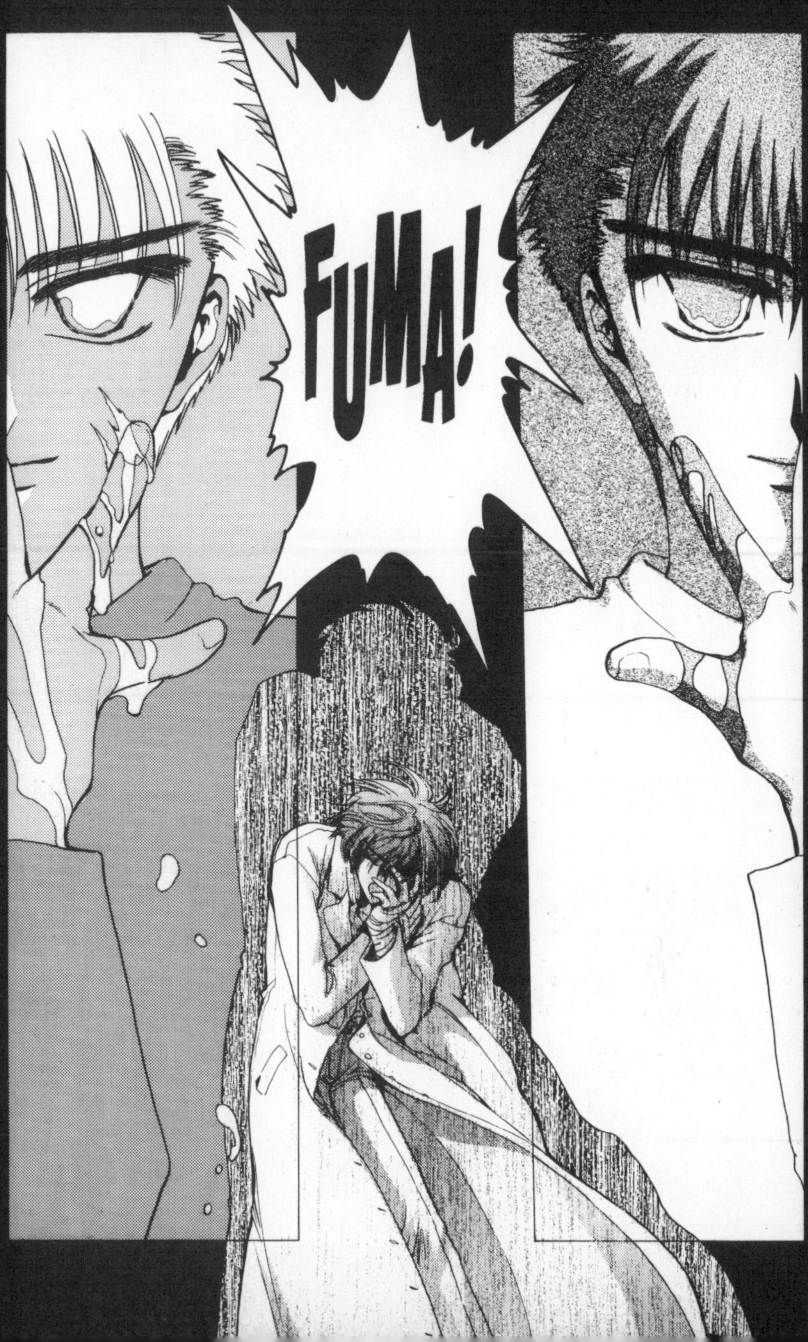
FUMA!

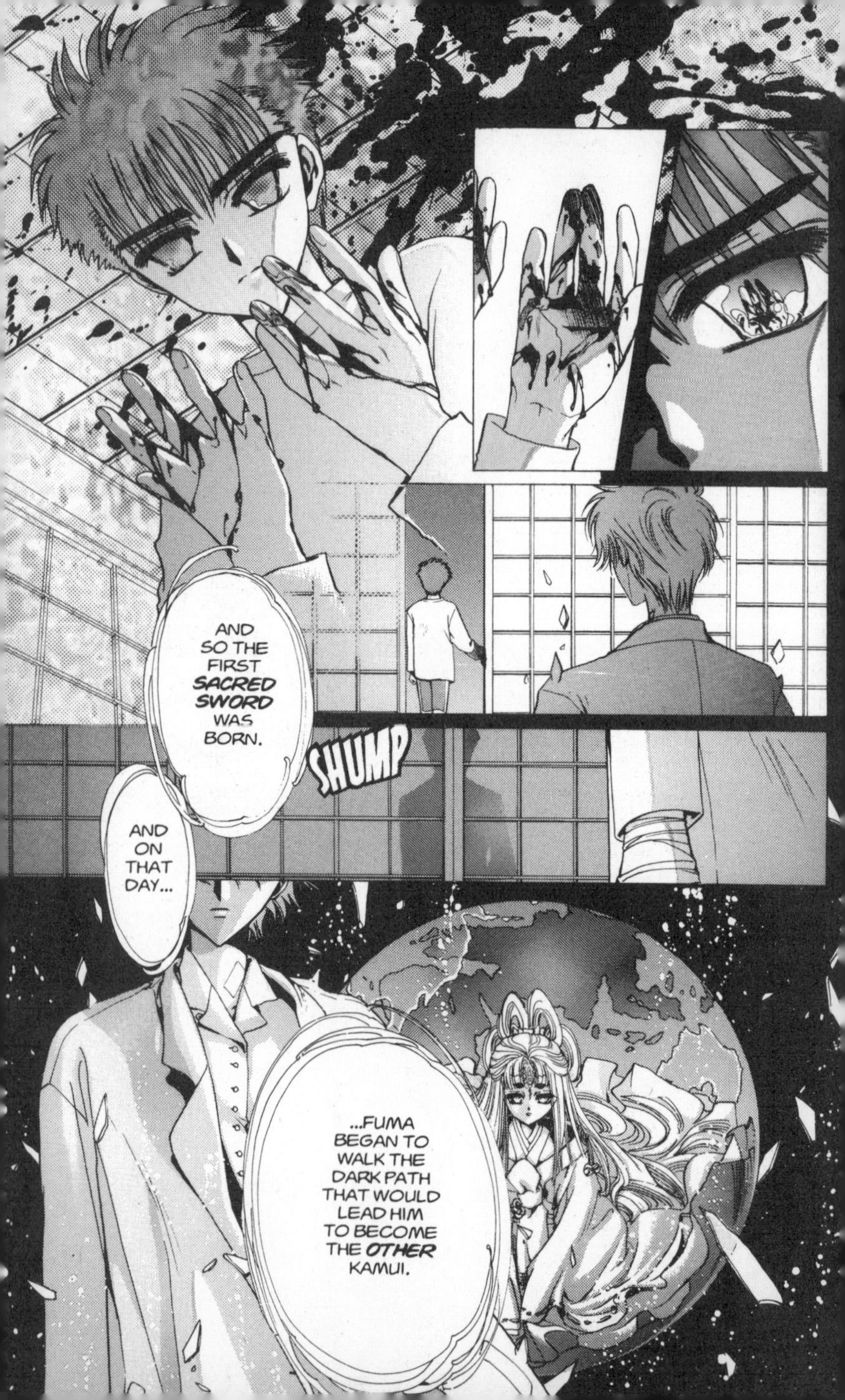
AND SO THE FIRST SACRED SWORD WAS BORN.
SHUMP
AND ON THAT DAY...
...FUMA BEGAN TO WALK THE DARK PATH THAT WOULD LEAD HIM TO BECOME THE OTHER KAMUI.

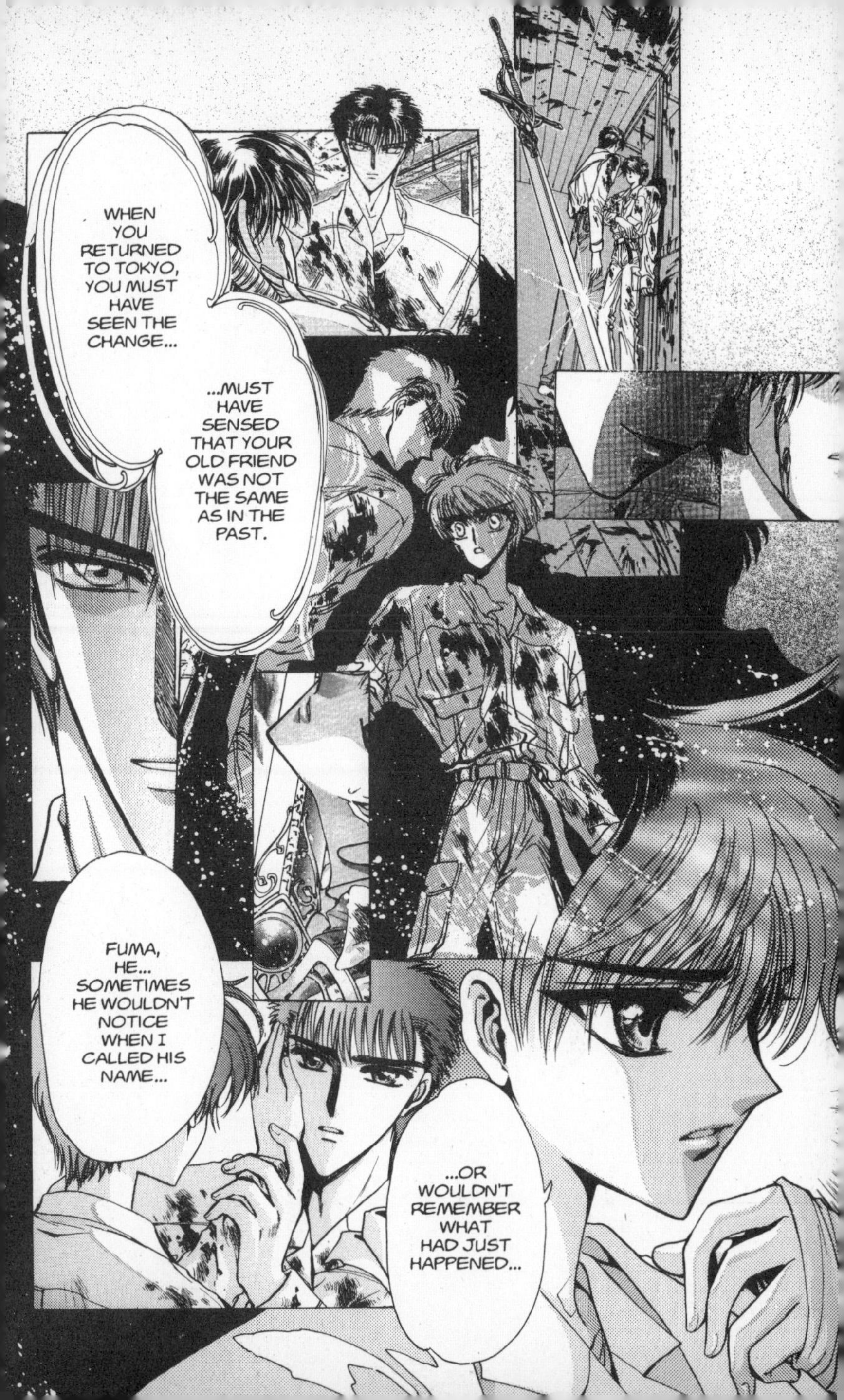
WHEN YOU RETURNED TO TOKYO, YOU MUST HAVE SEEN THE CHANGE...
...MUST HAVE SENSED THAT YOUR OLD FRIEND WAS NOT THE SAME AS IN THE PAST.
FUMA, HE... SOMETIMES HE WOULDN'T NOTICE WHEN I CALLED HIS NAME...
...OR WOULDN'T REMEMBER WHAT HAD JUST HAPPENED...

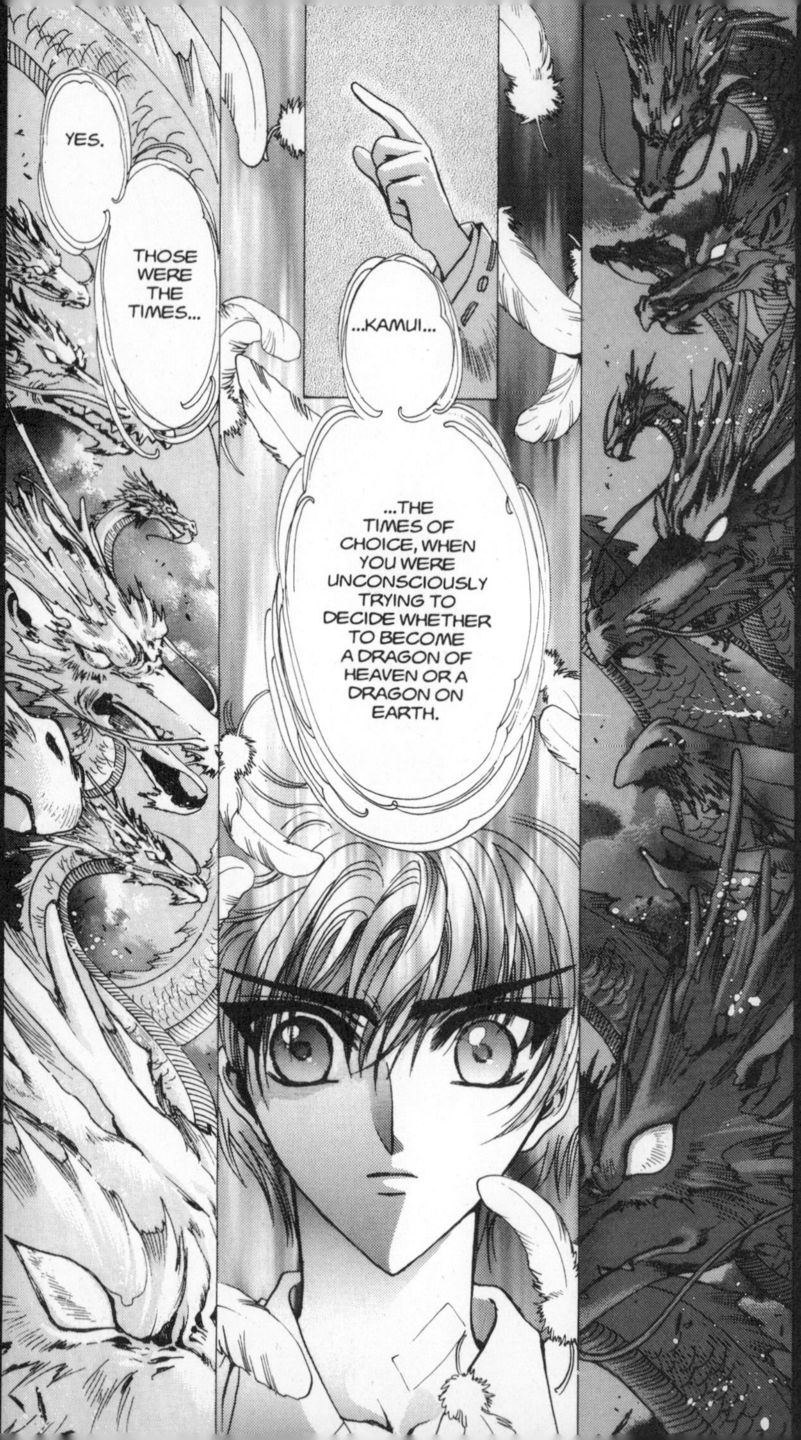
YES.
THOSE WERE THE TIMES...
...KAMUI...
...THE TIMES OF CHOICE, WHEN YOU WERE UNCONSCIOUSLY TRYING TO DECIDE WHETHER TO BECOME A DRAGON OF HEAVEN OR A DRAGON ON EARTH.

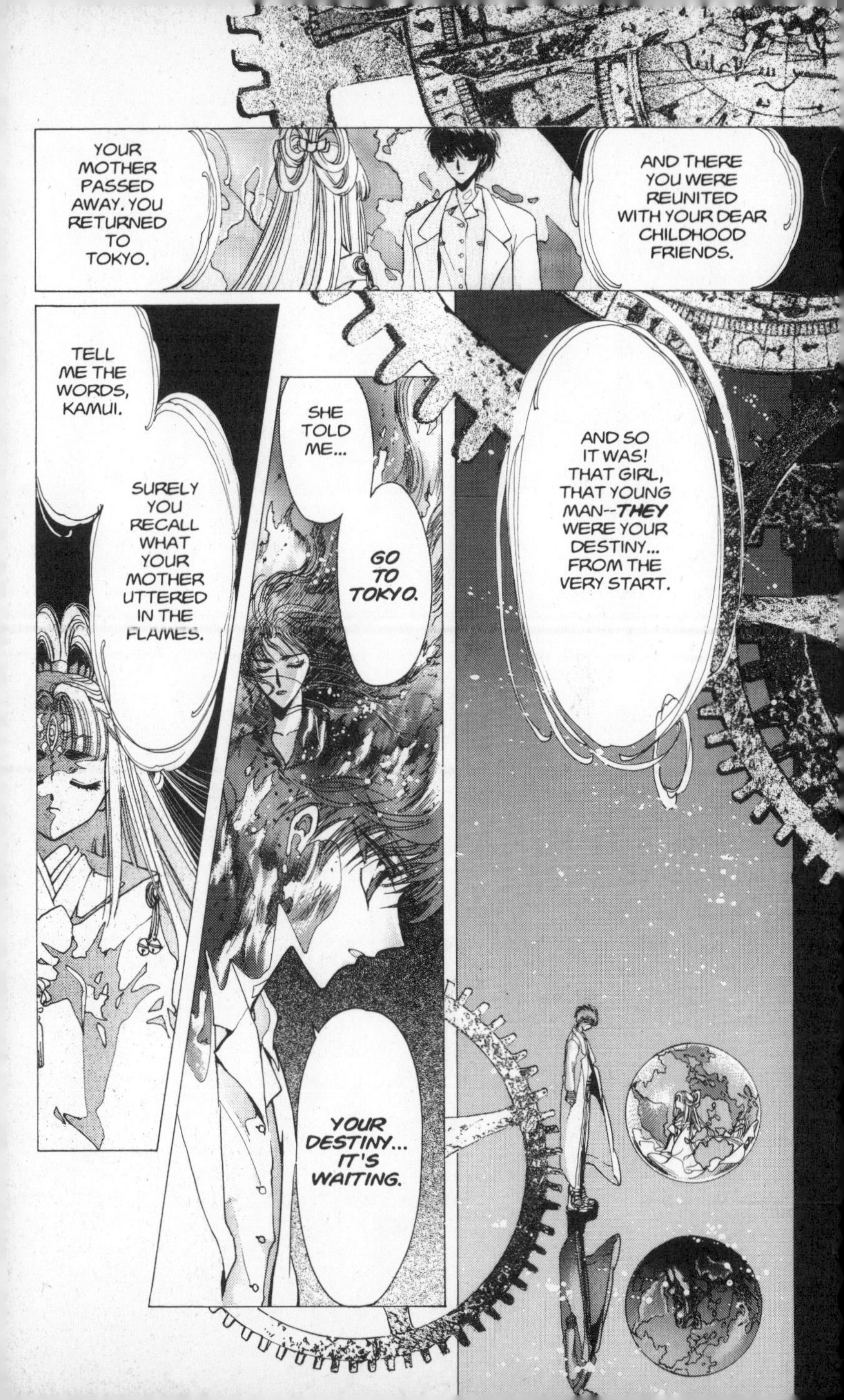
YOUR MOTHER PASSED AWAY. YOU RETURNED TO TOKYO.
AND THERE YOU WERE REUNITED WITH YOUR DEAR CHILDHOOD FRIENDS.
TELL ME THE WORDS, KAMUI.
SURELY YOU RECALL WHAT YOUR MOTHER UTTERED IN THE FLAMES.
SHE TOLD ME...
GO TO TOKYO.
YOUR DESTINY... IT'S WAITING.
AND SO IT WAS! THAT GIRL, THAT YOUNG MAN--THEY WERE YOUR DESTINY... FROM THE VERY START.

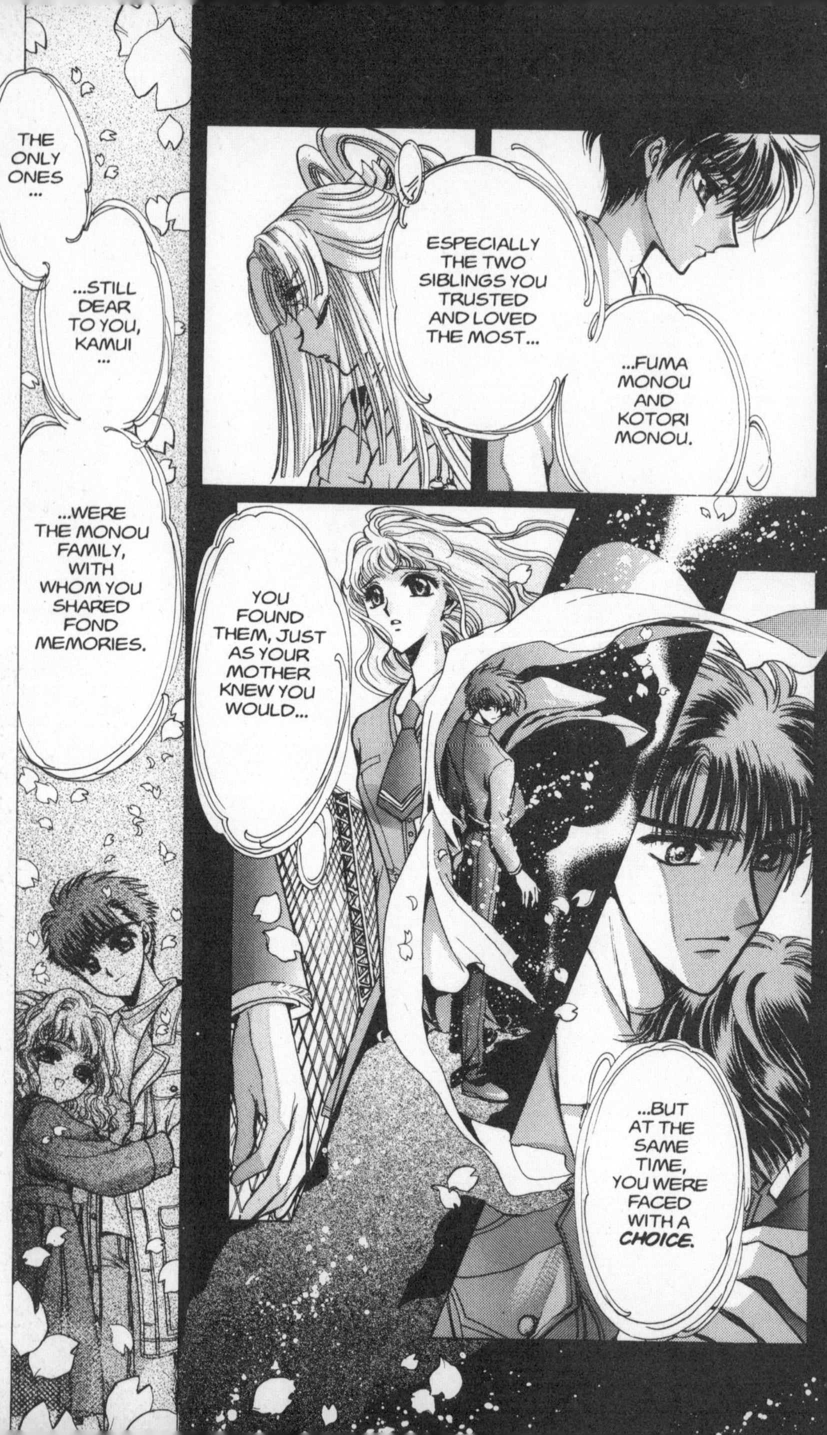
THE ONLY ONES ...
...STILL DEAR TO YOU, KAMUI ...
...WERE THE MONOU FAMILY, WITH WHOM YOU SHARED FOND MEMORIES.
ESPECIALLY THE TWO SIBLINGS YOU TRUSTED AND LOVED THE MOST...
...FUMA MONOU AND KOTORI MONOU.
YOU FOUND THEM, JUST AS YOUR MOTHER KNEW YOU WOULD...
...BUT AT THE SAME TIME, YOU WERE FACED WITH A **CHOICE.**

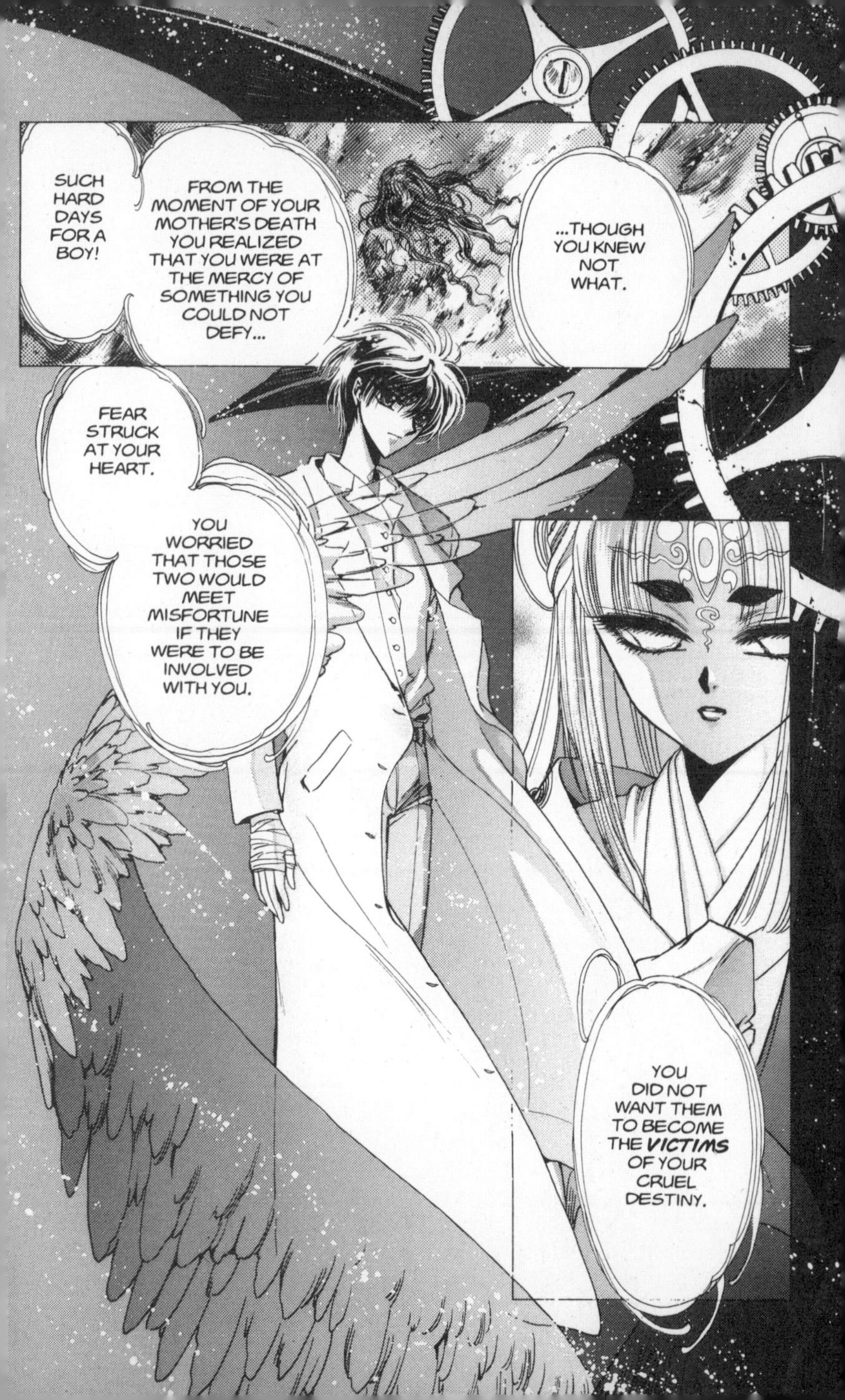
SUCH HARD DAYS FOR A BOY!
FROM THE MOMENT OF YOUR MOTHER'S DEATH YOU REALIZED THAT YOU WERE AT THE MERCY OF SOMETHING YOU COULD NOT DEFY...
...THOUGH YOU KNEW NOT WHAT.
FEAR STRUCK AT YOUR HEART.
YOU WORRIED THAT THOSE TWO WOULD MEET MISFORTUNE IF THEY WERE TO BE INVOLVED WITH YOU.
YOU DID NOT WANT THEM TO BECOME THE ***VICTIMS*** OF YOUR CRUEL DESTINY.

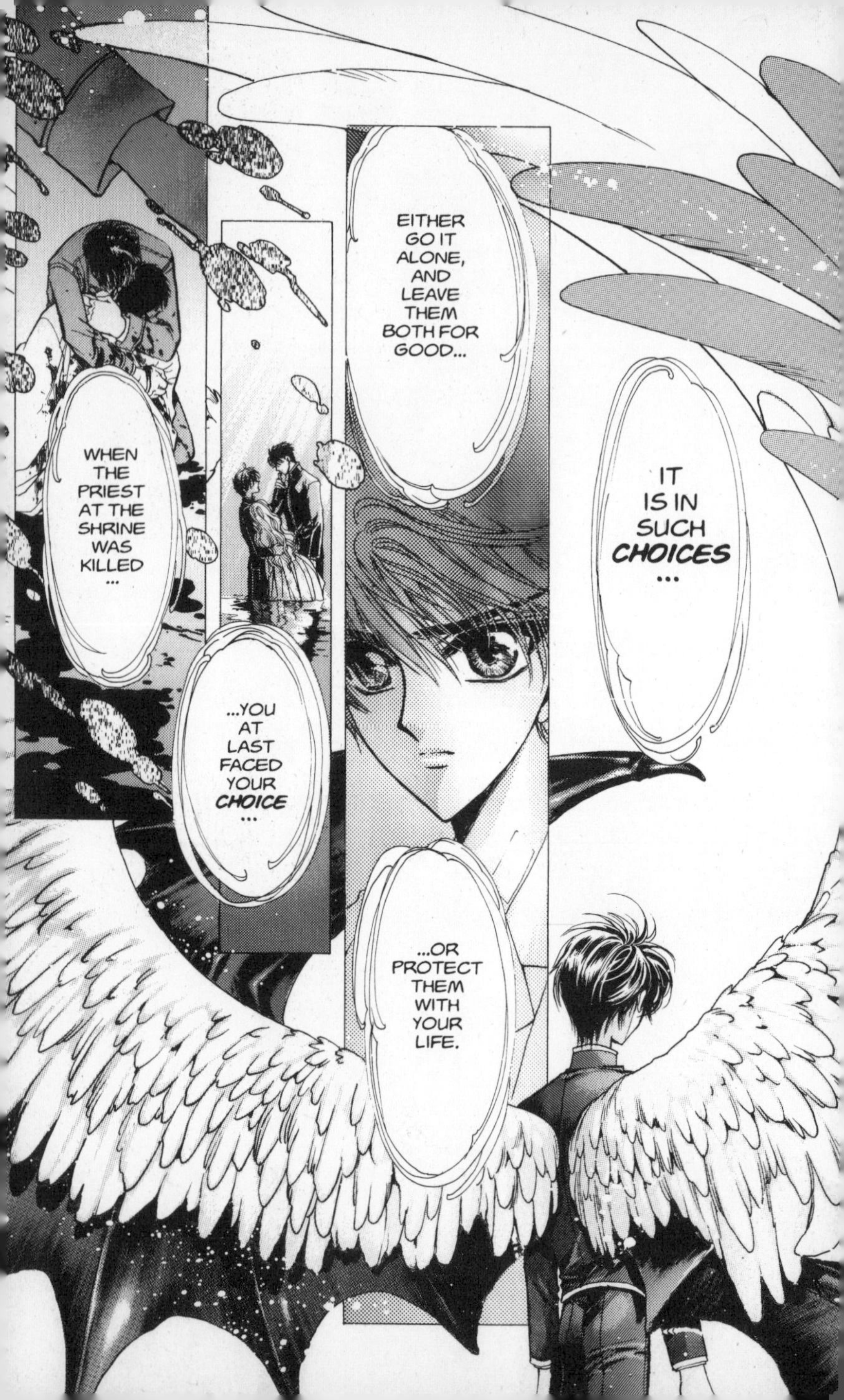
WHEN THE PRIEST AT THE SHRINE WAS KILLED...
...YOU AT LAST FACED YOUR CHOICE...
EITHER GO IT ALONE, AND LEAVE THEM BOTH FOR GOOD...
...OR PROTECT THEM WITH YOUR LIFE.
IT IS IN SUCH CHOICES...

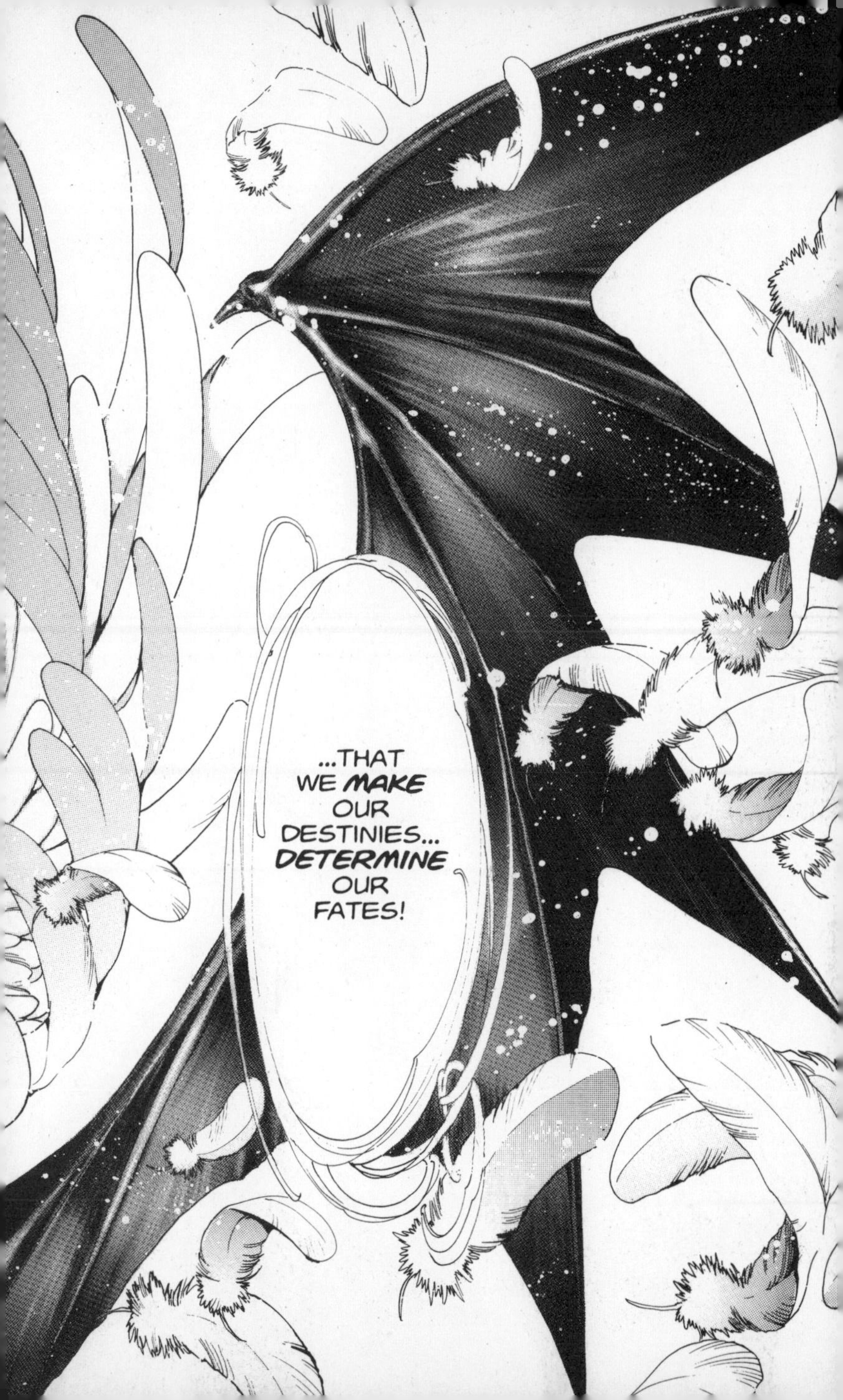
...THAT WE *MAKE* OUR DESTINIES... *DETERMINE* OUR FATES!

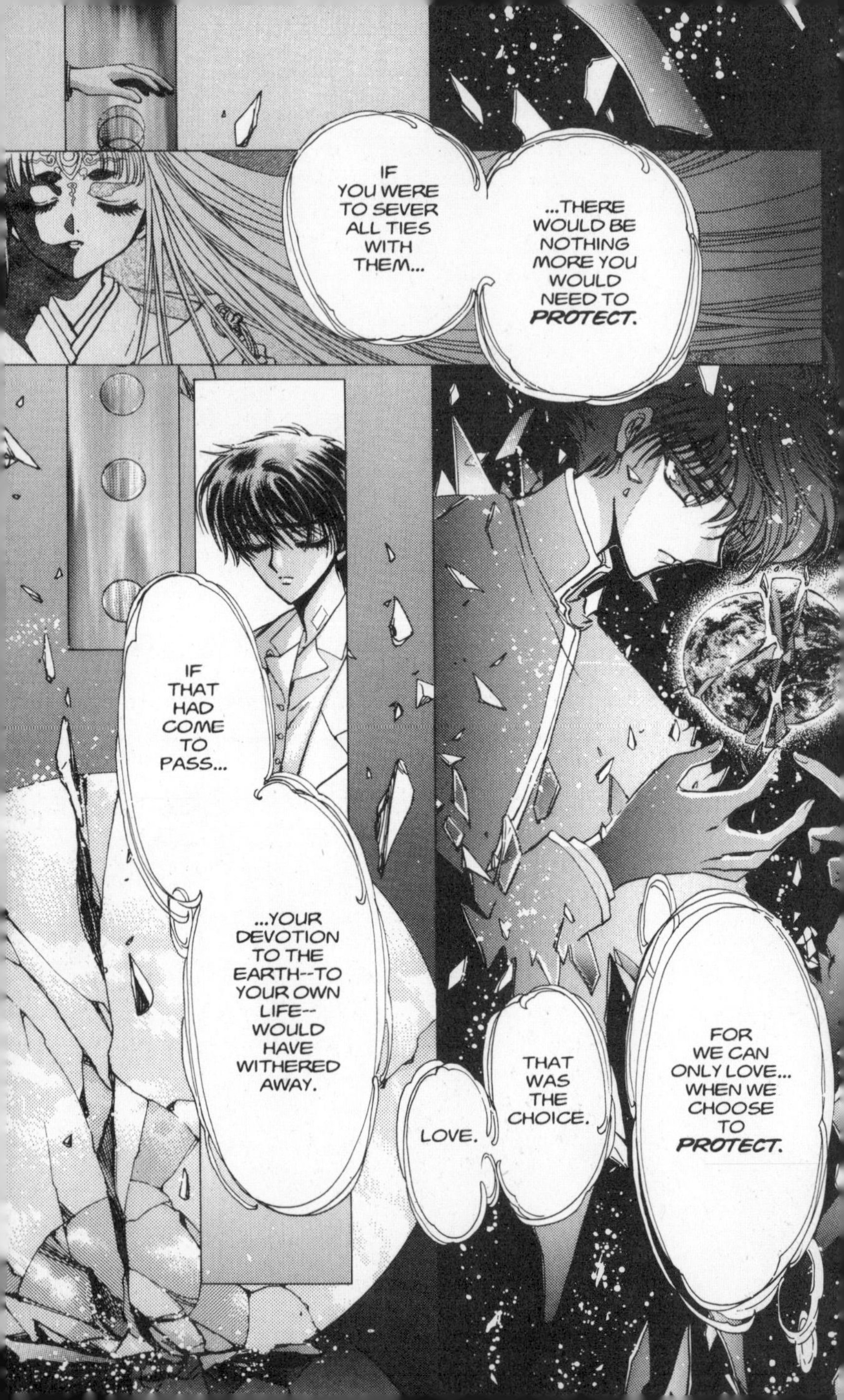
IF YOU WERE TO SEVER ALL TIES WITH THEM...
...THERE WOULD BE NOTHING MORE YOU WOULD NEED TO *PROTECT*.
IF THAT HAD COME TO PASS...
...YOUR DEVOTION TO THE EARTH--TO YOUR OWN LIFE--WOULD HAVE WITHERED AWAY.
LOVE.
THAT WAS THE CHOICE.
FOR WE CAN ONLY LOVE... WHEN WE CHOOSE TO *PROTECT*.

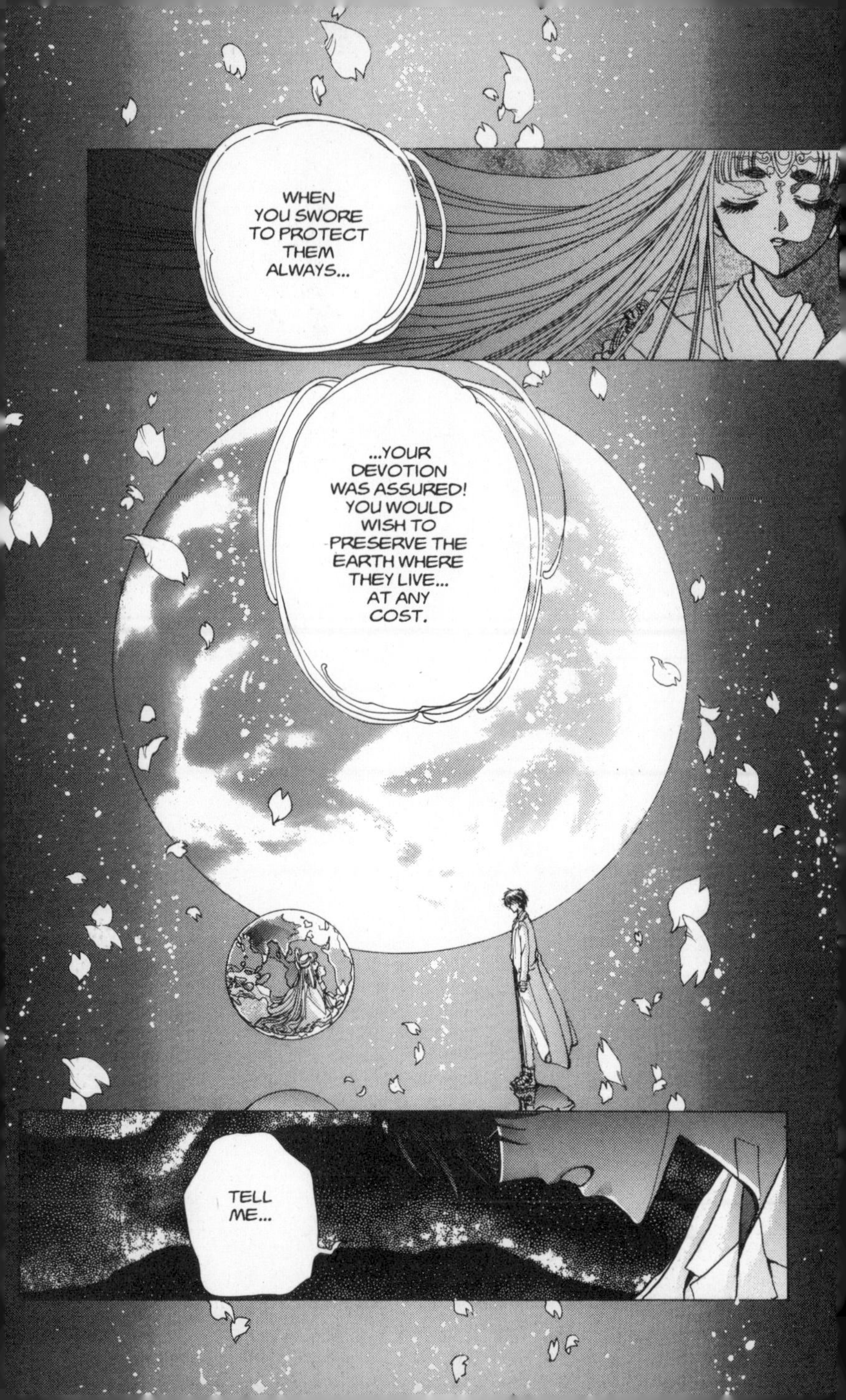
WHEN YOU SWORE TO PROTECT THEM ALWAYS...
...YOUR DEVOTION WAS ASSURED! YOU WOULD WISH TO PRESERVE THE EARTH WHERE THEY LIVE... AT ANY COST.
TELL ME...

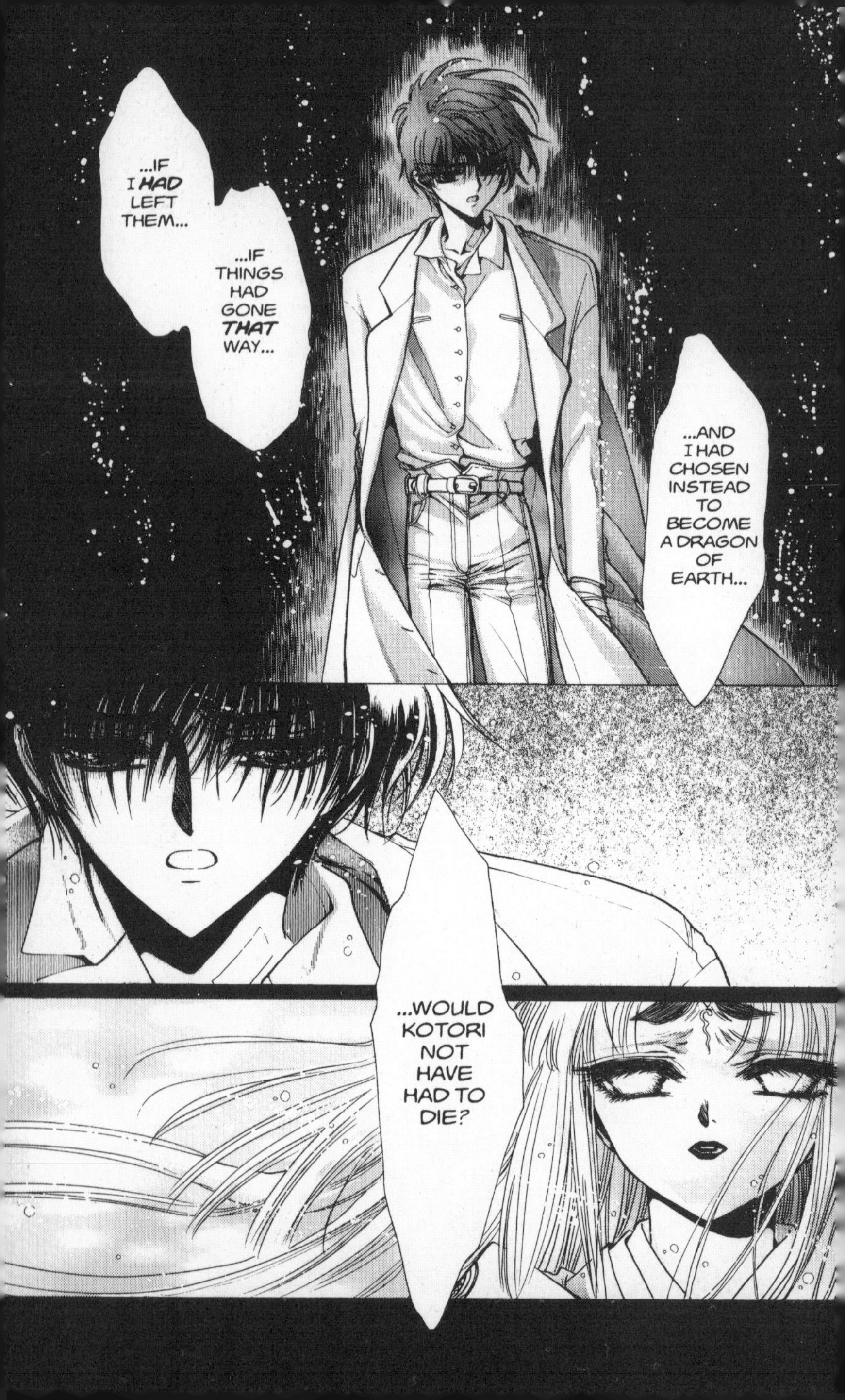
...IF I HAD LEFT THEM...
...IF THINGS HAD GONE THAT WAY...
...AND I HAD CHOSEN INSTEAD TO BECOME A DRAGON OF EARTH...
...WOULD KOTORI NOT HAVE HAD TO DIE?

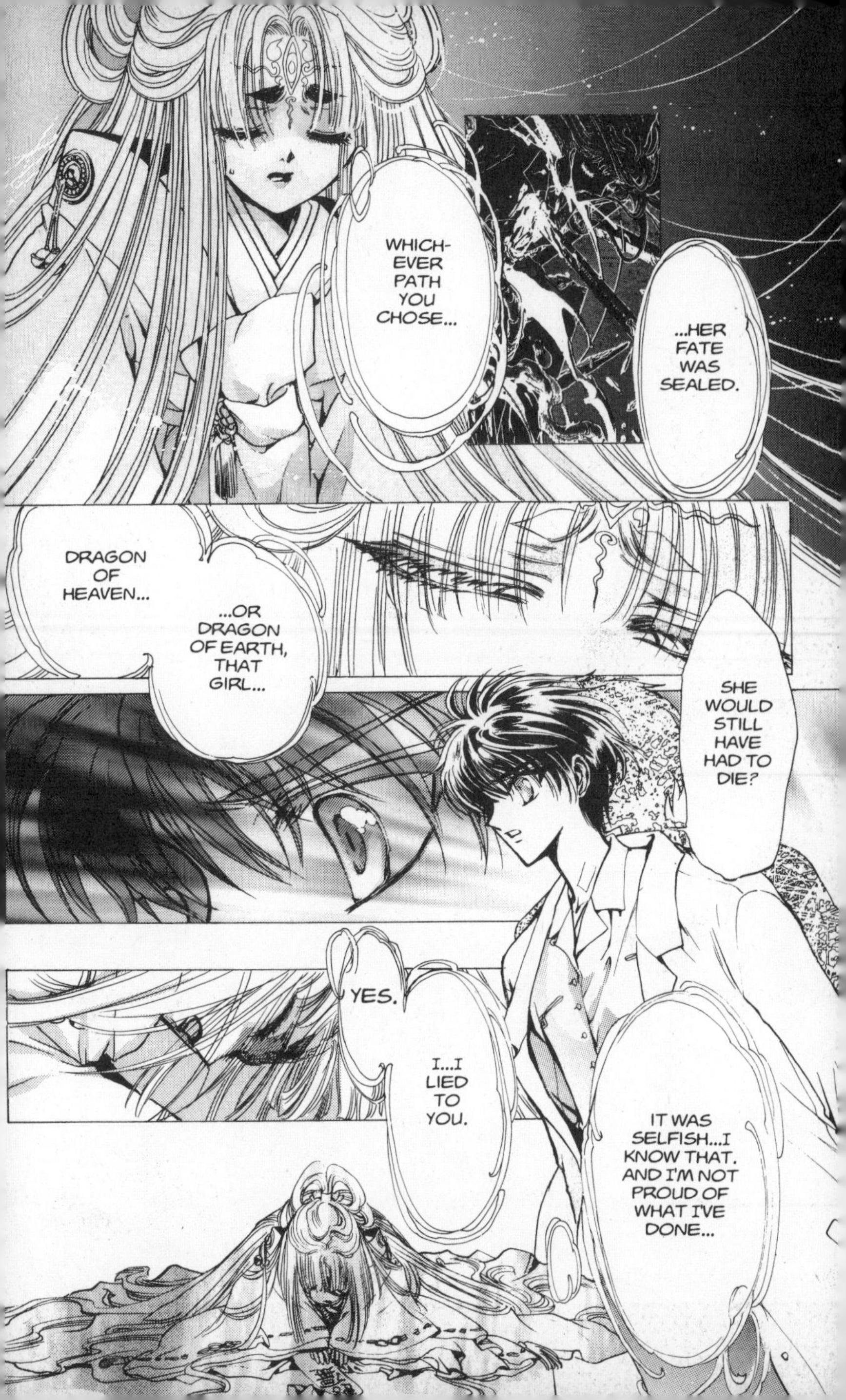
WHICH-EVER PATH YOU CHOSE...
...HER FATE WAS SEALED.
DRAGON OF HEAVEN...
...OR DRAGON OF EARTH, THAT GIRL...
SHE WOULD STILL HAVE HAD TO DIE?
YES.
I...I LIED TO YOU.
IT WAS SELFISH...I KNOW THAT. AND I'M NOT PROUD OF WHAT I'VE DONE...

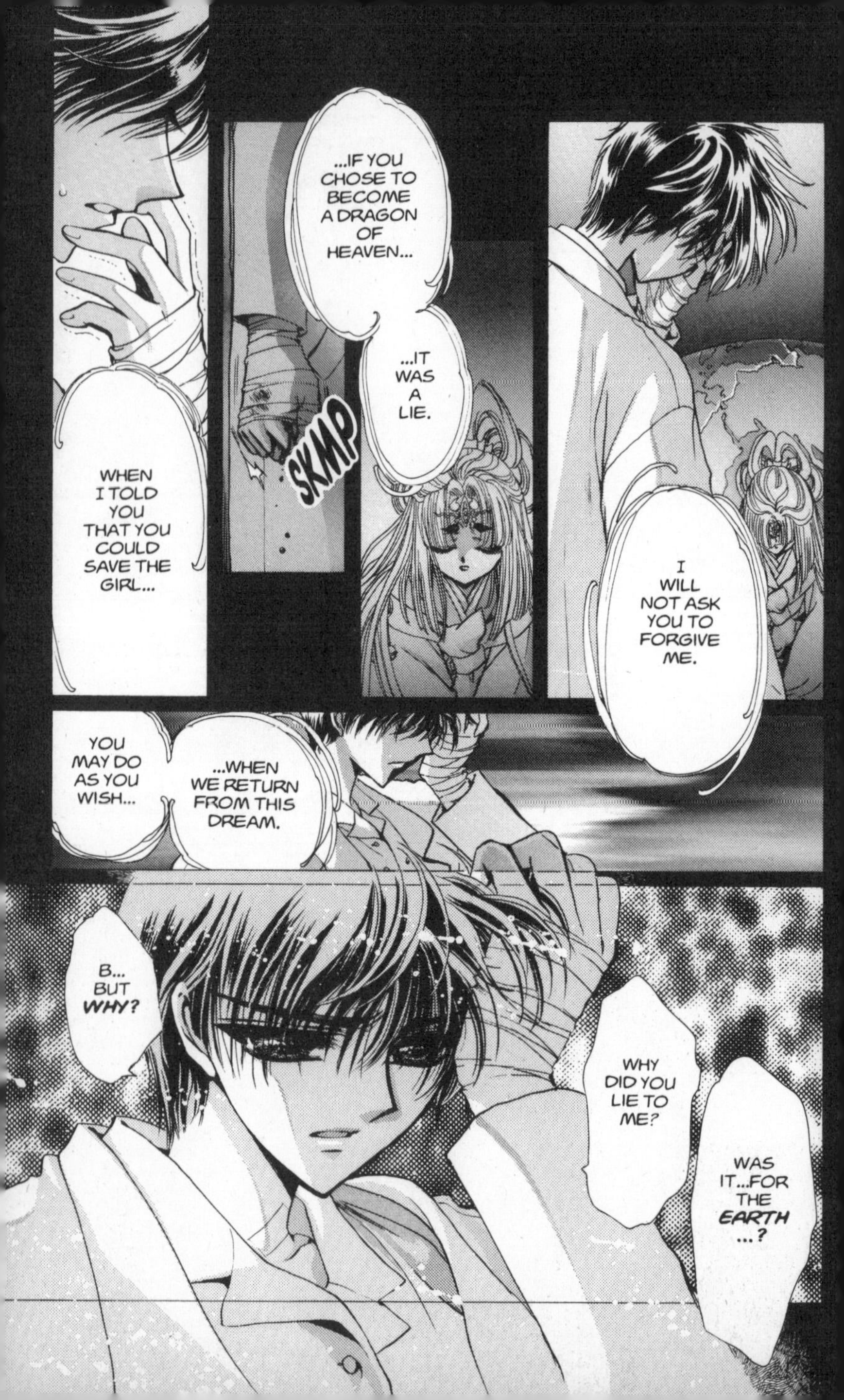
WHEN I TOLD YOU THAT YOU COULD SAVE THE GIRL...
...IF YOU CHOSE TO BECOME A DRAGON OF HEAVEN...
...IT WAS A LIE.
SKMP
I WILL NOT ASK YOU TO FORGIVE ME.
YOU MAY DO AS YOU WISH...
...WHEN WE RETURN FROM THIS DREAM.
B... BUT *WHY?*
WHY DID YOU LIE TO ME?
WAS IT...FOR THE *EARTH* ...?

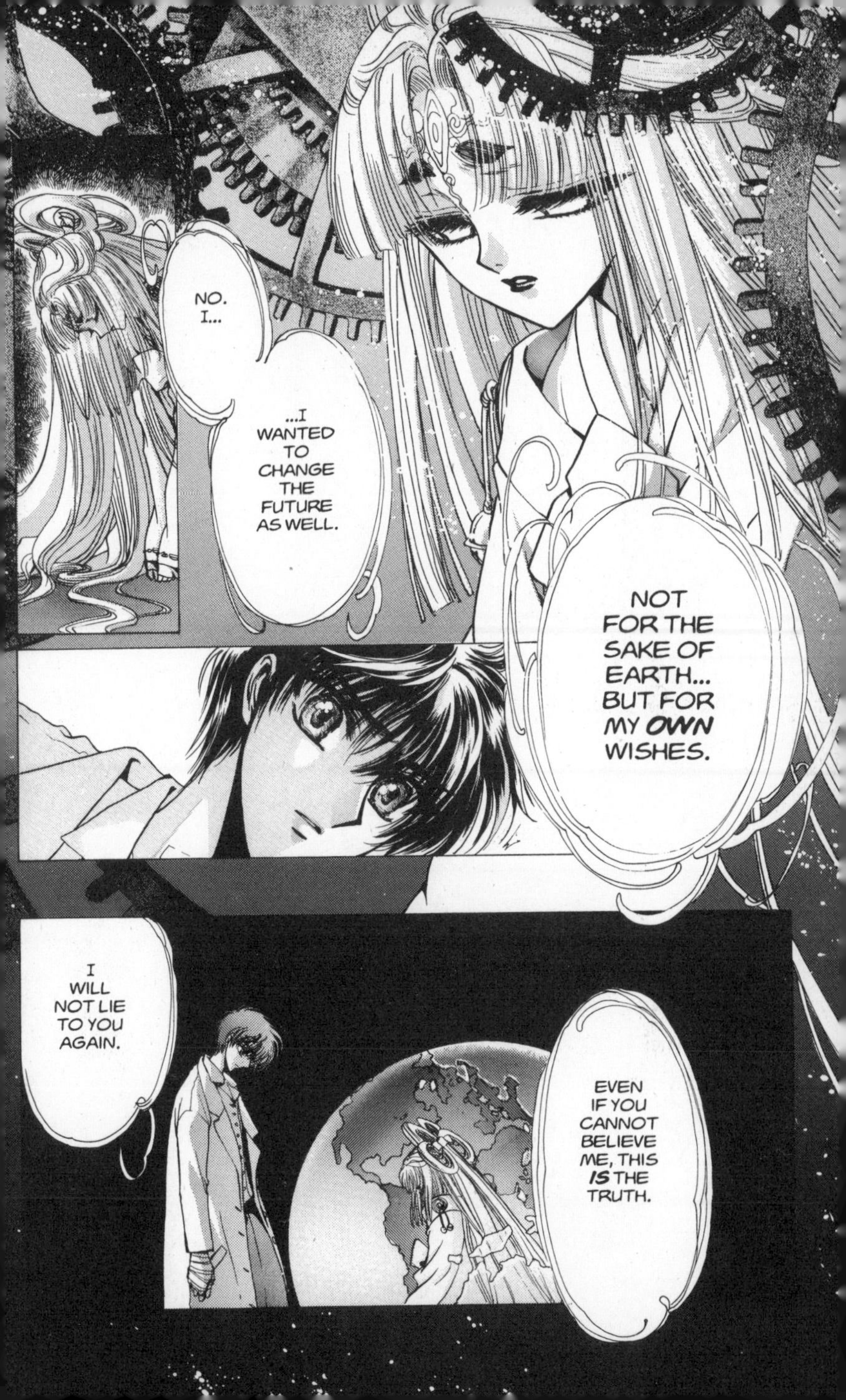
NO. I...
...I WANTED TO CHANGE THE FUTURE AS WELL.
NOT FOR THE SAKE OF EARTH... BUT FOR MY *OWN* WISHES.
I WILL NOT LIE TO YOU AGAIN.
EVEN IF YOU CANNOT BELIEVE ME, THIS *IS* THE TRUTH.

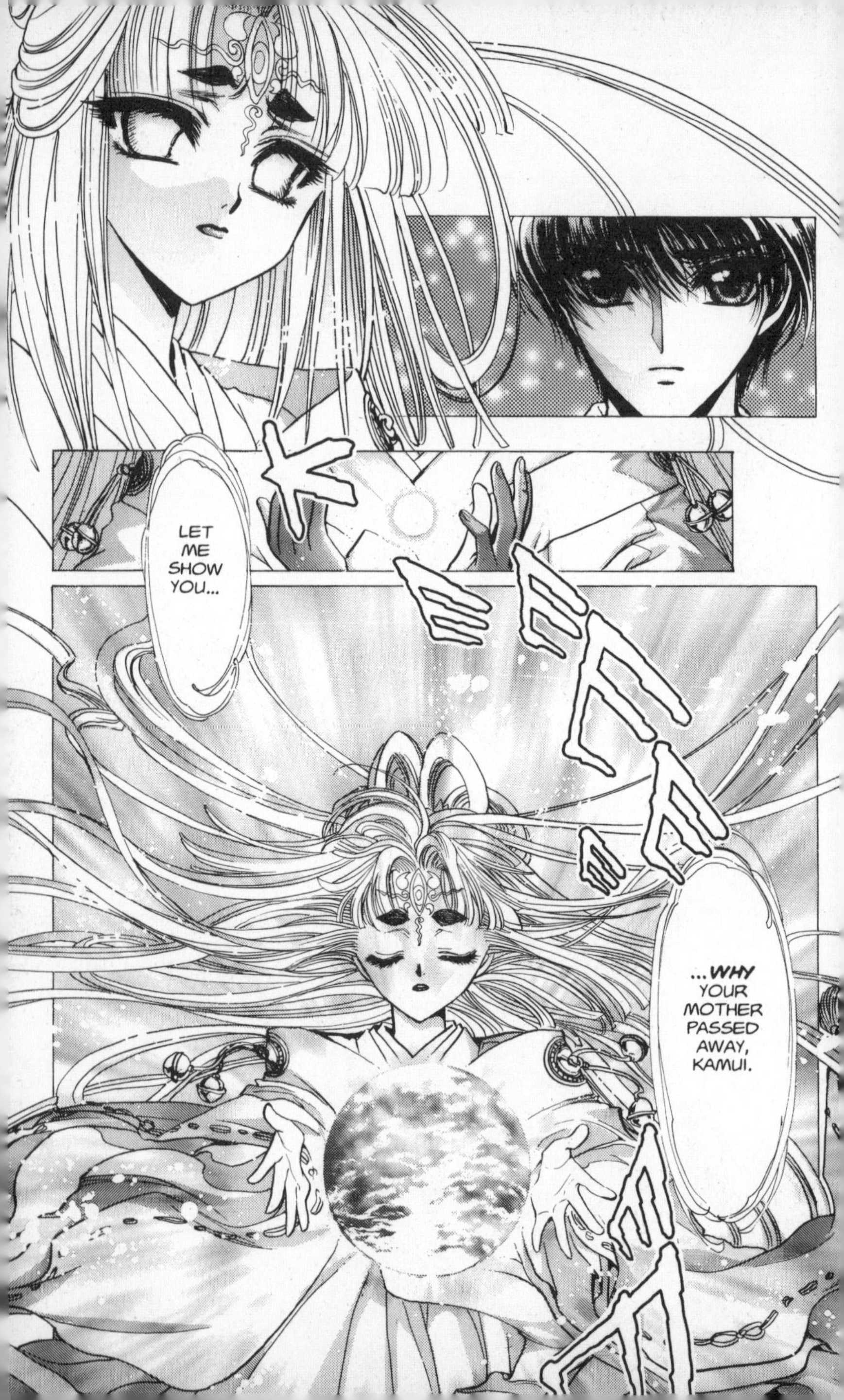
LET ME SHOW YOU...
...WHY YOUR MOTHER PASSED AWAY, KAMUI.

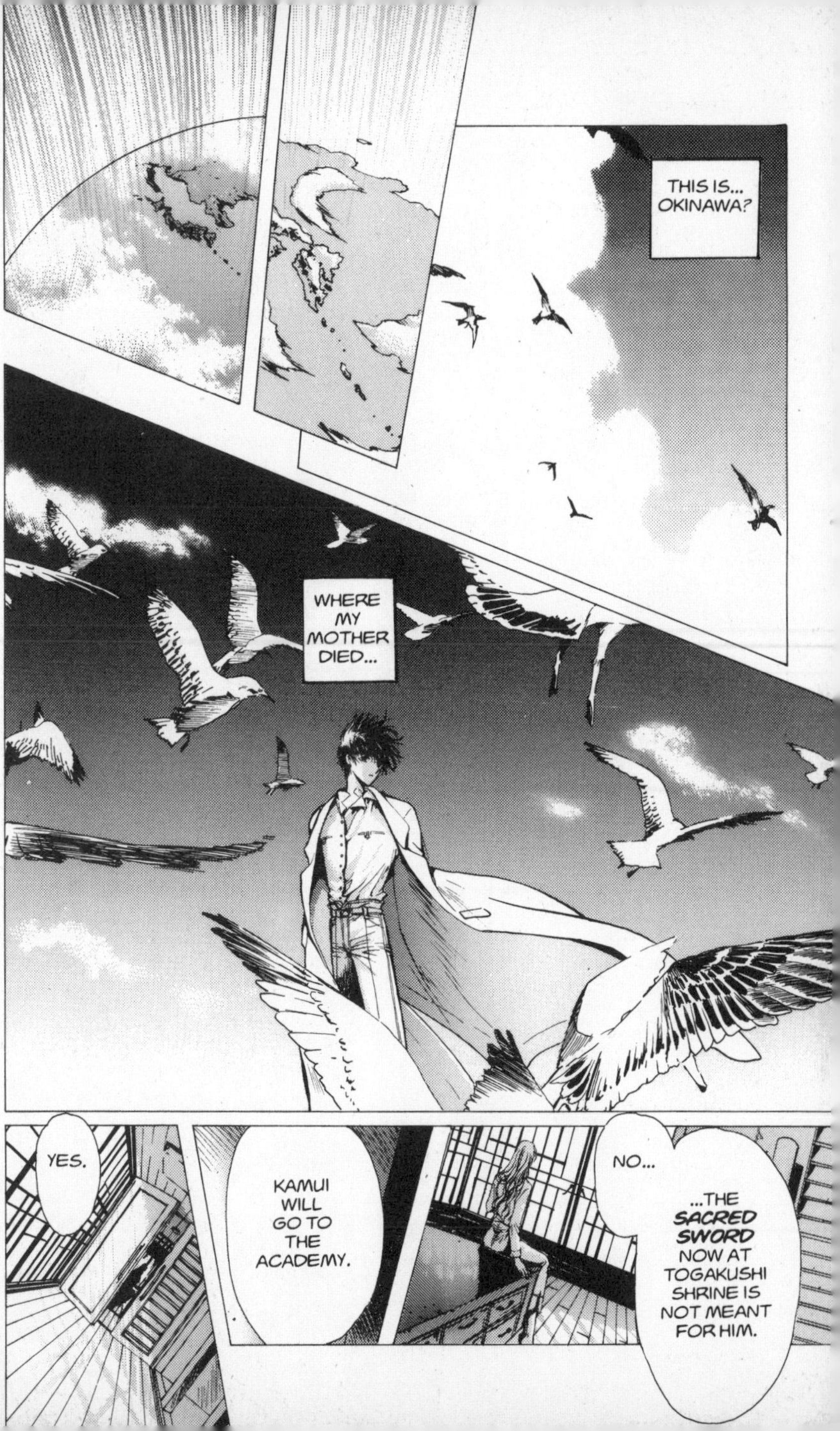
THIS IS... OKINAWA?
WHERE MY MOTHER DIED...
YES.
KAMUI WILL GO TO THE ACADEMY.
NO...
...THE SACRED SWORD NOW AT TOGAKUSHI SHRINE IS NOT MEANT FOR HIM.

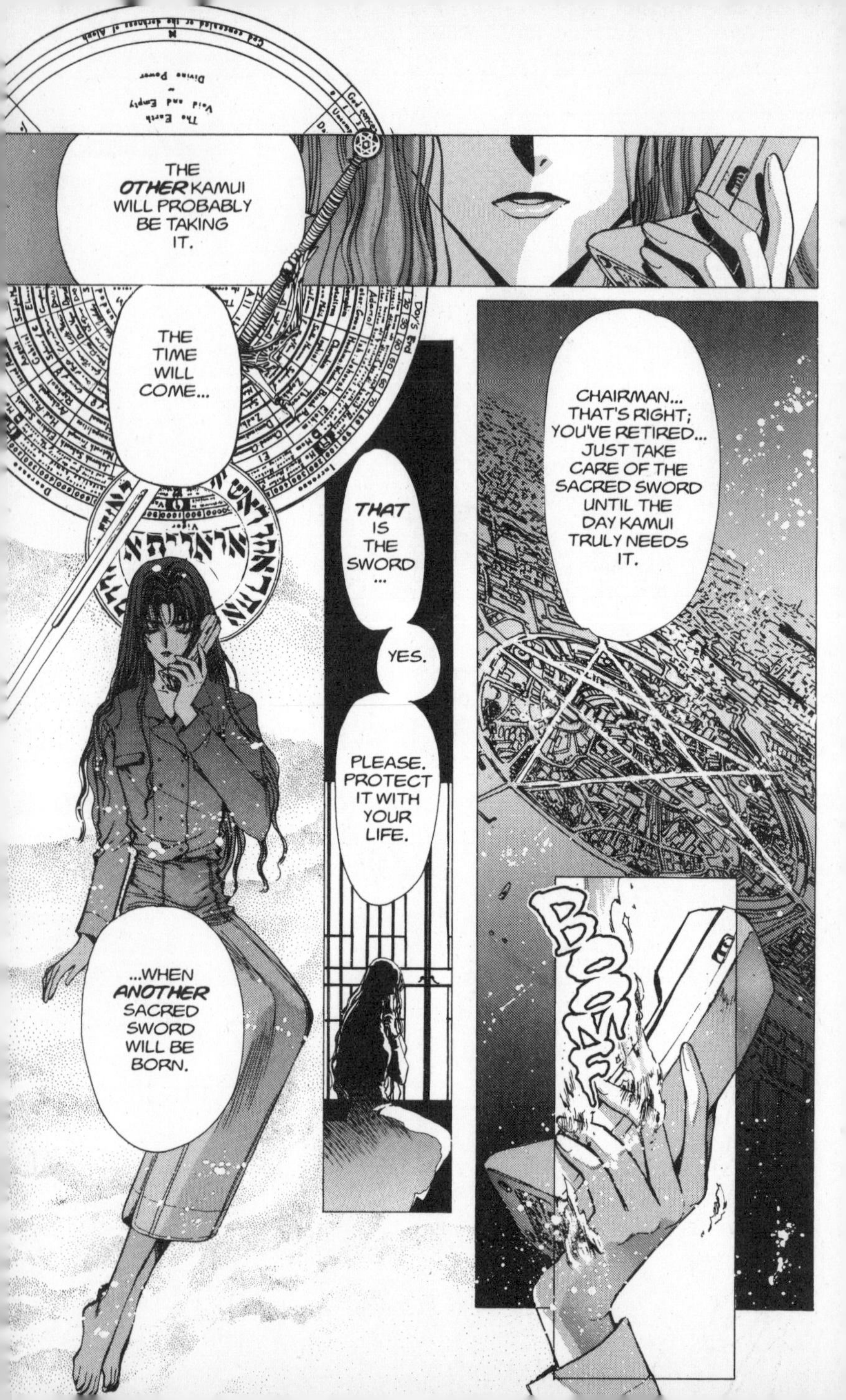

THE OTHER KAMUI WILL PROBABLY BE TAKING IT.
THE TIME WILL COME...
...WHEN ANOTHER SACRED SWORD WILL BE BORN.
THAT IS THE SWORD...
YES.
PLEASE. PROTECT IT WITH YOUR LIFE.
CHAIRMAN... THAT'S RIGHT; YOU'VE RETIRED... JUST TAKE CARE OF THE SACRED SWORD UNTIL THE DAY KAMUI TRULY NEEDS IT.
BOOOM

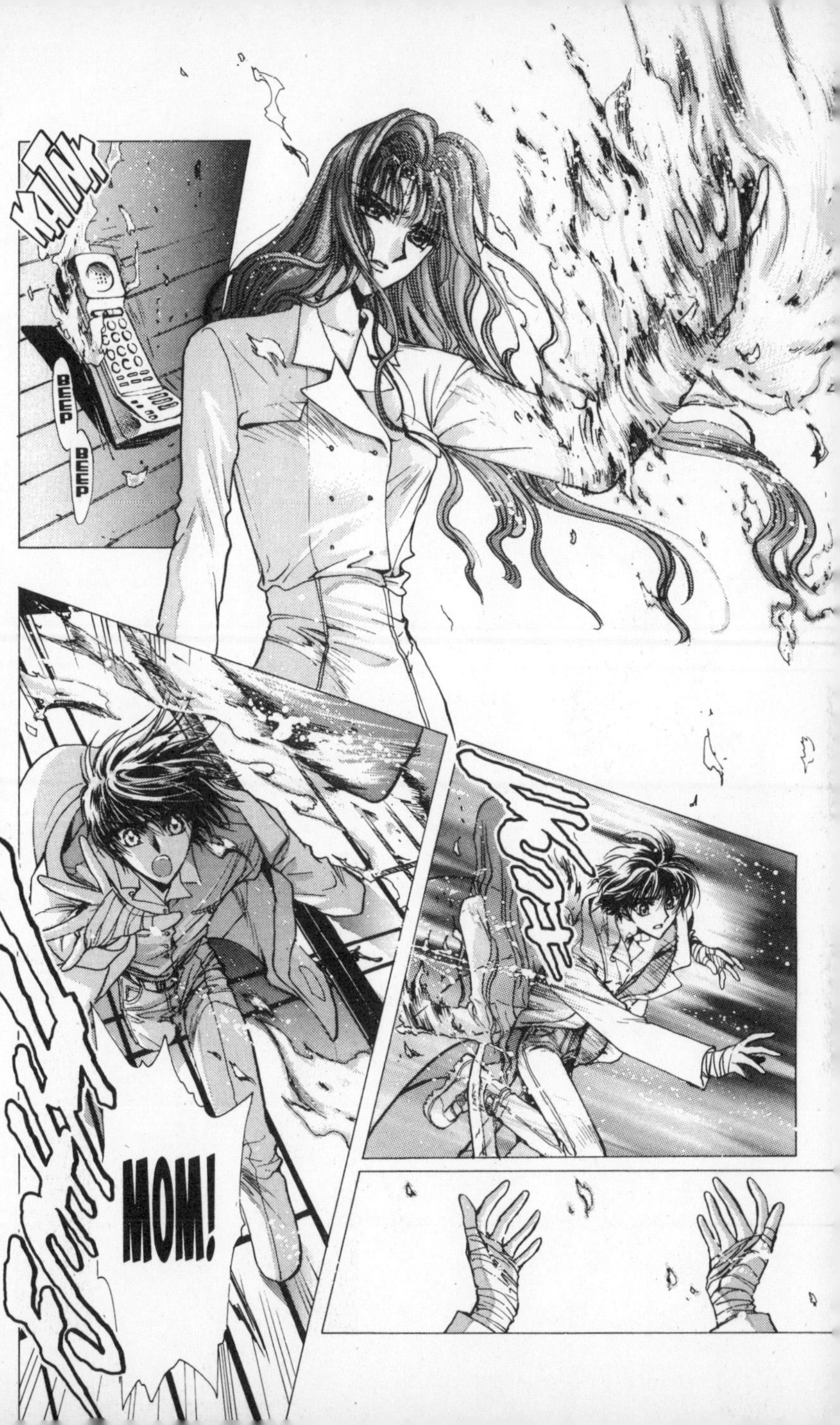
KATINK
BEEP
BEEP
BEEP
MOM!

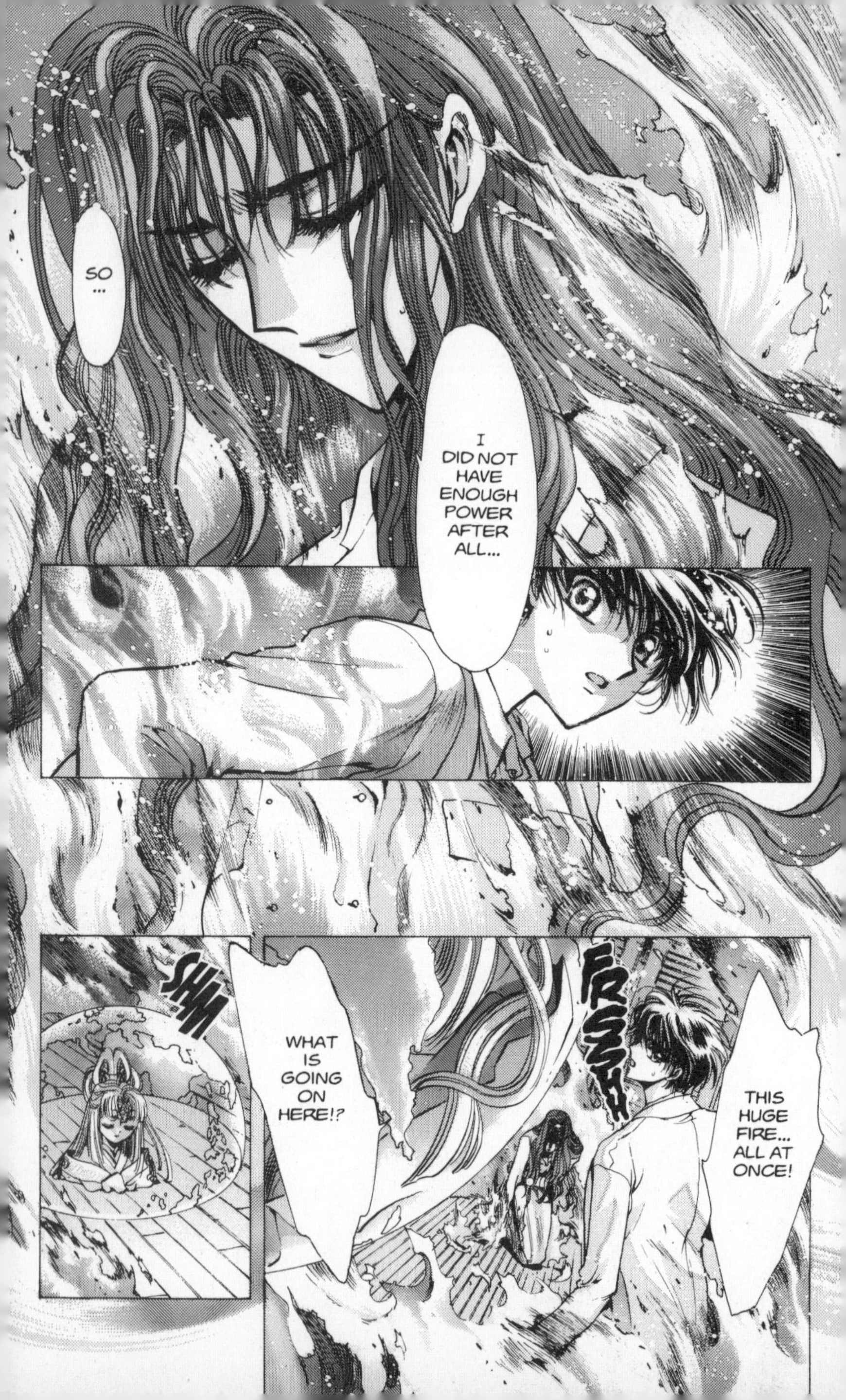
SO ...
I DID NOT HAVE ENOUGH POWER AFTER ALL...
SHM
WHAT IS GOING ON HERE!?
FRSSSH
THIS HUGE FIRE... ALL AT ONCE!

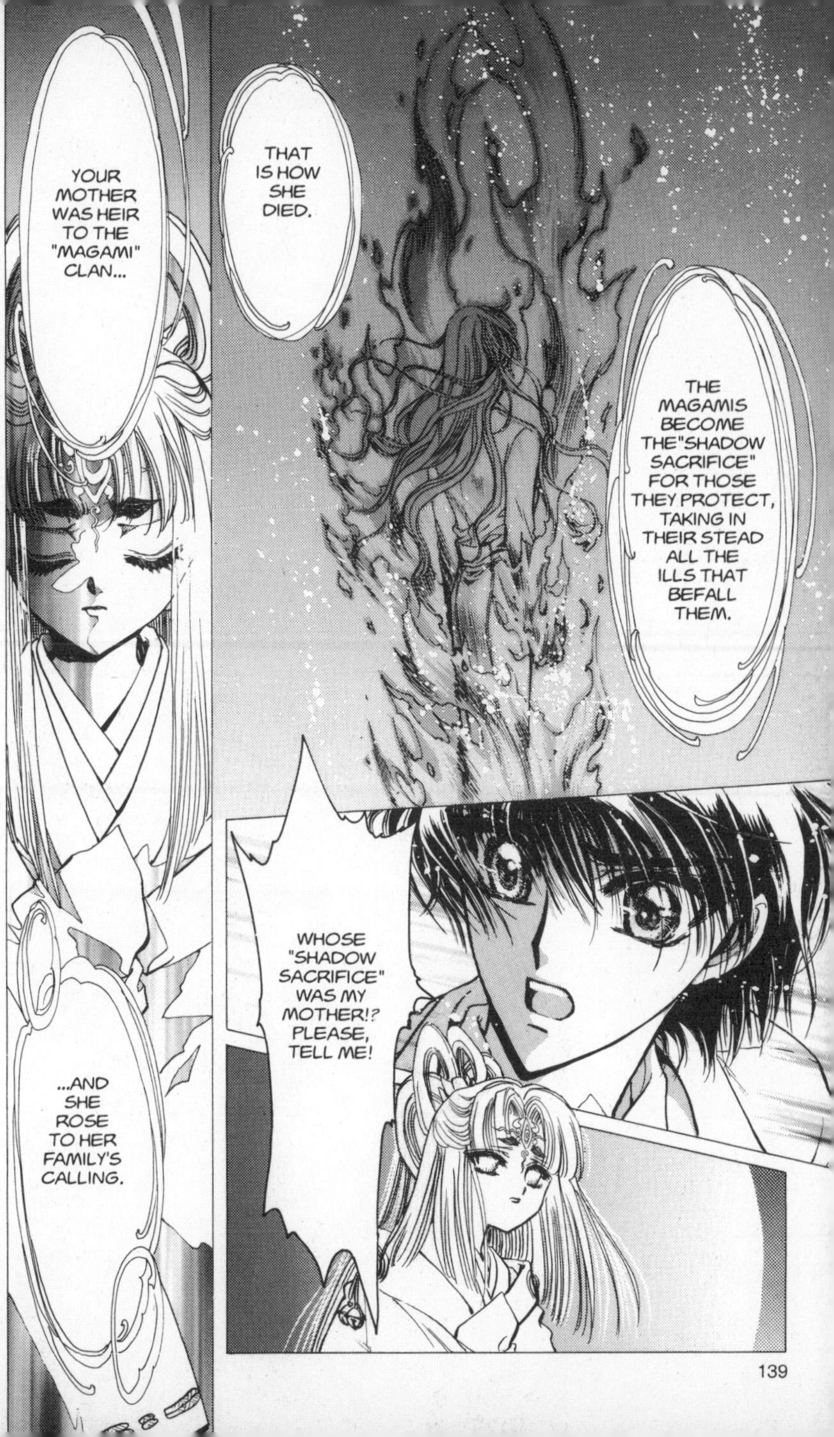
YOUR MOTHER WAS HEIR TO THE "MAGAMI" CLAN...
...AND SHE ROSE TO HER FAMILY'S CALLING.
THAT IS HOW SHE DIED.
THE MAGAMIS BECOME THE "SHADOW SACRIFICE" FOR THOSE THEY PROTECT, TAKING IN THEIR STEAD ALL THE ILLS THAT BEFALL THEM.
WHOSE "SHADOW SACRIFICE" WAS MY MOTHER!? PLEASE, TELL ME!

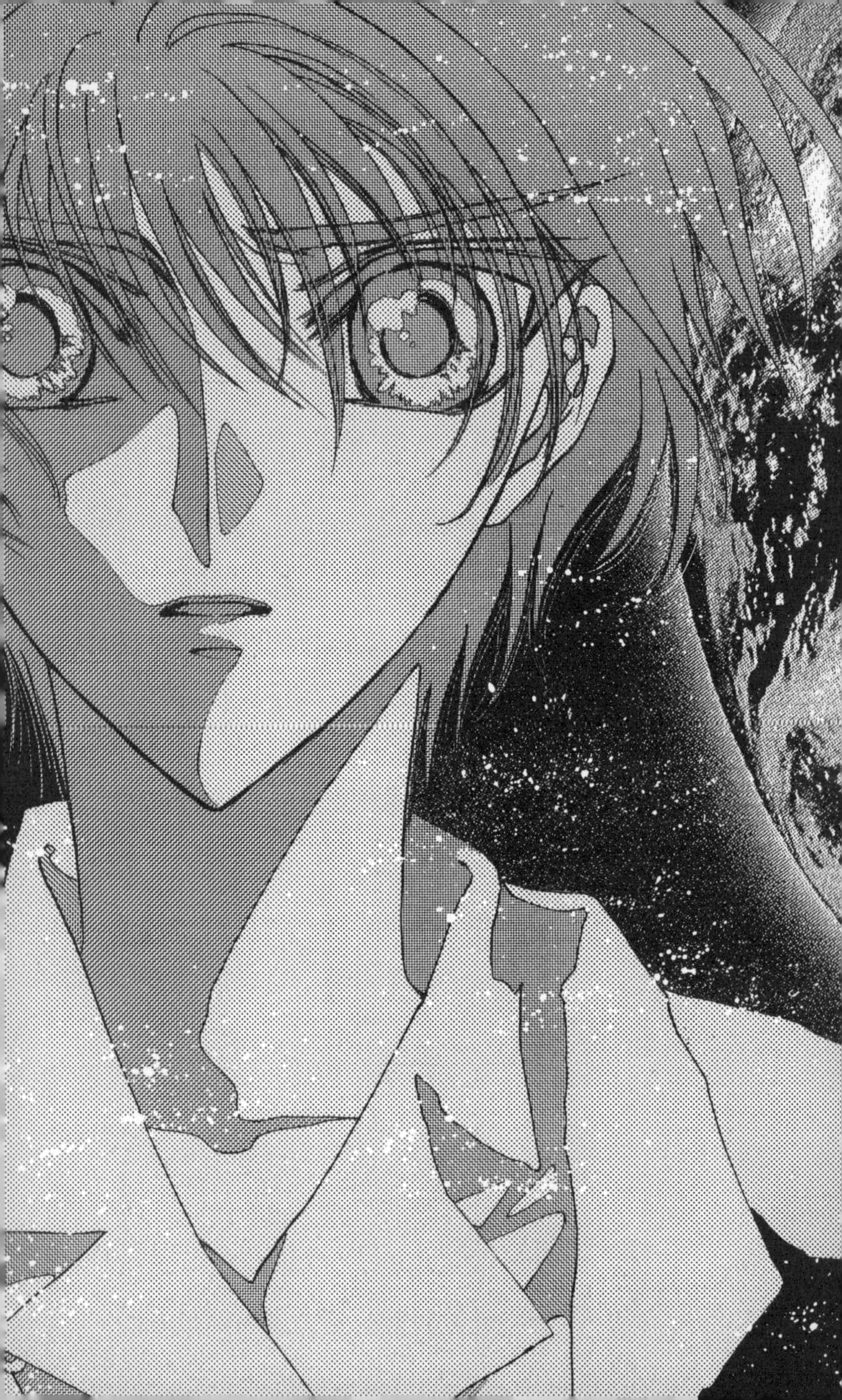

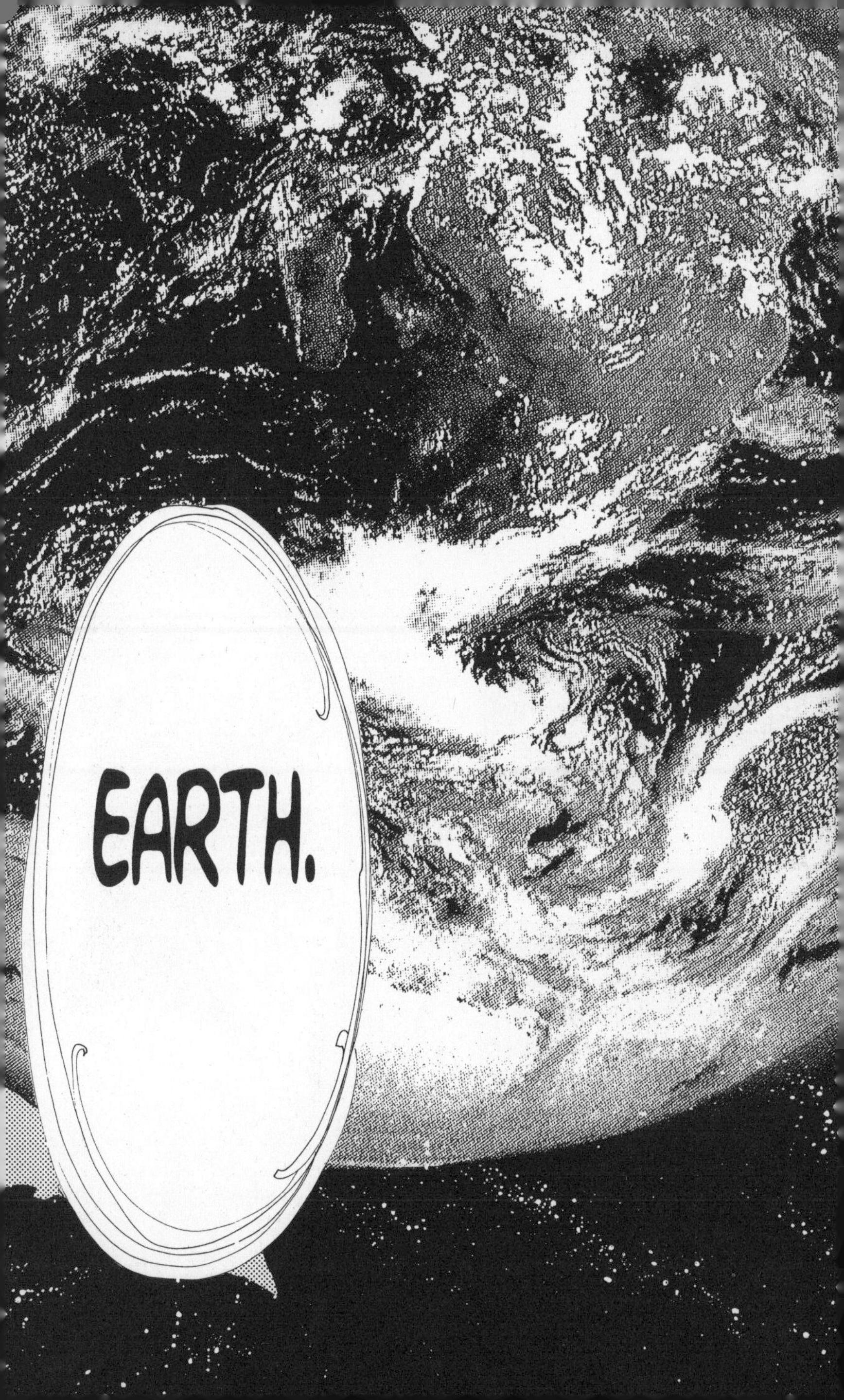
EARTH.

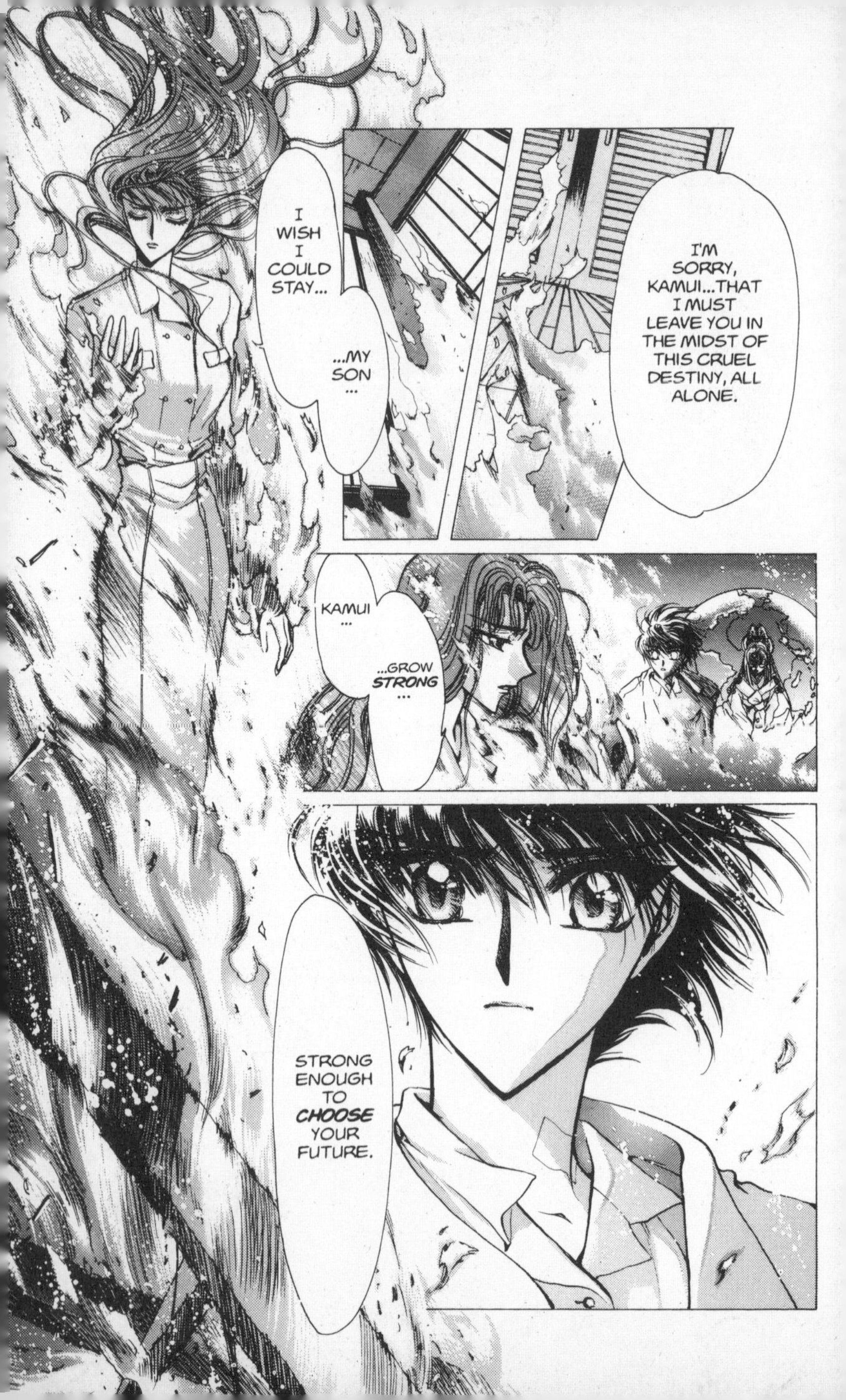
I WISH I COULD STAY...
...MY SON ...
I'M SORRY, KAMUI...THAT I MUST LEAVE YOU IN THE MIDST OF THIS CRUEL DESTINY, ALL ALONE.
KAMUI ...
...GROW **STRONG** ...
STRONG ENOUGH TO **CHOOSE** YOUR FUTURE.

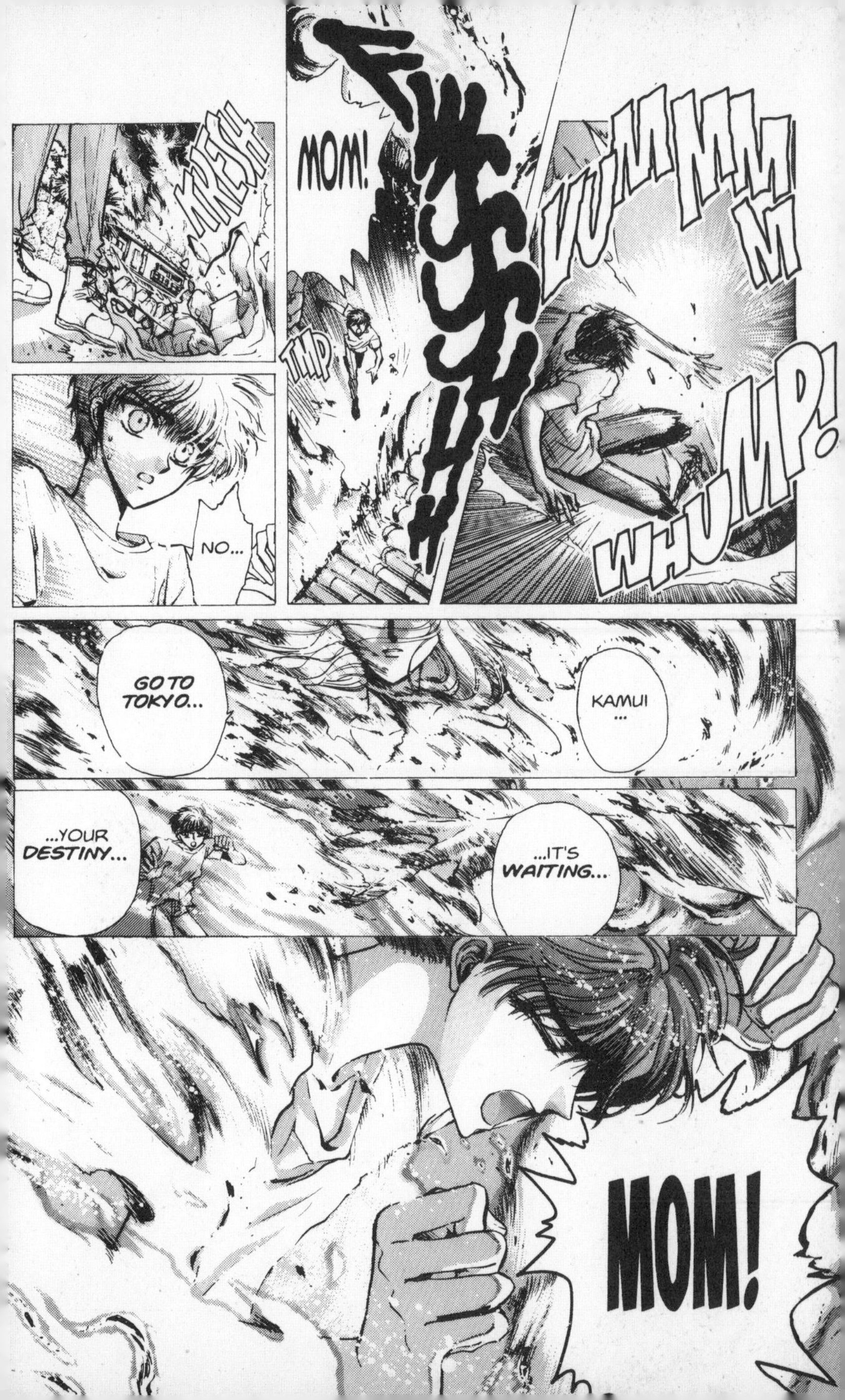
KRESH
NO...
MOM!
TMP
WHUMP!
GO TO TOKYO...
KAMUI ...
...YOUR DESTINY...
...IT'S WAITING...
MOM!

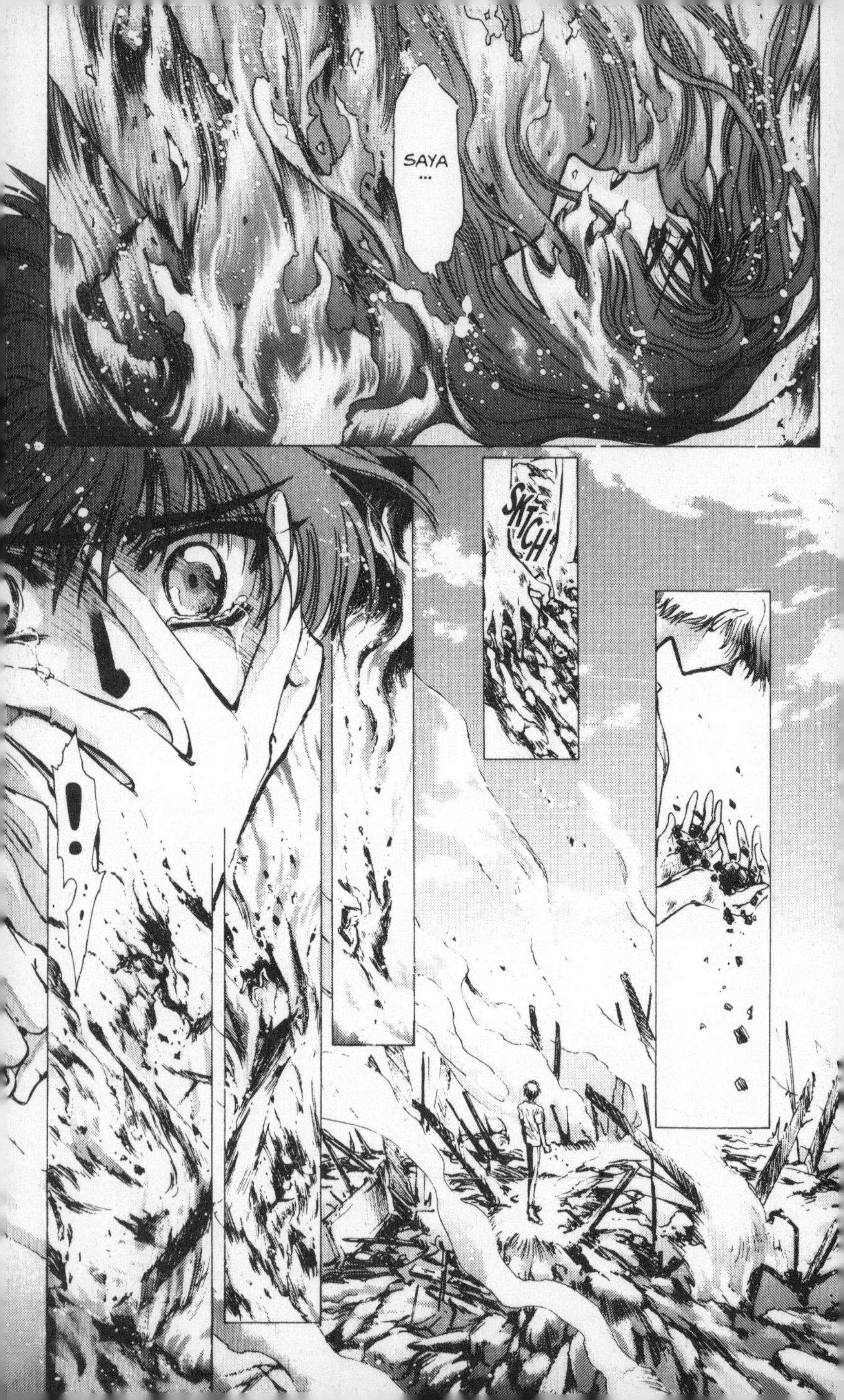
SAYA
...
!
SKTCH

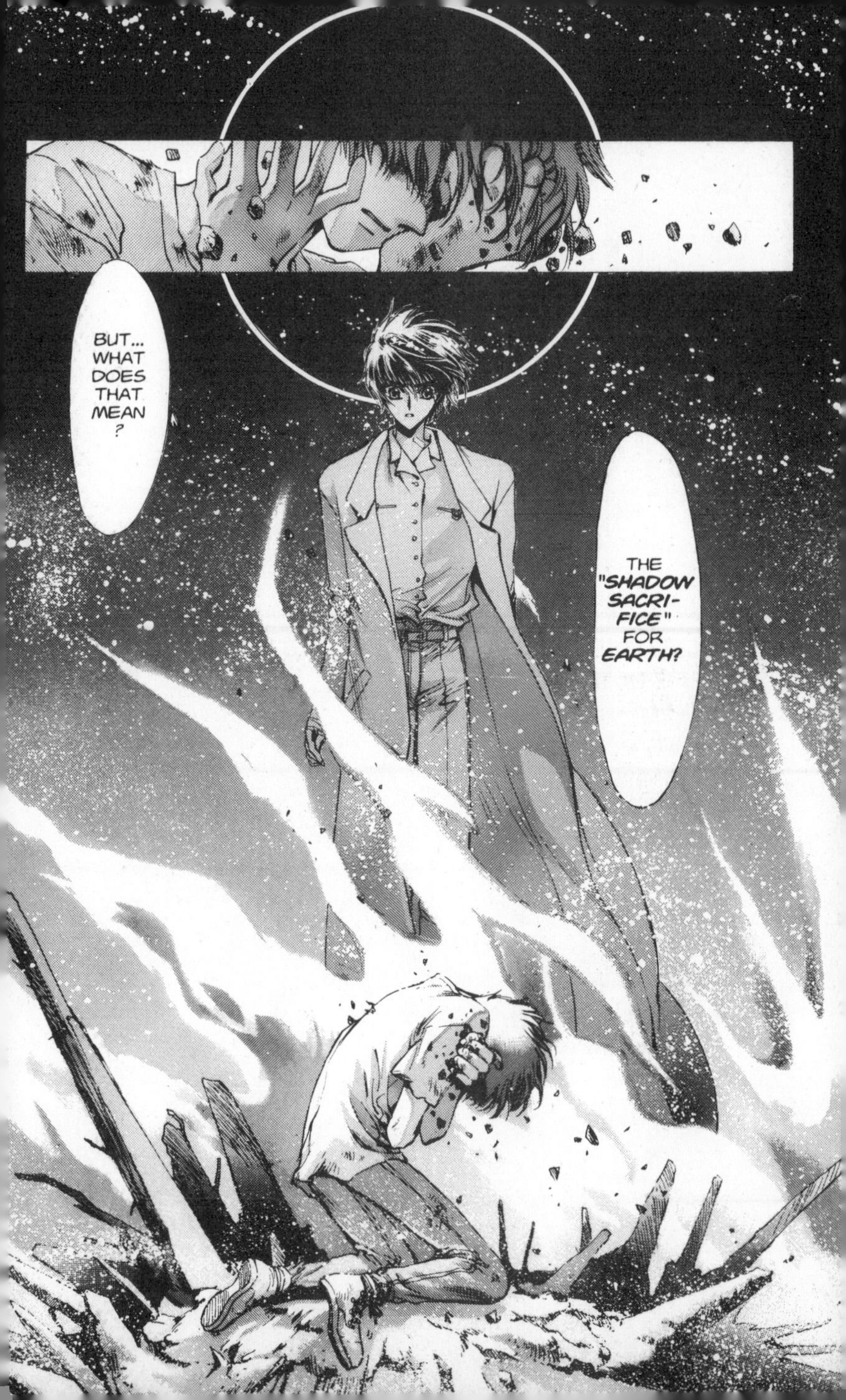
BUT... WHAT DOES THAT MEAN?
THE "SHADOW SACRI-FICE" FOR EARTH?

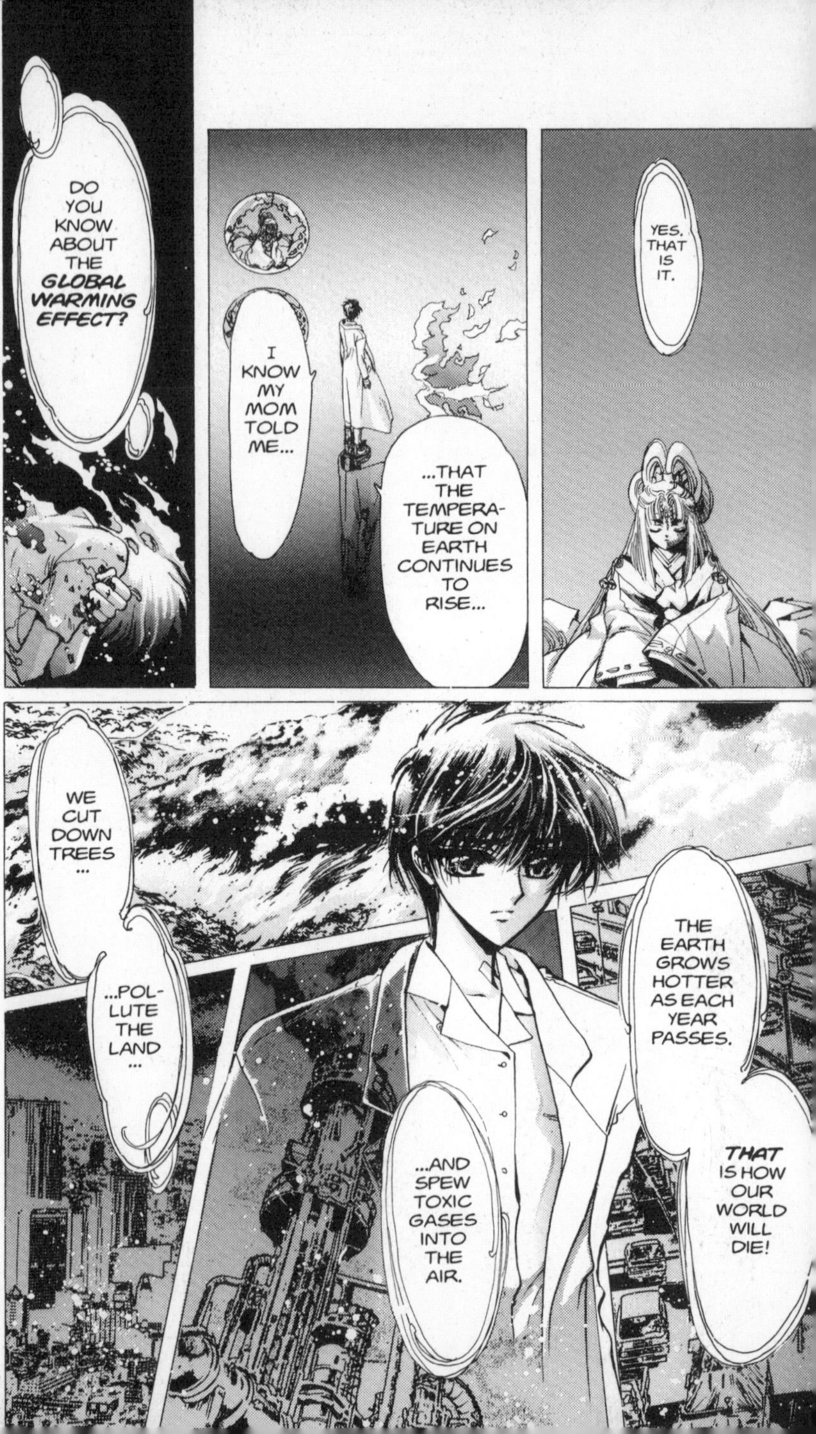
DO YOU KNOW ABOUT THE ***GLOBAL WARMING EFFECT?***
I KNOW MY MOM TOLD ME...
...THAT THE TEMPERA-TURE ON EARTH CONTINUES TO RISE...
YES, THAT IS IT.
WE CUT DOWN TREES ...
...POL-LUTE THE LAND ...
...AND SPEW TOXIC GASES INTO THE AIR.
THE EARTH GROWS HOTTER AS EACH YEAR PASSES.
THAT IS HOW OUR WORLD WILL DIE!

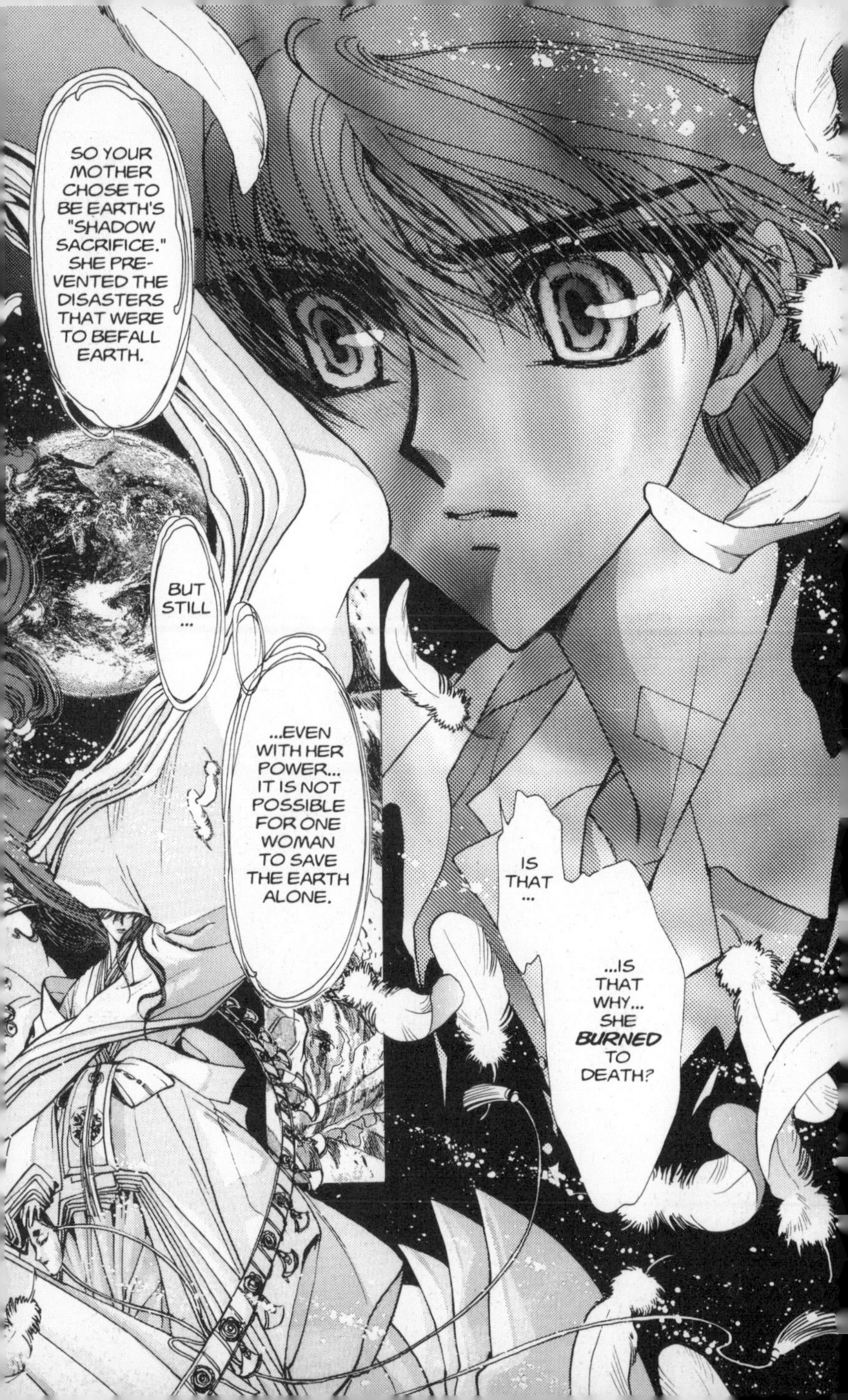
SO YOUR MOTHER CHOSE TO BE EARTH'S "SHADOW SACRIFICE." SHE PRE-VENTED THE DISASTERS THAT WERE TO BEFALL EARTH.
BUT STILL ...
...EVEN WITH HER POWER... IT IS NOT POSSIBLE FOR ONE WOMAN TO SAVE THE EARTH ALONE.
IS THAT ...
...IS THAT WHY... SHE **BURNED** TO DEATH?

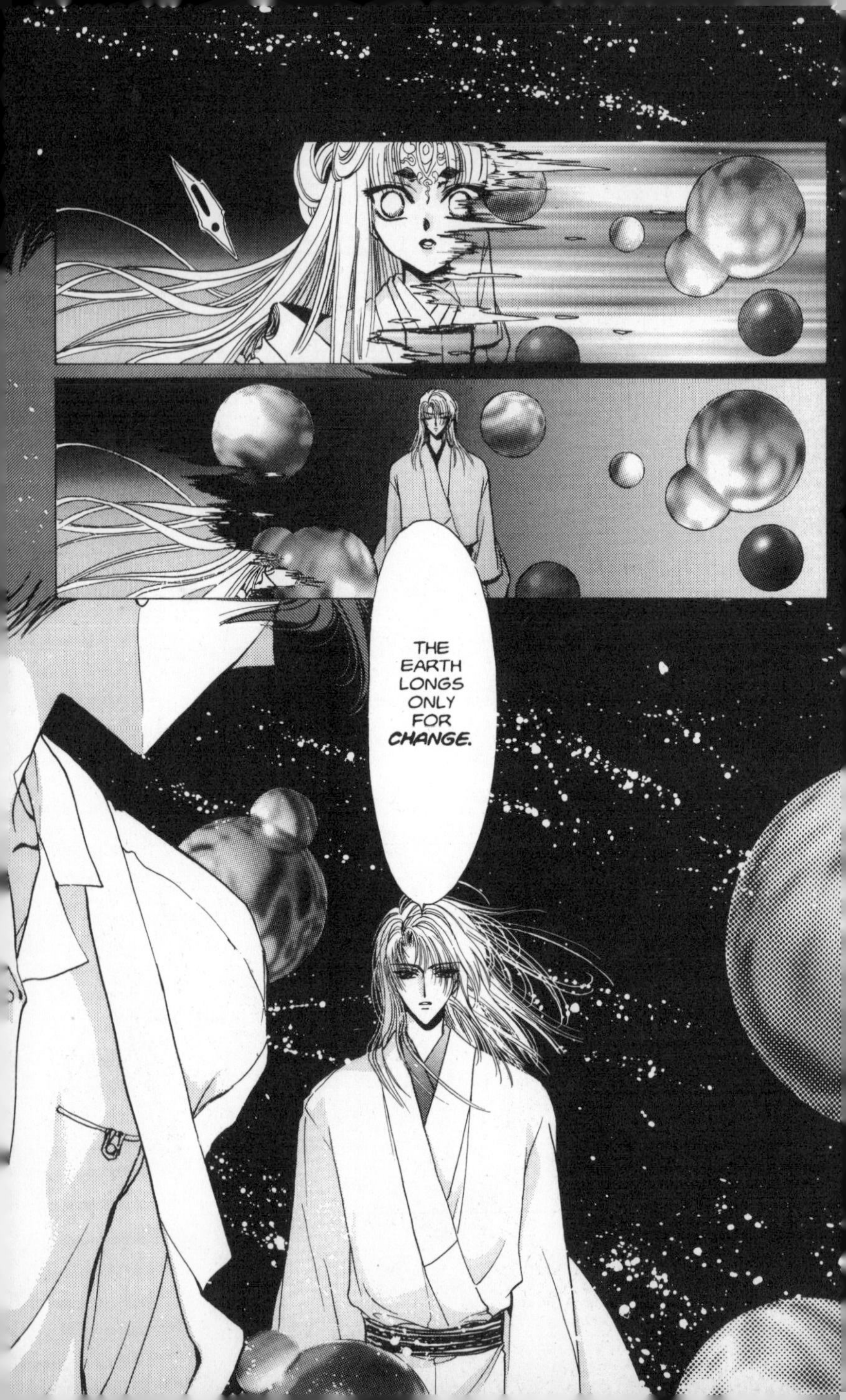
THE EARTH LONGS ONLY FOR CHANGE.

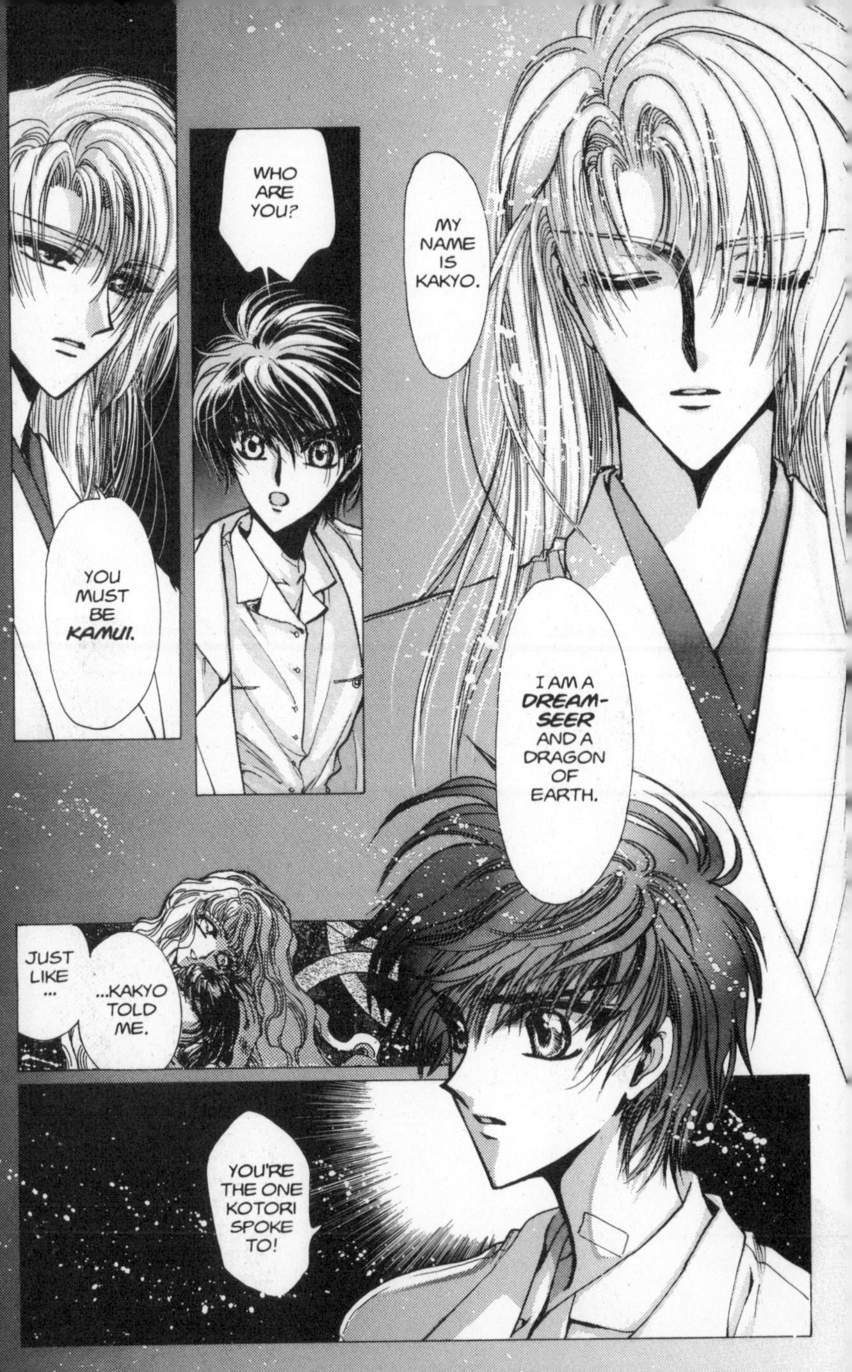
YOU MUST BE *KAMUI.*
WHO ARE YOU?
MY NAME IS KAKYO.
I AM A *DREAM-SEER* AND A DRAGON OF EARTH.
JUST LIKE ...
...KAKYO TOLD ME.
YOU'RE THE ONE KOTORI SPOKE TO!

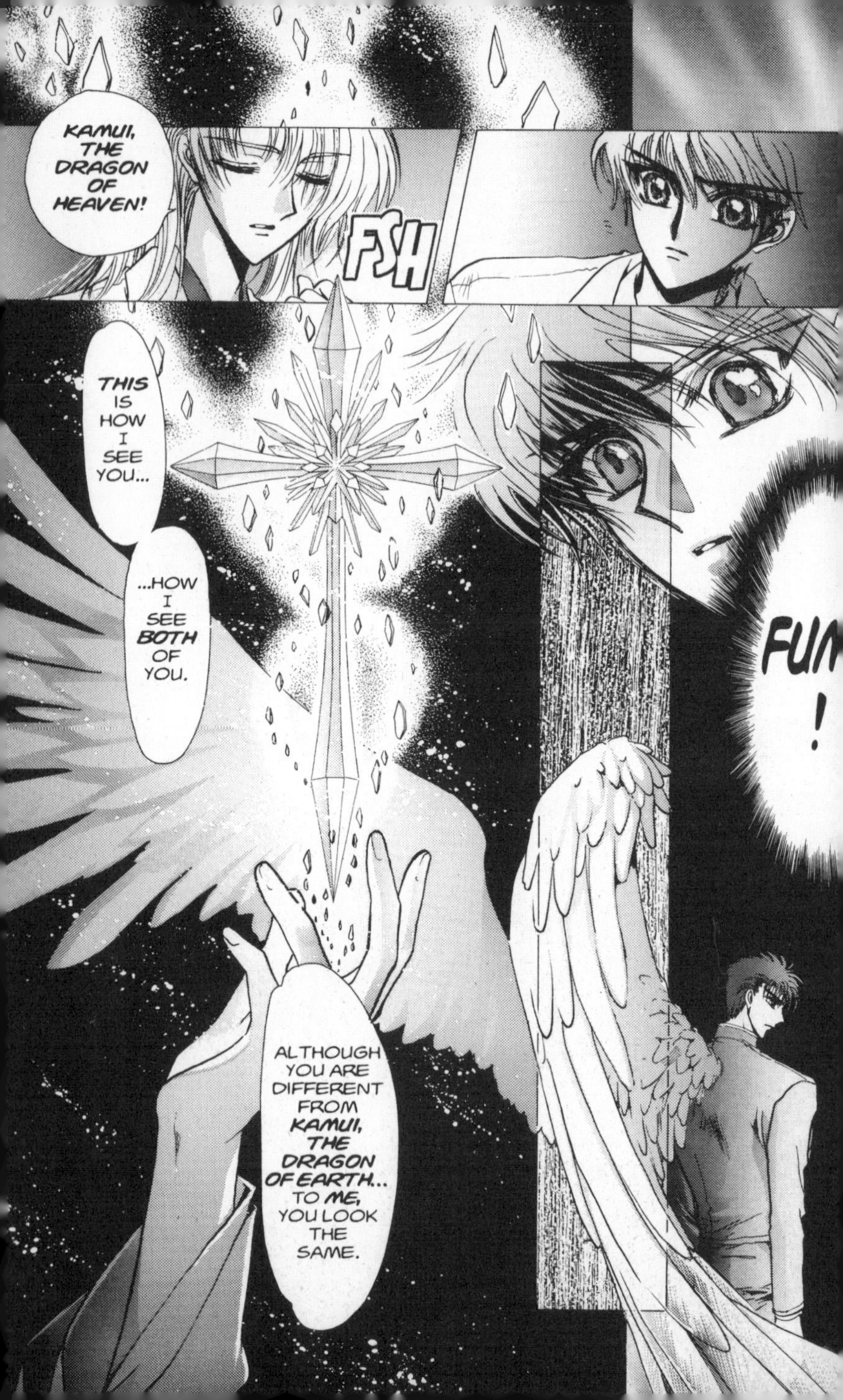
KAMUI, THE DRAGON OF HEAVEN!
FSH
THIS IS HOW I SEE YOU...
...HOW I SEE BOTH OF YOU.
FUN !
ALTHOUGH YOU ARE DIFFERENT FROM KAMUI, THE DRAGON OF EARTH... TO ME, YOU LOOK THE SAME.

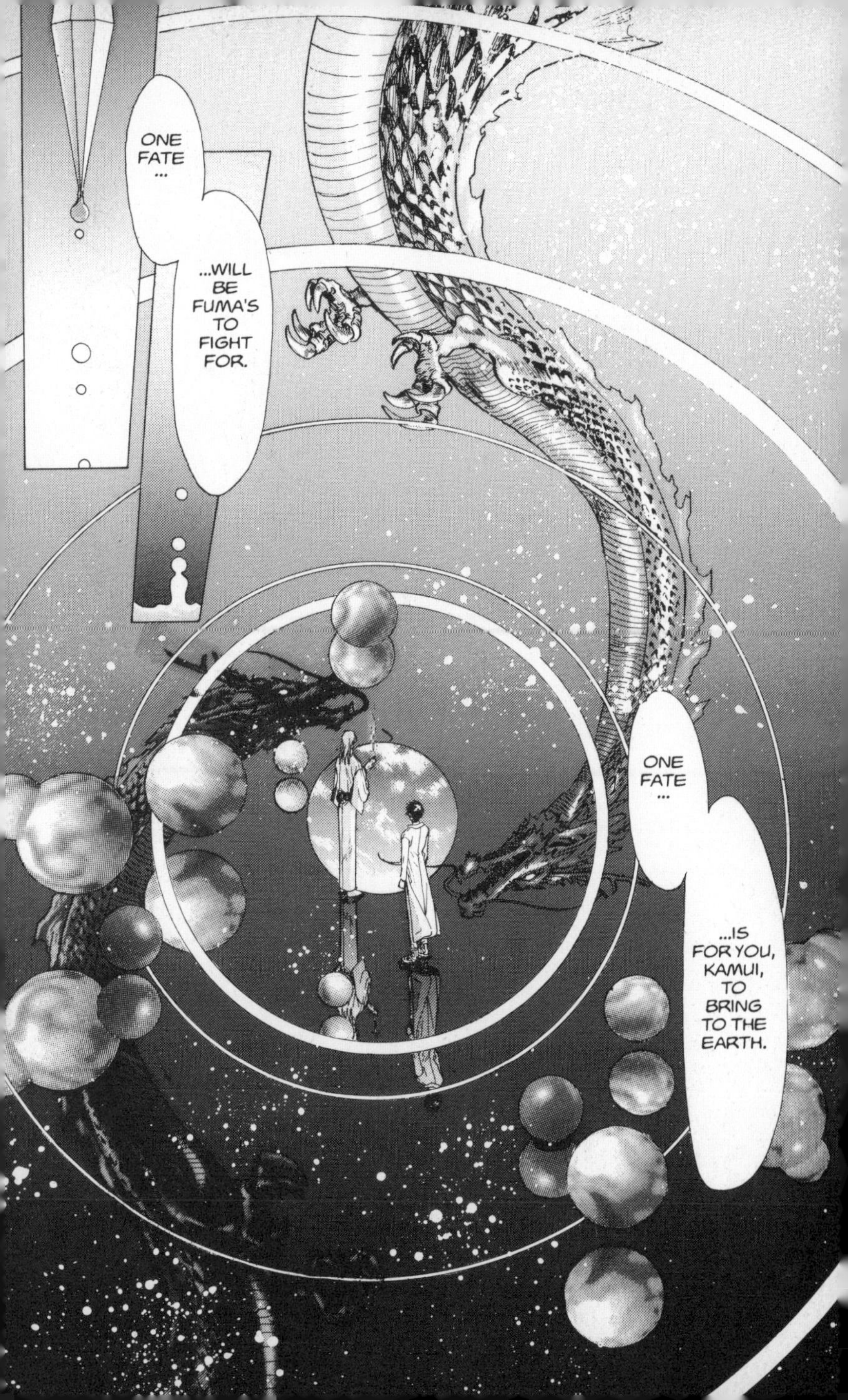
ONE FATE ...
...WILL BE FUMA'S TO FIGHT FOR.
ONE FATE ...
...IS FOR YOU, KAMUI, TO BRING TO THE EARTH.

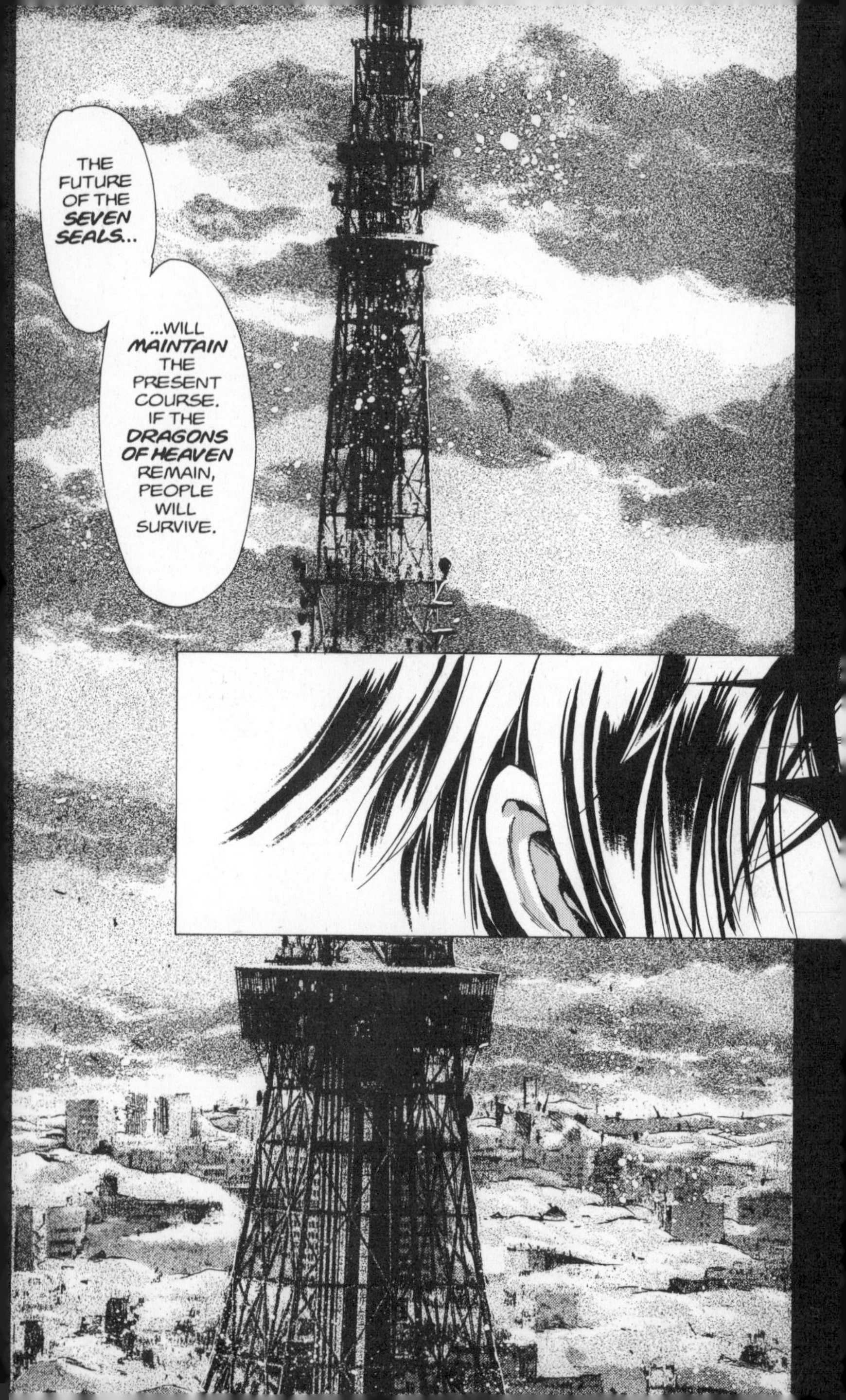
THE FUTURE OF THE SEVEN SEALS...
...WILL MAINTAIN THE PRESENT COURSE. IF THE DRAGONS OF HEAVEN REMAIN, PEOPLE WILL SURVIVE.

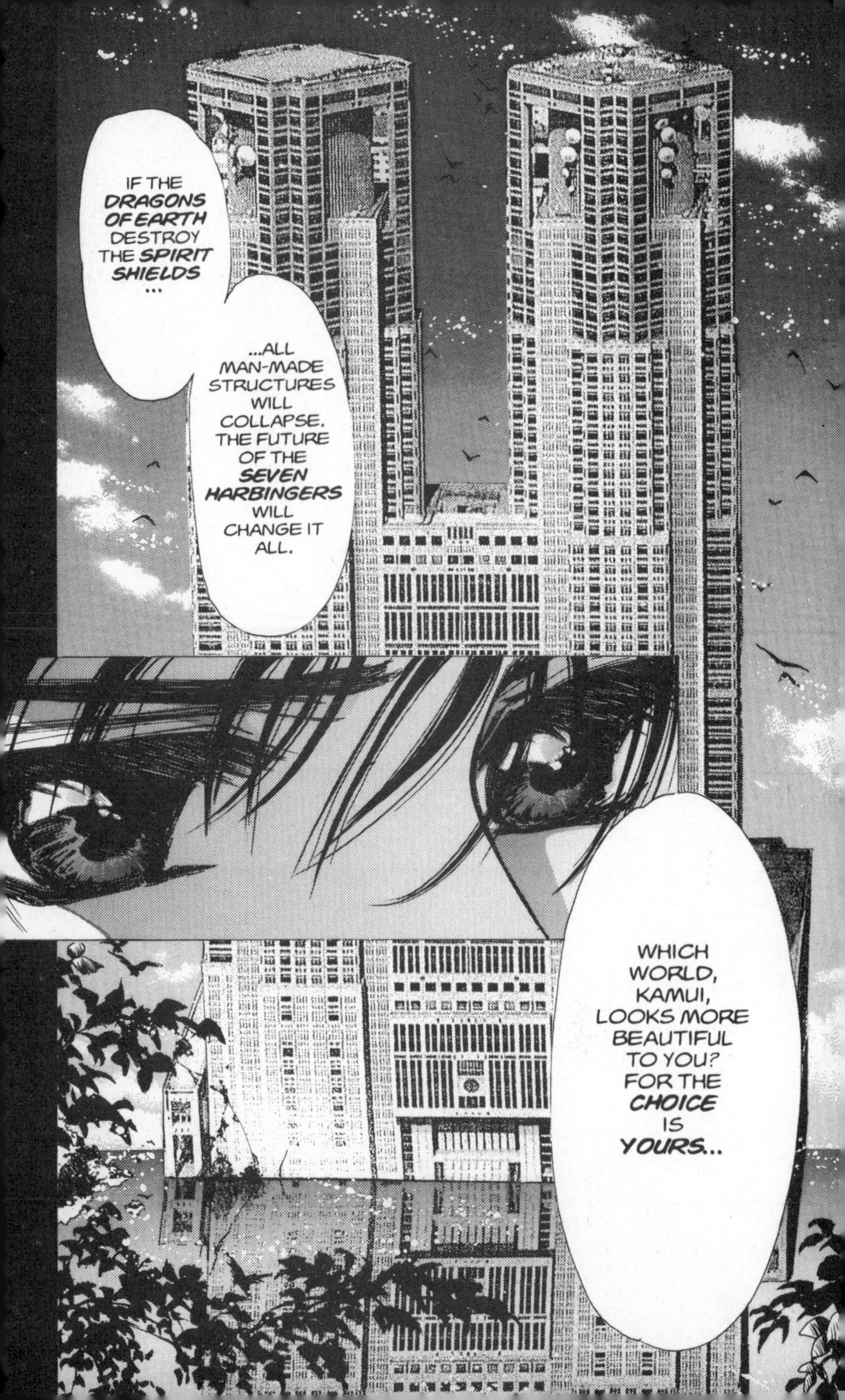
IF THE DRAGONS OF EARTH DESTROY THE SPIRIT SHIELDS ...
...ALL MAN-MADE STRUCTURES WILL COLLAPSE. THE FUTURE OF THE SEVEN HARBINGERS WILL CHANGE IT ALL.
WHICH WORLD, KAMUI, LOOKS MORE BEAUTIFUL TO YOU? FOR THE CHOICE IS YOURS...

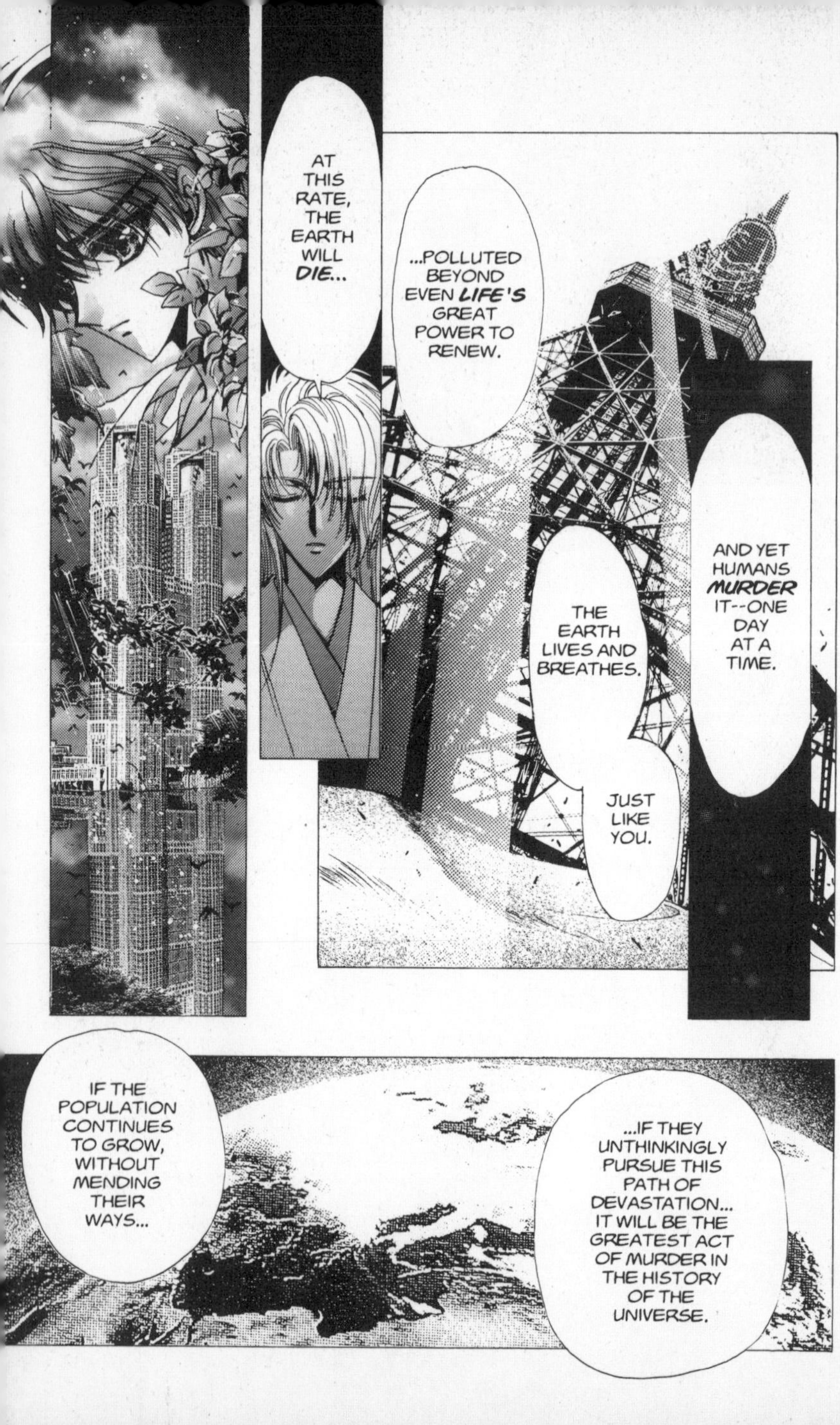
AT THIS RATE, THE EARTH WILL *DIE*...
...POLLUTED BEYOND EVEN *LIFE'S* GREAT POWER TO RENEW.
THE EARTH LIVES AND BREATHES.
JUST LIKE YOU.
AND YET HUMANS *MURDER* IT--ONE DAY AT A TIME.
IF THE POPULATION CONTINUES TO GROW, WITHOUT MENDING THEIR WAYS...
...IF THEY UNTHINKINGLY PURSUE THIS PATH OF DEVASTATION... IT WILL BE THE GREATEST ACT OF MURDER IN THE HISTORY OF THE UNIVERSE.

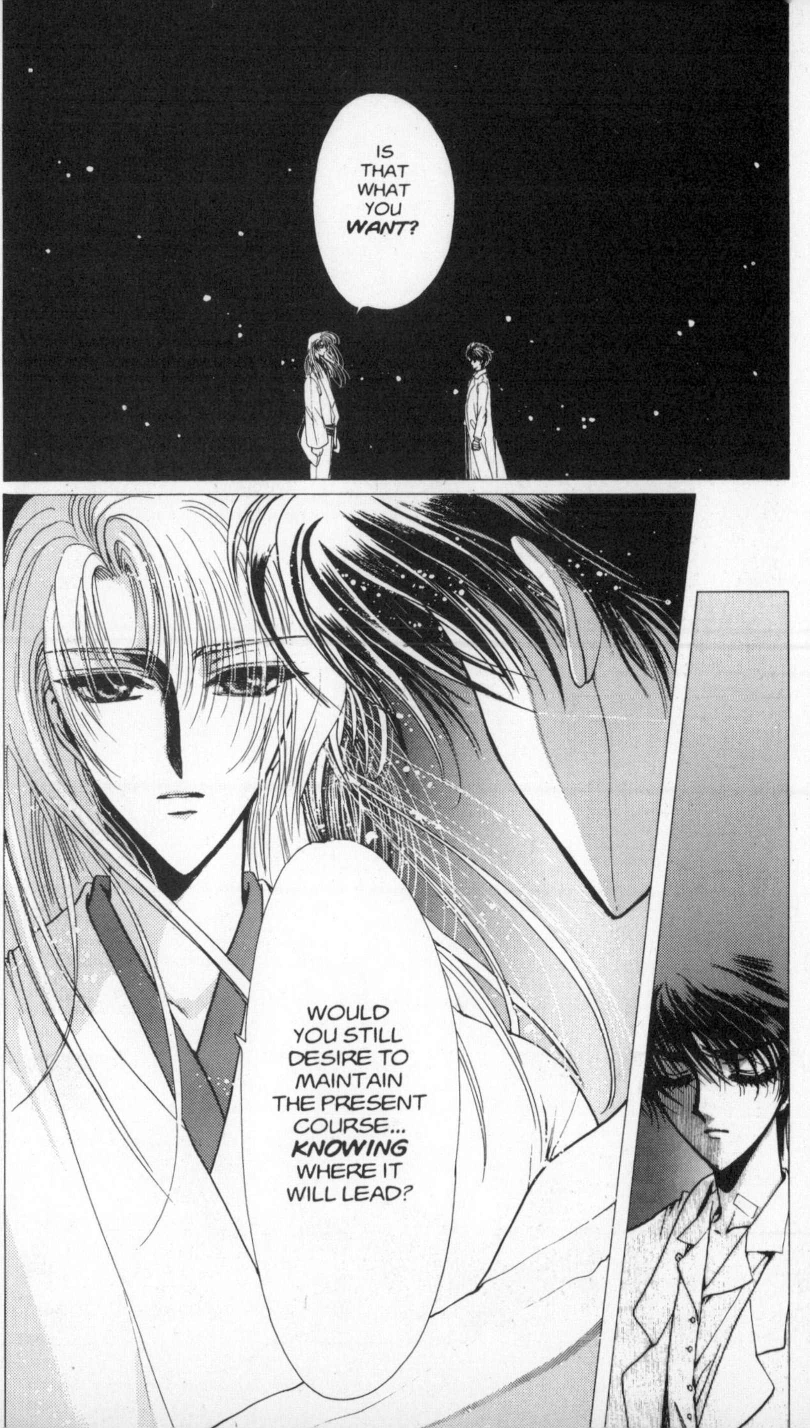
IS THAT WHAT YOU *WANT?*
WOULD YOU STILL DESIRE TO MAINTAIN THE PRESENT COURSE... *KNOWING* WHERE IT WILL LEAD?

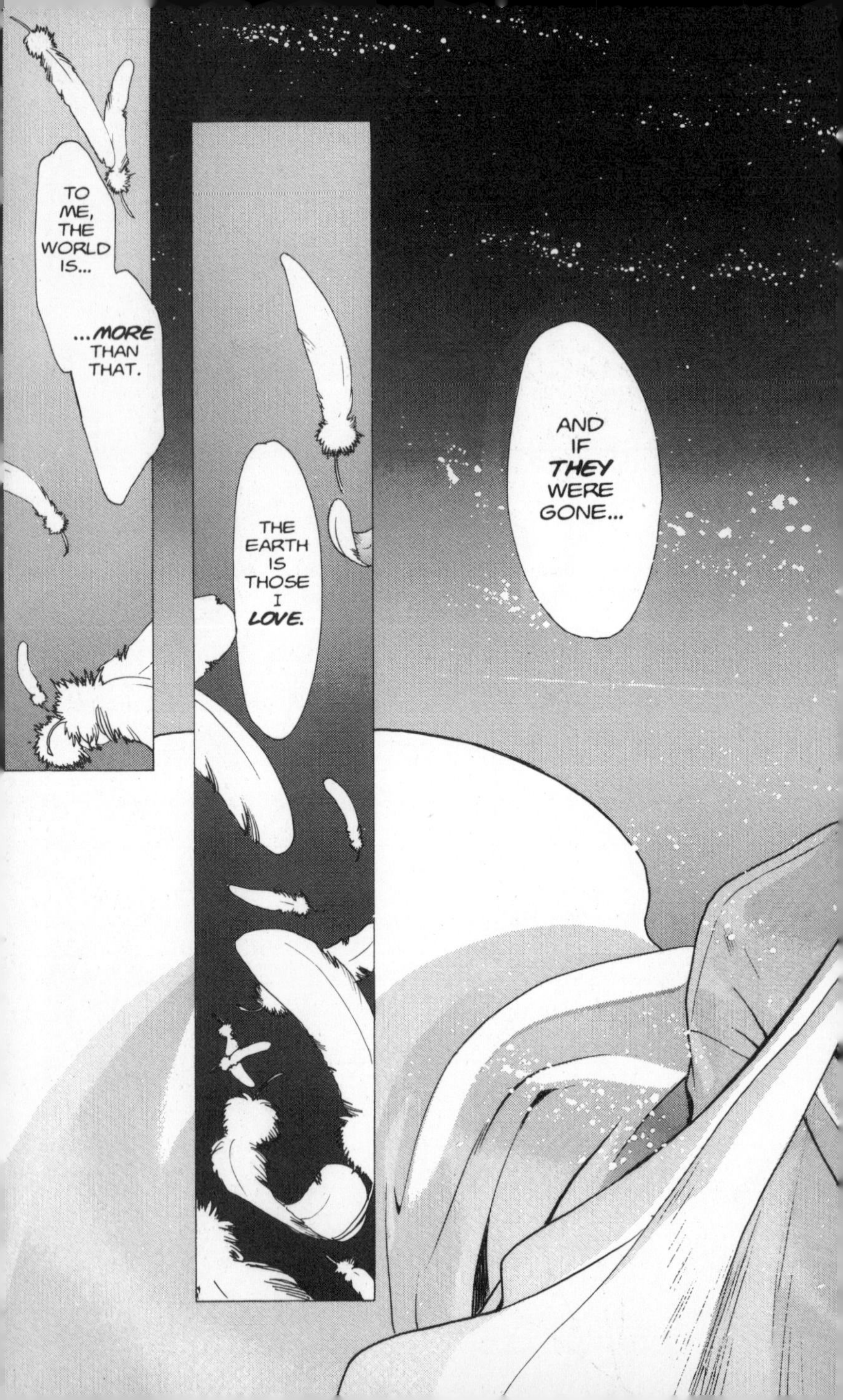
TO ME, THE WORLD IS...
...MORE THAN THAT.
THE EARTH IS THOSE I LOVE.
AND IF THEY WERE GONE...

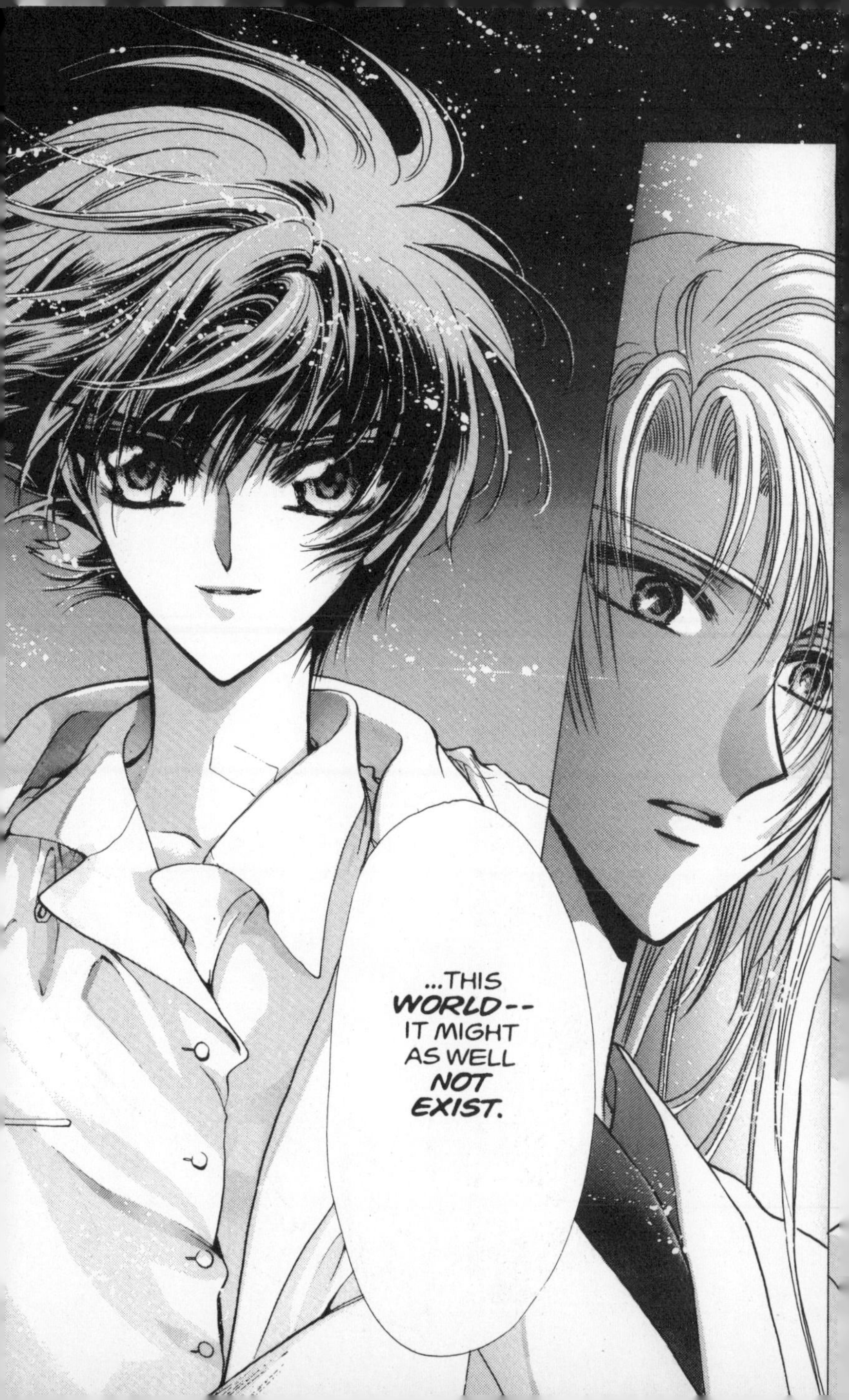
...THIS WORLD-- IT MIGHT AS WELL NOT EXIST.

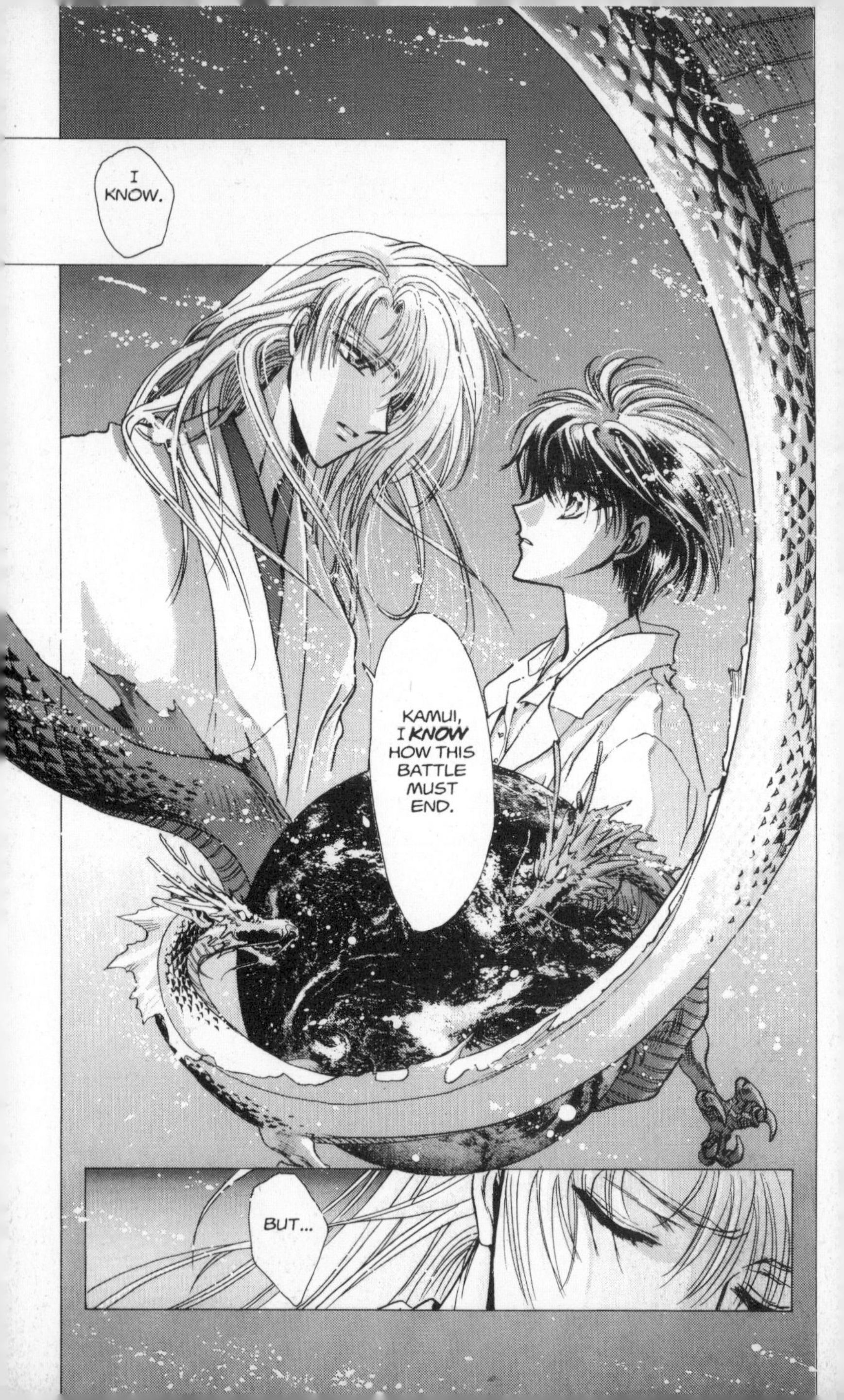
I KNOW.
KAMUI, I **KNOW** HOW THIS BATTLE MUST END.
BUT...

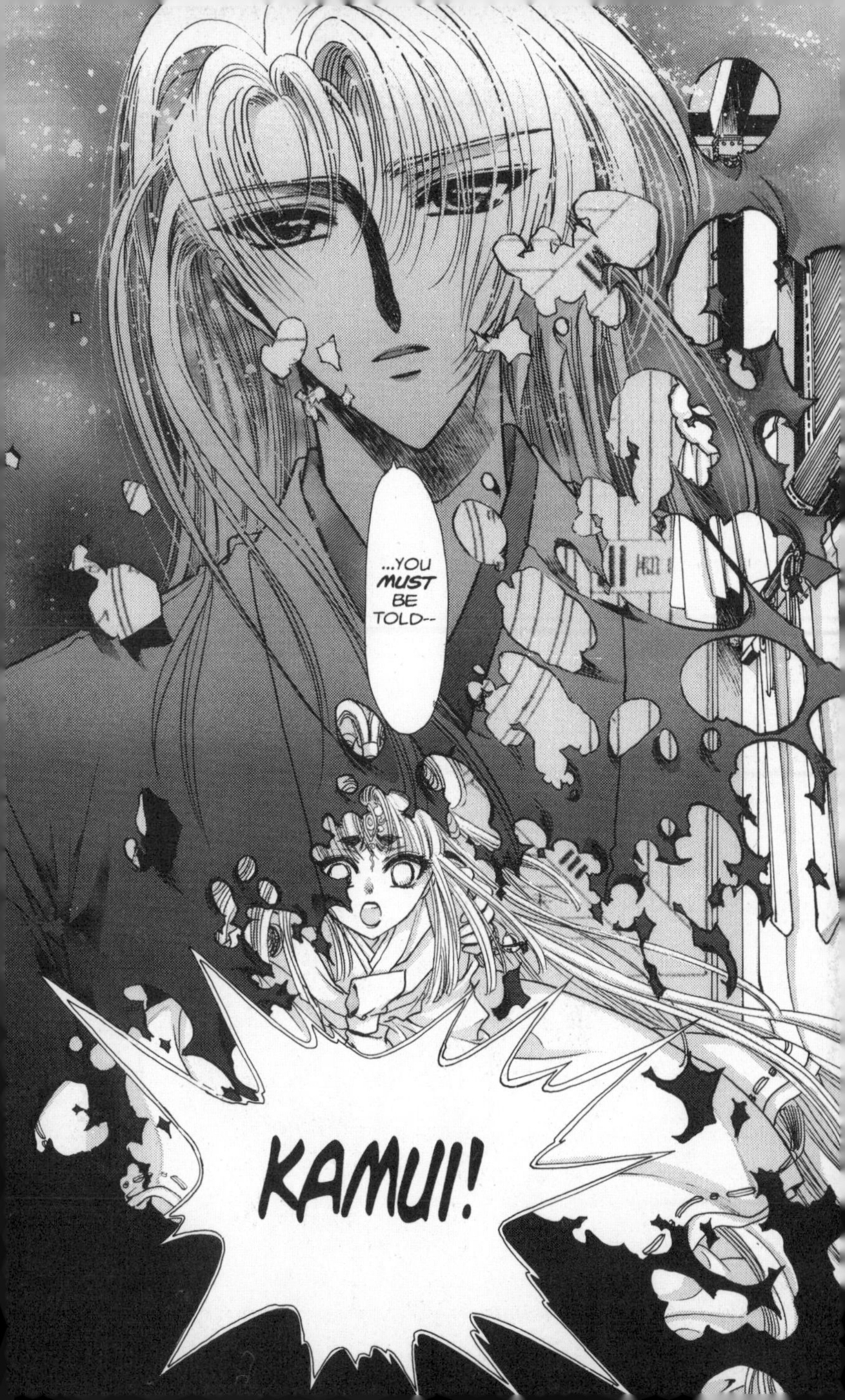
...YOU *MUST* BE TOLD--
KAMUI!

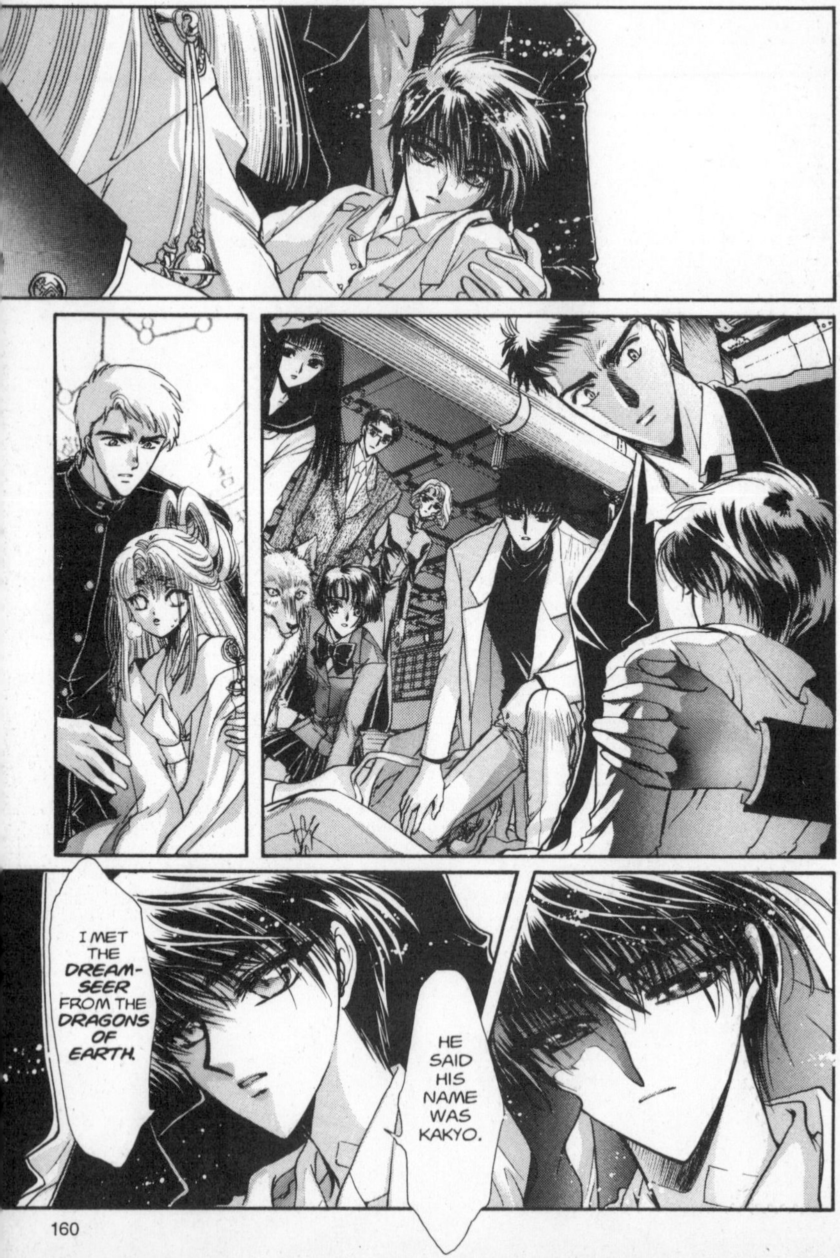
I MET THE DREAM-SEER FROM THE DRAGONS OF EARTH.
HE SAID HIS NAME WAS KAKYO.

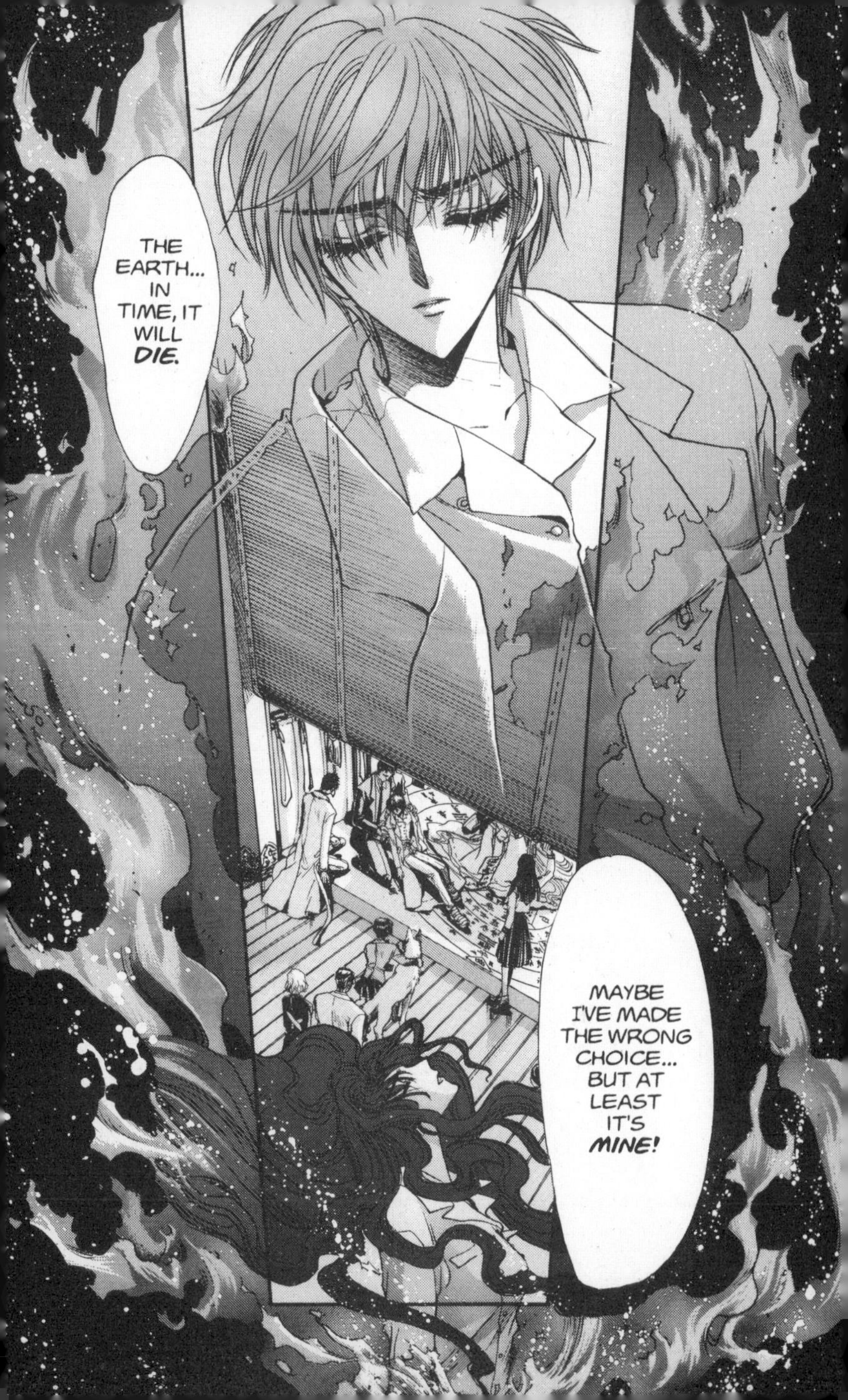
THE EARTH... IN TIME, IT WILL DIE.
MAYBE I'VE MADE THE WRONG CHOICE... BUT AT LEAST IT'S MINE!

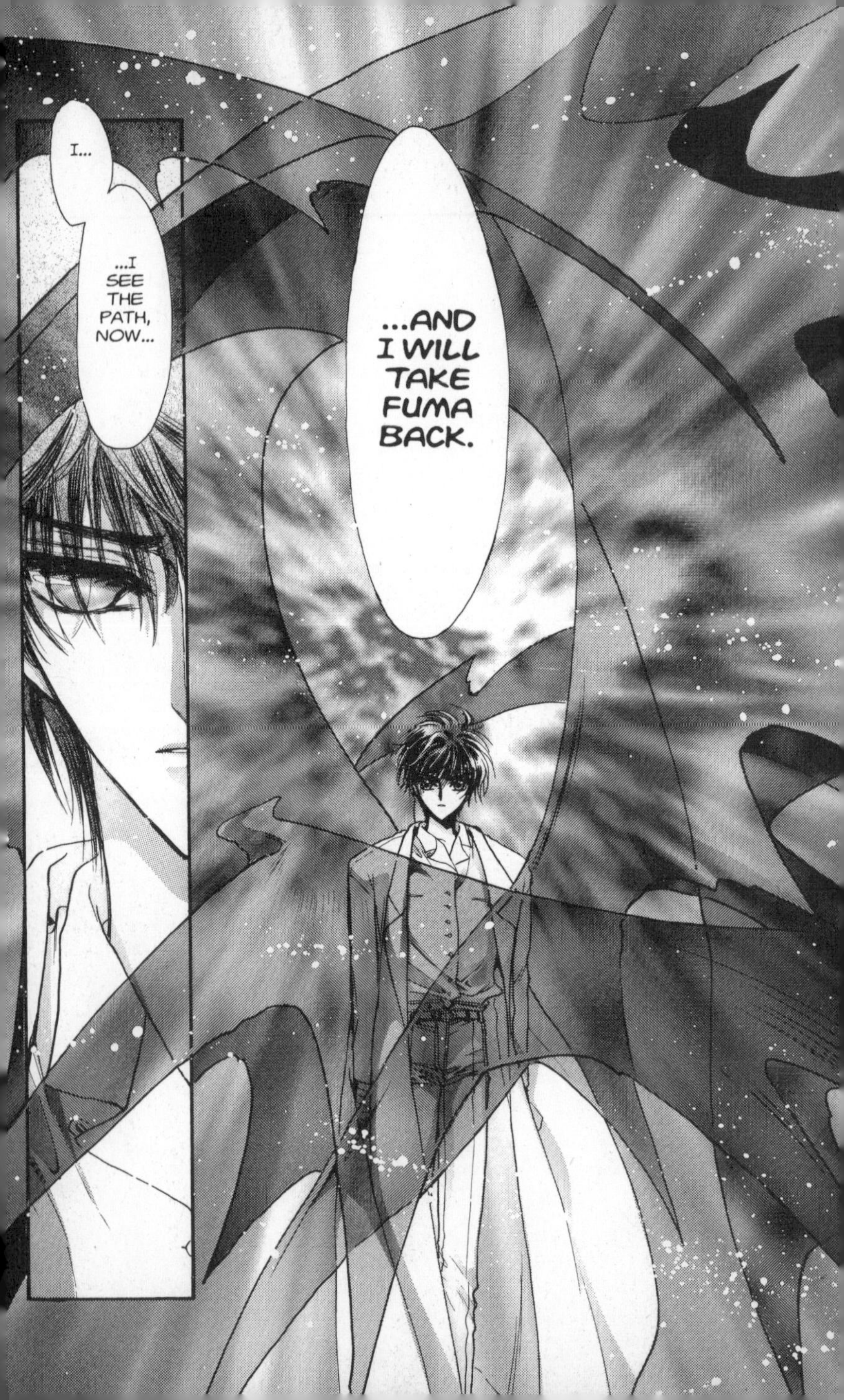
I...
...I SEE THE PATH, NOW...
...AND I WILL TAKE FUMA BACK.

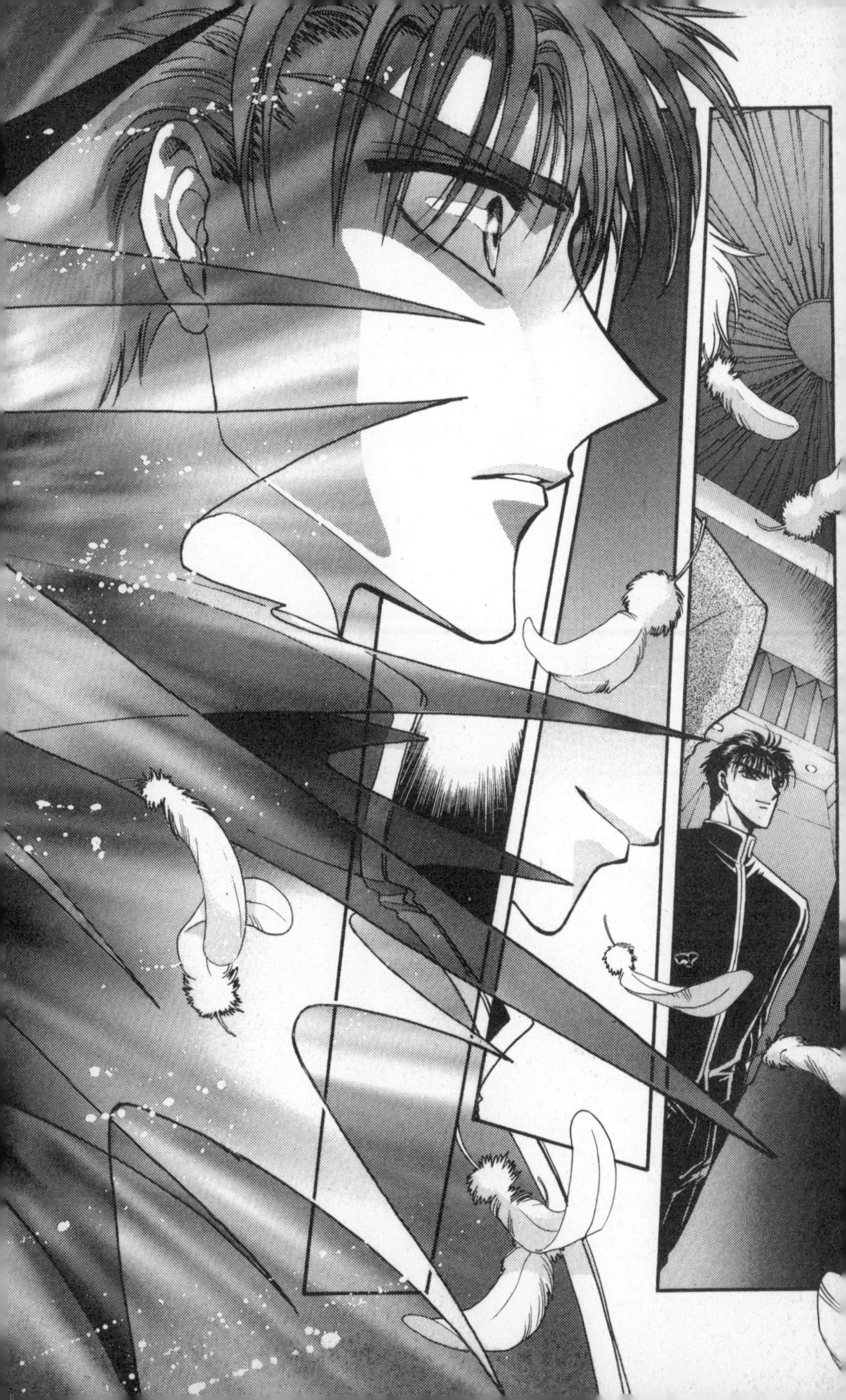

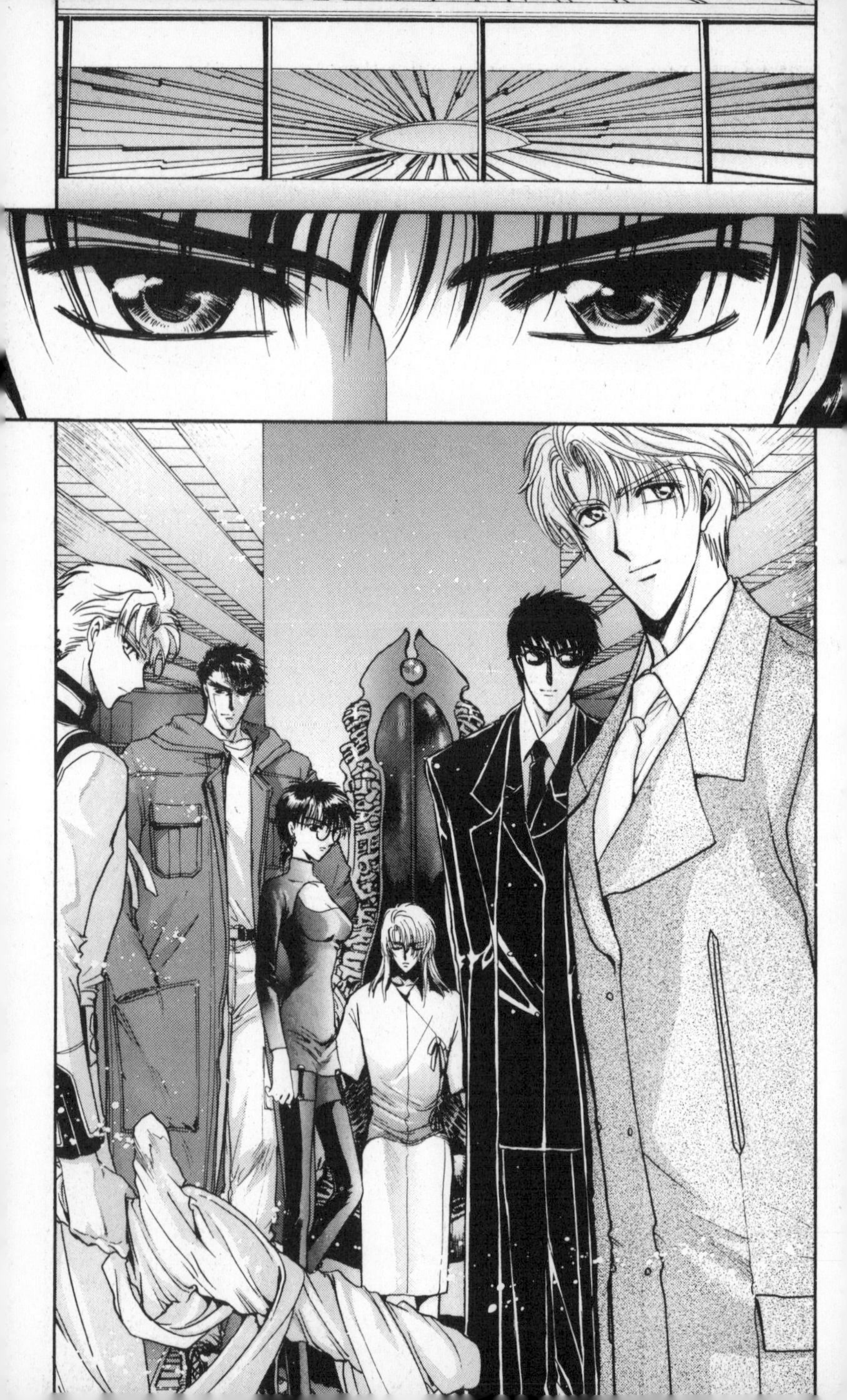

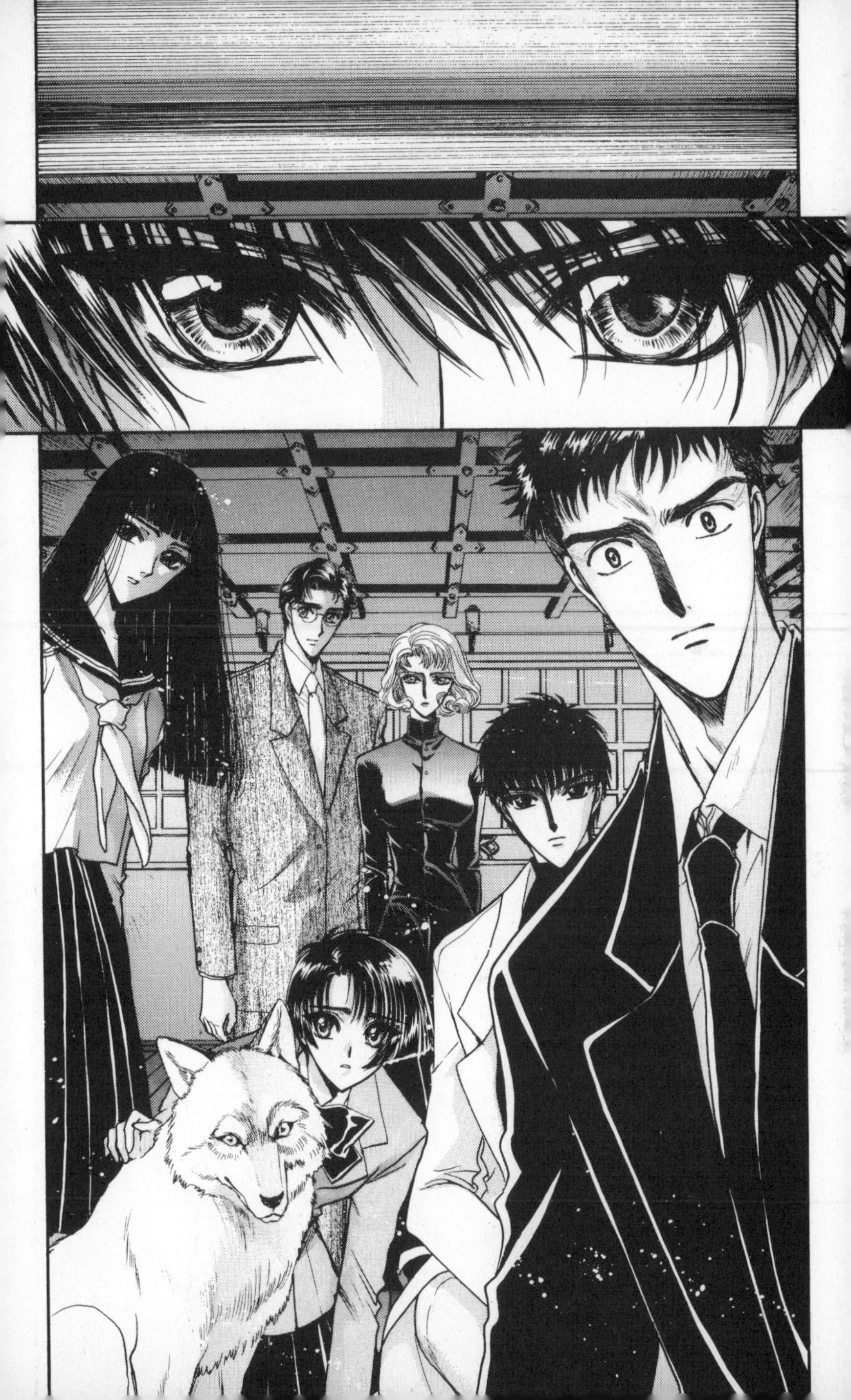

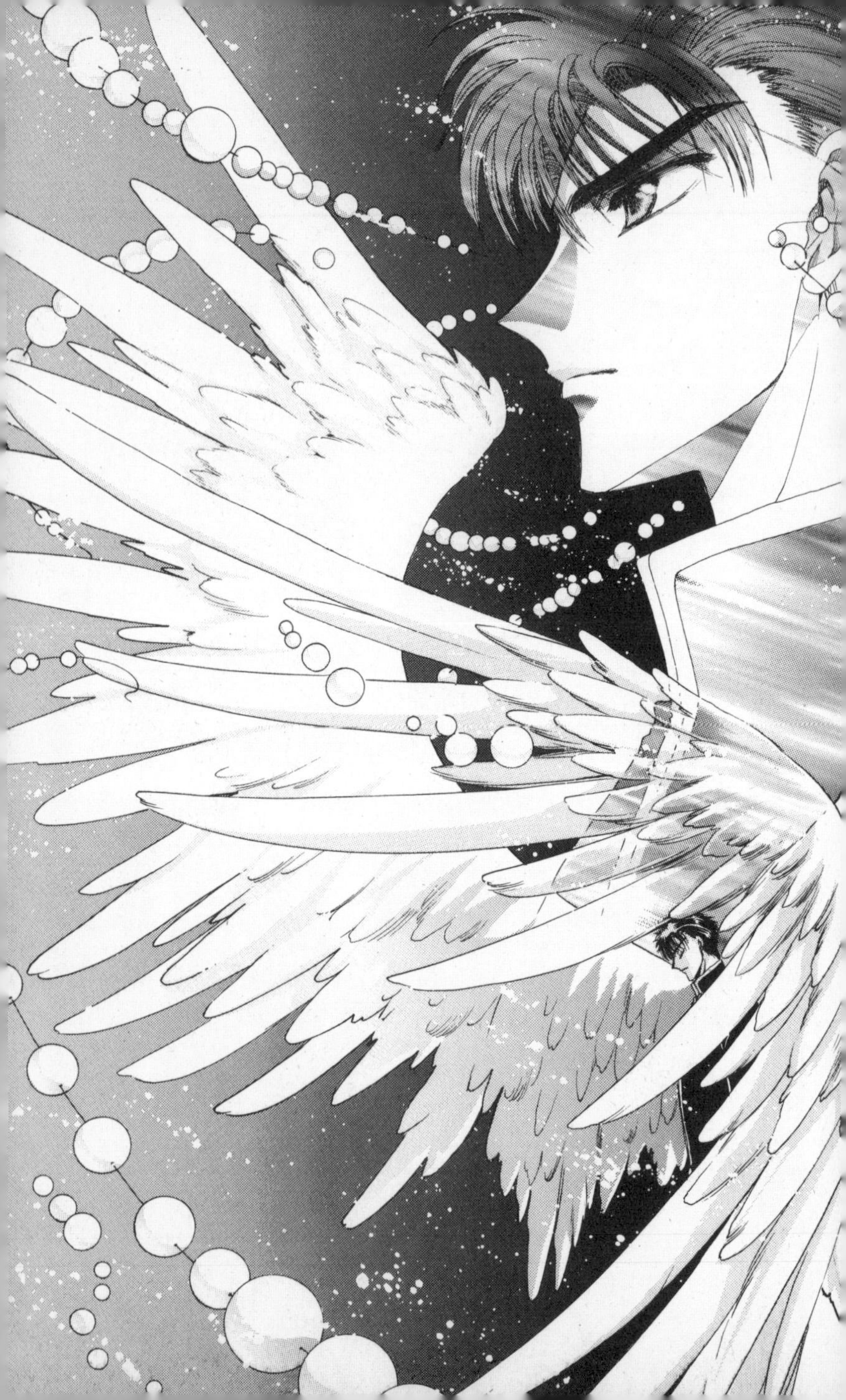

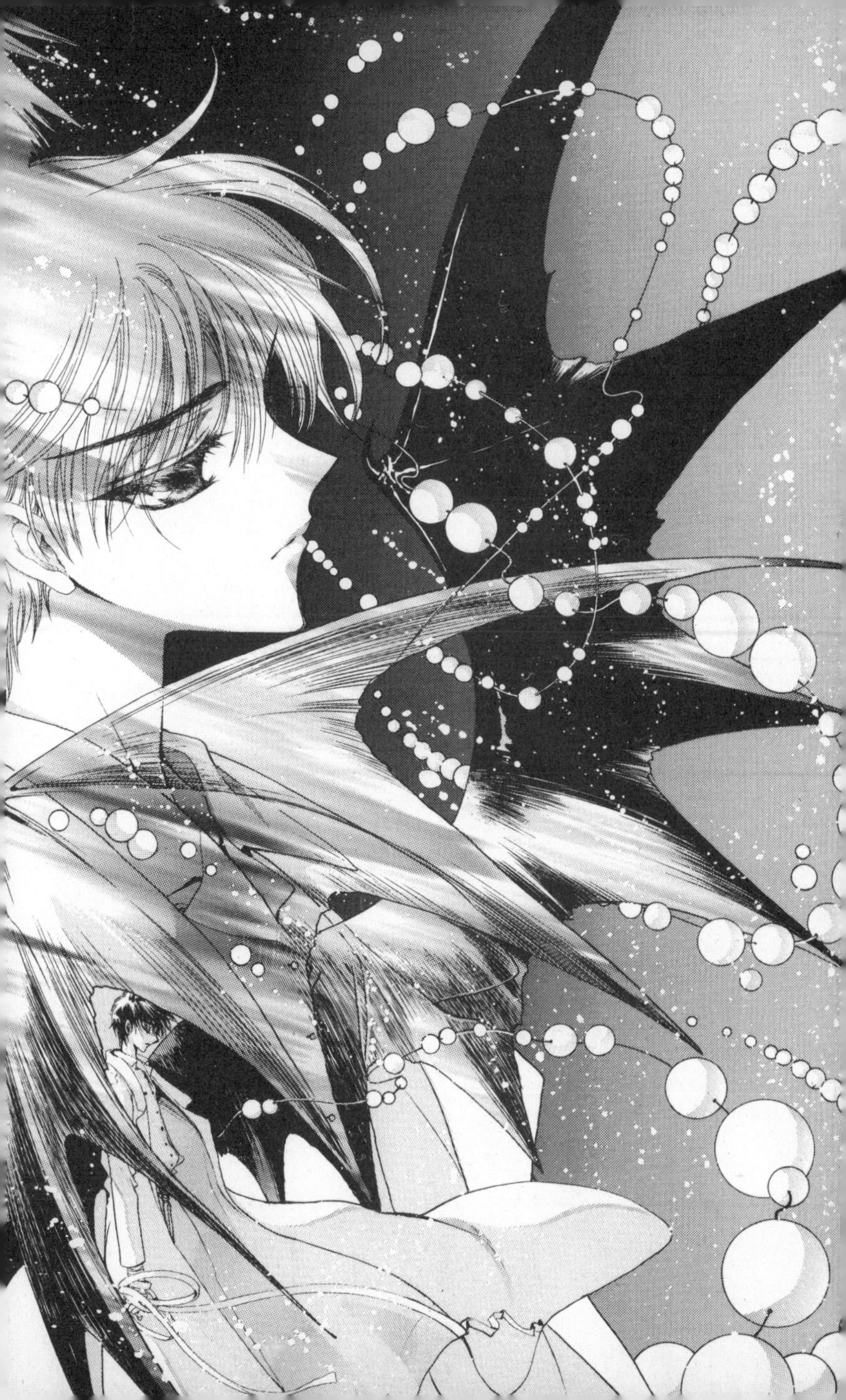

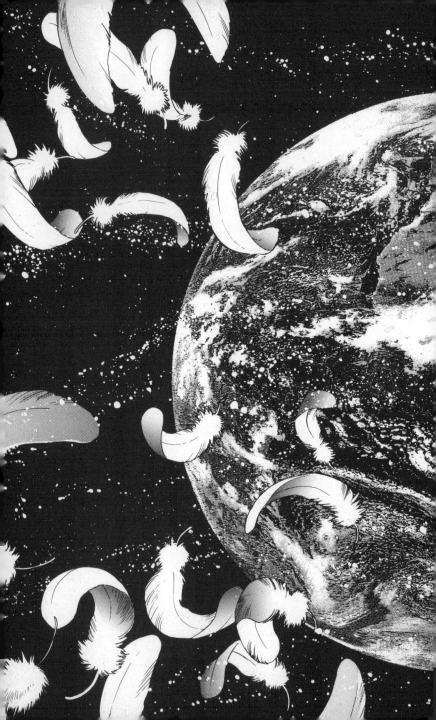

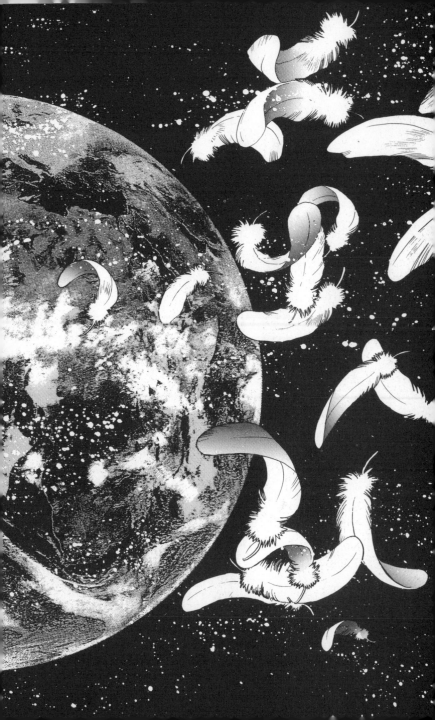

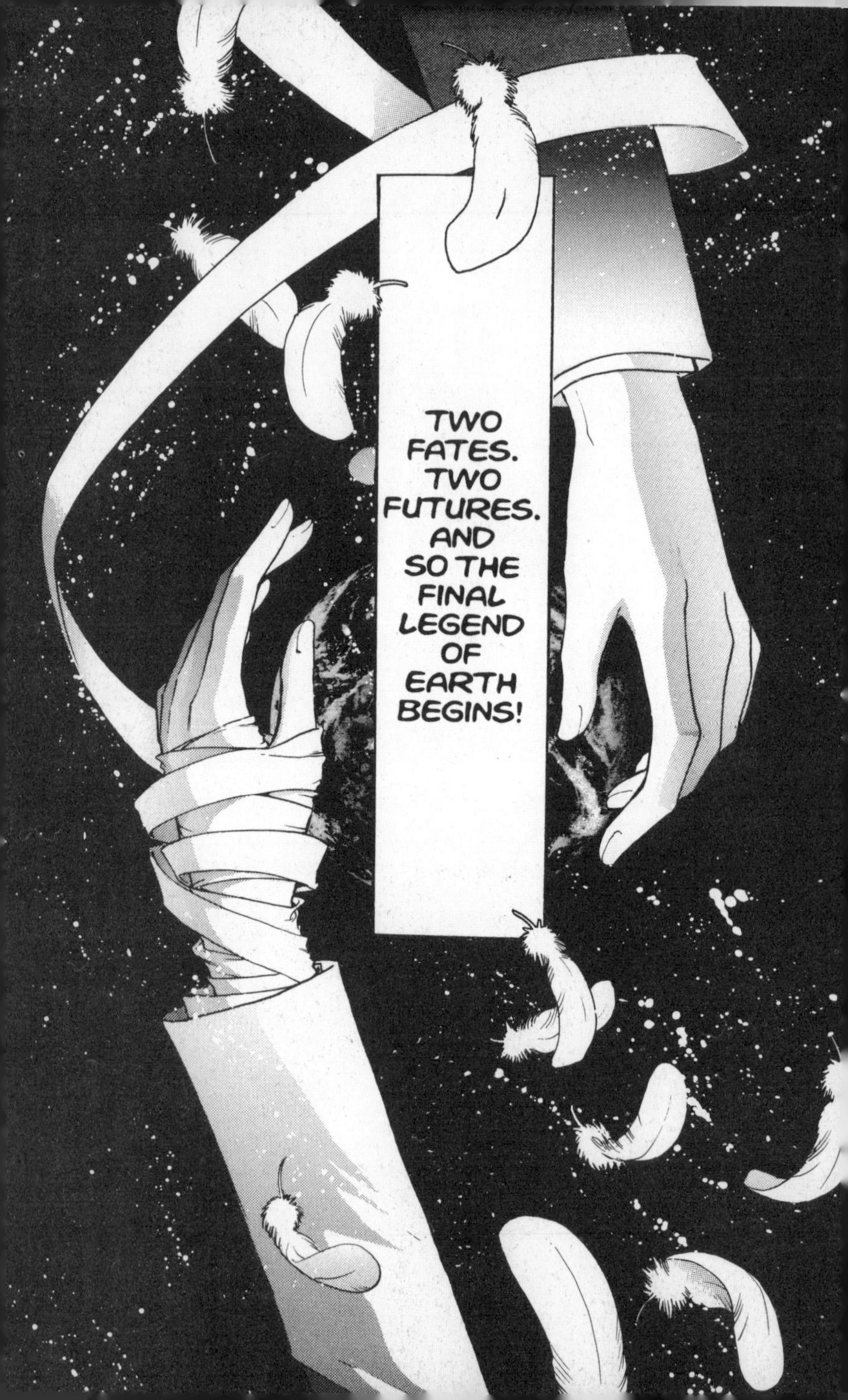
TWO FATES. TWO FUTURES. AND SO THE FINAL LEGEND OF EARTH BEGINS!

X

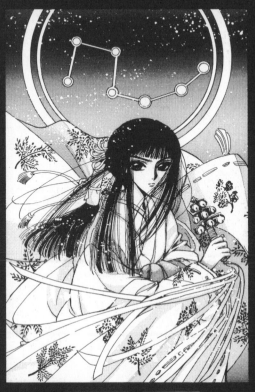

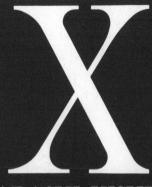

ARASHI KISHU

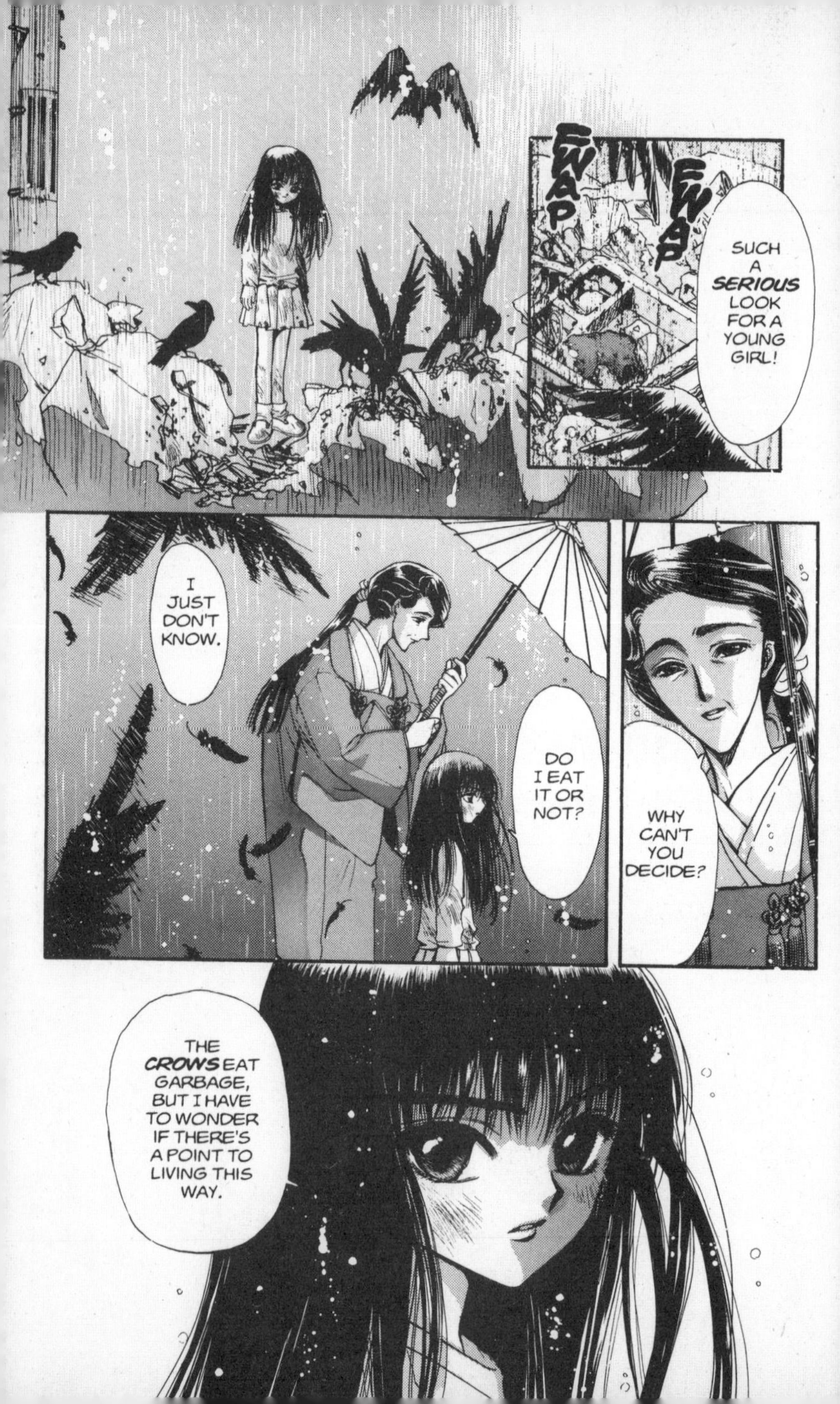
FWAP
FWAP
SUCH A SERIOUS LOOK FOR A YOUNG GIRL!
I JUST DON'T KNOW.
DO I EAT IT OR NOT?
WHY CAN'T YOU DECIDE?
THE CROWS EAT GARBAGE, BUT I HAVE TO WONDER IF THERE'S A POINT TO LIVING THIS WAY.

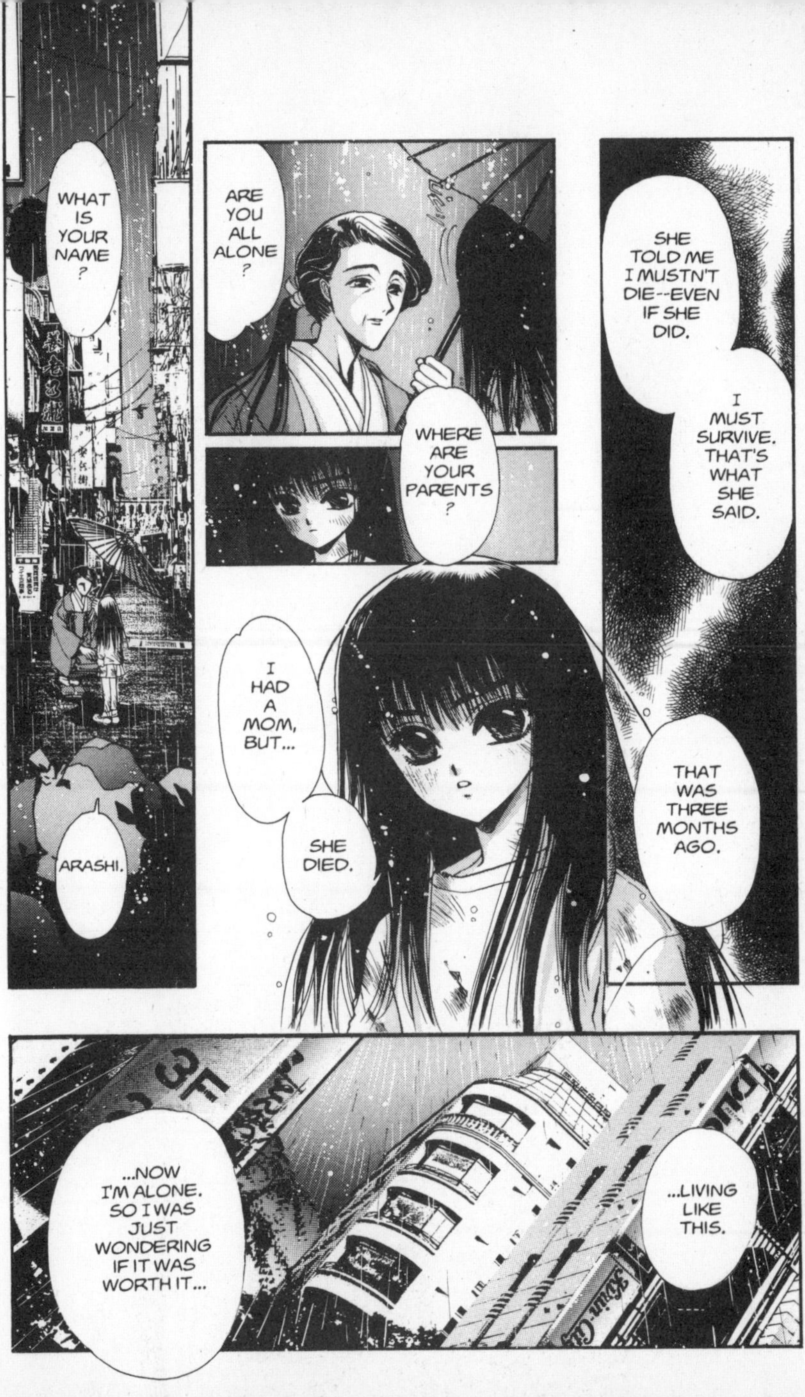
WHAT IS YOUR NAME?
ARASHI.
ARE YOU ALL ALONE?
WHERE ARE YOUR PARENTS?
I HAD A MOM, BUT...
SHE DIED.
SHE TOLD ME I MUSTN'T DIE--EVEN IF SHE DID.
I MUST SURVIVE. THAT'S WHAT SHE SAID.
THAT WAS THREE MONTHS AGO.
...NOW I'M ALONE. SO I WAS JUST WONDERING IF IT WAS WORTH IT...
...LIVING LIKE THIS.

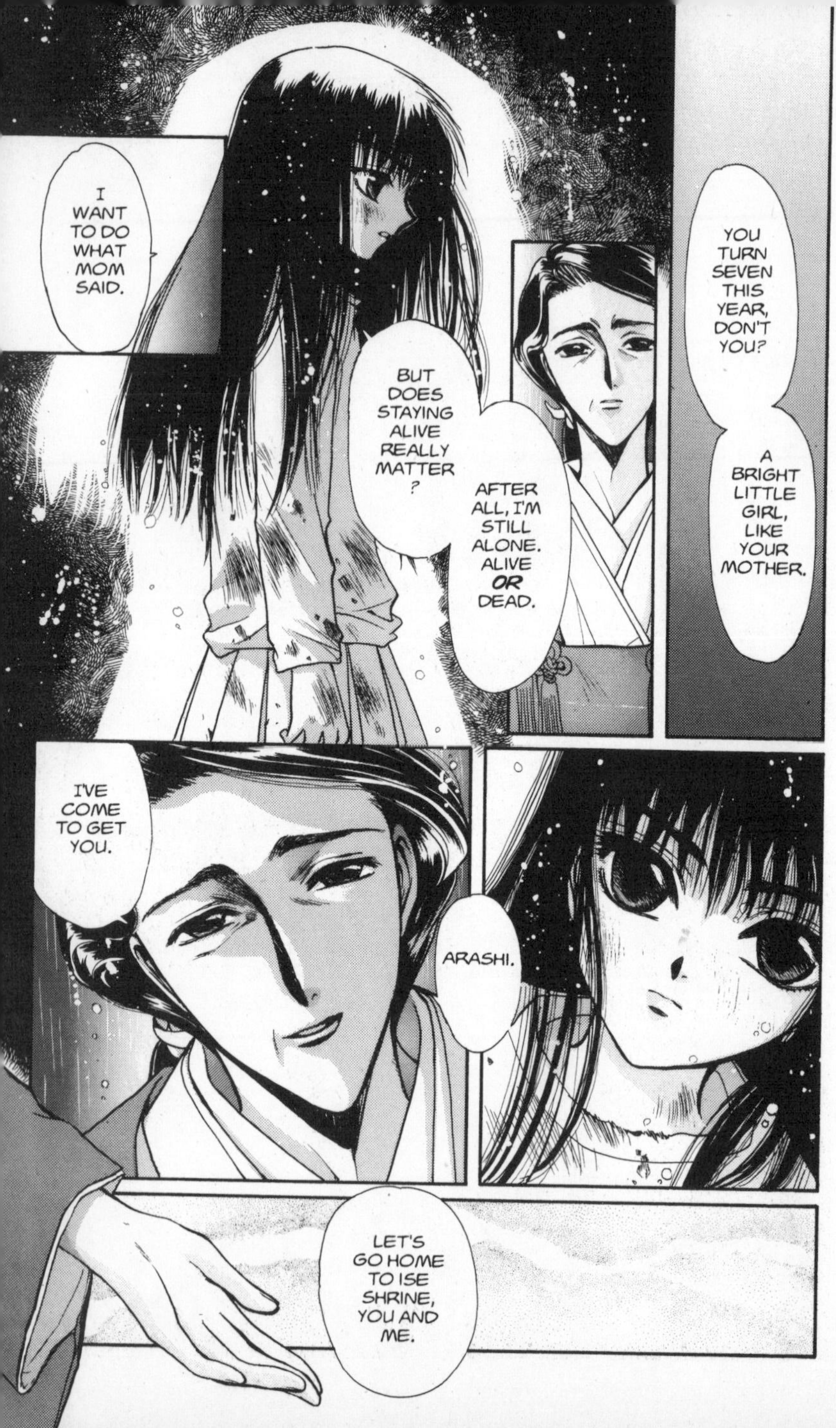
I WANT TO DO WHAT MOM SAID.
BUT DOES STAYING ALIVE REALLY MATTER?
AFTER ALL, I'M STILL ALONE. ALIVE **OR** DEAD.
YOU TURN SEVEN THIS YEAR, DON'T YOU?
A BRIGHT LITTLE GIRL, LIKE YOUR MOTHER.
I'VE COME TO GET YOU.
ARASHI.
LET'S GO HOME TO ISE SHRINE, YOU AND ME.

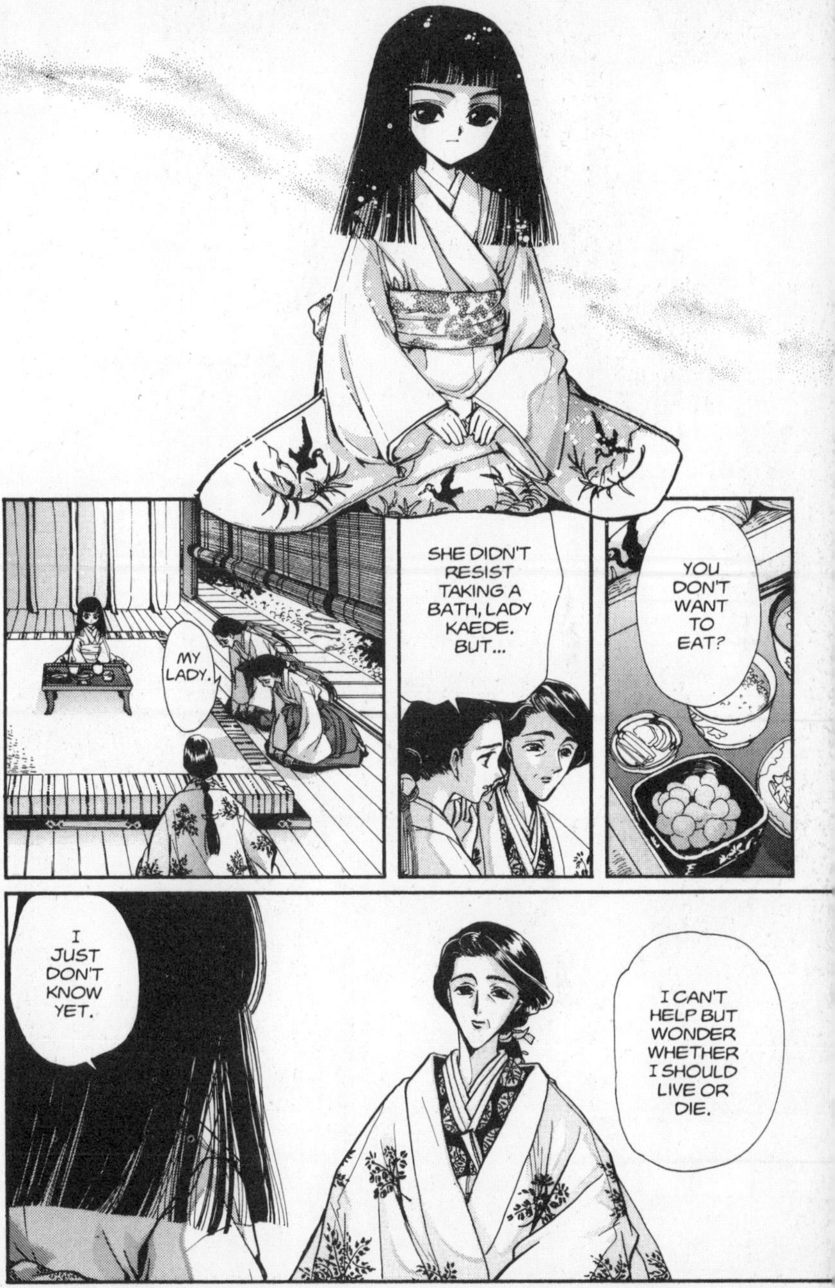
MY LADY.
SHE DIDN'T RESIST TAKING A BATH, LADY KAEDE. BUT...
YOU DON'T WANT TO EAT?
I JUST DON'T KNOW YET.
I CAN'T HELP BUT WONDER WHETHER I SHOULD LIVE OR DIE.

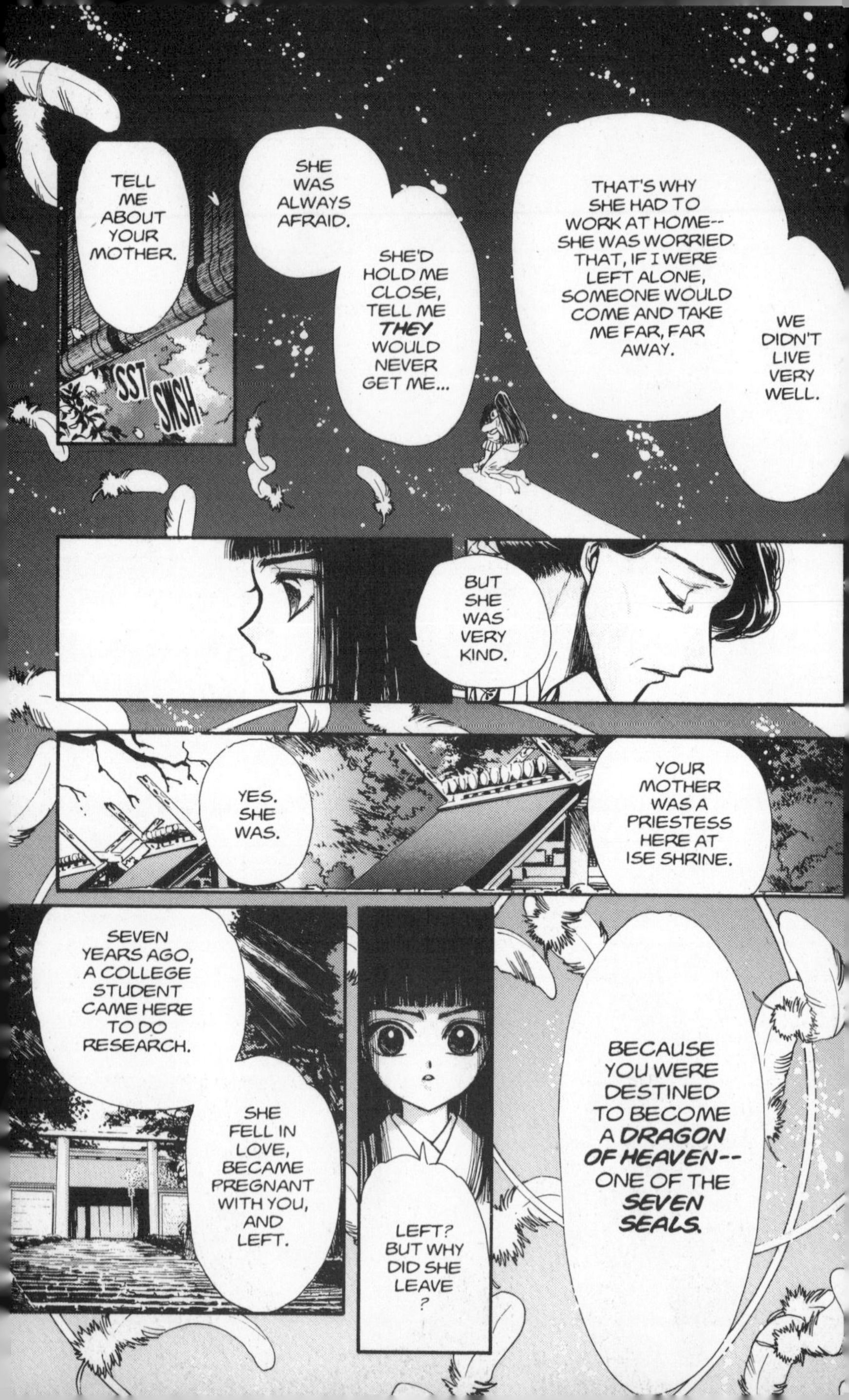
TELL ME ABOUT YOUR MOTHER.
SST
SWSH
SHE WAS ALWAYS AFRAID.
SHE'D HOLD ME CLOSE, TELL ME *THEY* WOULD NEVER GET ME...
THAT'S WHY SHE HAD TO WORK AT HOME-- SHE WAS WORRIED THAT, IF I WERE LEFT ALONE, SOMEONE WOULD COME AND TAKE ME FAR, FAR AWAY.
WE DIDN'T LIVE VERY WELL.
BUT SHE WAS VERY KIND.
YES. SHE WAS.
YOUR MOTHER WAS A PRIESTESS HERE AT ISE SHRINE.
SEVEN YEARS AGO, A COLLEGE STUDENT CAME HERE TO DO RESEARCH.
SHE FELL IN LOVE, BECAME PREGNANT WITH YOU, AND LEFT.
LEFT? BUT WHY DID SHE LEAVE ?
BECAUSE YOU WERE DESTINED TO BECOME A **DRAGON OF HEAVEN**-- ONE OF THE **SEVEN SEALS.**

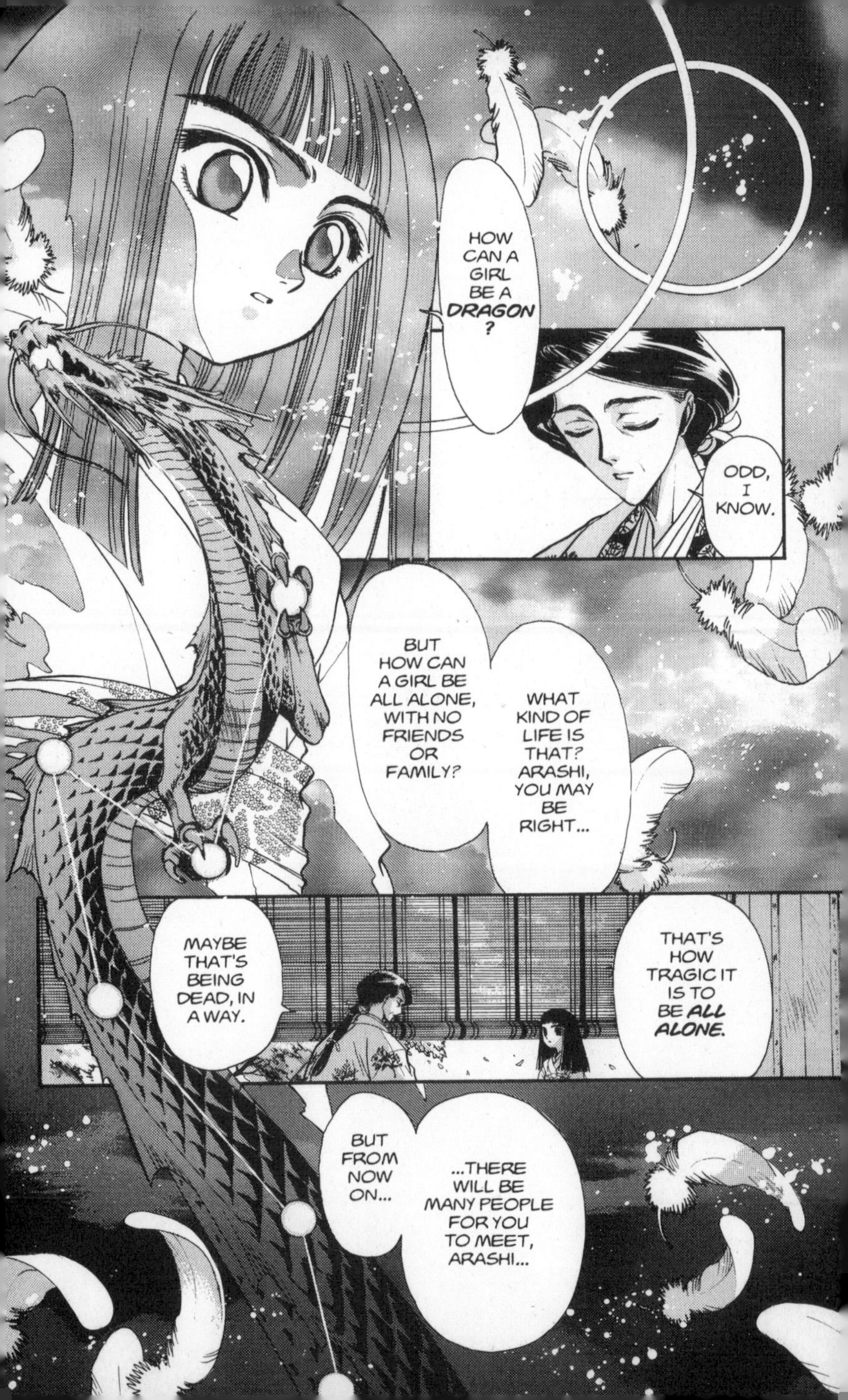
HOW CAN A GIRL BE A DRAGON?
ODD, I KNOW.
BUT HOW CAN A GIRL BE ALL ALONE, WITH NO FRIENDS OR FAMILY?
WHAT KIND OF LIFE IS THAT? ARASHI, YOU MAY BE RIGHT...
MAYBE THAT'S BEING DEAD, IN A WAY.
THAT'S HOW TRAGIC IT IS TO BE ALL ALONE.
BUT FROM NOW ON...
...THERE WILL BE MANY PEOPLE FOR YOU TO MEET, ARASHI...

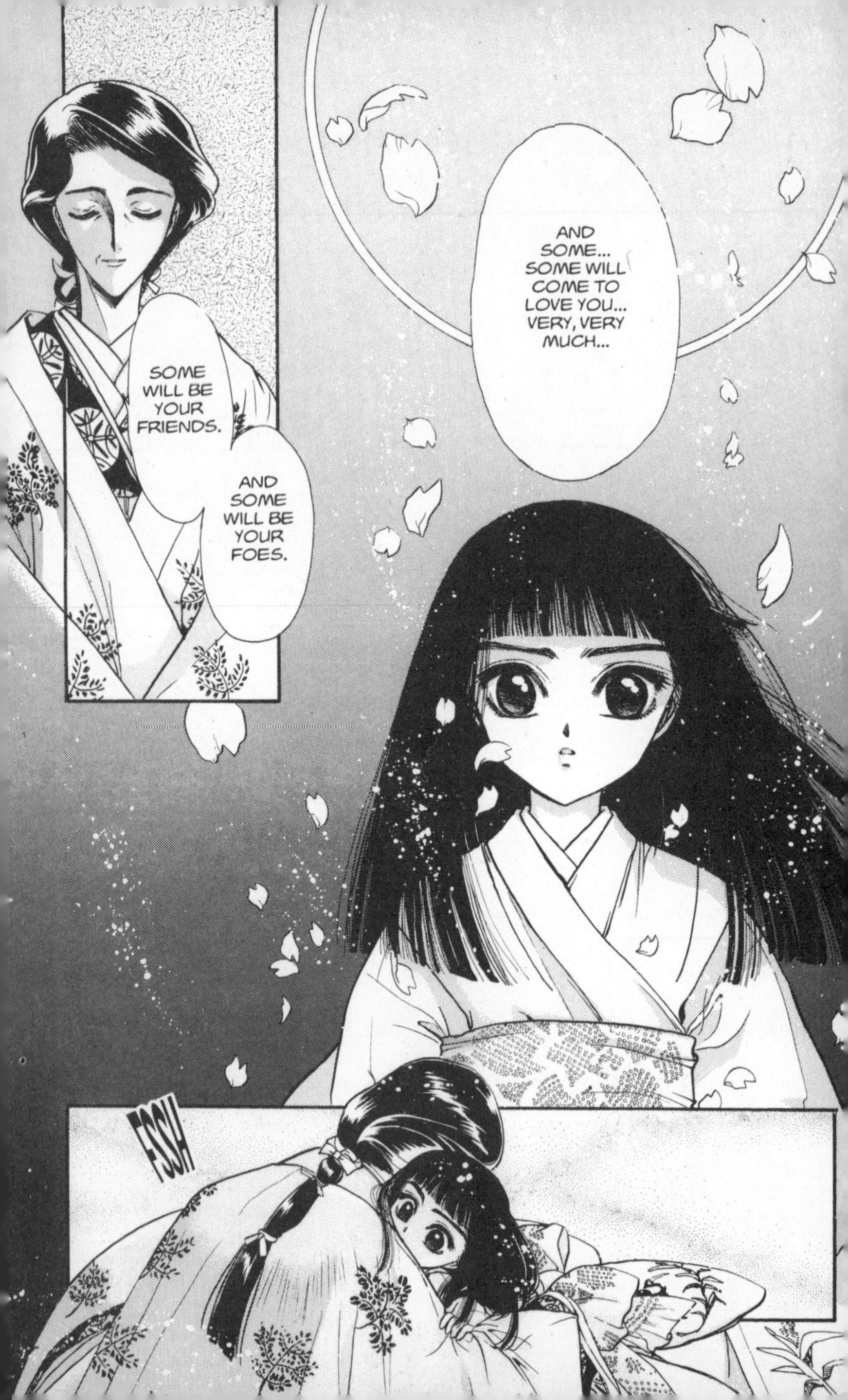
SOME WILL BE YOUR FRIENDS.
AND SOME WILL BE YOUR FOES.
AND SOME... SOME WILL COME TO LOVE YOU... VERY, VERY MUCH...
FSSH

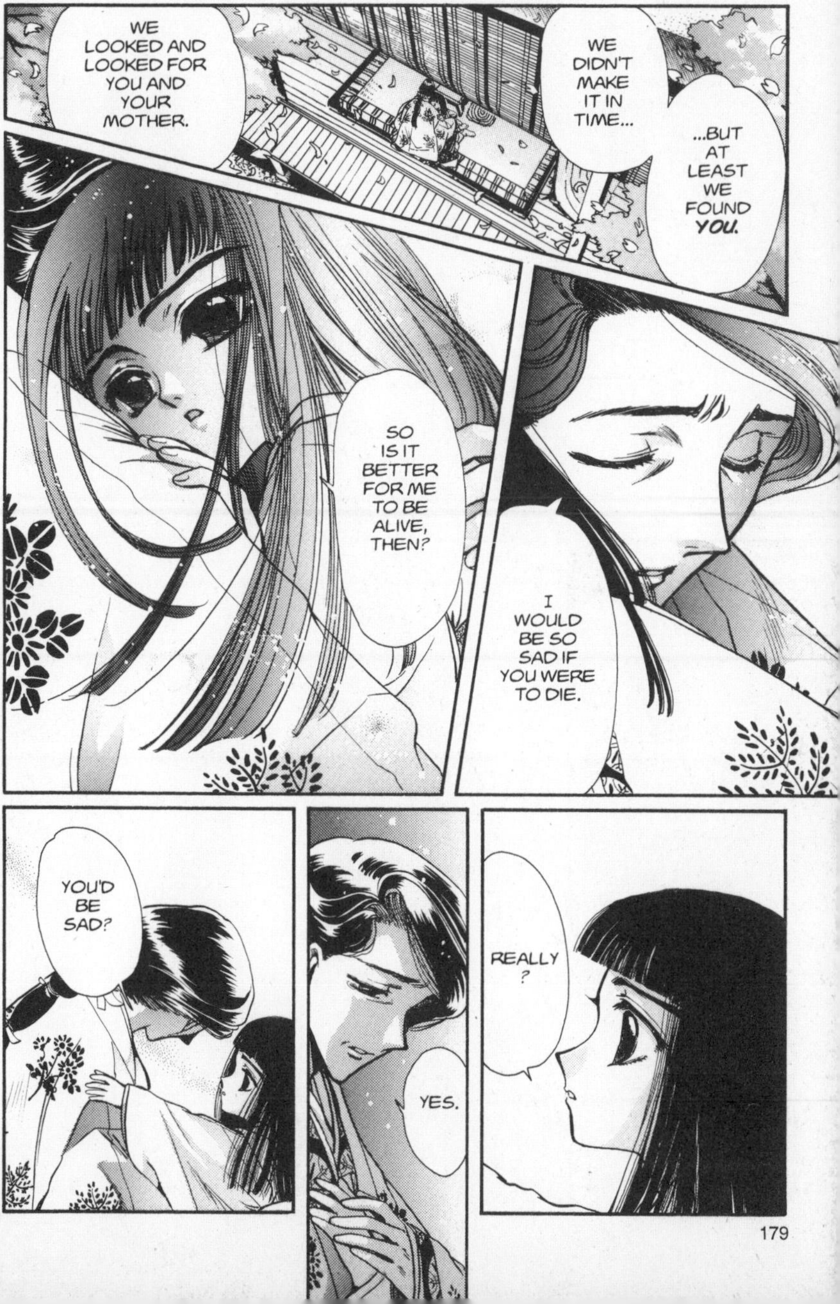
WE LOOKED AND LOOKED FOR YOU AND YOUR MOTHER.
WE DIDN'T MAKE IT IN TIME...
...BUT AT LEAST WE FOUND *YOU.*
SO IS IT BETTER FOR ME TO BE ALIVE, THEN?
I WOULD BE SO SAD IF YOU WERE TO DIE.
YOU'D BE SAD?
YES.
REALLY?

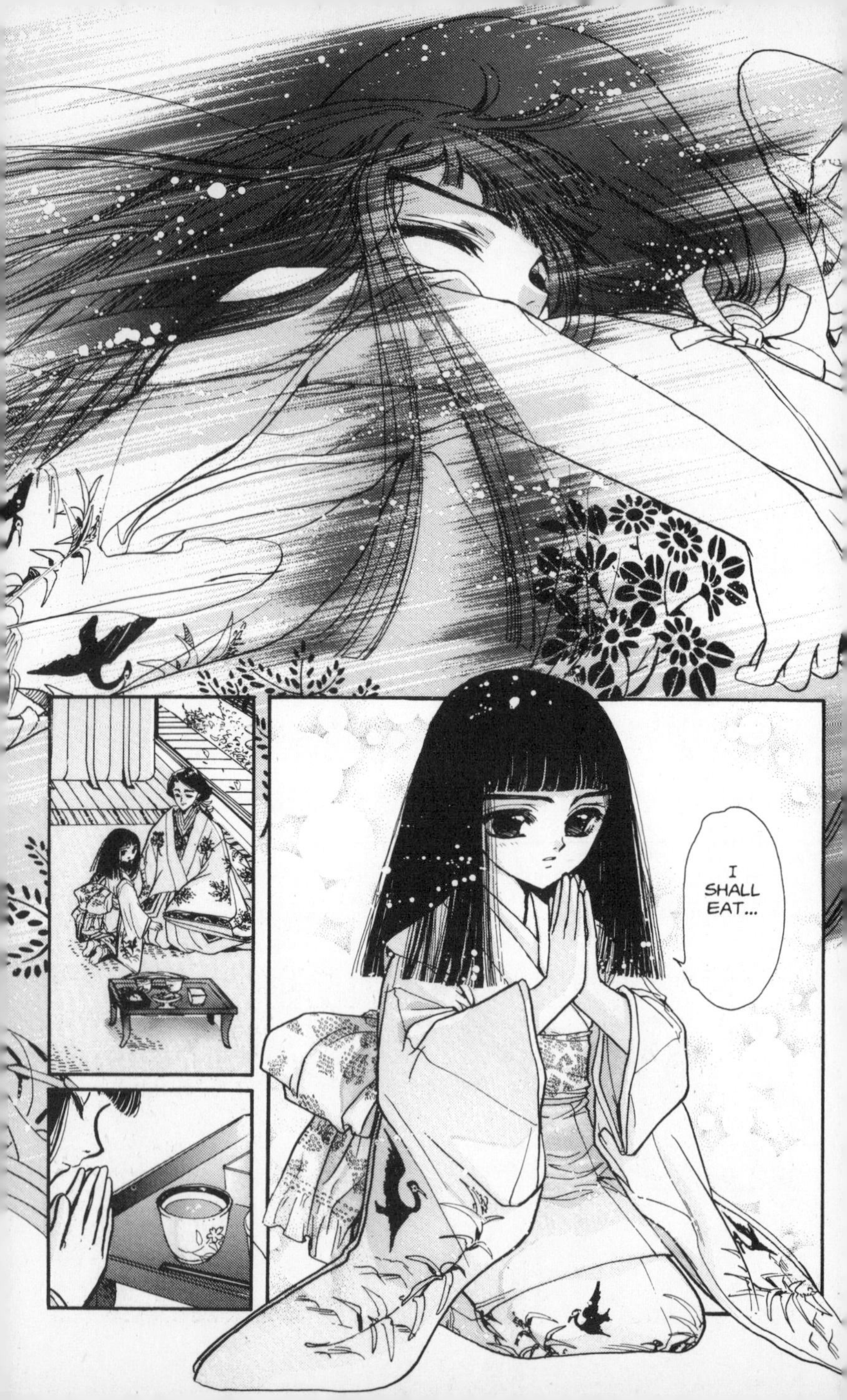
I SHALL EAT...

COMPLETE OUR SURVEY AND LET
US KNOW WHAT YOU THINK!

☐ Please check here if you DO NOT wish to receive information or future offers from VIZ

Name: _____

Address: _____

City: _____ State: _____ Zip: _____

E-mail: _____

☐ Male ☐ Female   Date of Birth (mm/dd/yyyy): ___ / ___ / ___   (Under 13? Parental consent required)

What race/ethnicity do you consider yourself? (please check one)

☐ Asian/Pacific Islander   ☐ Black/African American   ☐ Hispanic/Latino

☐ Native American/Alaskan Native ☐ White/Caucasian   ☐ Other: _____

What VIZ product did you purchase? (check all that apply and indicate title purchased)

☐ DVD/VHS _____

☐ Graphic Novel _____

☐ Magazines _____

☐ Merchandise _____

Reason for purchase: (check all that apply)

☐ Special offer   ☐ Favorite title   ☐ Gift

☐ Recommendation   ☐ Other _____

Where did you make your purchase? (please check one)

☐ Comic store   ☐ Bookstore   ☐ Mass/Grocery Store

☐ Newsstand   ☐ Video/Video Game Store ☐ Other: _____

☐ Online (site: _____)

What other VIZ properties have you purchased/own? _____

_____

How many anime and/or manga titles have you purchased in the last year? How many were VIZ titles? (please check one from each column)

ANIME
- ☐ None
- ☐ 1-4
- ☐ 5-10
- ☐ 11+

MANGA
- ☐ None
- ☐ 1-4
- ☐ 5-10
- ☐ 11+

VIZ
- ☐ None
- ☐ 1-4
- ☐ 5-10
- ☐ 11+

I find the pricing of VIZ products to be: (please check one)

- ☐ Cheap
- ☐ Reasonable
- ☐ Expensive

What genre of manga and anime would you like to see from VIZ? (please check two)

- ☐ Adventure
- ☐ Comic Strip
- ☐ Detective
- ☐ Fighting
- ☐ Horror
- ☐ Romance
- ☐ Sci-Fi/Fantasy
- ☐ Sports

What do you think of VIZ's new look?

- ☐ Love It
- ☐ It's OK
- ☐ Hate It
- ☐ Didn't Notice
- ☐ No Opinion

THANK YOU! Please send the completed form to:

NJW Research
42 Catharine St.
Poughkeepsie, NY 12601

All information provided will be used for internal purposes only. We promise not to sell or otherwise divulge your information.